1587, A YEAR OF NO SIGNIFICANCE

The Meridian Gate (Wu Men), main entrance to the Forbidden City.

1587

A YEAR OF NO SIGNIFICANCE:
THE MING DYNASTY IN DECLINE

RAY HUANG

NEW HAVEN AND LONDON : YALE UNIVERSITY PRESS

Published with assistance from the foundation established in
memory of Calvin Chapin of the Class of 1788, Yale College.

The preparation of this book was aided by a fellowship grant
from the John Simon Guggenheim Memorial Foundation.

To be published in Chinese under the title *Wanli Shiwunian*
[The fifteenth year of Wan-li] by Zhonghua Shuju, Beijing,
People's Republic of China.
(For romanizations of the title and publisher in the Wade-
Giles system, see Library of Congress Cataloging in Publication
Data below.)

Designed by Sally Harris
and set in Zapf International type.
Printed in the United States of America by
The Murray Printing Co., Westford, Mass.

Figure 13 (air photo of the Altar of Heaven) is reproduced by
courtesy of Dmitri Kessel, *Life* Magazine. © 1955, Time, Inc.

Library of Congress Cataloging in Publication Data

Huang, Ray.
    1587, a year of no significance.

    "Published in China under title Wan-li shih-wu nien (The
fifteenth year of Wan-li) by Chung-hua shu-chü, Peking."
    Bibliography: p.
    Includes index.
    1. China—History—Ming dynasty, 1368–1644.
I. Title.
DS753.H79813   951'.026   80-5392

ISBN: 0-300-02518-1 (cloth)
        0-300-02884-9 (paper)

10   9   8   7   6   5   4   3   2

For Gayle

C ONTENTS

ILLUSTRATIONS

Frontispiece   The Meridian Gate (Wu Men), main entrance to the Forbidden City. (Courtesy National Palace Museum, Taipei)

Following page 74

The Wan-li emperor, Chu I-chün. (National Palace Museum, Taipei)

Lady Wang. (National Palace Museum, Taipei)

Woodcut of man and woman embracing. (*Chung-kuo Pan-hua Shih-lüeh* [Peking, 1962]. Courtesy Jen-min Mei-shu Ch'u-pan-she, Peking)

Mandarin square breast-patches. (*Ta-Ming Hui-tien*, 1587 ed.)

Chang Chü-cheng. (*Chung-kuo Li-tai Ming-jen Hua-hsiang Lei-pien* [Taipei, 1978]. Courtesy Wei-wen Books & Publication Co., Taipei)

Shen Shih-hsing. (*Wu-chün Ming-hsien T'u-chuan-tsan*, Harvard-Yenching Library, Cambridge, Mass.)

The Cheng-te emperor. (National Palace Museum, Taipei)

The emperor's armed guard, with dragon flags. (National Palace Museum, Taipei)

Drawing of Cheng-te. (*Hsiu-hsiang Ta-Ming Cheng-te Huang-ti Yu-chiang-nan Chuan*, Gest Library, Princeton, N.J.)

Lithograph of water-control project. (*Hung-hsüeh Yin-yüan T'u-chi*, 1886 ed.)

Woodcut of floor-plan of the Altar of Heaven. (*Ta-Ming Hui-tien*, 1587 ed.)

Stone arch of the Altar of Heaven, showing symbolic clouds. (Detail from photo by Brian Brake, New Zealand)

Air photo of the Altar of Heaven. (Dmitri Kessel, *Life* Magazine. © 1955. Time, Inc.)

Wan-li's mausoleum: entrance building. (*Historical Relics Unearthed in New China*, Peking: Foreign Language Press, 1972); interior of vault; and detail of stone door panel. (Photo by Ann Paludan. Courtesy Ann Paludan)

Line drawing of Hai Jui. (*Hai Jui Chi* [Peking, 1962]. Courtesy Chung-hua Shu-chü, Peking)

Magistrate trying law case. (*Erh-pe-sa Hsiao-t'u*, 1875 ed.)

ACKNOWLEDGMENTS

Over the last fifteen years I have seldom written anything without asking L. Carrington Goodrich to review the manuscript before I submitted it to a publisher. Fu Hsien-sheng always performed this task for me with personal concern and patience. In the case of *1587, A Year of No Significance*, he not only read the entire manuscript, but also sat down with me on several occasions to help me iron out the rough spots. Those occasions were not only to my benefit but were also a source of enjoyment. I have been particularly impressed by his broadmindedness, as this book contains a number of variations in detail from his own *Dictionary of Ming Biography*, among them my harsh indictment of Chang Chü-cheng which, however, does reflect the opinion of his contemporaries.

I am grateful to Frederick W. Mote for his encouragement and his advice about style. I also wish to thank the group of young scholars working under his direction, among them Jim Geiss, Tom Bartlett, and Ellen Soulliere.

Derk Bodde read chapter 1 of the first draft and urged me to complete the book. Denis C. Twitchett was in close touch with me all through the time of the manuscript's preparation, and I am most grateful for his constant encouragement.

Another scholar who supported my early proposal to write a description of Late Imperial China was Arthur F. Wright. I do not claim that he and I always agreed in our ideas about this period of history. But this fact never prevented us from having productive discussions of what we agreed or disagreed about. It is in the spirit of friendship that I remember him here.

The theories expressed in this book had their origin in an article written by me and Joseph Needham in 1974. I wish to remind my readers, however, that as early as 1944 Needham had argued against adopting a moralistic attitude toward historical conflicts of great complexity and advocated a synthetic approach that gives just weight to all the elements involved. This I have attempted to do.

Inevitably, in the course of writing this study I have encountered many technical problems. I am grateful to the friends and colleagues who helped me with these details. Henry Serruys identified the Mongol leader referred to in the Chinese sources as "Huo-lo-ch'ih" as Qulaci. Hon H. Ho found for me a picture of the plant known as *tu-ching (Vitex cannabifolia)* that was used to make the "whipping clubs" frequently mentioned in the text. Gianni Azzi read me passages from the Italian version of Ricci's journal. L. Carrington Goodrich supplied me with eleven pages of handwritten notes taken from a partial English translation of Antonio de Gouveia's journal by J. M. Braga of the National Library of Australia. Following Braga's practice, I have referred to him as Gouveia rather than de Gouveia.

I also want to thank George C. Potter and Chui-chun Lee for their tireless efforts in solving my bibliographical problems—George especially for locating the portrait of Shen Shih-hsing. I am indebted to Edward L. Farmer for sending me xeroxed materials concerning Hung-wu's ruling on imperial succession.

Barbara Folsom of Yale University Press has contributed a great deal by improving my English style. Her meticulousness in handling technical problems is equally commendable. For both I am very, very grateful.

R. H.

FOREWORD

Ray Huang's concentration on a single year near the end of the Ming dynasty gives the reader a remarkable glimpse into the workings of the Chinese leadership of that time. But this account must not persuade us that the bitter sufferings of the Chinese people in general, both then and since, have all been a huge mistake—that from now on China must discard her entire past experience and imitate the West in whatever way possible to make up for lost time. This is not the author's message. To indict China's bureaucratic system is not to negate the whole range of Chinese culture. A balanced view is essential; there is much to conserve. Historians may re-examine the mistakes of the past in the hope of providing warnings for the future but at the same time caution their readers to preserve what is of value. Presumably, for China the experiences of both East and West must be drawn upon. It is essential that the historian lay everything on the table. This is what Ray Huang has done.

With confidence I believe that this work will contribute to a general understanding of China's modern history. As the first reader to have examined the manuscript with considerable care, I sent word to the author at once, giving my impression of it. I see no reason why my words to him may not be reproduced here to conclude this foreword: "It is top-hole, full of information, and a first-rate argumentation as to how China got the way it did. I know of none better."

L. Carrington Goodrich

Spuyten Duyvil, New York City
May 2, 1980

xiii

1
THE WAN-LI EMPEROR

Really, nothing of great significance happened in 1587, the Year of the Pig. China was not facing a foreign invasion, nor was the country engulfed in a civil war. Even though the capital district did not have sufficient rain during the summer and epidemics broke out in those months, and though drought was reported in Shantung, and flood in South Chihli, and earthquakes took place in Shansi in the autumn, none of these disasters occurred in alarming proportions. For an empire as immense as ours, such minor incidents and setbacks can only be expected. On the whole, the Year of the Pig would go down in history as an indifferent one.

Can we therefore omit that year from history books?

Not quite.

During the year preceding the defeat of the Armada in the Western world, many seemingly unimportant events took place in China that were closely linked to both her past and her future. At the time it was hard to say for certain whether any isolated incident was merely a passing episode or a crucial turning point, but in fact these interlinking events made history. Moreover, it is precisely those commonplace occurrences which historians have been inclined to overlook that often reflected the true character of our empire.

Let me begin my account with what happened on March 2, 1587, an ordinary working day.

It was a sunny day. The trees in Peking were still leafless. The ground on the unpaved streets, after intermittent snow in past months, remained frozen. The air was not terribly cold, but it was not yet warm enough to make outdoor work comfortable.

Around lunchtime hundreds of governmental functionaries, civil officials as well as army officers on duty with the capital garrison, raced toward the imperial palace. Word had spread that the emperor was to meet his court at noon. The message caught everyone unprepared. The privileged few riding in sedan chairs still had time to tidy their belts and robes during the journey; but the majority, on foot, were too exhausted from the one-

1

mile dash between their offices and the palace to pay attention to such details.

It was unclear how the guards at the Gate of Greater Brilliance came to allow the crowds to enter. Perhaps seeing the swarms of silk-robed officials, they too were convinced that an important state function was at hand. But once past the gate, the crowd entered the Imperial City. By then they must have realized that the courtyard was too quiet for the occasion. No preparations seemed to have been made on and below the towers of the Meridian Gate. The imperial furniture was not on display. There was no bell-ringing or drum-beating. There were not even any extra guards and officials to serve as marshals. Could all this be a mistake?

Apparently someone made an inquiry of the palace eunuchs inside. It was confirmed that indeed the emperor had never ordered the audience. The crowd began to disperse, relieved yet still excited. They could not help spending a good part of that afternoon and evening discussing the ridiculous false summons; but no one could explain why he himself had been so credulous.[1]

The emperor may have found this little disturbance not at all unamusing. But as sovereign he had to take serious action. Soon his verbal orders were passed to the eunuchs on duty, committed to writing, and directed to the Ministry of Rites and the Court of State Ceremonial. These two offices were in charge of ritualistic proceedings, the former for designing them to conform with the cosmic spirit and historical precedents, and the latter for actual coordination. They should have known that an imperial audience had not been held at noon for 160 years and that there was no existing procedural code for it. How could the session have been called for without either preparation or rehearsal? When the rumor of the audience was circulated, members of these two offices should have helped to clarify the situation and stopped the stampede. For their failure to do so, all of them were to forfeit their salaries for two months. Moreover, an investigation was to be conducted promptly to find out who had first circulated the false message.

The investigation turned out to be inconclusive. The court reported that the whole thing had started with a large number of people simultaneously running toward the palace; it was therefore impossible to pin down the responsibility. Upon receiving this report, the emperor extended the suspension of salary to all governmental functionaries in the capital.

How severe this punishment was might not have been fully realized by the emperor. He had suspended salaries before to penalize officials for dereliction of duty and for submitting irritating memorials to the throne, but such a measure had been applied only to individuals. The group penalty covering the entire body of capital officials was unprecedented. Indeed, because emoluments for the bureaucracy authorized by the dynasty were fixed at very low levels, many officials, especially those in the higher echelons, did not live on their regular pay. A minister, rank 2a, was entitled to an annual salary of 152 ounces of silver; in practice he might receive cash gifts from provincial governors of ten times that amount on a single occasion. Aware of this custom, the emperor may have imagined that all officials received such perquisites. There was no evidence that he understood the difficulties of the office-holders in the lower ranks, who extended their personal resources to accumulate seniority and wait for provincial assignments, meanwhile often languishing in debt. For a secretary in a ministry, rank 6a, the annual compensation of thirty-five ounces of silver had to be counted as an essential item in the household budget, even though it might not pay the rent. So the harsh punishment must have brought distress to many such households.[2]

The action taken by the throne was nevertheless considered to be just and final. With all its pomp and grandeur, the imperial court was supposed to preserve its impeccable and meticulous manners as an inspiration to the nation. It was absolutely unbecoming for the entire court to run chaotically toward a wrong destination at a wrong time. Both the sovereign and his bureaucrats realized that to fulfill their functions they had to do well in two areas: personnel management and ceremonial procedure. Of course, not many practical problems could be solved this way, but it was essential to managing an immense empire from one center. There was a limit to the number of practical problems that could be perceived, understood, analyzed, and discharged by our literary bureaucracy that governed many millions of peasants. So discipline and decorum had to be emphasized; the example set by the emperor's court became paramount. Rewards and punishments remained effective means to underline this emphasis.

The Wan-li emperor, now turning twenty-four, was himself a veteran of ceremonial proceedings. By March 1587 he had been the Son of Heaven for almost fifteen years. Even before his enthronement, when not yet nine years old, he had gone through the ritual of capping, which prematurely ushered in his manhood. Thereafter he was no longer considered a child, at least not in public.

Wan-li still remembered that winter day when he was led into a screened cubicle temporarily erected in the courtyard, from which he emerged three times, always clad in a new set of garments. Each time he was crowned with a different hat. The assortment of headgear and robes was the regalia designated for various ceremonial functions into which he, as heir apparent, must be initiated. Between the changes in wardrobe, he was instructed to kneel down, stand up, turn around, hold a scepter, and drink wine from a special cup—all to the accompaniment of music and the chanting of ceremonial officials. The proceedings took the whole morning. The next day the boy sat stiffly to receive the formal congratulations of the court officials.[3]

Several months later came the death of his father, the Lung-ch'ing emperor. As heir designate he met the imperial court in mourning. The assembly of officials had prepared polished pieces of literature declaiming the urgent reasons why he must now take over the vacant throne. Twice Wan-li, who had been carefully coached, declined on the ground that he was too grief-stricken. Only to the third round of persuasion did he give his assent. From that moment on ceremonies became inseparable from his life.

During the past fifteen years the emperor had sacrificed to heaven and earth, performed ritual motions of farming, and celebrated New Year's Day and the ferry boat festival that fell on the fifth day of the fifth lunar month. He had sacrificed to imperial mausoleums and the family temple and meticulously observed the birthdays and dates of death of all preceding emperors and empresses of the dynasty. He received missions from foreign tributaries and retiring officials who bade him farewell. He reviewed troops, issued battle banners, and accepted prisoners of war after the imperial army's major and minor battles.

The disposal of war prisoners was usually one of the most awe-inspiring occasions of the emperor's court. He sat on the tower atop the Meridian Gate overlooking the granite-paved courtyard, flanked by general officers who held noble titles. Lined up next to them was a full battalion of imperial guards, soldiers of gigantic stature clad in shiny armor and helmets adorned with red tassels. Down below, while thousands of court officials and soldiers watched, the prisoners, in chains and red cloth with holes cut out for their necks, were forced to kneel on the stone pavement. Then the minister of justice came forward to read aloud a list of the crimes those prisoners had committed against humanity. Upon completion of the charges, he petitioned the emperor that the prisoners be executed in the marketplace. The reply from the throne—"Take them there; be it so ordered"—could not have been heard by all present. The order, however, was repeated by the two nobles standing immediately next to the sovereign and then echoed in succession by four, eight, sixteen, and thirty-two guardsmen, until it touched off a thundering shout of the same order by the entire battalion of soldiers, their chests inflated.[4]

Every year, in the eleventh lunar month, the emperor received the following year's calendar and proclaimed it to the populace, so that they would know when to plant their seeds for food and when to sweep their family graves. With the same degree of solemnity he received all important literary works compiled by the Han-lin Academy. Every work accepted by the throne was made official writ. It was placed on a portable lectern and carried through all the ceremonial gates and the entire length of the courtyard, accompanied by academicians and musicians and escorted by porters who carried burning incense.[5]

With full formality, the emperor granted princely ranks to his cousins and remote relatives, authorized their weddings, and bestowed honors upon their wives. He had, upon his succession, named his principal mother, the former empress, the August Empress Dowager Jen-sheng, and his natural mother, formerly the imperial consort, the August Empress Dowager Tz'u-sheng. The latter was particularly important to him, perhaps the only person in the world who had given him the kind of love due to a child.[6] Many years later, on her birthday in the eleventh lunar month, he still went to the Imperial Polar Gate to accept the good wishes of his courtiers on her behalf, even though by that time he had discontinued many ceremonial proceedings.

But ever since his capping Wan-li had become a public personality. When he constructed a palace building for her, the dowager's appreciation was not expressed orally but was incorporated into a letter of thanks solemnly read to him while he lay prostrate on the ground. The letter was then kept in an imperial archive as a state paper. When Wan-li entertained his two mothers with stage plays by a palace troupe, he had to kneel in the courtyard awaiting their arrival, rising only when the empresses dowager had dismounted from their sedan chairs.

Thus, in becoming emperor, Wan-li lost much of his personal identity and had little private life. Even when he moved about inside the palace compound, he was accompanied by a large retinue led by eunuchs who cleared the path with whips.

When he decided to elevate his favorite concubine, Lady Cheng, to the position of imperial consort, the proceedings were announced beforehand so that the ceremony might be prepared. This act caused a supervising secretary to protest on the ground that the honor should go to Lady Wang, who had given birth to the emperor's first son, whereas Lady Cheng was the mother of only his third son. This objection started a controversy that was to alienate the monarch from his court and rock the dynasty for the rest of its duration. At the time, however, the ceremony proceeded as planned. The sovereign did not personally hand out the honor. As tradition prescribed, he commissioned his deputies to do so. With credential and patent they conferred the title upon the designated woman. The emperor sanctified the first haircuts of his infant sons and ritualistically gave them their names.

In performing these functions the Wan-li emperor found that he had to change clothes often, sometimes several times a day. Ming emperors wore no metal crowns. The most formal hat worn by the sovereign was a rectangular black mortarboard, with the shorter edges facing front and rear. Dangling from each of the two edges were twelve strings of beads. The curtainlike beads in front of his eyes and behind the nape of his neck must have made the wearer uncomfortable, compelling him to remain solemn and steady and to move very deliberately. To match the mortarboard the emperor wore a black jacket and a yellow skirt, both elaborately embroidered. Over the skirt was an apronlike knitted band. Along with two tassels, the band was hung on a jade belt. Red socks and red ankle-boots completed his attire.

Garments of the second degree of formality were red; they could be considered the emperor's military uniform. The headgear was a shell-like helmet, complete with chin strings in accordance with military tradition. But in place of the metal studs on the headpieces worn by soldiers, the emperor's red helmet was lined with leather and decorated with rows of jewels. The yellow dragon robe that was conventionally regarded as the emperor's standard costume, because he wore it so often, was in fact for occasions of even lesser degrees of formality. When retiring from public functions, the emperor changed into a black dragon robe with green borders.

The symbolic value of the office of the monarchy was amply illustrated by the ritualistic farming performed by the emperor every spring in front of the Altar of Earth. About two hundred farmers were called in from the two counties surrounding Peking to form an assembly. Actors dressed up as deities of wind, clouds, thunder, and rain. Two officials led an ox; two older farmers held a plow. Other peasants carried farm implements and barrels for human fertilizer. The emperor, however, touched neither the tools nor the draft animal. His left hand holding a whip and his right hand a ceremonial plow carved with a dragon and painted in gold, he was flanked by two elders. The procession marched across the field three times. Then the ruler retired to the tent to watch his courtiers, led by the minister of revenue, repeat the process. Seeding was performed by the prefect of

Shun-t'ien and his staff. No sooner was the soil covered than actors in peasant clothing presented five principal grains to the emperor, simulating a good harvest. The sovereign was then congratulated by all present.[7]

Most other state functions were less interesting; they could be very tiresome indeed. The daily audience with the court, for instance, was loathed even by the most diligent statesmen. It was a chore that several predecessors of the present emperor had found unbearable. Although now much simplified, the procedure still remained a heavy burden on Wan-li.

In order to attend the audience, even before daybreak all civil officials and all army officers in the capital and the members of the local government within the metropolitan district had gathered outside the palace. The gates were opened after drum-beating and bell-ringing. The participants assembled in the courtyard in front of the ceremonial hall. Civil officials faced west; military officers faced east. Four imperial historians were posted around the emperor to record the proceedings. Censors acting as marshals took the roll and wrote down the names of those who coughed, spat, stumbled, or dropped their ceremonial tablets. Whips were cracked to call the ceremony to order. At the chanting of the master of ceremonies, the assembly turned around, bowed to the emperor once, and kowtowed three times. The chief minister of State Ceremonials announced the names of those officials who were about to leave the capital for retirement and provincial assignments; these dignitaries then paid the sovereign special homage in farewell. Then officials ranked 4b and above filed into the ceremonial hall. The various departments and ministries made reports to the emperor; at times he asked questions and gave oral instructions. All proceedings were expected to be completed before dawn.

In the early years of the dynasty the court audience was repeated at noon and in the evening. There were 185 kinds of official business that could and must be reported to the emperor in person. Until the end of the fifteenth century at least, the morning audience had been very seriously regarded. When the sixth emperor, Cheng-t'ung, ascended the throne at the age of nine, a new rule was put into effect to limit the oral report to eight items of business a day, those having been brought to His Majesty's attention in advance in writing. But the audience was never postponed because of rain or snow. On those days officials were permitted to wear raincoats over their silk robes. A regulation of 1477 further permitted umbrella-carriers to accompany officials to the courtyard. Only very rarely were senior statesmen, men over seventy years old, excused from attendance. Even emperors could not easily excuse themselves from the daily event. Once in 1498 the ninth emperor, Hung-chih, virtually begged his senior grand-secretary to call off the morning audience at the last minute for just one day. The night before there had been a palace fire; because of loss of sleep the sovereign did not feel physically fit to go through the proceedings. The morning audience was suspended only from one to three days upon the death of a relative of the emperor or an important statesman. Even then, while the emperor temporarily absented himself, the court officials were still required to proceed to the Meridian Gate to bow to the throne. During the period of state mourning the emperor and his court changed into somber-colored robes for the ceremony, omitting the gold and silver and ivory dress belts.[8]

The first to break with this tradition was Cheng-te, the tenth Ming emperor and the present emperor's granduncle. Conscious of his ability to assert himself, Cheng-te was determined to carry out his own concept of monarchy rather than that of his courtiers. After 1517 he frequently absented himself from the capital for prolonged periods. As the bureaucrats refused to cooperate, he gathered around himself a staff of eunuchs. During his absences the office of the grand-secretary was maintained by him mainly as a center for transmitting messages, and he made little use of civil officials for decision-making. When he returned to Peking he put forth many bizarre proposals, such as that court audiences be held late at night followed by state banquets. Such suggestions seemed to the bureaucracy merely provocative.

It would be difficult to imagine what would have happened had these conditions continued, but Cheng-te died without issue in 1521. He was succeeded by the Wan-li emperor's grandfather, the Chia-ching emperor. The succession marked the first time in the dynasty's history that a prince from a lateral branch of the imperial family had ascended the throne. The courtiers took advantage of the opportunity to terminate the influence of the eunuchs; the most notorious ones were put to death. For about twenty years Chia-ching attended to his office conscientiously; he even instituted many revisions in court rituals, which he considered to be closer to the classical model. But when approaching middle age, he grew tired of public life. Withdrawing to a villa inside the Imperial City, he became infatuated with Taoist formulas for manufacturing elixirs. Another twenty years passed and the court audience was virtually abandoned. Unfortunately for the dynasty, Chia-ching's reign was the longest until that of the present emperor; it lasted almost forty-five years.

The Wan-li emperor's father, Lung-ch'ing, left a colorless record in history. He ruled for less than six years. For the first year after his enthronement the morning audience was held regularly. But the emperor merely sat there, cold and numb. Even the routine utterances were made by his grand-secretaries on his behalf. Then, in the next four and a half years, even this lifeless performance was suspended, or held very sporadically.[9]

In 1572, at the accession of the present emperor Wan-li, Grand-Secretary Chang Chü-cheng arranged to have the morning audience with the court held on the third, sixth, and ninth days of every ten-day cycle; other days the young emperor devoted to his schooling.[10] Now, almost fifteen years later, the routines had not been completely abandoned, but the cancellation of both the morning ceremony and the study sessions had been more frequent in past months. The offering of a sacrifice was usually presided over by appointed representatives. Under these conditions the false alert for an audience at noon sounded even more ridiculous.

The morning audience held by the Wan-li emperor was in fact an abridged form. Very rarely did the court move into the ceremonial hall. Except for special occasions it avoided even the Meridian Gate. The proceedings took place at the Gate of Brightening Administration because of its unpretentious surroundings and simple effect. The horses and elephants that usually manifested imperial grandeur were absent. The oral report by officials was no more than a formality. Among the items of business submitted in advance to the emperor, only those issues requiring public attention were selectively presented.

Ever since his enthronement the Wan-li emperor had impressed his courtiers with his majestic countenance. His voice was deep, his pronouncements clear and loud, ending in powerful tones which "seemingly came from his diaphragm." More than once this had been cited as an invaluable asset for the occupant of the throne, especially when he was a child emperor.[11] Anyone could see that Wan-li was precocious. Some years later he himself disclosed that at the age of five by Chinese count—which put his actual age between three and four—he had already learned to read.[12]

In the early years of his reign, when he was instructed to refer to a slip of paper on his sleeve that reminded him how to respond to various requests and proposals, Wan-li had only a vague idea of what he was doing. He knew that he had to do these things because he was emperor; and for the same reason nearly everyone had to kowtow to him. In his world he had yet to meet an equal. He liked his brother Prince Lu, but the child was five years younger than he. Beyond that, there was not even a playmate at court except for a handful of eunuch attendants. Two persons he had learned to respect: Tutor Chang and Big Companion Feng. Both seemed to be good men, well regarded even by Empress Dowager Tz'u-sheng. Their conjunction with Wan-li's life was an act of destiny bound deeply to affect a nation of many millions.

Chang Chü-cheng, with his wide-set eyebrows and long beard, was always a source of authority and wisdom. Always well-groomed, he seemed to wear a new robe every day, with its creases well kept.[13] His mind was just as sharp and meticulous as his clothing and manners. Whenever he said something it always hit the mark—clear, definite, and incisive.

The Wan-li emperor and his two dowager mothers had a particular reason to feel grateful to Tutor Chang, whom Wan-li sometimes referred to as the "Senior Counsellor." When the Lung-ch'ing emperor died, the first grand-secretary had been Kao Kung. Having handled public affairs for Lung-ch'ing for some time, Kao took it for granted that he was still in command. He was overbearing enough that the first time he was approached by the emperor's messenger he questioned in public how a nine-year-old could actually assume that he was master. If Kao Kung were allowed to behave so arrogantly, what else would he be capable of? And if the Son of Heaven was treated by him like any other nine-year-old, did he have any respect for the two empresses dowager? It was under Chang Chü-cheng's confidential advice that the problem was quickly dealt with and solved for good. On that summer day of 1572, all officials were called to assemble in front of the palace at short notice. A eunuch arrived with a piece of yellow paper signed by the two empresses dowager and the emperor. When it was read in front of the kneeling officials, Kao Kung was shaken and lost countenance. The imperial order stripped him of his rank and position, and commanded him to return to his home region that very day. Thereafter he was to remain under the surveillance of the magistrate of the district for life. Thus, the imperial family felt that Tutor Chang had secured the throne for the young emperor at a difficult time. With Kao Kung dismissed, Chang's succession became a matter of course; he had more than earned the position of first grand-secretary.

But in addition to being the chief counsellor, Chang Chü-cheng was also in charge of the emperor's education. Wan-li's five lecturers, two calligraphy instructors, and one academician attendant were all appointed by him. Tutor Chang supervised their instruction personally, sometimes took over the lecture himself, and supplemented the textbooks with his own writings.

Ever since the autumn of 1572, Wan-li's schoolday had consisted of three separate periods devoted to basic Confucian classics, calligraphy, and history. During the rest period he retired to his lounge and the instructors to theirs within the same building. Between the first and second periods, however, Big Companion Feng Pao and other eunuchs would bring to the throne the day's memorials awaiting the emperor's approval, with attached rescripts already drafted by the grand-secretaries. During that hour, Wan-li exercised his sovereign right by wielding a vermilion brush on the state papers, always assisted by a half-dozen eunuchs under Feng Pao's direction; all civil officials, including even Tutor Chang, had to stay away unless called for questioning.[14]

The emperor completed his studies and the day's work at noon. He ate his lunch in the library and had the afternoon free, except that he must further practice his handwriting in his spare time, and learn the verses in the classics and the dates, names, and events in history by heart. These lessons Wan-li never took lightly because he knew that the next morning Tutor Chang might ask for a recitation. If the emperor had prepared his lessons well, the grand-secretary was ready to kneel and murmur that the dynasty was blessed to have such an enlightened sovereign; but he was equally capable of casting a pair of fiercely inquisitive eyes on the lonely and helpless pupil if he had not.

Until his wedding in 1578, Wan-li had shared his palace quarters with Empress Dowager Tz'u-sheng. She was very much involved in her son's duties and functions as emperor. On the days he was supposed to meet his court, it was she who woke him in the morning. His conduct and education were always important to her. Feng Pao, the eunuch who had taken care of her son for many years, remained her contact outside the palace. As a young prince Wan-li had ridden on Feng's shoulders and started calling him "Big Companion." Now promoted to Director of Ceremonies, Feng was the head of the palace staff. His direct access to the empress dowager transformed Wan-li's affection for him into awe, as a bad report from him could prompt Tz'u-sheng to order him, even as emperor, to kneel for long periods of time.[15]

Under such strict discipline and guidance Wan-li progressed well with his studies. He had learned that the primary duties of the ruler were to venerate heaven and to follow the precedents established by his ancestors. Less than four months after his accession, a supernova later known as "Anno 1572" suddenly appeared in the sky, the size of a saucer and orange in color.[16] Before it dimmed its light in early 1573 and vanished a year later, the heaven-sent portent made a strong impression on Wan-li. On the advice of Tutor Chang, he fully examined himself for bad thoughts, speech, and conduct. Since even the regularity of the universe depended upon the young emperor's character and wisdom, he had no choice but to be thrifty, diligent, sincere, and courteous on all occasions.

The children's game that Wan-li played with eunuch attendants was regarded as unbecoming for the emperor; thus any crowd had to disperse at the approach of the footsteps of the Big Companion. Now the emperor had developed an intense interest in calligraphy, which was also the favorite hobby of Mother Tz'u-sheng and of Feng Pao. In early 1574, barely ten, Wan-li was able to execute characters one foot high. On several occasions he asked Tutor Chang and other grand-secretaries to watch him work with the brush and gave them his long sheets of artistry as souvenirs. Chang Chü-cheng accepted his with thanks; but the next day he came to admonish the young emperor to the effect that His Majesty's brushwork had already exceeded expectation. Calligraphy, he further argued, was after all a minor art which in itself added nothing to the empire's well-being. Sage rulers in Chinese history excelled only in virtue, not in aesthetic skills. One should keep in mind that Ch'eng-ti of Han, Yüan-ti of Liang, Hou-chu of Ch'en, Yang-ti of Sui, and Hui-tsung of Sung were accomplished musicians, painters, poets, and writers. Yet, with all their talents, none of them escaped dynastic decadence and tragic ends. The moral of this lecture was that even harmless hobbies could develop into undesirable distractions that sent rulers to their ruin. To stress this point, by the end of 1578 Chang had eliminated calligraphy from Wan-li's curriculum.[17]

The practice of frugality started with palace expenditure. At Tutor Chang's suggestion, the lantern decorations and fireworks that had illuminated the imperial gardens and buildings after every new year over the past century were discontinued. The emperor had ordered the redecoration of two palace buildings as the new living quarters of his two mothers. The order was rescinded because of Chang Chü-cheng, who decided that the conditions of the two buildings were good enough as they were. At one time Wan-li complained that numerous palace women around him all loved self-adornment and he did not have enough jewels to give them. The grand-secretary urged him to think first of food and clothing for the populace: emperors should never be preoccupied with pearls and precious stones, as they can in no way dispel cold and hunger.[18]

Yet, the fundamental problem of the enormous expenditure of the imperial household was its size. The Forbidden City, an area of a quarter of a square mile, was covered with blocks of glaze-tiled palatial buildings and ceremonial halls and gates, marble terraces, and endless painted galleries.

It was surrounded by the Imperial City, an area of no less than three square miles, also closed to the public. Within the enclosure were numerous avenues and several artificial lakes. In addition to imperial villas, temples, and residences of eunuch officials inside the compound, there were also supply depots and material-processing plants. Among them was the Court of Imperial Entertainments, which had the capacity to serve banquets for up to 15,000 men on short notice. Next to the bakery, distillery, and confectionery were the emperor's stable, armory, printing-office, and book depository.

In sum, the palace was completely self-sufficient; all materials needed to support the Forbidden City were either deposited or being manufactured in this huge maintenance area, whose parklike surroundings were also used for sports and recreation. Moreover, certain articles consumed at sacrificial services and distributed to the personnel outside the palace, including wax and incense, as well as cotton cloth and cotton wadding for making the uniforms of the capital garrison, were also stored in the warehouses within the Imperial City. With few exceptions, all those supply depots and installations were supervised by eunuchs, who were organized into twenty-four departments.[19] During the early years of Wan-li, there were close to 20,000 eunuchs, counting those holding official ranks on a par with top bureaucrats down to messengers and household attendants; the number was still increasing steadily. The palace staff also included 3,000 women.[20]

To make things worse, this huge staff, like the bureaucracy, was grossly underpaid. This situation reflected the system established by the dynastic founders. Since the emperor owned all that was within the Four Seas, there was no need for him to maintain substantial estates. Instead, he derived from tax proceeds large quantities of material and manufactured goods—from silk to metal ingots and from lumber to sesame seeds—and these were deposited immediately next to his palatial quarters, what was then the largest logistical base in the world. Officials, who were expected to live in extreme austerity, were from time to time handed out some of the goods set aside by the emperor, either as a bonus after a sacrificial ceremony or as outright bestowals from the throne.

But by the sixteenth century officialdom no longer lived in austerity. The top-ranking eunuchs carried on a life style differing little from that of the top bureaucrats. Feared and venerated, they too kept magnificent mansions within the Imperial City, staffed with household managers, personal secretaries, and domestic servants. By custom, palace women lived with them as if they were married. Although obviously without offspring, they patronized adopted sons, nephews, and sometimes junior eunuchs.[21] Their methods of gaining irregular income also resembled conventional bureaucratic practices.

For the rank-and-file palace attendants, a major source of personal gain was their control of supply depots. Every month delivery agents from the provinces would arrive with assorted materials in lieu of tax payments. Unless these were found to fulfill specifications, the cargo would not be accepted and the deliverers, unable to discharge their responsibility, would be stranded in Peking. This quality control could, however, be drastically modified by paying a fee. Usually the delivery agent would approach an intermediary, who received the money and guaranteed acceptance of the cargo in question. During Wan-li's reign, the most influential intermediary agent operating around the supply depots was Li Wei, earl of Wu-ch'ing, Tz'u-sheng's own father—or, to put it bluntly, in private life the reigning emperor's maternal grandfather.

As the earl, in collaboration with the palace eunuchs, continued to turn in substandard materials for profit, the army personnel became angry, for the cotton cloth thus checked in was issued to them for their uniforms. In 1577, the young emperor was persuaded to take one bolt of the inferior cloth and complain to Tz'u-sheng. Humiliated, the empress dowager wanted the case settled by law. At this point Tutor Chang interceded. Instead of going to court, Li Wei was summoned to stand in front of the palace to receive a reprimand. After the event Chang Chü-cheng was jubilant. He seized the opportunity to place dozens of eunuchs in charge of the supply depots; the demand for "cushion money" at those installations came to a halt. Throughout the maneuver Chang had the cooperation of Director of Ceremonies Feng Pao. Nevertheless, this heroic act was to have repercussions later.[22]

Affairs of state in the first decade of Wan-li's reign, from 1572 to 1582, showed a remarkable improvement over the conditions of the previous hundred years. Nomadic invasions no longer threatened the northern frontier. Pirates disappeared from the eastern coasts. After a prolonged period of peace, imperial coffers were well stocked with silver bullion, thanks to Chang Chü-cheng's administration. This was more than a boy emperor and his secluded mother could have hoped for. No wonder that when Tutor Chang had a minor stomach disorder, Wan-li volunteered to fix him a bowl of noodle soup! Tz'u-sheng's deference to the grand-secretary was even more complete. A very religious person, she had made up her mind to contribute from her own purse to the construction of a temple in honor of a certain goddess; it was at Chang Chü-cheng's advice that the project was abandoned. The alternate plan of constructing a stone bridge outside Peking with the same money was presented to her without prior consultation. Similarly, when Wan-li caught the measles, the empress dowager promised to offer upon his recovery an altar for masses in thanks for Buddha's mercy. Because of Chang's objection, this promise was never fulfilled either. More than once Tz'u-sheng wished to have the annual autumn execution of prisoners suspended in the name of mercy; Chang Chü-cheng argued that such extreme leniency had no genuine basis in Buddhist teaching. Not all such rulings had been easy for the empress dowager to accept, especially in 1574, when, after her intercession failed, more than thirty prisoners were beheaded the next day.[23]

On an ordinary working day the emperor acted upon two to three dozen documents that were brought to his attention. Each was written on a long sheet of paper folded screen-fashion to form a pamphlet of four, eight, twelve, or more pages. The documents differed from one another in format, according to their classification, the number of characters on each page, and style of writing. But in general they fell into two major categories. Those submitted by capital officials in the name of their offices, along with reports and petitions from the provinces, carried imprints of official seals; they had to go through the Office of Transmission. When they reached the palace, duplicates had already been delivered to the Office of Supervising Secretaries at the two wings of the Meridian Gate. Very rarely would such public documents cause serious disturbances in the emperor's court. Capital officials, however, were entitled to submit memorials to the emperor as individuals, sometimes delivered by the writers themselves and received by palace eunuchs at the Gate of Polar Convergence. Without duplicates until the emperor's rescript was attached and sent to the supervising secretaries for publication, these personal petitions and their contents remained confidential, unknown even to the writers' superiors. Many a controversy was caused by papers in the latter category.

When Wan-li was in his early teens, he merely followed Big Companion Feng's instructions, affixing his own rescripts in vermilion ink on certain papers to make official the drafts in black submitted by Tutor Chang's office. The documents that he personally worked on involved simple replies such as *Approved* and *Acknowledged*. When the rescripts required complicated phraseology, the work was, as a rule, delegated to Feng Pao's squad of assistants. These proceedings were completely in agreement with the dynasty's established practice. An instruction written in red in the emperor's presence carried the authority of the throne. On the other hand, any unauthorized use of the vermilion brush constituted falsification of imperial order, a crime subject to the mandatory death penalty.

It must have been some time before the young emperor grasped the mechanics of the institutional process, of which he himself was the central figure. There is no evidence, for instance, that, when in those early days he carried out his official duty in a way not fundamentally different from taking calligraphy lessons, he fully understood the import of his own re-script *Acknowledged*, which really meant that the suggestion or request expressed in the paper had been politely rejected, and that, considering the noncontroversial nature of the proposal, no action would be taken against the writer of the paper or others mentioned therein. One duty Wan-li could not delegate had to do with his power of appointment. The problem was solved in this way: whenever there was a vacancy in a high office, Tutor Chang and the ministers always submitted more than one candidate for the emperor's selection. When he circled one name with his vermilion brush, that person was appointed, and the emperor had ostensibly made a deci-sion of his own. However, he had early been indoctrinated to believe that the person whose name topped the list was best qualified.[24]

Until Wan-li reached his adolescence, about the time, in 1575, when he performed the ceremony to report to his ancestors that thereafter he was to wear his hair long, his understanding of his own role was limited to several simple notions: that he had become emperor not by merit but owing to the will of Heaven; that this will would continue to hold true as long as he kept the populace content and happy and the world in harmony; that in order to do so he must put good men in office and get rid of evil ones; and that in all these areas Tutor Chang's advice must be followed because he always knew best. It must therefore have been a shock to Wan-li when, soon after his long-hair ceremony, he began to receive memorials naming Chang Chü-cheng an impostor and criticizing him for meting out penalties to others, not in the interests of the empire but to suit his own selfish designs. The most disturbing fact was that one of those remonstrating papers put the blame on the emperor himself. The three years' reign of His Majesty, the memorialist claimed, was noted for harshness toward those who worked tirelessly for the throne. This was contrary to the teaching of the ancient sages, who had repeatedly stressed that moral leadership starts from kind-ness and gentleness, that only through forgiveness will the good feelings under Heaven be nurtured and promoted. The present state of affairs indi-cated that the emperor was under the influence of evil counsel.

Faced with direct attacks and indirect charges, Chang Chü-cheng turned in his resignation to comply with the principle that, be the criticism just or unjust, a public figure with self-esteem should never cling to his position when being criticized. After all, his usefulness had already been nullified when he was openly proclaimed an obstacle between the imperial throne and public confidence. But the emperor absolutely refused to listen to these arguments. He was predisposed, rather, to punish the critics. A confidential meeting with Tutor Chang and the Big Companion further confirmed his suspicion that the memorialists were destructive and malicious. At this point Chang Chü-cheng pointed out that anyone working immediately under His Majesty was obliged to mete out punishments, call them what one wished. Good men must be rewarded and evil men punished. Otherwise how could state affairs be managed?

Thus the imperial decision was made. The first official who had raised the question of Tutor Chang's ill management was deprived of his rank and discharged from the Civil Service. The second challenger, knowing the likelihood of imperial displeasure over the remonstrance yet obstinately persisting in his argument, had in fact committed an act disrespectful to the throne. It was ordered that he be arrested, stripped of his robe before the Meridian Gate, and beaten with whipping clubs for a hundred strokes. A standard instrument for chastising insubordination, these clubs, with their rough sectional joints, had claimed many lives and left permanent scars on the thighs and hips of those who survived.[25]

But Chang Chü-cheng had no intention of letting the emperor go to such extremes. He interceded by petitioning the sovereign to omit the beating. The offender was exiled to the frontier instead. At this point the Wan-li emperor was much impressed by the magnanimity of his tutor, who would even beg for clemency on behalf of someone who had unjustly criticized him. He did not know, yet at least, that a person who gave offense to Chang Chu-cheng had to endure all kinds of harassments at the hands of numerous governmental functionaries, who believed that any additional injury they could inflict on the victim would ingratiate themselves with the grand-secretary, someone who could really deal out punishments. Only much later did the emperor learn that this second offender, though he escaped beating at the Meridian Gate, was tormented by everyone on his way to his exile and eventually died at the frontier post under most mysterious circumstances.

As time went by, however, Wan-li's understanding of his own surroundings was broadened by his study of history. Gradually he realized that monarchy under the Ming differed from that of previous dynasties. In any other period when the emperor was a minor, a regency would have been established for him. An uncle or a cousin would have acted as prince regent. This was not permitted under the Ming dynasty's constitution. A standing procedure established in the very early years of the dynasty had demanded that all imperial princes, including the emperor's uncles, cousins, younger brothers, and sons except for the heir apparent, be permanently removed from the capital upon reaching maturity. They were given territorial titles, palatial mansions, and annual stipends for life. But, settled in the provinces, they could never enter into politics; and without the emperor's explicit approval they could not even travel. The fundamental idea was to free the monarchy from interference by cadet branches of the imperial family.

A similar preventive measure dictated that imperial consorts must be selected from families of humble origin, not from those of social distinction. Wan-li's own maternal grandfather, Li Wei, had been a commoner of meager means. Only after Tz'u-sheng's elevation from palace woman to imperial consort did Li receive noble titles. Yet even then his earldom gave him no more than an honorific commission in the army with a modest stipend, accompanied by neither land grant nor active service. The only governmental functions in which he took part were ceremonial. It was to supplement his insufficient family income that Li Wei chose to be an intermediary between tax deliverers and palace eunuchs. One of his three sons became a palace eunuch himself.[26]

The dynasty had had only three prime ministers; they were all executed by the dynastic founder. Since the last one had been put to death for treason, no one had ever again been appointed to that position. The employment of grand-secretaries to fill the gap involved a certain ambiguity. A grand-secretary was an accomplished literate, having won high placement at the Civil Service examinations and, as a result of his talents, sent on to the Han-lin Academy for advanced study. Once appointed grand-secretary at the Literary Depth Pavilion, his duties were confined to putting the emperor's declarations and rescripts into an elegant prose style. At the beginning it was never conceived that a grand-secretary would become a policymaker. Because of its long-term continuity, the influence of the office steadily expanded during the middle period of the dynasty. Yet, until the reign of the Chia-ching emperor, the present emperor's grandfather, in their limited capacity of providing counsel to the throne, the three to six grand-secretaries had still worked as a team. The monarch might see a senior grand-secretary at more frequent intervals, but this did not demote the others to subordinate rank.[27] By the time Chang Chü-cheng became senior grand-secretary, however, he was indeed chief. The appointment of other grand-secretaries, all nominated by him, carried Wan-li's specific instruction to serve under Tutor Chang. This change undoubtedly sparked controversy.[28]

The essence of the constitutional arrangements and practices was that imperial power could not be delegated and in theory never had been delegated. But the principle could never have been enforced to the full, especially while the emperor was still a boy. Many years later Wan-li could laugh at the thought that his courtiers expected him to make his own decisions on numerous state issues when he was only twelve. At that time, if he remembered at all, he merely referred to Tutor Chang those instructions he had received from Big Companion Feng, and to the latter those rescripts drafted by Chang. That was why both of them were so indispensable. It would not have occurred to Wan-li that the close affiliation between the senior grand-secretary and the eunuch director in charge of the palace staff might also raise a controversial issue.

Despite the general misconception, eunuchs in Ming times could not be accurately labeled as domestic servants who rose to meddle in state affairs. It was true that every eunuch had to go through the process of self-castration before being selected to enter the palace, and for this reason eunuchs as a group usually gave an impression of being lowly born. But it would be a gross mistake to believe that none of them had achieved prominence by merit. Even during the reign of the first emperor, Hung-wu, eunuchs were frequently dispatched to tributary states as the sovereign's personal envoys and to the provinces as tax auditors.[29] After the middle period of the dynasty, their service as the emperor's personal secretaries had become essential to the palace operation, as by then several dozen memorials required imperial attention every day. Those papers were as a rule lengthy, with technical discourse mingled with doctrinal polemics. Even with careful reading, it was difficult to grasp the main issues and peripheral subtleties, not to mention the number of administrative terms and long lists of proper names. The Director of Ceremonies, who handled the papers, employed several senior eunuchs to examine these documents before reporting to the throne.

Few of the papers were held inside the palace or acted upon directly. The majority were dispatched to the grand-secretaries at the Literary Depth Pavilion for rescript writing. To sustain this process it was vital that the eunuchs in charge be prepared to brief the sovereign the next morning. Often they had to take turns working until midnight.

During their closed-door session with the emperor in the morning, it was the duty of these half-dozen eunuchs to advise the sovereign either to read the complete text of the memorial or merely to scan the significant parts of it, giving close attention to certain names and arguments. The emperor could approve the rescripts drafted by the grand-secretaries in toto or sometimes with minor revisions, especially in phraseology. In theory he could also reject the draft altogether and produce a rescript of his own. This sovereign right, however, was rarely exercised in practice. One implication of such a practice was that, under those circumstances, the grand-secretary concerned would be compelled to resign; and that should be prevented from happening for as long as possible. Normally, grand-secretaries were expected to hold office for life. Good emperors should induce their grand-secretaries to draft rescripts that were to their liking.

Although it was not impossible for an illiterate eunuch who had won the emperor's favor to break into this inner circle by becoming the Director of Ceremonies, such cases were few. Most of those in elevated positions had qualified for and earned them. A dominant majority had graduated from the Inner Palace School, which they first attended when they were no older than ten. Already screened for unusual talent and potential, they were given a classical education in no way different from that of the bureaucrats. In fact, their tutors were often the best talent of the Han-lin Academy. Not regular members of the Civil Service, those specially selected eunuchs nevertheless had gone through many rounds of competition among themselves as well as learning on the job as assistants and understudies to senior eunuchs before attaining their own seniority. Some of them had the skill to improve the style of writing of the grand-secretaries and to correct the wrong radicals of the characters. Since the emperor customarily signed only several documents a day, most state papers carried finishing touches by those eunuchs. If they did not inject their own ideas into the work, they at least kept the emperor informed of His Majesty's own doings, which was in itself a significant task.

This small group of confidential secretarial personnel, like other senior eunuchs, wore red robes, not black, which was the color of palace attendants. The most distinguished among the half-dozen, the Director of Ceremonies included, wore jackets with special designs authorized by the emperor, thus commanding prestige and influence above ministerial officials. From time to time one or two were even granted the special privilege of riding horses on avenues within the palace compound. Still better, the pinnacle of palatial honor was to be carried in a sedan chair—a most coveted privilege that was nothing short of viceregal significance. But when the system functioned well, the small party of eunuchs confined their ostentation to the palace. Separated from the bureaucracy and holding office at the emperor's pleasure, they were responsible to the sovereign himself. Their work remained anonymous; they would forever be unsung heroes within the governmental structure.[30]

Because of his closeness to Chang Chü-cheng, however, Feng Pao was not destined to remain unsung. Until the Wan-li emperor reached maturity he had not the slightest suspicion that his Big Companion would one day fall into the classic pattern of evil eunuchs, whose personal ambitions could ruin dynasties—a lesson he had come across often in his historical studies. On the contrary, Feng Pao was discreet and unassuming. Not an accomplished scholar, he nevertheless loved books and calligraphy, and indulged in such gentlemanly pastimes as playing the lute and chess. It was because of such attitudes that he earned Tz'u-sheng's confidence. Moreover, he had come a long way to reach his present distinction. A personal secretary to the Chia-ching emperor, he was in charge of the Eastern Depot during the reign of Lung-ch'ing, Wan-li's father. That agency, with the Silk Robe Guard under its control, was responsible for the security of the capital and for the supplying of secret information to the throne. After holding that sensitive position, Feng's promotion to Director of Ceremonies was only to be expected according to the dynasty's custom. But he was put aside by Kao Kung for a number of years. After Kao's dismissal he had finally advanced to this position, the highest any eunuch could hope to attain.[31]

In the autumn of 1577, the emperor's court was put to a serious test. Imperial Tutor Chang Chü-cheng's father had died in Hukwang. Standard procedure would have required the grand-secretary to relinquish his position and return to his native district to observe the period of mourning for twenty-seven months.[32] When his request for relief from duty came, Wan-li did not take it seriously, however. The emperor had already conferred with his two mothers and decided that Chang was irreplaceable. It could not be otherwise. His Majesty had recently celebrated his fifteenth birthday; both state affairs and his own education still required Tutor Chang's supervision. With the help of Feng Pao, he composed his own rescript in a mixed tone of command and entreaty urging Chang to stay in office. The grand-secretary resubmitted his request to leave two more times; Wan-li in his turn repeated the order, holding that Chang's service could not be suspended and denying the request for leave. In his last rescript he also added that this was the empress dowager's wish. The correspondence, sent back and forth between the palace office and the Literary Depth Pavilion not more than a thousand yards away, served a public purpose. Along with other documents, the papers eventually turned up at the Office of Supervising Secretaries for publication, where dozens of clerical workers made copies from the originals so that the entire court could read the full texts.

But there was little indication that the public was convinced either of Chang Chü-cheng's genuine desire to leave office or even that the wish to retain him had truly come from the imperial family. Official historians and readers-in-waiting of the Han-lin Academy, conscious of their position as members of the literary-educational branch of the government and therefore morally bound to keep the emperor's court in harmony with the teaching of ancient sages, were deeply disturbed. They realized that the dynasty stood upon its moral character, which was its strength. Otherwise it would never be able to govern the people. The secret of administering an enormous empire such as ours was not to rely on law or the power to regulate and punish but to induce the younger generation to venerate the old, the women to obey their menfolk, and the illiterate to follow the examples set by the learned. In all these areas the example set by the emperor's court was of paramount importance. Many of those Han-lin academicians had come from rural communities themselves. They knew that government by law had its limitations. But when a person was moved by the principles of loyalty and filial piety he would always remain upright and law-abiding. He would align himself behind his village leaders and kinship groups and conduct himself properly. These principles must nevertheless be repeatedly stressed, promoted, and expounded. What would the imperial subjects think now, if the emperor's own tutor regarded the requirement of mourning for a deceased parent as a mere gesture, to be performed only as long as it served his purpose and dispensed with when it did not?[33]

While the emperor remained unaware of it, scores of Han-lin academicians invited the minister of personnel to join them and marched him to Chang Chü-cheng's residence for a personal interview and appeal. They wished to persuade the grand-secretary to give up his pretension to being indispensable. Even for his own good, he should retire from active service for the required twenty-seven months in order to gain credibility for many years to come. The confrontation, however, was fruitless. The emperor, Chang argued, had personally commanded him to stay. How could a self-appointed committee come to his house and advise him to act to the contrary? Furthermore, Minister of Personnel Chang Han was in fact Chang Chü-cheng's protégé, having received his present position through the grand-secretary's intervention, which had put him ahead of two more qualified candidates. In the past four years he had also worked closely with Chang Chü-cheng in placing the grand-secretary's other protégés. After this short interview Chang Han was impeached by several censors—not for this private meeting at the grand-secretary's house, but for some unrelated matters which otherwise would never have been brought up—and was forced into retirement. This hardly made the dissatisfied academicians happy. They knew that the censorial-supervisory branch of the government, involving some 110 investigating censors and 52 supervising secretaries, had long since been turned into a tool subservient to Chang Chü-cheng.

One more line of action was open to the academicians, however: they could submit their own impeaching memorials. Though such a move would be, strictly speaking, outside their domain and open to the risk of retaliation, their offering of loyal and disinterested advice to the throne was nevertheless justified by the unusual circumstances. The thousands of pages from the most fundamental works which they had learned to recite and write about assured them of the absolute correctness of their action. In the dynasty's history, similar group remonstrances had been organized before. The initial petition was submitted by the lowest rank-holders among the bureaucrats, in mild language, to be followed by stronger arguments. If the sovereign were angered and decided to punish the memorialists, as was anticipated, the colleagues and superiors of the remonstrators would eventually have to intervene. Petitioning for mercy on behalf of the offenders, they would find it inevitable to speak on the case at issue in such a way that the entire court would be forced to take a stand. Even if the remonstrance did not prevail, the public agitation produced by it would have achieved its purpose. The organizers of the campaign would then feel that they had done their best, and their deeds would in due course be registered in history.

The attempted impeachment of Chang Chü-cheng proceeded in such a fashion. The first two memorials were submitted by two Han-lin academicians. They merely argued that Chang, grieving over the demise of his father, could not manage public affairs with his usual wisdom. It was therefore both cruel and unwise for the imperial family to compel him to remain in office. A stronger tone was taken in the two succeeding papers, signed by junior members of the Ministry of Justice. Imperial Tutor Chang was said to be brazenly shameless to hang on to his sinecure; this would do irreparable damage to the dynasty's revered traditions. Since Chang was unwilling to return to Hukwang, His Majesty the Emperor should issue him a stern order demanding his immediate departure and requiring him to remain at his father's burial site in repentence. Only then could the atmosphere of the imperial court be cleared.

No one can say for sure how the subsequent events in late November of 1577 developed and were given the finishing touches. Eunuchs ran back and forth between Tutor Chang's house and the palace. Inevitably some of them relayed messages to the second grand-secretary, who was acting on Chang's behalf while the case awaited the emperor's decision. It is unclear what Feng Pao reported to the empresses dowager. The emperor himself probably knew less than anyone; several years later, when he reviewed the sequence of events, he would think that indeed he had known very little. But the record testifies that imperial rescripts in vermilion ink called for severe punishments to the petitioners. They had openly defied the throne and showed their contempt for it.[34]

The first two memorialists were beaten sixty strokes in front of the Meridian Gate with whipping clubs. After the punishment their names were removed from the Civil Service register. The other two remonstrators were dealt twenty more strokes than the first two offenders because of their bold arguments. Furthermore, they were exiled to the frontier for life, ineligible for future pardon. The soldiers at the Silk Robe Guard always had a political sense of how exactly the beating should be administered, and in this case the wrath of the grand-secretary was carried out in full force. Thus the first dozen strokes had already ripped the skin of the victims; the successive blows simply kneaded human flesh with blood-soaked whipping clubs. One of the victims lost consciousness; it was a miracle that he survived. Another survivor, it was noticed, lost one buttock. After the beating the soldiers carried the offending memorialists away on canvas sheets and dumped them on the pavement outside the Imperial City. Their families were permitted to take them home. But others who looked after and comforted them had their names taken by the secret agents of the Eastern Depot. Many of these people were later summoned to the depot for further questioning.

The action taken by the throne came so suddenly and with such resoluteness that other remonstrators never had a chance to carry out their part of the plan. A declaration, duly signed by the Wan-li emperor, charged the remonstrators with directly countering his expressed wishes, thus exhibiting contempt for the throne. They were in reality taking advantage of his own youthfulness. Using morals and ethics as a pretext, they had attempted to deprive the emperor of his needed counsel so that they could do what they wished to satisfy their selfish purposes. The declaration went on to say that the punishment so far meted out was only a token penalty. Should the conspirators wish to proceed further, it promised to deal with them even more sternly. Thus a predetermined charge of treason awaited subsequent protestors. None came forth and the case was closed—at least for the next five years.

Chang Chü-cheng now attended his office in a cloth robe and a belt lined with ox-horn to express mourning. His salary was suspended as he had requested. But the emperor directed that portions of rice, tea, salt, vegetable oil, candles, firewood, and charcoal be regularly delivered to his residence. Wine and delicacies were supplied him by the Court of Imperial Entertainments every day. In protest dozens of disgruntled courtiers submitted their resignations. Since they pleaded only poor health and family reasons, the requests were routinely granted with no questions asked. The Secret Police had no reason to report to the emperor the handbills denouncing Chang Chü-cheng as a traitor which now appeared in the streets of Peking. Unsuccessful in making arrests, they could only quickly destroy the subversive literature that fell into their possession.

Grand-Secretary Chang changed into a red robe with a jade belt to celebrate Wan-li's imperial wedding in early 1578, then changed back into mourning dress to return to his native Chiang-ling for a vacation from mid-April to mid-July. His official duties were not interrupted, however. On important state matters the emperor dispatched the essential documents to him by special couriers who covered a distance of roughly one thousand miles.

Most likely, at that time the emperor had no inkling of the luxury in which Tutor Chang traveled. With the Secret Police under Big Companion Feng's supervision, such reports never reached the throne. But others knew that during the journey Chang was carried in a specially designed sedan chair which could have foreshadowed the railroad cars to come many centuries later. It was large enough to be divided into a bed-chamber and a reception room, staffed with two attendants and hauled by thirty-two bearers. The grand-secretary's bodyguards included a contingent of musketeers furnished by General Ch'i Chi-kuang. Enroute the emperor's chief counsellor was not only a guest of honor of civil officials, but also was greeted by imperial princes in residence who broke tradition to come out from the city

walls to welcome him. In Honan he visited his old adversary now in retirement, the former grand-secretary Kao Kung, in order to make peace with
him. Kao, already ill, correctly believed that he had only several months to
live. Chang Chü-cheng, in turn, pointed out that the hair at his own temples had turned gray, even though he was only in his early fifties. During
this reunion Chang never anticipated that their antagonism had yet to be
laid to rest, or that it would take its toll when both men were in their
graves.[35]

For Chang Chü-cheng, it was heart-warming that he continued to hold
the confidence of the emperor. The tutor explained to the young sovereign
that he himself was unpopular merely because he wanted to give the throne
his devoted service. The emperor replied that he understood; and he appreciated his tutor's loyalty and dedication, which "could penetrate the
sky." Before he took leave in April, Chang's farewell in the palace was a
moment of truth. Both the grand-secretary and the emperor shed tears. The
three months' separation seemed to last much longer. Upon Chang's return
Wan-li was very pleased as well as relieved. That autumn Chang
Chü-cheng's mother also arrived in Peking. She was immediately rushed to
the imperial palace, where the two empresses dowager drew her into their
inner circle and showered her with gifts. On that happy occasion neither
mother nor son realized that imperial favor was an expendable thing; when
it was used up there was an end to it, and as such it lacked the lingering
effect of the good will of common people under ordinary circumstances.[36]

The imperial wedding in early 1578 was not an exciting event. The emperor was only fourteen years old; his bride, daughter of a commoner
hastily given an army commission, was barely thirteen. Needless to say, this
was not a union of love. Wan-li merely abided by his mother's wish to have
many grandchildren as soon as possible. The installation of a principal wife
to the ruler legitimated his nuptials with other consorts, of whom two were
declared official only ten days after the wedding ceremony.

Most unfortunate was Empress Hsiao-tuan, as she is known to history.
She was, from her wedding day, permanently encased in palatial pomp and
comfort; yet, by the cruel exigency of tradition, her marriage was only a
state necessity, reducing her to an accessory to an institution, entitled to all
kinds of meaningless honors but to little satisfaction as a wife. She bore the
emperor a daughter and lived almost as long as he did. But at no time did
she in any way affect the course of his life. As the principal daughter-in-law
to Jen-sheng, the emperor's principal mother, she had both the privilege

and the obligation of attending her in public, such as helping her from her sedan chair, a task Hsiao-tuan performed exactly as required, thus earning for herself a reputation for filial piety. Inside the palace, however, she was better remembered as a ruthless mistress who frequently ordered her chambermaids beaten, sometimes to death.[37]

Yet, if Wan-li paid little attention to Hsiao-tuan, neither did he show much interest in the other two consorts. The important women in his life were yet to enter the picture, almost four years after his wedding to Hsiao-tuan, by the end of 1581 and later.

In the meantime the adolescent monarch was restless. The palace compound was magnificent but also oppressively monotonous. Even with those balustrades, incense burners, sculptured birds, and bronze lamps on stone bases, the Forbidden City comprised by and large the same architecture and routines over and over again. On fixed dates, the platoons and battalions of attendants changed from fur-lined robes with ear-covers, into silk, and then into light-weight gauze for the summer. Flowers were taken out from winter storage, leaves were raked, and ditches dredged—all according to a prearranged schedule. Yet palace life remained timeless and seasonless, lacking either the thrill of surprise or the excitement of anticipation. As emperor, Wan-li could not venture outside the palace compound. He could not even think of dropping in to visit his courtiers at home; no ritualistic proceedings to govern such behavior had been established in the dynasty's history.

But after his wedding Wan-li was at least free from Tz'u-sheng's daily supervision. Soon he discovered that life could be slightly more interesting. Sun Hai, a eunuch attendant, advised him to organize drinking parties with other attendants in the villas within the Imperial City. This was not exactly a city in the ordinary sense. The western portion of the enclosure was an immense park, with lakes, marble bridges, and white stone towers. The more than one thousand cranes hovering near the Lamaist temple in particular gave the area a feeling of warmth and informality, in contrast to the regimentation within the Forbidden City. Now the emperor often loitered both in and outside the gardens for fun, wearing tight-sleeved garments and carrying a sword, frequently under the influence of alcohol. One night in 1580, at seventeen, during one such merry hour Wan-li demanded that two palace women sing songs they were not familiar with. For their failure to obey the imperial order they were sentenced to death on the spot—a penalty carried out only symbolically, by cutting off tassels of their hair. Other attendants who tried to intervene were beaten. The incident was eventually reported to Tz'u-sheng by none other than Big Companion Feng Pao.

The empress dowager decided that such misconduct on the part of a monarch called for dethronement. She announced that Wan-li would be replaced by Prince Lu. Preparation had been made for herself, stripped of all regalia of honor because of her failure to provide her son with proper guidance, to report the decision to the family temple. At this point Wan-li knelt down before her in repentance. Only after holding out for over an hour did she accept his apology, on the condition that he would settle the case of misconduct with Chang Chü-cheng.

The grand-secretary made the sovereign pledge, in writing, to rectify himself. The attendants who had led him astray were ordered to report to the army. A review of the palace roster of personnel made with Feng Pao ended with the mass discharging of the emperor's favorite eunuchs, many of them merely because of their interest in sports. Tutor Chang further made himself responsible for the emperor's conduct even within the palace and free to advise the throne on private matters. Beginning in early 1581 he daily assigned four Han-lin academicians to keep company with the emperor, as an aid to His Majesty's effort toward "settling the mind and cultivating virtue."[38]

One area, however, Chang's surveillance could not reach. The hundreds of palace women were the emperor's property; no relationship involving them with him was illicit, because any liaison could be legitimated by granting the lady in question the title of secondary wife. The Ruler of All Men was entitled to one empress, usually one principal consort, a number of associate consorts, and still more concubines. Ever since the Cheng-te emperor had died without an heir, it had been generally recognized that the throne must widen the possibility of producing male offspring to assure regular succession.

Palace women were selected from the general population around Peking. Sometimes as many as three hundred were admitted to the imperial household as a group. Between the ages of nine and fourteen, the young girls were nominated by the precinct and village elders according to quotas assigned to the communities, and subsequently went through many rounds of screening and selection before they entered the palace gate, which to most of them was a point of no return for the rest of their lives.

Those nymphs inside the Forbidden City became a frequent topic of erotic literature. They were likened to sculptured jade yet said to be freshly fragrant, appearing either as voluptuous as fully blossomed peach trees glowing in the morning sun, or as slender and delicate as jasmine vibrating in an evening breeze. In reality, palace women were never unpleasant to look at, yet hardly so glamorous and disturbingly beautiful as the romantic poets described them because eye-catching quality had never been the standard for selection.

The tears and loneliness of the girls who grew up within the palace compound must, however, have been real. Unless a palace woman caught the fancy of the emperor, the only male in the palace (as Tz'u-sheng herself had done, and thus was elevated to what she was today), her life was forlorn indeed. Having wasted her flourishing years as a chambermaid, she either had to find the sympathy of a compatible eunuch in her middle age or be sent to the northwest corner of the palace to perform miscellaneous labors. Upon her death her remains would be cremated and buried in an unmarked grave to assure that neither rumor nor legend could arise around one who theoretically had been accessible to emperor or emperors in her lifetime. With so slim a chance of eliciting imperial favor, the lot of palace women was so uninviting that when an impending selection was announced, many thoughtful parents quickly married off their young daughters to eliminate their eligibility.[39]

But in the winter of 1581 that slim chance befell one of Tz'u-sheng's chambermaids, later known as Lady Wang. She captured Wan-li's fancy and became pregnant. For some time the liaison was kept from the empress dowager, as it was feared that the illicit connection would incur her displeasure. In March 1582, when the emperor chose nine concubines one day at his mother's direction, Lady Wang was not even included. But soon afterward, when Tz'u-sheng discovered the liaison and Lady Wang's pregnancy, she was far from displeased. On the contrary, she was elated by the prospect of a grandson. In July, the title of Consort Kung was conferred upon Lady Wang to enable her to give birth in late August with ample legitimacy to the Wan-li emperor's first son, Ch'ang-lo, later known to the courtiers as "the eldest imperial son." To celebrate the event, the imperial decree announcing the good tidings also proclaimed a general amnesty and tax remission throughout the realm. Special envoys were dispatched to Korea, the nearest tributary state, to break the news. Yet nowhere was Ch'ang-lo referred to as an imperial prince. By tradition, until the title was formally conferred, he was not one.[40]

With all this going on, 1582 was a year crowded with events. Its climax was the death of Chang Chü-cheng. In order to effect a basic cure of the empire's fiscal administration, the senior statesman had, in the name of the Wan-li emperor, ordered a national land survey; but his death came before the returns were consolidated. When Chang was first ill, it was disclosed that he had some difficulty in moving his bowels and laxatives were all that were needed. The sudden demise of such an energetic and alert person at the age of fifty-seven came as a profound shock to many, although it made others rejoice. Hardly nine days before, already seriously ill, Tutor Chang had been granted the title of Grand Preceptor, the highest honor any civil official could hope to attain—in fact, an honor that had not been conferred upon a living soul over the past two hundred years. Chang did not live long enough to put his additional prestige to work, to add more substance to his administration; nor did he have the opportunity to congratulate the emperor on the arrival of a son before his nineteenth birthday.[41]

In this connection, the installation of nine imperial concubines that year was important, as among them was Lady Cheng, then fourteen years old. How could an emperor of eighteen, with every desirable female within arm's length, prefer a romantic love affair with such an innocent little thing—one among at least a dozen who had been chosen for the sole purpose of providing the dynasty with reserve heirs—to his union with the woman who had infatuated him and given birth to his first son? More inscrutable still was the fact that this love was later said to have lasted throughout the rest of their lives and became a major cause of the "constitutional crisis" that was destined to make a prosperous empire unhappy. In fact, Lady Cheng at no time monopolized the emperor's attention. He was yet to have eight sons and ten daughters born of eight wives. He had a daughter by Lady Wang twenty-seven months after meeting Cheng. Furthermore, the emperor was later known to have been very much in love with another consort, Lady Li. Only her early death prevented her from leaving a significant impression on his life.[42]

Whether Wan-li's relationship with Lady Cheng should be called romantic love is debatable. The stories leaked out about her through palace eunuchs never established her as a great beauty. But she was said to have been intelligent, well-read, and strong-willed. Above all, she must have shared certain interests in life with Wan-li. Those qualities enabled her to satisfy his emotional needs.

Immediately after Tutor Chang's death, the emperor freed himself from the daily surveillance by the Han-lin academicians. Becoming a father that summer, he must have felt the relaxation of control by mother Tz'u-sheng. Yet his new sense of freedom never again induced him to keep company with rowdy eunuchs. He had truly come of age. It was about this time that he turned into an avid reader. Not only did he order his grand-secretaries to provide him with copies of the *Veritable Records* of the reigns preceding his own, but he also let his eunuch attendants purchase in Peking any newly published books they could lay hands on, including poetry, collections of essays, medical books, plays, novels, and detective stories. His delight in these printed pages was shared with Lady Cheng.[43]

Some of this reading material was marginally pornographic. What made a woman a woman? Was she supposed to enjoy sexual acts in bed? What made her part her lips and close her eyes? Did a flower love to have its ovary sucked by a honey bee? Popular literature, which rose phenomenally during His Majesty's reign, was full of sensual suggestion, though the vulgarity was as a rule made less offensive by poetry. How deeply did the emperor himself become involved in this development?

For many years to come Wan-li was to be criticized by his bureaucrats for his preoccupation with the "pleasure of women." His critics never seemed to understand, however, that imperial polygamy was basically utilitarian. Such pleasure as it yielded was at a low level. The ecstasy of love-making created by a freeing of body and mind in unison was hardly possible between a demigod and his terrified subject; for the latter in all likelihood had been awed to numbness beforehand. Even Wan-li's attraction to Lady Cheng could not have been primarily physical. If it had been, with all the alternatives available to him, his fondness for her could never have been so enduring. On a later occasion he confided to Grand-Secretary Shen Shih-hsing that Lady Cheng took good care of him. That must have been what gave him a sense of emotional security.

Lady Cheng had come into Wan-li's life at the right moment to fill a void. Overnight she must have grasped the reality that, beneath the dragon robe he wore, was a lonesome and defenseless human being. Even his own mother was determined to run him like an institution. Realizing this, Lady Cheng quickly kept her rendezvous with destiny and attained instant womanhood. While other ladies distanced themselves from the emperor out of submission and fear, she teased him, laughed at him, and joked with him. If she had not put herself on an equal footing with him and appeared as more than his equal, how could she have provided the strength and assurance he wanted so badly? Now eunuchs reported that the emperor and Lady Cheng visited the temples and villas in the Imperial City together, a favor that he was not known to have extended to other consorts. On at least one occasion they were seen praying together in a chapel. If the word of the eunuchs can be trusted, Lady Cheng was frequently unhappy about the emperor's indecisiveness. In such instances she would shout at him, "You *are* an old lady!"[44]

Being feminine and irresolute was something Wan-li had to shake himself loose from. In those hectic days of 1582 he strove to be diligent and attentive to his office, making a string of important decisions himself, especially on high-level appointments. Perhaps it was around this time that he watched his palace troupe put on a play called *A Pardon Granted on the Hua Mountains,* in which an unhappy emperor on stage chants: "My government is in the hands of the Ning family; and here I am, left to attend to ceremonies!" Eye-witnesses reported that the emperor in the audience was very disturbed, appearing to be as unhappy as the emperor onstage.[45]

But how to become a monarch with full authority, to rule as well as to reign? In Wan-li's case he still had to react to the memorandums brought to his attention, either to believe or disbelieve the arguments presented to him. Who were the memorialists? They were either followers of the deceased Grand Preceptor—those who owed him their career advancement, who had believed that he should be retained in office when his father died, and had prayed for his early recovery when he was ill—or else they were his enemies—those who believed that Chang Chü-cheng had been an impostor, a tyrant, and a hypocrite. In 1582, before the youthful emperor could fully appraise the situation, the pendulum in his court had swung back to favor the latter group. He had no knowledge that the official who had succeeded Chang Chü-cheng as first grand-secretary, Chang Ssu-wei, himself a protégé of the senior Chang, was a close friend to his own maternal grandfather, Li Wei, earl of Wu-ch'ing, and an archenemy of the chief eunuch, Big Companion Feng Pao. Still less did he realize that Chang Ssu-wei, reading public opinion correctly, was ready to reverse what Chang Chü-cheng had done to make himself popular.[46]

The movement to conduct a purge of the policies of the late Grand Preceptor started without a fuss. Although Chang Chü-cheng's name was not mentioned, an imperial decree acknowledged his national land survey to be a failure, as it had coerced provincial and local officials to over-report the cultivated acreages in their districts.[47] Caught unaware, Wan-li accepted the argument that seemingly had been advanced in order to publicize his thoughtfulness as sovereign. The moment he put his vermilion brush to paper, hundreds of officials who had worked diligently for the project, especially those who had reported significant acreage increases, were exposed to shame; on the other hand, those who had ignored or discounted Chang's instructions emerged as public heroes.

Encouraged by this event, in the next few months many inconspicuous figures went about impeaching other inconspicuous figures. It so happened that the censured were always in one way or another connected with the deceased Grand Preceptor. As their misdeeds were exposed, Chang Chü-cheng's record appeared to be more and more questionable. The momentum increased; accusations grew bolder and more direct in molding public opinion as it was stirred up. Slowly but irrevocably, Chang Chü-cheng emerged as having been very treacherous and deceitful. The purge gradually affected his close lieutenants, causing several with ministerial ranks to be removed. By the end of the year Chang was said to have cheated the emperor, plagued the population, accepted bribes, sold governmental offices, advanced his henchmen, let his household servants dominate and harass the officials, and even to have arranged marriages to perpetuate the association of his cohorts.[48]

The emperor now finally realized that his trust had been misplaced. Most difficult for him to accept was the fact that Tutor Chang, despite his endless lectures on frugality, had for all those years lived to a great extent in luxury. He had even filled his house with curios and rare paintings of all kinds. Although Chang had been widowed for a number of years, he had apparently maintained a harem of young women, some of them noted beauties who had been gifts offered by his lieutenants to gain his favor. Wan-li in quick succession felt saddened, wounded, humiliated, and enraged. Just to think that during all the years when he himself, the emperor, had felt he could not afford the necessary gifts for the palace women, and such gifts had had to be entered into the books in the form of vague promises to be kept some time in the future—to think that his grandfather had been forced to make a profit on tax cloth as a middleman and to suffer the humiliation of being scolded in public for wrong-doing—while Chang Chü-cheng, the saintly preacher, had all along been taking advantage of him and reaping all the benefits!

During the last days of 1582 and the early months of 1583, the emperor's mind remained disturbed. That winter Grand-Secretary Chang Ssu-wei suggested that he select a site for his future mausoleum, which provided some distraction.[49] In the early spring the triennial palace examination for the Civil Service candidates was due; Wan-li presided over the proceedings. The essay question was a short essay in itself, consisting of close to five hundred characters. In tune with the traditional custom of self-criticism, the sovereign asked the competing scholars why it was that the more he tried to tighten the administration, the more official corruption and breakdowns in law and order increased. Was it because he did not have sufficient kindness and gentleness within himself? Or had he been indecisive and irresolute? Undoubtedly the quiz had been prepared by the literary educational officials. The emperor's mind was nevertheless at work when he selected it over several alternative questions, thus revealing his own uncertainty.[50]

His court was not so hesitant in promoting the denunciation of Chang Chü-cheng's movement, however. During the winter practically all the surviving offenders against the deceased Grand Preceptor had been recalled from banishment and exile and reinstated in office, whether they were misfits, inefficient, or men of solid character who had refused to compromise.[51] But this movement could not go further and remain secure if Chang's close associate, Feng Pao, continued to occupy the sensitive position of Director of Ceremonies, with the Secret Police under his control. Two senior eunuchs, none other than Feng's immediate assistants, were chosen to approach the sovereign. His Majesty must be made to understand that among his confidants Feng Pao was the most deceitful. The bribes he received from civil officials and top army officers were prodigious. In fact, on the day Chang Chü-cheng died, Feng went to Chang's household and removed five curtains, all made of pearls. He also took nine pearls, some as large as eggs, that gave off light in the dark. The emperor was persuaded to press charges and confiscate the property. What remained unspoken was that, afterward, the two informing eunuchs were to receive as their spoils the offices vacated by Feng and his deputy, one for his directory and the other for the Eastern Depot.

Wan-li was still undecided.

"What would happen," he asked, "if Big Companion came to the throne room and started a fuss?"

The eunuchs replied, smiling: "He can't, Your Myriad Years. The moment your order is read to him he has to leave."[52]

Eventually Feng Pao, stripped of his rank and title, was ordered to report to the mausoleum of the dynastic founder in Nanking. The charge against him, "deceiving the emperor and preying upon the nation," needed no further substantiation. Since the legal concept was that all worldly goods belonged to the emperor and that individuals held property only at his pleasure, confiscation was a natural recourse when imperial pleasure was withdrawn.

The takeover of Feng Pao's household goods delighted yet saddened the sovereign. They were not as fabulous as the informers had claimed them to be, but they were substantial enough. There were gems and bullion, musical instruments and art works of historical fame. Although nominally the emperor owned everything within the Four Seas, in reality the possessions of a eunuch could make him envious! Some of the confiscated items might come in handy, as the wedding of his own brother, Prince Lu, was approaching.[53]

The next logical step was to confiscate Chang Chü-cheng's property too; it was said to exceed Feng's in value. For a long time Wan-li could not take such a step. Whenever he thought about Tutor Chang, he had mixed feelings, which brought back memories from his boyhood and adolescence. On one of the memorials about Chang Chü-cheng which the courtiers urged the emperor to sign into a proclamation, he wrote that he did not wish to be ungrateful to someone who had served him diligently for a decade.

Had Lady Cheng in any way affected his decision? Were her nagging and stubbornness, which according to the courtiers ruined not only the reign of the present emperor but later those of a son and a grandson as well, factors that hardened his heart? No one could say for sure. But in the summer of 1583 she was promoted by Wan-li from imperial concubine to Consort Te; and two and a half years later he advanced her to imperial consort, thus putting her above all his secondary wives and making her inferior in rank only to the empress. There is little doubt that from this point on she held more of the emperor's attention than anyone else. It was therefore unlikely that any important decision made by him was kept from her.

And there was Empress Dowager Tz'u-sheng. Before the deposed grandsecretary Kao Kung died, he made numerous approaches to Li Wei, her father, in the hope that the earl would help him to reopen his case. But as long as Chang Chü-cheng was alive the latter could do little. In fact, his clandestine contact with Kao Kung had already been reported by the Secret Police.[54] But this situation changed rapidly when Chang was dead and buried. In three months' time, the earl of Wu-ch'ing became the marquis of Wu-ch'ing. His influence could no longer be overlooked when the wind in his grandson's court had turned so much in his favor. What he confided to his daughter remains unknown. But she was, at least on one occasion, overheard to mention the enormous assets of Chang Chü-cheng.[55]

Now a book supposed to have been written by Kao Kung, called *Last Words on the Sick Bed*, was found in print.[56] In this memoir Kao insisted that he had been singled out in 1572 by the late Lung-ch'ing emperor as the principal guardian of the present emperor, then the heir designate. At the time, Kao had contemplated the removal of Feng Pao because the eunuch was known to have sold several official positions for profit. More serious still, on the first day the present emperor met the court, Feng, having escorted the sovereign designate to the dragon seat, did not step aside. Thus, when the officials kowtowed to the future emperor, they actually kowtowed to Feng Pao too. The eunuch, by using such a tricky maneuver to build up his own prestige, had already exposed his cynicism and contempt for the emperor. But before Kao could act, Feng had conspired with Chang Chü-cheng to secure from the imperial mothers the order of Kao's removal. The author did not deny outright his own remarks about the present emperor at the age of nine; but he claimed that he had been speaking of his fear that the new young sovereign might be misled by his eunuch attendants, as his granduncle, the Cheng-te emperor, had been when he ascended the throne before the age of fourteen.[57]

Kao, a master of deceit himself, could not have presented in this volume all the facts as they had occurred even if his authorship were genuine, which is very much in doubt. But it made little difference. The publication of the memoir was well timed; it captured the moment when many readers would seize upon it as nothing but the truth. Its many references to the names of witnesses had the tone and color of authenticity. But most of these witnesses were no longer alive when the book was published.

Last Words on the Sick Bed had yet more damage to render Chang Chü-cheng over the capture of Wang Ta-ch'en, said to have taken place on February 20, 1573, or about a half-year after Wan-li's accession and author Kao Kung's banishment. This case was not merely fabrication. Official records corroborated that on that day, in the early morning, a man disguised as a eunuch had been seized by the guards at the main palace gate. Interrogation established that he was Wang Ta-ch'en, who had been a household servant but was then unemployed. The case was by no means unprecedented. Despite the vigilance at the palace gates, once in a while intruders managed to enter. It was unclear what Wang's intention was. Kao Kung asserted in his memoir that Wang came from Ch'i Chi-kuang's command, and the exposure of his connection with the general would have embarrassed Chang Chü-cheng, who was then patronizing Ch'i in the face of strong criticism. At the same time, Feng Pao, having put Kao Kung under house arrest on the basis of distorted reports and false charges, was afraid that the dismissed grand-secretary would one day come forward to testify against him. The two decided to use Wang Ta-ch'en to frame an attempt on Wan-li's life so that Kao Kung could be permanently silenced. According to the memoir, Feng Pao had supplied the palace intruder with what appeared to be weapons for assassination but promised him immunity and a generous reward if he would confess that he had been sent there by the malcontent Kao Kung. To protect the scheme from discovery, Chang Chü-cheng was to arrange for a rapid trial and quick return of verdict so that Kao could be implicated and dealt capital punishment.

The scheme went awry because, first, the bureaucrats whom Chang Chü-cheng had canvassed refused to cooperate, and then, Wang Ta-ch'en, realizing at last the enormous risk he was taking, backed away from the arrangement at the preliminary trial at the Eastern Depot. Instead he threatened to tell the truth. Now Feng Pao, in desperation, ordered that poisonous wine be served to the prisoner that night until his vocal cords were destroyed. The public trial two days later produced only a speechless and defenseless prisoner. He was sentenced to death, and the sentence was immediately carried out to relieve the anxiety of the conspirators, whose plan had nearly backfired.

Now, a decade later, was the emperor to believe all this or to dismiss it as hearsay? There must be some substance to the story. He still vaguely remembered that at age nine he had been told that a bad man had sneaked into the palace compound. Tutor Chang's warning still appeared in the journals. At one point the puzzled sovereign called for the files on this case of Wang Ta-ch'en. The papers, however, revealed little. They merely indicated that the trespasser by that name who had two daggers concealed under his robe was executed on March 25, 1573. Yet Kao Kung's friends were so convinced of the authenticity of the intrigue that they engraved the story of the plot on Kao's tombstone.[58]

Wan-li ordered an inquiry to find out the truth. Only on the advice of Grand-Secretary Shen Shih-hsing was the order withdrawn. Except for Feng Pao, all principal characters referred to in the case, including the trial judge, had died within the ten-year period. The investigation was likely to create serious disturbance without arriving at adequate conclusions. Yet, in one way Kao Kung's memoir had already achieved its purpose. Never again could the Wan-li emperor think of his deceased tutor with even mixed respect and affection. He and his mothers had thought that Chang had secured the throne for him while he was helplessly young. It turned out that Chang Chü-cheng had worked only for the benefit of Chang Chü-cheng! If for a slight personal advantage he had been willing to sacrifice a former friend and colleague by judicial murder, what else could one have expected from him?

Early that year Wan-li had revoked the Civil Service ranks of Tutor Chang's three sons. In April 1573, when further conspiracies of Chang with

Feng Pao were brought to his attention, he decreed that Chang Chü-cheng's title of Grand Preceptor be posthumously eliminated.[59] The anti-Chang group then circulated the story that before his death the grand-secretary had actually intrigued to usurp the throne. Ch'i Chi-kuang was to make his army available at the right moment. A provincial examiner in Chang's confidence had placed before the candidates an essay question which insinuated that the imperial throne belonged to the most virtuous and most talented. This was now construed to have been put forth to test public opinion and to create the atmosphere for an impending takeover. This last news item had disturbed the Wan-li emperor so much that he had the quiz found in the records and showed it to Grand-Secretary Shen Shih-hsing. The latter had considerable difficulty in assuring the sovereign that the essay topic, quoted from classical sources, could not have such implications.

Yet, as more of Chang Chü-cheng's life was laid bare, the emperor was even less at ease with his ghost. It had become clear that when the grand-secretary was alive, he had surrounded himself with cronies who constantly flattered him as a statesman of imperial timber and a leader of majestic vision. Chang, smiling pleasantly, had made no gesture to deny their flattery. His having taken their comments for granted led to the speculation that the imperial throne was indeed what he was aiming for.[60] Even such presumptuousness Wan-li might have tolerated. But more unforgivable was the fact that Chang Chü-cheng had also allowed his followers to call him I Yin. Who was I Yin? He was a sagelike statesman in ancient Shang times. Having assisted Ch'eng-t'ang to become ruler of all China, he had held the regency for his heir and grandson, T'ai-chia. But as the latter grew immoral, I Yin dethroned him and took over the sovereignty himself. He acted as ruler for three years, returning the throne to T'ai-chia only after the latter had shown repentance and made amends.

With all its insinuations, this story could well cause the Wan-li emperor's face to turn alternatively red and white with humiliation and rage.[61] Yet for a time he still tried to forget the whole thing. It was only in May 1584 that he finally authorized the confiscation of Chang's properties. The action was touched off by an incendiary petition submitted by an imperial princess who charged that when Chang Chü-cheng was alive he had not only wrongly stripped her husband of his aristocratic title but also seized their family estate for personal gain. The emperor's order of confiscation, however, involved some technical difficulties. Almost two years had slipped by since Chang's death. The decree must produce what had been in his possession as of two years ago and not be limited to what was now found on the deceased's premises. This meant that an effort had to be made to uncover what was hidden and what had been carried away. In such a case the judiciary procedure called for a fair estimate of the assets, based not on evidence but on the general reputation of the accused and his standard of living. His kin must then be forced to make up the difference.[62]

Now Chang Chü-cheng's high style of living had been so well publicized and the emperor's anger so inflamed that the officials executing the confiscation order dared not produce less than what seemed to be logically adequate. Chang's house in Peking was assessed at 10,000 ounces of silver. His brother and sons, under arrest in Chiang-ling, had together surrendered assets in excess of 100,000 ounces of silver plus gold and silver jewelry. When more was demanded from them, the eldest son, already badly beaten, confessed that he had indeed hidden three times that amount somewhere. The next morning he was found dead; he had hanged himself. Several days later a household servant followed suit.

Chang's household goods, loaded on 110 carrying trays, were delivered at the palace. Among the effects were four sheets of calligraphy done by His Majesty the Emperor and given to his cherished tutor several years before to commend his loyalty and devotion. No prizes of excessive value were said to have been produced by the confiscation proceedings. If Wan-li personally checked those effects, his reaction is not recorded. The only person who could have interceded in the case was Empress Dowager Tz'u-sheng; apparently she did not make the move. It was about that time when her own father, the marquis of Wu-ch'ing, died. He was posthumously honored as a duke; the aristocratic title was, moreover, inherited by the first son.[63] Entirely unprecedented, the conferring of honor to imperial in-laws on such an extravagant scale would never have been possible during the era of Chang Chü-cheng, who, if alive, would certainly have argued against it in the interest of the dynasty.

After the confiscation of family properties, two persons pleaded mercy for Chang's mother. As a result, Wan-li ordered that a cottage along with 160 acres of land be set aside for her use. Yet one of the petitioners, Grand-Secretary Shen Shih-hsing, received a mild reprimand from the throne for siding with the Chang family. The other was less fortunate. Minister of Justice P'an Chi-hsün was subsequently dismissed from the Civil Service for exaggerating the hardships of the Changs.[64]

Having gone this far, it would have been difficult for the Wan-li emperor to retreat from his position. But there was no basis upon which to build a case of treason or usurpation; nor would such charges serve the interest of

His Majesty the Emperor. A general proclamation was nevertheless required. It came another four months later. In September 1584, after the imperial censorate had listed all the wrong-doings of Chang Chü-cheng, Wan-li declared that his former tutor and grand-secretary had abused power, perverted governmental operation, silenced public opinion, and withheld information from the throne. All these, added to gross disloyalty in managing state affairs, would have justified "the reopening of his coffin and desecration of his remains." It was only in consideration for his many years of service that this penalty was omitted. Instead, Chang's offenses were posted in every corner of the realm. One of his brothers and two sons were exiled to remote frontiers in perpetuity.

With Tutor Chang posthumously disgraced and Big Companion Feng Pao banished, the emperor had fully regained the reins of his government. But soon he was to discover that the freedom of action he had anticipated was as illusory as ever. After all, to become Son of Heaven was to fulfill an institutional requirement only.

What was the true meaning behind this anti–Chang Chü-cheng movement? It gradually became clear to Wan-li that those who spoke against Chang were of two different types. Some of them were of solid character but also very conservative and inflexible. As soon as the case with Chang was settled, they, among them remonstrators who had previously been beaten at the Meridian Gate and were now reinstated, lost no time in memorializing to censure the emperor himself. Now His Majesty was criticized for being extravagant, indolent, pleasure-seeking, and unfair to his wives—for example, in putting Lady Cheng ahead of Lady Wang. They were determined to make him appear anything but himself. There was another group of officials who, also speaking with moral tongue, pretended that they alone had the strength and vision to expose this Chang-Feng combination and to save the throne from the results of its conspiracies. Having eliminated a few top officials whom they disliked, they now busied themselves with clues as to who had married whose cousin and who had been seen with whose household manager, so that the charge of guilt by association could be extended; and in so doing they created more vacancies in the government and at the same time promoted their own influence. This practice came to a halt only after the emperor, smarting from their censure, reversed himself and demoted some of the agitators, reassigning them to remote provinces.

Now in 1587 His Majesty the Wan-li emperor was still only twenty-four years old; but he had been ruler for fifteen years. The time-span seemed even longer because of so many repetitious and tiring routines. A year earlier Lady Cheng, now imperial consort, had given birth to Ch'ang-hsün. A son born of the woman he loved should have given Wan-li some comfort. But Ch'ang-hsün, called by the courtiers the "third imperial son," turned out to be a heavy burden ever after his birth. Alert observers could tell that the emperor was either tired or bored or both. He had chosen as essay topic for the last palace examination a theme related to the Taoist doctrine that good government could be maintained while the ruler did nothing.[65]

Yet his reign, destined to be the longest of the dynasty, still had a long way to go, crowded with many events. The Year of the Pig was only an insignificant interlude. That July the former imperial tutor, Chang Chü-cheng, had been dead exactly five years. It suddenly occurred to Wan-li to ask what had happened to the house in Peking that had been confiscated from Chang's family and was assessed at a value of 10,000 ounces of silver? Was it occupied? By whom? Or had it been sold or rented? He was curious enough to ask the Ministry of Works to give him an answer. But whatever the reply was, it was not entered in the state records. Apparently the chroniclers felt that by merely writing down the emperor's questions they had faithfully reported his state of mind. The issue itself was too trivial to merit following up.[66]

2 SHEN SHIH-HSING, FIRST GRAND-SECRETARY

For Shen Shih-hsing the moral burden was heavy every time he drew close to the Literary Floral Hall, a yellow-tiled building on the eastern side of the palace compound where the emperor held his private and public study sessions. It was there that one day in 1574 he had watched the Wan-li emperor, then ten years old, execute a sheet of calligraphy, *Present Me to Goodness and Purify Me*.[1]. The scroll was a message for Shen. He had been touched to receive a unique personal gift from the throne so precociously and appropriately composed. Thirteen years later, Tutor Shen still had the imperial handwriting hanging in his residence; but now, alas, the early promise of a brilliant reign by Wan-li might never come to fruition.

Although Shen Shih-hsing was not one of the five instructors who had taught the crown his basic subjects, he had lectured before the emperor longer and more often than anyone else.[2] Now, as first grand-secretary, he also had overall responsibility for the latter's study sessions, which is why the reigning monarch addressed him as "My Dear Tutor." Seldom did a whole month slip by without his receiving something from the throne as a reward for his service. These imperial gifts were sometimes tokens in the form of two samli, baskets of arbutus, folding fans, and branches of mugwort—articles of seasonal significance merely to remind the instructor that he was not forgotten on special occasions. But sometimes they could be quite substantial, consisting, for example, of pieces of silver and rolls of silk fabric in palace designs.[3]

Whether or not the gifts from the throne had financial value, it was the courtesy of the emperor that counted, with its implication of the recipient's prestige and influence. Indeed, in these days to be appointed an emperor's instructor was a crucial turning point in a bureaucrat's career. Not everyone so appointed was destined to reach the highest office; but few of those who had not received the appointment could even hope to arrive at the top. To be a lecturer at the public sessions attended by the emperor himself especially attested a court official's unchallengeable erudition. He must be a highly qualified theoretician of statecraft if not a simultaneous practitioner of it.

By tradition the emperor's private study sessions started as soon as he was designated imperial heir, or when he reached six years old; at that time he was introduced to the Han-lin academicians. His public study sessions followed the enthronement and lasted throughout his reign. Held in the spring and autumn when the weather was comfortable, the public sessions took place three times a month. Attendance by all six ministers, two chief censors, all grand-secretaries, and other dignitaries, including the top aristocratic title-holders nominally on duty with the imperial army, was mandatory. The crowd was augmented by six supervising secretaries and ceremonial officials, all in their embroidered robes.

The session started very early in the morning, right after sunrise. To stress the solemnity of the occasion, the emperor arrived with twenty bodyguards. Although not in armor as during other rituals, they carried their ceremonial weapons. First the sovereign took his seat in the study hall facing the doorway on the south. At his command the assembly of officials entered the Literary Floral Gate. In the yard at the top of the granite staircase they kowtowed to the emperor. Only then were two lecterns carried in by the ceremonial officials and placed before the emperor, one just in front of him and the other facing it two steps away, for the lecturers. By this time the participating officials had filed into the building. According to rank and function, they flanked the path extending from the imperial seat to the doorway, including the lecterns.

Like all ceremonies, this one achieved audio and visual symmetry and balance. Each session was to begin with the exposition of selected verses from the *Four Books*, to be followed by a lecture based on another classical work, often historical. Two identical sets of textbooks, together with lecture notes neatly copied and submitted one day in advance for His Majesty's preview, had been placed on the lecterns. A volume of the *Four Books* was always on the sovereign's lefthand side. At the chanting of the master of ceremonies, two lecturers in red robes and two librarian assistants in dark blue, all Han-lin academicians, broke from the ranks of lined-up officials to take their positions, the lecturers with backs to the doorway facing the emperor, the librarian assistants on two sides facing each other. Now the lecturers performed their own round of kowtowing. That done, the librarian assistant on the left came close to His Majesty's lectern and knelt. He turned to the exact page of the copy of *Four Books* and spread out his lecture notes. Simultaneously the lecturer on the left advanced one-and-a-half steps to the center and started his discussion. When he had finished, the copy of the *Four Books* was duly closed. The two performers retreated in good order to make way for their counterparts on the right. The entire proceedings occupied a good portion of the morning, through which the emperor, the only one seated, remained motionless and at attention.[4] If he should inadvertently cross his legs, the lecturer was obligated to quote classical sources asking the question: Can the ruler himself neglect the principle of propriety? The question was repeated until it elicited a silent answer. The sovereign, awed by the reprimand, would revert to his original posture.[5]

With all its ritualistic trappings, the lecture was a vital state institution. Though elucidating classical works, the lecturers were expected to relate their messages to the current affairs of the state. Not only were the dictums about the primary duties of the Son of Heaven, including his concern for the well-being of the people and the absolute importance of maintaining general moral standards, immediately applicable to the entire audience—not least the seated sovereign; but citing historical events was a way of comparing past with present, and thus of reiterating the close relationship between ethics and public well-being. A good lecturer must achieve this purpose. Imperial tutors who merely presented perfunctory lectures or used them to flatter the throne were considered disloyal, and in some cases in the past had been dismissed.

When criticizing the emperor, the lecturer had, of course, to choose subtle approaches to make his inferences least offensive. The sovereign was entitled to ask questions and even to add comments of his own. But to challenge the speaker during the course of the lecture would have been a serious breach of decorum. Even if the instructor should go wrong because of poor preparation, imperial displeasure must be held back for the time being, to be expressed later at some opportune moment, and indirectly. This immunity of the lecturer had been observed even by Cheng-te, the present emperor's granduncle, who had broken many traditions but never this rule. Though he loathed the remarks on his personal conduct repeatedly implied in the lectures, he nevertheless managed to maintain his forbearance. His only retaliatory measure took the form of sudden promotions of his most critical instructors to the remotest posts of the empire.[6]

Now no longer a performer at the study sessions, Shen Shih-hsing was their planner and coordinator. His office of the Grand-Secretariat at the Literary Depth Pavilion was also located inside the Meridian Gate. However, many interior gates and partitions separated it from the throne hall and the emperor's living quarters. On any working day the sovereign and his chief counsellor might not be more than a thousand yards away from each other, but it was the longest thousand yards in the world. Aside from the morning audience and the study sessions, the emperor rarely saw his grand-secretaries. Their intercommunications were conducted on paper, although sometimes imperial orders were relayed verbally by eunuchs. Very seldom did Wan-li summon a grand-secretary for consultation. When Shen Shih-hsing held the position, he was summoned on the average less than once a year. And the last time an emperor had visited the office of the Grand-Secretariat was 160 years earlier.

The Literary Depth Pavilion consisted of a main hall housing a statue of Confucius. It had four offices in addition to library facilities on the sides and in the attic. A bungalow across the yard provided working space for clerical assistants. As the nerve center of a large empire the layout was notably unassuming. But it had already been greatly improved from what it used to be during the earlier days of the dynasty when, in fact a "pavilion," it had served as little more than a place for the emperor's document officers to sit. The extension of office space, additional furnishings, and employment of clerical personnel marked the maturity of the secretariat. Only now it was not so clear whether the pavilion was a liaison office between the Civil Service and the throne, a command post over the ministries, merely an advisory body, or even an arbitrating agency. A great deal of its work could be described as the application of abstract principles to real problems. Often when, with the emperor's approval, it made a decision about personnel management or something else, the published justification for the move possessed moral overtones which blurred the practical issues behind it. This departure from the true points at issue resulted from a lack of statutory guidance that could deal with the legal technicalities of specific details. But the practice made public discussion of classical works even more vital, as they supported these moral overtones.[7]

Shen Shih-hsing had no reason to enjoy these public lessons any more than anyone else did. The sessions were much too long, the proceedings too formal. The themes chosen from classical sources had never been astoundingly interesting. To be on time for the assembly, he had to get up well before daybreak. Like all the other participants, before the middle of the session he felt tired and would be looking forward to the food and wine to be served in the reception room at the Left Concord Gate immediately afterward. But even this treat had to wait until the lecterns were removed, all the participants had filed in good order from the lecture hall, and had kowtowed once more to the emperor in the yard outside the building. At the gate room the banquet had been prepared in advance; yet it took a long time to seat everyone. The ranks and positions of the participants must be observed; nevertheless, exceptions were made for the lecturers, librarian assistants, and copyists who had duplicated the lecture notes, who took seats of higher honor over those of the same grade as themselves.

As the first grand-secretary, Shen Shih-hsing was personally responsible for maintaining the session in perfect order. He would feel disturbed if the Wan-li emperor showed signs of fatigue during the proceedings, a lecturer did not perform as well as expected, or something else went wrong with the ritual. By 1587, the Year of the Pig, he must have attended such lectures more than a hundred times, as prior to Wan-li's reign he had lectured in front of the Lung-ch'ing emperor. On the granite apron outside the Literary Floral Hall he had prostrated himself so often that he practically recognized its every stone. Not to mention the long hours of standing inside!

Sometimes Shen wondered why he had to be the one to argue that the study sessions must continue. Would not he, for his own sake, also love to be excused from the agonizing routine? The same thing applied to the emperor's morning audience. Even Censor-in-Chief Keng Ting-hsiang, a vigorous man, confessed in one of his essays that he had great difficulty during the predawn event. It was worse on cold winter days. Like Keng, Shen Shih-hsing had originally come from the south where the weather was never like that of Peking. When, the previous winter, on a bitterly cold morning, he had overheard his colleagues saying that one man's white face had turned red and another's red face had turned black, he knew that his own admonition to carry on the audience proceedings would never make him popular.[8]

In 1587 Shen Shih-hsing was fifty-two years old. As he had pointed out in one of his memorials to the emperor, his hair and beard had already started to turn gray when he was still in his forties.[9] As first grand-secretary, wearing a robe of the python design, he had also reached the highest rung of the Civil Service ladder.[10] And then, there was the prior example of Chang Chü-cheng. Why not relax and take things as they come?

Relax indeed he could; he was never known as an impetuous man. But take things as they come he must not. In providing the best leadership to an empire such as ours, there was no substitute for ritualistic proceedings. The emperor did not have a formidable army at his command; he did not even have a large land base. He remained the Son of Heaven only because everybody believed that he was. This belief required the ritualistic exercises involving the sovereign and his chief ministers to be enacted with vigor and regularity, completely in a public spirit, and accompanied by aesthetic and moral overtones. Pageantry or not, the many rounds of kowtowing reaffirmed imperial supremacy; yet merely the fact that the emperor attended the ceremonies indicated that he was subjecting himself to the cosmic order and moral law. It was precisely because the messages taken from the basic classical sources were dull and trite that one must be prepared to listen to them again and again. The heat and cold and the predawn hour only tested the human will. This idea of discipline and endurance had been emphasized by Censor Keng. Even in the emperor's farming ritual obviously a degree of make-believe was involved; but make-believe is not necessarily unreal. One must realize how powerful an instrument of government it was when all the participants shared a belief in it. The emperor's public study sessions symbolized an even more concrete meaning: the occupant of the throne and his best policymakers were seeking classical and historical guidance to arrive at an enlightened administration.

Thinking this way did not help Shen Shih-hsing to feel any easier, because in 1587 there was little evidence that his tutorship over the emperor was a success. If it was, why had the twenty-four-year-old Wan-li emperor twice within the past twelve months declared that he had suffered from blackout when rising early in the morning and therefore had to have his audience with the court and the study sessions suspended for unspecified periods of time? Why had this happened both times in early autumn, when a new series of lectures had just gotten under way?[11] More disturbing still was the fact that, though Wan-li had said he was unwell, the eunuchs revealed that His Majesty had been horseback-riding at the palace stable. He might even have been thrown from a horse and injured his forehead, which he did not want the courtiers to see.[12] News of the incident had circulated widely, causing a secretary from the Ministry of Rites to remonstrate against the emperor for his negligence of duty and failure to take care of himself as the Son of Heaven. This fuss had hardly died down when in the early spring Wan-li again asked to be excused from public functions, this time saying that, owing to an overabundance of the fire element in his body, he had taken some cooling medicine, which, however, had driven the burning discomfort down to his feet, causing such unbearable itching that his resultant scratching had torn his skin. In the meantime stories persistently leaked out that the monarch was drinking to excess, was staying out too late at night, and was overly involved with the palace ladies.[13]

There was little that Tutor Shen could do. With care he spread the stationery on his desk to compose a most persuasive memorial pleading with His Majesty, for the sake of the Imperial Shrine, to take good care of himself. In it he nevertheless pointed out that the founder of the dynasty, the Hung-wu emperor, had carried on his public study sessions to the very end of his reign, by which time he was close to seventy.[14] Would this message sway the young sovereign? The first grand-secretary was not sure.

In an anxious and gloomy moment, Shen Shih-hsing once wrote diagnosing the ailment of the empire as "a cleavage between the top and the bottom," which, he went on to explain, meant "the separation of the interior from the exterior." "Never since ancient times," he continued, "has a state under these conditions managed to remain in peace and order for long."[15]

But Shen Shih-hsing did not like to give up easily. At times he confided to his close friends that he found himself in an impossible position. He also wrote poems blaming himself for his own failure and expressing his wish to retire so that he might enjoy the leisure of a gentleman-farmer in his native Soochow.[16] Once such feelings had been vented, however, he turned his attention back to his office. If the emperor said that his trouble was itching feet, then the first grand-secretary had to believe him. He should be grateful that the sovereign disclosed his discomfort at such length. This in itself was a good sign, and his absence could not be more than a temporary setback, as even according to the emperor's own description his was not a serious illness. Having appointed the new librarian assistants, Tutor Shen was ready to resume the lectures any time the emperor was. But while he waited he also pondered the possibility of whether Wan-li could be persuaded to continue his studies at some later time of day, such as mid-morning, if getting up early was too much for him.[17]

The first grand-secretary was an effective persuader. As such, he must be prepared to be a believer. Unless he convinced himself that certain methods would work, it would be deceitful and pointless to solicit the commitment of others to them. In a situation where things needed to be done, he could not wait for others to make the initial move before he joined them. He must be willing to take the plunge without reservation. This prior commitment, called by him "sincerity," would then enable him to inspire others and be ready to accept only partial commitment on their part. In a letter to his friend, he disclosed that he was mustering his maximum sincerity to win the heart of the emperor.[18]

In reality a state of mental assertion, or the mobilization of will power in a group effort, this quality of sincerity was cited in the opening paragraphs of the *Four Books*. It was to put this citation and other doctrines from the classics to work that the services of academicians like Shen Shih-hsing had been enlisted.

In 1587 Shen Shih-hsing had been the first grand-secretary for four years. He had attained that position because of what seemed to be a capricious sequence of events.

When Chang Chü-cheng died in 1582, his position had passed to Chang Ssu-wei. But in less than a year the second Chang's father also died. It would have been absolutely impossible for him to maneuver to remain in office. In his absence, Shen Shih-hsing, not too long ago the junior grand-secretary, was ordered to act on Chang's behalf, as very shortly before then death and illness had eliminated all those senior to him. Most unexpectedly, Chang Ssu-wei was never to return. His mourning completed, he himself fell ill and never recovered.[19]

In 1587, Shen Shih-hsing was in the prime of life despite his constant references to his gray hair. Since his parents had been buried for a number of years, his career was never to be interrupted by mourning. But neither was he as ambitious as his predecessors; in fact, to be mild and gentle was his ambition. His biographers went to great lengths to describe him as reserved and unpresumptuous, and as "a man who refused to stand on precipitous cliffs."[20] It was destiny that made him first the emperor's chief counsellor and then the center of a controversy which eventually forced him to turn in his resignation no fewer than eleven times before he was permitted to leave his high post.

True, being labeled as Chang Chü-cheng's protégé was a handicap. Yet immediately after 1582 who in the high echelons of government was not? It might even be said that Shen Shih-hsing had earned Chang Chü-cheng's trust more by merit and less by maneuver than had Chang Ssu-wei; and once Chang Chü-cheng was dead and thus unable to fend off the variety of charges against him, Shen Shih-hsing recognized Chang's mistakes but refused to make the deeds of his former mentor appear worse than they were. These sterling qualities were recognized by his fellow officials, and undoubtedly also by the Wan-li emperor.

Like most grand-secretaries, Shen Shih-hsing had started his official career within the literary-educational branch of the government. Ever since he had distinguished himself in 1562 by winning first place among 299 successful candidates at the palace examinations, he had been assigned to the Han-lin Academy.[21] He served there for fifteen years, first as a literary editor and finally as a reader-in-waiting. Before his appointment to grand-secretary in 1578 the only nonacademic position he had ever held was that of vice-minister for seven months. Like his predecessors Chang Chü-cheng and Kao Kung, he never held office outside the capital.

Did top academicians automatically become superb statesmen? How would court historians and great prose-writers qualify as the emperor's personal advisers? Where and how would they gain administrative experience? Twenty-five years earlier Han-lin bachelor Shen Shih-hsing could have asked the same questions. But now Grand-Secretary Shen Shih-hsing no longer had any doubt about these issues. Why? Because our empire was created to be controlled from the center by documents; field experience or the lack of it made very little difference.

There were 1,100 counties within the realm, of which each magistrate was appointed by His Majesty the Emperor. Could any one sitting in the capital really control how these magistrates managed their districts? Of course not. The best he could do was to investigate their characters, and through personal evaluation at periodic intervals divide the magistrates into categories and earmark them for promotion and demotion. Only occasionally, at best, were outstanding accomplishments promptly cited along with those who had achieved them, and the worst cases of mismanagement and negligence immediately dealt with. This meant that the greater part of governmental business involved personnel management and was basically settled on paper according to general standards.[22]

Moreover, even though some magistrates could fully utilize their talents and work conscientiously, their enlightened administration was by no means efficient government in any ordinary sense. For instance, people in a district might speak a dialect the magistrate did not understand; the local population might even have customs that made no sense to him. Even in a populous county, he never had more than six assistants, who, like himself, held Civil Service ranks. The rest of the office help consisted of perhaps a dozen locally recruited clerks. Serving a three-year term as magistrate, the individual official was simply not commissioned to innovate and to carry out specific policies. Often he found the best he could hope for was that the district would remain in reasonably good order and its tax quota be fulfilled. In discharging these responsibilities he actually implemented a kind of indirect rule: he must invite and inspire the support of the local gentry. This group of retired officials—students of imperial universities, nominated scholars, and some purchasers of rank—being men of substance in rural communities, could be induced to make their influence prevail over the populace until taxes were paid on time, disputes settled behind the scenes rather than flaring up in lawsuits, the poor taken care of by their clans, widows never remarried, and the filially pious commanded respect in the district and were imitated. Only under these conditions would the district earn its reputation of being "pure and honest," and its magistrate make his own name as a good "parental official," not one who was "frivolous and unstable." Yet all these objectives involved the human touch, no strange organizational principle.[23]

As a Han-lin academician Shen Shih-hsing knew the human approach only too well. He had drafted letters of commendation for the emperor to award to chaste widows and men of age and virtue. He had lectured before the Wan-li emperor that a ruler should see to it that in good years the population had enough to eat and in bad years at least not die of starvation, and that the kingly way of ancient times, still applicable to the present day, was no more than to promote faith and harmony and elect good men to office. When these goals were accomplished, the state was already acting in the cosmic spirit, even though it might continue to follow the established ritualistic proceedings to ensure auspiciousness.

Of course sometimes technical decisions had to be made. At a specific time and in a specific place, a tribal chieftain on the frontier might better be pacified rather than pressed militarily. There could be advantages—or fewer disadvantages—if in certain areas the Yellow River could be slightly diverted to the south rather than following its present channel. The ratio between horses and tea traded on the frontier might need readjusting. But again, decisions such as these could be made by governors-general and imperial commissioners on the scene rather than by the emperor and his grand-secretaries in the capital. Although by tradition these issues must be referred to the throne for approval, such approval could be a matter of routine if capable men had been assigned the tasks. Once more this meant that the essence of the business in the imperial court was the management of personnel. Indeed, the structure demanded grand-secretaries to equip themselves with at least a working knowledge of geography and history, which only enhanced the qualifications of the former members of the Han-lin Academy. They had, after all, spent years familiarizing themselves with these subjects. In fact, the best geographical and historical works about our empire were compiled by the Han-lin academicians.

Before becoming grand-secretary in 1578, Shen Shih-hsing had participated in and supervised the preparation of the *Veritable Records* of the two reigns preceding the present emperor's and the *Collected Institutes* covering the entire span of the dynasty. This assignment required him to read all state papers chronologically arranged for decades. It would have been difficult to find a better way to prepare himself to be the emperor's counsellor.[24]

Shen was now regarded by his colleagues as an elder statesman. This had little to do with his chronological age, which actually put him at eight years younger than Second Grand-Secretary Hsü Kuo and one year younger than Third Grand-Secretary Wang Hsi-chüeh. Shen Shih-hsing was nevertheless recognized to be "mellow" and "stable," having derived his seasoned experience from long study and reflection. This accumulated wisdom enabled him to think that when a proposal was useful to our empire, usually it was not because the idea was original or logically convincing, but because it suited our constitution. In order to be acceptable, it must agree with the general practice of the Civil Service. A line of action would be of little use unless it fulfilled the long-term interests of the empire. Localized schemes promising short profit, even if ingeniously conceived, often produced illusory and even adverse effects.

The empire was not set up to wage wars, to reconstruct its own society, to conduct a national program of any kind, nor even to improve the standard of living of the populace aside from taking preventive measures against famine. Its purpose was to maintain peace and stability. How could this desired peace and stability be preserved? One certainly could not work directly with the peasants: they were the governed, not the governing. In any case, illiteracy excluded them from any meaningful dialogue. There was also a limit to which a grand-secretary could go by approaching the gentry. For Shen Shih-hsing, anything he wished to accomplish could only be accomplished with the bureaucrats.

In 1587, the Year of the Pig, 3,000 peasants in Shantung had taken up banditry. The left censor-in-chief reported that the White Lotus Sect, taking advantage of the poor harvest of the previous years, was enlarging its membership. The situation was alarming.[25] But being alarmed was of little help; nor could the problem be solved by dealing with these 3,000 bandits alone. The basic solution had to rest with the ability of the entire bureaucracy to work together as a team, in harmony and mutual trust. Failing that, there was no way to direct the 1,100 county magistrates and tell them how to manage their districts, parental officials though they were supposed to be. Yet before the bureaucrats could work together with mutual confidence and a common purpose, their morale had to be improved.

Politics and government, as the first grand-secretary saw it, was no more than culture. As such it was part of daily life and subject to the rule of common sense. If the bureaucrats in the capital did not even see the emperor for months, it would be difficult for them to believe that he still had everything under his firm control. Next they would question whether he really cared about their problems. In the end they would seriously doubt that their work was even appreciated. Suspecting this, they would be unlikely to attend to their offices with dedication and devotion. This meant that sincerity would soon be lost. The empire would have "a cleavage between the top and the bottom," and there would be "a separation of the interior from the exterior," as Shen Shih-hsing had warned. When these conditions prevailed, banditry would increase; and in the future more poor harvests would drive more hunger-stricken peasants to join the various popular religious sects, which would, in turn, start more uprisings.

In order to work with thousands of governmental officials, Shen Shih-hsing simply had to pledge his own sincerity. He might be called a great compromiser. But it was clear that unless he acted the way the officials wanted, they might not function the way he wanted. This was tantamount to saying that while the bureaucracy was created to carry out governmental functions, the most pressing problem it had to handle was none other than the bureaucracy itself—a simple and fundamental fact which, ironically enough, with all his maneuvers and brilliance Chang Chü-cheng had overlooked.

By definition the bureaucracy included both army officers and civil officials. But in practice the military bureaucracy had never been politically important; the officers' corps was not even politically conscious. With the exception of the period under the first two founding emperors, during the Ming dynasty civil dominance over the military was complete. An army general was purely a technician. His prestige having sunk to the lowest level in history, he might have his moment of glory in attending a special court ceremony. But in ordinary times he was regarded by the civil officials with disdain and excluded from decision-making.[26]

At the time when Shen Shih-hsing was first grand-secretary, the Civil Service, the only element to be reckoned with, had about 20,000 members.[27] About one-tenth of them held offices in the capital. It was always a spectacular scene when they assembled in their service robes, rank 4b and above in red and rank 5a and below in blue. They all wore black lacquer-treated hats with wings protruding sideways. Their black boots had very thick soles, the sides of which were trimmed with white lacquer. Their ceremonial belts, more like loops dangling loosely from their waists but never drawn tight, were backed with jade, rhinoceros horn, and gold and silver pieces that added splendor to the sight of the assembly as they glittered in the sun, showing the grades of the wearers' ranks.

The badge of rank itself was called the "mandarin square," a chest-piece embroidered with elegant birds, always in pairs. The top rank (1) was represented by two stately cranes soaring above clouds, the lowest rank (9) by a couple of earthbound quail pecking the grass. During certain state ceremonies, army officers were authorized to wear the same service robes, except that their breast-patches carried images of fierce animals—lions and tigers, bears and panthers, and so on. The censorial-supervising branch of the government had its own badge of identification. As civil officials, its members, regardless of rank, all wore embroidered breast-patches showing a legendary animal called *hsieh-chih*, which according to tradition could distinguish good from evil. Completely harmless to men of virtue, the hsieh-chih could allegedly smell an immoral character from a distance and would instantly leap at him and tear him to pieces. Another exception to the general rule was that a handful of civil officials, army officers, and chief eunuchs wore robes with designs of pythons and flying fish. Only authorized personally by the emperor, these badges of honor elevated the wearer above all service ranks. Shen Shih-hsing had received his Order of the Python two years before, in 1585.[28]

With very few exceptions, members of the Civil Service had qualified for it through the competitive examinations held once every three years. Those who passed the examination at the provincial level were awarded licentiate degrees, which made them eligible for appointment at the lowest rank, 9b, unless they preferred to take the higher examination at the capital or to enter imperial universities for further study. Those who passed the upper level of examinations were awarded doctoral degrees and were usually eligible for grade 7b. Counting the screening tests and qualifying examinations at the county level which the candidates had to pass before they were even admitted to the contest, the system, when in operation, must have involved close to one million aspirants to official positions, and included virtually all of the empire's literary talent.

An important aspect of the examination system was that, aside from the Civil Service, avenues for individuals to gain prominence and demonstrate their creative energies were extremely limited, in many cases nonexistent. It was not unusual for the success of a candidate to depend upon the concerted effort of his whole family. Although when success came he could go from rags to riches in his lifetime, his way to good fortune had as a rule been paved by his parents or even his grandparents, whose foresight and single-mindedness had enabled him to attain the necessary education. The self-sacrifice of widowed mothers and devoted wives remained a common theme behind such success stories, as attested by numerous emotion-packed tombstone inscriptions written by worthy sons and sad but grateful husbands in tribute to them. Aware of such concerted efforts, many counties routinely erected stone arches in front of the houses of native sons who had just received their licentiate degrees. Imperial conferring of honors on meritorious officials usually included their ancestors for three generations back and their wives. It often happened that most of them were no longer alive. Their honorary ranks and titles of Imperial Lady were nevertheless engraved on new tombstones and erected to replace the old. Artists were commissioned to paint their portraits reconstructed from memory and oral instructions, complete with silk robes and mandarin squares, which they were unlikely ever to have caught sight of in their own lifetimes. Special orders of commendation issued by the emperor to honor the deceased were very much prized, because these letters could be passed on to posterity. Not only did they redound to the credit of the ancestors cited, but to that of the descendants of those who had earned the citations as well. Sometimes a ranking official petitioned the throne to have his own promotion deferred in exchange for such a patent of honor.[29] Shen Shih-hsing could not have forgotten all these details. As a Han-lin academician he must have composed dozens of such imperial eulogies for the throne. Recently he had also handled a petition by the second grand-secretary, Hsü Kuo, who wished to defer his promotion in order to honor the memory of his parents and wife, all dead for many years.[30]

With so much in common, the corps of civil officials had to be a coherent body, especially the capital officials, who were the cream of the crop. All of them had learned from childhood to recite the text of the Four Books along with the officially approved commentaries by Chu Hsi. Therefore they were thoroughly familiar with the doctrine that the essence of government is compassion, by which it was meant that a cultured gentleman, aware of his own concern over the necessities of life and his preoccupation with his own family, could not help but extend this concern and preoccupation to serve others, who also had their needs to fulfill and their loved ones to take care of. Moreover, being educated, these civil bureaucrats were all bound by propriety. They knew, for instance, that one must care about and respect one's sister-in-law at a distance. Yet for every sacred rule there were exceptions: if one's sister-in-law happened to be drowning one would naturally be expected to put aside daily decorum long enough to jump in the water and save her if one could. In this respect morals were no more than common sense. A world of order would be in sight if every individual followed his native instinct to do good.

Besides being enlightened, officials could also be jovial; on occasion they had the pleasure of mimicking the several masters of ceremony. They would demonstrate how one knew only how to mew and another only how to wail. Although solemn at ritualistic proceedings, they often had a good laugh afterward at having seen a minister of some state ceremonial miss a turn himself, or more shocking still, a dignified general in his service robe suddenly kneel to the emperor before the chanting had called for it, which could throw the entire assembly into a state of confusion.[31]

Yet were these capital officials, all 2,000 of them, really and at all times good-natured and congenial with one another, full of humor and compassion, and acting as a team in accordance with propriety and good common sense? Had this been the case, they could have transformed the outlook of the provincial and local officials, who in turn would have improved the administration in their districts until all had been declared pure and honest. Certainly had such ideal conditions existed, the severe penal code that prescribed death by torture for so many offenses could have been eliminated, continual evaluation of personnel within the bureaucracy would not have been required, and there would never have been the need to dress up so many civil officials as hsieh-chih monsters in order to police the bureaucracy itself. As for Shen Shih-hsing, if such official harmony had become a reality, his life would have been much simpler and far more pleasant, and the scandal of Chang Chü-cheng might never have occurred.

Shen Shih-hsing's subscription to sincerity, however, did not cause him to ignore reality. He understood that differences always exist between theory and practice. In the main, the doctrine of compassion was too simple to untangle the knotted threads of human motivation, which had already been complicated by the size of the bureaucracy and the wide span of our empire. The first grand-secretary labeled the professed moral tone of government that enabled the bureaucrats to justify their lines of action the *yang*, and their hidden desires and motivations the *yin*. The mixing of yang with yin being a matter of degree, adherence to principle therefore varied not only from one person to another but from time to time within the same person.[32] Not aiming at the impossible, Shen declared the "goal" of his administration, if he could use that term, as "merely to provide something for the virtuous men to rely upon and the evil-minded to be afraid of." This in itself was a difficult task; it would be impracticable to set a higher standard.

One factor underlying the unmentioned desires and motivations was that to occupy an official position was regarded by the public as a profitable business, even though most office-holders would deny it and almost none admit it. It was often reported that once a person passed his higher examinations and received his doctorate, he would be approached for many kinds of pecuniary purposes, including usury, land purchase, and allowing his public influence to be privately managed. Moneylenders in Peking offered selective loans to junior officials in the capital, expecting to make a handsome profit when those officials were transferred to provincial posts. It was generally said that public finances were tight; but with a large amount of silver passing through his hands, an office-holder always found the means to benefit himself if he wished.[33]

The surrender to such temptations on the part of bureaucrats was also extremely uneven. While the majority would accept from sources of twilight legitimacy only what they considered to be a reasonable amount to supplement their nominal salaries and to keep up a standard of living in line with their station, there were also notorious characters whose family fortunes were a legend. Yet at the other end of the spectrum were a handful of rugged individuals who would not tolerate any infraction of the moral code. Their cause had recently been advanced by the eccentric model official, Hai Jui. This unevenness made central management most difficult, placing the bureaucracy in constant tension.

Shen Shih-hsing's task was not made easier by the networks of personal ties within the bureaucracy, which could be considered a necessary evil of the centralized administration. Fundamentally, to manage the affairs of an enormous empire from the center had many drawbacks. A severe handicap was that exact conditions at the operational level could never be ascertained. It took a whole month to deliver a report from a remote province to the capital, which might turn out to be the most splendid and ornately constructed prose ever written on the topic but at a time when the vital statistics of that district had not been revised for over a hundred years. Thus, with little exaggeration one could say that the administration was accumulating every sort of ambiguity and anomaly from the bottom up.[34]

In the meantime the bureaucratic system had no way of making its established lines of responsibility more flexible. When something went awry in an official's district he was charged with it. It was not so much that he was adjudged legally guilty, as that administratively he had failed to maintain a flawless record—something that could not be overlooked. Even censorial investigation worked on this premise. If 3,000 brigands formed a war-band, some local officials had to be found at fault. They were charged either with failure to suppress the outlaws before the situation got out of hand or with the opposite: cruelty and ruthlessness in their attempts to deal summarily with the case, which then provoked the desperados into open revolt. Technically it would be too difficult to investigate more contributing factors and to trace responsibility to persons other than the immediately involved officials. Understandably, once such "side issues" were admitted to the inquiry, the case could be argued endlessly, and the postponement of a settlement could paralyze the operation of the entire bureaucracy.

The standing procedure governing personnel evaluation of the Civil Service demanded that provincial and local officials report to the capital at three-year intervals, when their records were thoroughly scrutinized by the Ministry of Personnel and the censorial-supervising functionaries. Capital officials were evaluated once every six years. Individuals reached the end of their careers if on such occasions they were labeled as "cruel," "unstable," "indiscreet," or similar descriptions. In the past a vigorous evaluation had resulted in as many as 2,000 officials receiving their orders of demotion, discharge, and retirement. Without purges of such dimensions the bureaucracy would be glutted. Yet such mass dismissals presented such a threat to the security of junior members of the service that they found it judicious to maintain close ties with their superiors. Persons from the same local district or those who had received degrees in the same year always felt a fraternal bond among themselves. The successful candidates, as a class, honored their examiners as mentors for a lifetime. Individuals who had already satisfactorily concluded their superior-subordinate relationship during one term of appointment would naturally continue this relationship on a personal basis when they encountered each other again in the course of assignment. There were also marital ties, of course, which linked many persons together beyond the scope of kinship. In this way patrons promoted their protégés, concealing their shortcomings and minimizing their mistakes. The latter, for their part, gave more devoted service to their benefactors, even to the extent of advancing their private interests.

From the vantage point of his experience, Shen Shih-hsing could see a dangerous tendency developing: the bureaucrats, instead of remaining a pool of civil servants ready to be assigned to the functionally divided departments and ministries, were establishing their own lines of communication and forming their own blocs. In part it was after viewing this situation that he designated the two kinds of motivation: the yin and the yang. Yet, being realistic, he never believed that all human frailty could or should be stamped out, having himself received the patronage of Chang Chü-cheng. As the emperor's chief counsellor, he saw that his urgent task was to help the young sovereign to reestablish public confidence, for mutual tolerance and mutual understanding were very much needed. He himself would do well to promote the yang rather than expose the yin. Committed to this purpose, every day he became more of a peacemaker than a policymaker.

One could always argue that the moral tone of government was a farce, or at most a facade the bureaucrats used to justify their lines of action. But there was no reason to believe that a facade had to be false, especially when men at the top were devoting their sincerity to maintaining it. The first grand-secretary had no alternative, because aside from morals, and aside from the common sense argued by the *Four Books* and Chu Hsi, there was no way to find a logical basis for and a working order behind our organization, to enable first the 2,000 capital officials, then the 20,000 members of the Civil Service and the one million aspirants for governmental offices, to say nothing of the numerous widowed mothers and foresighted grandparents, to arrive at a consensus—to decide what was right and what was wrong. Although private motivations were varied, indefinite, and uncertain—and in that respect no one person could speak of another for sure—moral laws were universally understood. They could be included in the emperor's study sessions, engraved on tombstones, and passed on to posterity. This fact was more than adequately demonstrated by the case of Tsou Yüan-piao.

Tsou, having passed the Civil Service examinations in 1577 at the age of twenty-six, arrived in court just in time to submit his memorial impeaching Chang Chü-cheng for his failure to mourn his father's death properly. For this bold move Tsou received eighty blows of the whipping club and was sent to the remote southwest as a common soldier, an exile that lasted for five years. In early 1583 he was recalled to Peking to become a supervising secretary, one of those wearing a hsieh-chih chest-badge. Since now remonstrance against the throne was part of his function, he lost no time in advising the Wan-li emperor to rid himself of many earthly desires and lead a pure and simple life. The imperial rescript on this paper, indicating that the counsel had been acknowledged, was as graceful as it could be under the circumstances. Not satisfied, however, Tsou returned with another memorial charging the throne with lack of faith. The implication was that Wan-li's personal conduct made him unfit to be a ruler. In conclusion Tsou quoted the proverb, "The best way to keep your bad deeds from the knowledge of others is not to commit them in the first place." This last sentence so infuriated the emperor that he was ready to give the memorialist a second beating at the Meridian Gate.[35]

Could a holder of rank 7b in the Civil Service, whose only recognizable merit was his earlier courageous impeachment of Chang Chü-cheng, be so brash as to set himself up as the spokesman of virtue and tell the throne what to do and what not to do, not even in a persuasive but in a commanding tone? Wan-li had his theory: being self-appointed authorities, Tsou and several others were by no means virtuous; neither were they loyal. What they were really after was instant fame. They were purchasing righteous names for themselves by paying the penalty of being disrespectful to him.[36]

The sovereign could very well have been right. Some bureaucrats, familiar with the classical pattern, had learned to live their lives in the light of history; for that the whipping club might not be too costly a price to pay. Yet, that being the case, it left the monarch and his first grand-secretary with even fewer alternatives: they too had to pursue a righteous name. Tsou Yüan-piao and his fellow remonstrators had proven that there was a universal standard venerated by learned men and sanctioned by history. Had a righteous name not been such a precious commodity, they would never have thought of buying it with their own flesh and blood in addition to their hard-won doctoral degrees and Civil Service ranks, not to mention the imperial commendations of their ancestors. This should have given the occupant of the throne and his cherished tutor something to think about. Unlike the junior officials, the emperor and his first grand-secretary were watched by the entire nation. Time, therefore, was not on their side and they could not afford to await the judgment of history.

When the first grand-secretary chose his role as peacemaker, his sincerity was appreciated by some but far from all the civil officials. He well knew that his critics were dissatisfied with his lack of resolution: "His head is moving in one direction and his tail in another."[37] At times he was also referred to as "that clerk who used to take orders from Chang Chü-cheng."[38] Occupying the desk left by Chang, Shen Shih-hsing was not entranced by these derogatory remarks, but neither was he seriously disturbed by them. Undoubtedly many others in his place would prefer to present themselves in a more decisive, dynamic, and authoritative manner. But as far as he could see, it had been exactly those heroic qualities that had brought down his predecessor. To follow Chang Chü-cheng's style at the top rung of the government would be to ignore the lesson of his failure.

As Shen Shih-hsing sat alone in the inner office of the Literary Depth Pavilion, he could almost hear his old mentor clearing his throat and issuing him instructions. Indeed, Chang had treated him more as a novice than as a partner. But this was the least of Shen's complaints. Clerk or novice, his inferior position had actually allowed him to grow and to progress. He also had to acknowledge that his former superior and master had been a very talented man. More than anyone else, Chang Chü-cheng was capable of remembering thousands of things in minute detail. It was a shame that a man of such ability and with such a passion to serve the empire should go down in history as a failure. Although Shen Shih-hsing had no intention of dwelling on the shortcomings of others, still less those of his own benefactor, he knew the Chang Chü-cheng story well and had learned his lesson from it. Chang's greatest fault had been that he could not practice humility, and because of that he tended to overlook the larger issues and in the end evolved into the kind of man Mencius had described as capable of seeing the barbs of a feather but unable to visualize a cartload of faggots.

This flaw was even more tragic because when Wan-li ascended the throne in 1572 Chang Chü-cheng was doing well. In those days no one was even gossiping about how he had maneuvered himself into becoming the master of the Literary Depth Pavilion and how he joined with Feng Pao to gain the empress dowager's favor. Everybody was tired of the deceitful Kao Kung. Chang Chü-cheng seemed to be a much better choice.[39] The events that followed had been unexpected; but in retrospect they were by no means incidental. In essence Chang Chü-cheng tried to impose a system on an organization the complexities of which could not be tidied up, and which, also by nature, had to operate under contradictory principles. He was bound sooner or later to meet opposition. He managed to chastise his critics in his lifetime; but his entire enterprise collapsed when he was dead and buried.

Chang was obsessed with the desire to improve governmental efficiency. He wanted a strong army, and in order to have one he had to fill up granaries and treasuries with food and silver. Financial administration was his area of specialization. But it was also in this area that he sowed the seeds of his own failure. The story is indeed complex.

Tax collection in our empire had numerous peculiarities. Anyone who was impatient with them could easily fall into their traps. Outwardly, the 1,100 counties were units on an equal footing. But appearance had little to do with reality. In practice, each county was assessed with a tax quota, which in most cases had not been revised for two hundred years. These quotas were extremely uneven: a rich county could turn out a total of tax proceeds several hundred times that of one of the poorest counties.

When a magistrate carefully scrutinized the affairs of the territory under his jurisdiction, he would to his surprise often find numerous unbelievable discrepancies between theory and practice. The native population, most of them illiterate, might use a set of units and measurements different from the official standard. Few of them understood governmental regulations aside from what they heard from their village elders. Many counties had not conducted a land survey for a long period, during which time land had been sold, rented, and mortgaged, and even the local topography had undergone changes. As a result, tax assessment might not correspond to actual holdings. In a number of cases it was difficult to determine who the legal owners were.

There were also many districts in which tax quotas were unusually low—so low, in fact, that at a glance one might wonder why the rates could not be increased. At least those districts should never have tax arrearages. But a more thorough investigation would disclose that because taxes were low, numerous small cultivators had acquired land of their own, yet their status as landowners by no means lifted them well above the starvation level. Large, rich, and absentee landlords all existed, but alongside them were also landlords who were just about as destitute as their own tenants. Essentially, the benefit of lower taxes had over a long time become indispensable to the livelihood of a significant segment of the population.

On the other hand, in a district where the tax quota was high, collection usually met with stiff resistance to a predictable degree, say about 60 percent in any particular county. In historical fact, the population in such districts habitually procrastinated about paying taxes, with the well-to-do landowners following the lead of marginal ones. They all knew that, up to a point, uncollected taxes would have to be written off, as no magistrate could struggle with thousands of delinquents forever. Chang Chü-cheng must have heard the report that sometimes taxpayers hired paupers to answer summons on their behalf, so that when the latter were flogged by the magistrate for delinquency, the former could let their payments lag further behind.[40] Shen Shih-hsing knew many such cases well, having come from Soochow himself, where tax collection had frustrated many a magistrate to the extent that Chang Chü-cheng called it "a demon's country" and "a district that had no conscience."[41]

The delivery of taxes to the higher offices was further handicapped by the practice on the part of many magistrates of collecting extras, called "customary fees," most of which they appropriated to compensate themselves and to pay adminstrative expenses. Under normal circumstances these extras had to be covered before the proceeds were turned over.

When Chang Chü-cheng insisted that all districts make their tax payments in full, he actually put undue pressure on the Civil Service at its operational level. His critics refused to be impressed by the silver bullion that he accumulated at state treasuries. They contended that in order to fill the coffers the magistrates had had to arrest a large number of peasants and beat many of them to death. The charge could have been exaggerated, but the loss of good will was real. The administration had also thus contradicted the benevolent tone it had adopted for itself and abandoned indirect rule through the local gentry.

In his drive toward efficiency Chang had ignored the dual chracter of the bureaucracy. Indeed, generally speaking, the civil officials, all 20,000 of them, were jealous protectors of their own sinecures, patrons of their associates, and supporters of local landholding and usurious interests. Yet their professed adherence to the *Four Books* could never be totally discredited. When inspired, persons like Tsou Yüan-piao would sustain every hardship and act of injustice meted out to them in order to uphold what they considered to be fundamental principles. They did not even consider loyalty to the throne as an end. They felt free to criticize the emperor because they did not want to see their own loyalty to principle wasted; it was the emperor's duty to translate that loyalty into action suitable to the doctrine of compassion. They could, of course, directly inspire others. It was this spirit which assured that the broken dikes on the Yellow River would be repaired, bandits suppressed, and barbarian invasions repulsed. In the officials' eyes, Chang Chü-cheng was replacing this spirit of selflessness with his improvised efficiency control, and when that was not enough, by practicing favoritism among his cohorts.

In fact, Chang Chü-cheng's partiality toward his close followers lay beyond his own choice. Fundamentally, the empire's transportation and communication could never be sufficiently improved to be systematized. Thus with all the power he could muster, Chang could not alter the basic character of the empire. While he was in office, tax quotas in the provinces remained unrevised, no new agencies were created, the salary schedule was retained intact along with its unrealistic features, and the local governments still lacked service support. The persistence of these conditions demonstrated that no administrator, talented or not, could sacrifice the human touch to neat organizational principles.

Still, in the Literary Depth Pavilion Chang Chü-cheng worked hard. He reviewed fiscal accounts, checked the strength of the troops, and personally directed the arrest and retirement of high officials who had violated the law. He even designed report forms and set up deadlines. For a decade he promoted a new group of ministers and governors who were all very brisk to act and very innovative in their own spheres. But it would be naive to believe that they were always honest and incorruptible, since they too had achieved their prominence through all sorts of irregularities practiced from the bottom up.

Because of his lack of authority, Chang had to coach his trusted governors and commissioners to submit to the throne the kind of memorial he wanted, and then, as the emperor's counsellor, he would approve the very recommendations he had worked out himself. Soon after he assumed office he found himself busily writing personal letters. To provide incentive, he included in his private correspondence to his followers suggestions for their career advancement. By exercising his grand-secretarial prerogative of appointing personnel in the name of the emperor, he thus created an institution of his own to compensate for the lack of system in the organization.

The case of Chang Chü-cheng fully exposed the weaknesses of the over-centralization of an enormous empire, whose technical problems exceeded its capacity to govern. There was a limit beyond which its administrative efficiency could not go, and to strive too hard in that direction could lead to peril. When the top administrator refused to accept this lower end of the efficiency scale as the standard, the bureaucrats became divided and technical problems turned into moral issues.

Inasmuch as Chang Chü-cheng had not abandoned the bureaucratic apparatus, he himself could not be consistent in his actions. What exposed him to the most criticism was his ostentatious style of living, which to his own way of thinking was no more than his due. It might have been justified under other circumstances. But in the present situation he was demanding from his fellow officials the kind of frugality that he himself did not practice. On one occasion, the unsuspecting emperor, hearing of Tutor Chang's intention of remodeling his house so that a new hall might be constructed to display the imperial calligraphy in his possession, directed that one thousand ounces of silver be contributed from his own purse to finance the project, as the sovereign assumed that his tutor must be a man of very limited means. Only years later did His Majesty learn that the actual cost of construction had run to ten times that amount.[42] Moreover, the design of this Peking residence was immediately copied by the officials in Hukwang, who duplicated the mansion for Chang in his hometown using public funds. In spite of Chang's declining gesture, the same officials also erected three stone arches in his honor. Chang Chü-cheng also made an issue of the hostel services provided by the Imperial Postal System. He wanted to reserve them for only the most essential trips on official business and declared a stiff penalty for abuses. Yet his own household servants and those of his close relatives were seen in several provinces, demanding transportation and porter service from the local magistrates. His own letters disclosed that his followers often offered him valuable gifts, including land and cash.[43]

All these incidents forced Chang Chü-cheng's sympathizers into silence, although they wished to defend him. With his experience, he should have known that he could still pass unnoticed if he merely talked less about frugality and lived a life neither modest nor really extravagant. But Shen Shih-hsing's predecessor had to be excessive on both counts. He made others uncomfortable as well as envious. Shen Shih-hsing could see that the charge of usurpation, if introduced alone, could easily have been dismissed, since technically Chang was obliged to assume responsibility when the emperor was still in his tender years. But when Chang Chü-cheng's lack of sincerity was exposed in so many cases and emerged as a pattern, anything said about him was no longer inconceivable. One could imagine the emperor's reaction to the news of many unpleasant details lately brought to his attention. As sovereign he had endured Chang's sanctimonious preaching on frugality for years.

Aware of his own weaknesses, Chang Chü-cheng became increasingly sensitive to criticism. Perhaps that was why he was impelled to offend so many men of letters. If Shen Shih-hsing had one personal complaint against his patron and predecessor, it concerned the unnecessary insults Chang had hurled at these men of influence. Like all the bureaucrats, these literary figures also needed recorded official careers to boost their social esteem. Having already disqualified them as unfit for public service, Chang Chü-cheng could have spared them his caustic remarks, which served no purpose other than to aggravate their already wounded pride, and which caused Shen, in their eyes Chang's successor, to bear the consequences years later.

For example, Wang Shih-chen, the prose writer of the century, had considered himself Chang's "classmate," as both men received their doctoral degrees in 1547. Denied a ministerial post, Wang made many overtures to the then first grand-secretary, writing eulogies of his parents and giving him substantial gifts, including an antique piece of calligraphy. Chang was not moved, however. His answering letter to Wang expressed his opinion of him with a degree of candor that was not calculated to ease the tension between the two. In part it read: "A shield made in Wu and a curved saber manufactured in Yüeh should be encased in boxes and treasured, so that their fine quality will be kept intact. It would be unwise to take them out and use them; they would inevitably break."[44] The recipient of this letter endured his humiliation to publish a most derogatory biography of his controversial classmate, in which he also tossed a few uncomplimentary remarks Shen Shih-hsing's way.

Another man of literary fame, Wang Tao-k'un, as vice minister of war had submitted an elegant essay transmitting his financial report. It is unclear whether his rhetorical extravagance or the discrepancies in his accounts annoyed Chang Chü-cheng more. He wrote Wang to inform him of his dismissal from the Civil Service, and why: "Orchids, yes even orchids, would have to be weeded out, we regret to say, if they should ever bloom in the middle of public avenues."[45] In both these instances Chang merely saw the bureaucrats involved as individuals whom he might or might not select for government service. What he failed to see was that the bureaucracy as a body, representing the empire's educated elite and long self-perpetuating, was a source of power in itself and, in a sense, was master.

In the last years of his life, Chang must have felt the mounting pressure of opposition, already intensified by the mourning issue in 1577. He began to see himself as a sort of martyr, to the point where he quoted Buddhist scripture to portray himself as "entering into the burning pyre in order to reach the gateway of soothing coolness."[46] Shen Shih-hsing, the novice, lacked his master's zeal for martyrdom; yet he also knew that such dramatic self-sacrifice would not be necessary if he could avoid making most of the mistakes of his predecessor, which he was more than aware had been committed at the same desk he now occupied.

He remembered that in the early years of Wan-li's reign, when the public placed great hope in Chang Chü-cheng, they did not expect him to take every item of governmental business into his own hands to create a system. Their concept of a superior statesman was one who could use his own personality and prestige to neutralize opposites. He should be firm and definite to a point; beyond that he must nevertheless let magnanimity and forgiveness take over, until men of varying talents all felt at home in the administration and the less virtuous and less competent would be inspired to do better. In sum, he should put the doctrine of sincerity to work.

Unless one could dismiss all the bureaucrats or replace the present Civil Service with another organization founded on a different set of principles, one had to work with the bureaucracy as a whole on its own terms. It had a logic for its professed virtue; it also had an underlying urge for self-gain. It was essential to see its dual character and to read accurately the consensus of its members—not least the opinions of the men of letters among them. Since circumstances had already guided Shen Shih-hsing, the present first grand-secretary, to his self-assigned role of a peacemaker, he should carry on as such. What others called him made no great difference, even though he always respected their opinions.[47]

In 1587, the Year of the Pig, few people would have suspected that the present first grand-secretary had any reason to feel insecure. But this had not been the situation in the first two years after he took over the Literary Depth Pavilion. In those days anyone who had had the slightest connection with Chang Chü-cheng was under attack. It took more than good luck for Shen Shih-hsing to survive his share of crises, among them the case of Kao Ch'i-yü. The experience must have strengthened his belief in humility. He knew that without being humble he would never have remained where he was today.

Shen's quiet and peaceful disposition had been well accepted. But his emergence as the first grand-secretary could not have escaped criticism. His close relationship with Chang Chü-cheng was not something that every courtier was willing to forget. When in those days he felt uncertain about himself, even his status as the emperor's tutor gave him little assurance. Everyone could see that Wan-li was no longer the delightful pink-faced pupil always ready to comply and please. He had passed through a period of awkward adolescence. Now, with a thin mustache and a few whiskers on his round chin, he made it unmistakably clear that the boy who had been a manipulated ruler had now awakened to vindicate himself. This made the position of his chief counsellor even more hazardous.

Shen Shih-hsing's apprehension was amply justified, both by the general atmosphere in the court and by the historical fact that of the eight first grand-secretaries who had preceded him, only two had completed their service without involving themselves or their family members in some criminal activities.[48] Outwardly, the punitive action always came from the throne. In actuality, however, on none of the occasions had the prosecution been separable from controversies among the bureaucrats, and it had been traceable to policy differences thoroughly tainted with personality conflict and wounded pride. When a private feud was transformed into public issues over which the final verdict had to be given in terms of absolute good and evil, in not a single case had the emperor acted with full knowledge of the reality.

In those two very vulnerable years stretching from the summer of 1583 to the summer of 1585, Shen Shih-hsing could almost see a ring closing in around him. Only lack of positive evidence that the young emperor was ready to discharge his newly appointed first grand-secretary inhibited Shen's adversaries from making an outright attack upon him. The "opposition," represented by many angry young officials, wanted to know why, of Chang Chü-cheng's four sons, three had been awarded doctoral degrees and two appointed members of the Han-lin Academy. It so happened that on one of these occasions Shen Shih-hsing was the examiner for the Chang brothers. When this inquiry failed to remove Shen, a motion was introduced to bar sons of grand-secretaries from all future examinations. Although defeated, the proposal was calculated to draw attention to Shen Yung-mou, Shen Shih-hsing's elder son. An impeachment of Minister of Personnel Yang Wei also failed to carry, although he was denounced in public for taking orders from the Literary Depth Pavilion when managing his office. The censure of the minister of rites by the same group of recalcitrants, on the other hand, did succeed. Hsü Hsüeh-mo was forced to retire. Ostensibly the ousted minister had not consulted enough of the geomantic specialists in the court before taking action, and as a result had selected an inferior site for the emperor's future mausoleum. But the real issue concerning the bureaucrats here was that, like Shen Shih-hsing, Hsü was marked as Chang Chü-cheng's protégé and had also recently married his daughter to Shen's younger son.

The pattern was too familiar to be overlooked. The enemies of the first grand-secretary were stripping away the outer layers to reach the core. Charges were made by association and implication; technical errors were amplified into moral issues; isolated incidents were interpreted as a concerted effort. As always, a bureaucratic campaign could be started by a slogan, a couplet or pun, an anonymous handbill, an examination question, a suspected murder, the impeachment of an insignificant figure, or a memorandum on water supply or a report on horse-tails. The object was to draw attention and gather a following. Whether those purposes were achieved through straightforward argument or through subtle insinuation was not the point. Once the initial move was made, others would follow. The overall effect was cumulative. The early skirmishes generally engaged only the lower echelon of the bureaucracy; later the battle would be taken over by the senior members, who stood behind the more vociferous and sanguine young officials. A final showdown was deferred until the time was ripe. In politics, this was a way of life. The hidden motivation of the yin had to be mixed with and dignified by the more legitimate and justifiable yang, so that, without satisfying any specific legal technicality, the campaign would nevertheless go forward because public opinion was in its favor. All these strategies took time.

In the case of Kao Ch'i-yü, for instance, Grand-Secretary Shen Shih-hsing was brought to the brink of peril. Yet because he survived the crisis, his position was ultimately buttressed; his meekness proved to be, after all, a source of strength. Kao had established an enviable record as a Han-lin academician and had served in turn as chancellor of imperial universities in Nanking and Peking. Only recently, at Grand-Secretary Shen's recommendation, was he given a vice minister's title and appointed lecturer at the emperor's public study sessions. If precedent counted as a reliable guide, one might assume that he was being groomed to be a future grand-secretary, or even eventually to become chief counsellor to the throne. But at this point fate dashed his hopes of reaching the summit of officialdom. Suddenly he was criticized for having handed out an examination question several years before, which, though asserting that the world belonged to the most talented and most virtuous, was actually a disguised message encouraging Chang Chü-cheng to usurp the throne, because at that time Chang was unabashedly posing as just such a superior character. This accusation had its serious implications. The charge was lethal: its shocking effect on the bewildered emperor was calculated, and the accused's association with the first grand-secretary was obvious. In an age when judiciary decisions depended more on logical deduction than on evidence, the accusers had reason to believe that they had handed over Shen Shih-hsing, along with the hapless Kao Ch'i-yü, to the vengeful-minded sovereign. As deliberation of the charges took place, Shen Shih-hsing, obviously involved, voluntarily suspended himself. When the second grand-secretary who was temporarily filling in pleaded on Shen's behalf, he too was promptly censured by the young opposing courtiers, and had to stay home.[49]

At this point the emperor hesitated. But it must also have been at this point that he began to grasp the true meaning of all these belated efforts to "save" the throne. More decisively, the senior members of the court, whom the young officials had expected to act as their leaders, wanted no part of it. Wang Hsi-chüeh, the third grand-secretary, even argued in public that Shen

Shih-hsing's mild and gentle manner should never be mistaken for a sign of weakness: it was statesmanship that held him back and made him so accommodating.

After a good deal of suspense the imperial decision was announced: Kao Ch'i-yü was dismissed from the Civil Service for handing out an "absurd" examination question. The imperial patent previously issued in honor of his ancestors was also withdrawn. The alleged usurpation, or the instigation for it, was, however, not questioned. As a mild way of showing disfavor to the accusers, the censor who had initiated the impeachment of Kao was not rewarded. Instead he was transferred to an obscure provincial post. Subsequently several agitators in the case were even demoted. However, the sovereign definitely wanted to retain the services of his two grand-secretaries. He dispatched eunuchs as his personal envoys to visit Shen Shih-hsing and Hsü Kuo at their residences and urged them to return to office.

Thus, in 1585, three years after his death, the case of Chang Chü-cheng was finally allowed to rest. Or at least when future controversies flared up in the court, the instigators had to find a justification different from exposing the lackeys of the deceased Grand Preceptor, whose title had already been rescinded and property confiscated.

Once the dust had settled, the first grand-secretary had the opportunity to reflect on the whole sequence of events. How many of his critics were genuinely concerned with the degrees conferred upon Chang's sons and the inferiority or superiority of the emperor's burial site? Possibly no more than a handful. There were some ambitious men who wanted to ride those controversies in order to move ahead. But again, those opportunists could not be many. The underlying fact was that Chang Chü-cheng had become an emotionally packed issue. Bare mention of his name could stir up antagonism, and one did not need to work very hard to arouse public anger toward persons labeled as Chang's close associates, like Hsü Hsüeh-mo and himself.

Why was Chang Chü-cheng so universally hated? Though he had meant well, he had been off balance. By putting everyone under surveillance and dismissing individuals according to his own standards, he had threatened the security of thousands who wore embroidered chest-patches from cranes down to quails, thus directly and indirectly affecting their patrons and protégés as well. Above all, Chang had misunderstood the functions of those who wore the hsieh-chih monsters. Instead of deploying them to imitate the Secret Police, he should have utilized the censors and supervising secretaries to assess public opinion. They should have been allowed to act according to public conscience after blending yin with yang.

For our empire an absolute standard was irrelevant. Peace and stability had to be derived from what the 20,000 degree holders wearing silk service robes considered fair and reasonable. When Chang Chü-cheng violated this principle, he threw the entire bureaucracy into a state of anxiety. Since most of the bureaucrats had arrived at their present stage of distinction through continued struggles aided by their families over generations, Chang, as his classmate Wang Shih-chen pointed out, had made himself a personal enemy of an entire empire.[50] Without the resultant repressed anger and hidden fear, this anti-Chang movement could never have come such a long way, attracted so many followers, and generated the energy to produce so many incidents.

If—with luck—by the summer of 1585 the emperor's decision had finally closed the case, Shen Shih-hsing was to make great efforts to ensure that such a disturbance would never occur again. He had already persuaded the Wan-li emperor to discontinue Chang Chü-cheng's efficiency control as a first step toward easing tension among the civil officials. His methodically minded predecessor had devised a scheme of having supervising secretaries tabulate the tax arrears and cases of banditry reported in the counties and provinces. He had issued a directive that back taxes must be paid in full and all bandits caught. The central government summarized any unfinished business monthly and semiannually. Unless a magistrate was cleared by the supervising secretaries' office, he could not be promoted or transferred. In some outstanding cases, officials were even called back from retirement to answer questions concerning undischarged responsibilities. This was totally unreasonable, Shen Shih-hsing argued. Tax collection involved so many factors that stood outside an official's control that its success or failure should never be arbitrarily accepted as a measure of his competence. Similarly, whether a bandit was caught or escaped was a matter of chance. The demand for total arrest only compelled magistrates to round up innocent suspects and torture them into confessing. These arguments alone eliminated the only institutional guide of Chang Chü-cheng's administration.[51]

To show his magnanimity, Shen Shih-hsing truly forgave the young officials who had moved to censure him, in several cases even recommending their promotions. His plea on behalf of Tsou Yüan-piao was especially unexpected, since Tsou, in addition to submitting outspoken memorials to infuriate the emperor, had also been instrumental in removing Minister of Rites Hsü Hsüeh-mo, father of Shen's own daughter-in-law. After considerable haggling on paper, he managed to secure Wan-li's permission to let the offending memorialist go without being beaten at the Meridian Gate. Yet no sooner had Tsou received his order of dismissal than the first grand-secretary started working on his second rehabilitation.

The spring of 1587 offered Shen Shih-hsing an even better opportunity to demonstrate his sincerity as a statesman, because in the Year of the Pig the evaluation of capital officials again fell due. Reversing his predecessor's mass dismissals during the same event in the Year of the Snake, he was determined to limit the changes to an absolute minimum. Good feeling was generated when the word spread that the first grand-secretary wanted everyone to stay. When the final results were announced, only thirty-three doctoral-degree holders were demoted and discharged, and none from the three vital departments: the Ministry of Personnel, the entire censorial-supervising staff, and the Han-lin Academy. Such leniency was unprecedented. His own position now more than secure, Shen was generally regarded as an elder statesman, mellow and stable.[52]

Shen's relationship with the sovereign also took a turn for the better. Cordiality had now progressed to a feeling of affection. As one of the envoys, he had, at His Majesty's command, conferred the title of Imperial Consort on Lady Cheng. He also made several trips to Ta-yü-shan to supervise the construction of the emperor's mausoleum. This service pleased Wan-li so much that he authorized the first grand-secretary to wear on the site a special jacket with the double image of the character *felicity* embroidered on the front, which signified a commission unique in both color and design and possessing a distinguished personal touch.

With increased confidence, and using his native gifts of maneuvering and persuasion, Tutor Shen also obtained Wan-li's consent to suspend his personal command of the army, to limit his travel outside the capital, and to restrain eunuch Chang Ching, who had taken over the Eastern Depot as head of the Secret Police. Although rarely mentioned, all these issues affected the sense of security of the civil officials. When a sensitive area was touched upon, their confrontation with the throne could be intense and bitter. Even though the bureaucrats never launched their protests by asserting their constitutional rights, the same effect was achieved when they submitted their humble pieces of advice and petitions telling the sovereign what he should never do. By foreseeing potential areas of contention and removing the causes beforehand, Shen Shih-hsing knew that he had fulfilled the role of a peacemaker.

But peacemaker or mellowed statesman, the first grand-secretary could never escape the criticism of being a great compromiser. What was the difference? A compromiser compromised. He abridged and discounted principles for the sake of expediency. Shen Shih-hsing could always argue that he needed to solidify his own position before he could put the emperor's court once again in workable order. This argument was valid only up to a point—that is, provided that it produced results. He had correctly perceived Chang Chü-cheng's error as overconfidence in imposing order and discipline. In contrast, he preached in favor of sincerity, to be arrived at through ritualistic exercises and the exposition of classical literature.

The proposition was reasonable enough. There were, as everybody recognized, technical gaps in managing the affairs of a large empire; and experience had proven that these could not be bridged by ruthless demands imposed from above. Moral inspiration for voluntary striving to fill the gaps remained the only alternative. But Shen's own record of four years as first grand-secretary could not convince his critics that the theory had been put into practice.

For one thing, he was now even unable to induce the emperor to attend ceremonial functions. Shen Shih-hsing must have been terrified at the realization that after the Chang Chü-cheng affair, with its charges and countercharges, His Majesty was growing more cynical every day. Yet how could he feel otherwise when, after years of taking Chang's instructions as literally true, he found that everybody was saying one thing and doing another? He never openly resisted playing the role of paragon of virtue because it was required by the *Four Books* and the instructions of his ancestors. But how could one be sure that, sensitive as he was, inwardly he did not consider it a trap which the officials had laid for him? Now he also had the woman he loved, even though exactly what influence she had over him was not clear. All these factors taken together, however, in no way made Shen Shih-hsing's position the slightest bit more defensible. After all, he was supposed to supply faith and guide the throne to perfection. As imperial tutor, he had lectured before the Wan-li emperor longer and more often than anyone else. In this hour, when he was mustering his maximum sincerity, would things begin to change? Or had he already exerted his maximum sincerity?

Only time would tell.

Time Shen still had, but not as much as he thought. By 1587 he had reached the mid-point of his occupancy of the Literary Depth Pavilion. Only four more years would pass before he was to face the fact that time had run out for him, and suddenly he found that he could not stay even one day longer.

The Wan-li emperor, Chu I-chün (r. 1572–1620), official portrait.

Lady Wang, Wan-li's consort and mother of his eldest son, Ch'ang-lo, official portrait.

A contemporary woodcut illustrating the fact that romantic love was becoming more popular in the late sixteenth century.

The "mandarin square" was the breast-patch worn by each
civil service official to indicate his place in the hierarchy.
The top rank was represented by two cranes soaring above
the clouds, the lowest by a pair of quail pecking at the grass.

Chang Chü-cheng, imperial tutor,
senior grand-secretary, and advo-
cate of "hard policies."

Shen Shih-hsing, his successor,
who was in favor of a "soft administration."

Official portrait of the Cheng-te emperor, Wan-li's granduncle and China's "Merry Monarch," who loved to travel incognito and indulge in amorous adventures.

The emperor's armed guard carrying dragon flags (detail from painted scroll).

Contemporary woodcut of Cheng-te appearing on the cover of a play and depicting him as a gentleman of leisure with flower in hand.

Nineteenth-century lithograph of an extensive water-control project. Flooding was a perennial problem of the imperial government through the centuries.

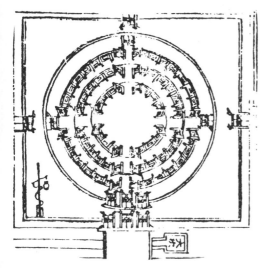

Woodcut of the ground-plan of the Altar of Heaven (1587) where Wan-li went on May 16, 1585, to pray for rain.

Stone arch of the altar decorated with symbolic clouds.

A recent air photo showing triple arches added to the other three sides.

Wan-li's mausoleum, one of the Ming Tombs: *above*, entrance building housing the stone tablet; *below left*, interior of vault; *below right*, stone door panel.

Line drawing of Hai Jui, memorializing bureaucrat and rigid moralist.

Decisions on legal cases involving capital offenses were often arbitrary and based only on the individual deductions of the local magistrate concerned.

The death penalty was meted out in public for its intimidating effect rather than as an act of retributive justice.

Women were discriminated against. The unexplained death of a male relative could constitute a serious threat to the life of a woman of the family.

Ch'i Chi-kuang, the lonely—and innovative—general.

Cavalry formation invented by Ch'i Chi-kuang, showing the defensive square consisting of abatises and wagons.

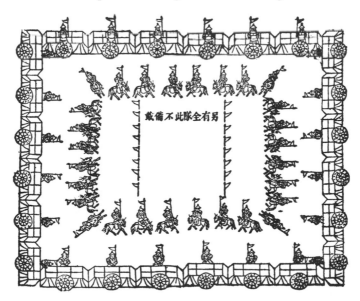

A symbolic depiction of Ch'i Chi-kuang's "mandarin duck" formation, showing the weapon carried by the infantryman in each position (a). A rattan shield and the bamboo tree (b) commonly used as an obstructive weapon by foot-soldiers, along with swords, antler-shaped metal spears, and lances (c). (Drawings are reproduced from Ch'i Chi-kuang's military handbooks.)

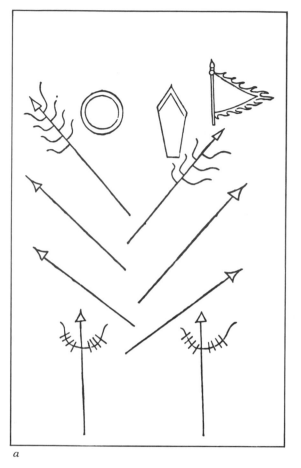

a

b

c

The *fo-lang-chi*, or *Feranghi*, a type of gun used in sixteenth-century China even though it was of European origin (a). The "generalissimo" with details (b).

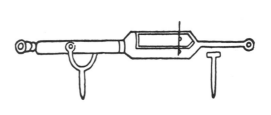

a

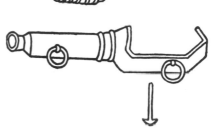

b

Banners and flags designed by Ch'i Chi-kuang, who used symbols and animals from astrology and folklore in order to build up the morale of his peasant mercenaries.

Woodcut of one of the defensive towers stationed along the Great Wall and manned with *fo-lang-chi*, another of Ch'i Chi-kuang's ideas. The largest tower could accommodate up to fifty men.

Modern-day photograph of the Great Wall.

Drawing of the Great Wall made by the Ming scholar Ku Yen-wu.

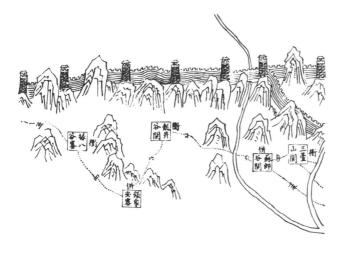

Contemporary portrait of Li Chih as
a Confucian scholar.

Li Chih conducting a seminar on the
front porch of his chapel, the "Hall
of Buddha in Fragrant Iris."

Present-day photograph of the side tower on the
Meridian Gate, which has remained virtually
unchanged for the past 400 years.

3
A WORLD WITHOUT
CHANG CHÜ-CHENG

In a world without Chang Chü-cheng the empire began to slide slowly but irrevocably into an abyss. It eventually found itself in a constitutional deadlock the breaking of which was beyond any human powers. At first the crisis was not even recognized. But as months stretched into years and years into decades, each worsening turn of events marked a point of no return. As an emperor who actually carried on a strike against his own bureaucrats over a long period of time, Wan-li has come down in history without any close parallel. He was vengeful because his courtiers frustrated his desire to make his third son his heir at the expense of his first, thus hurting the woman he loved. He was cynical because he knew that everyone else, like him, harbored his hidden yin behind his professed yang. Yet despite all these feelings Wan-li made no plans to abdicate or, on the other hand, to force his own wishes on his court. He did not even publicly announce his intention of making his third son heir, although to others it was as clear as though it were written. As a result, no attempt was made to impeach him; no civil war broke out; there was no rebellion. Yet for well over a decade the sovereign continued to engage in this odd struggle of endurance with the civil officials. If they would not let him install Ch'ang-hsün as his successor, he in turn would not authorize the investiture of Ch'ang-lo as heir designate. In fact, he even refused to let the eldest imperial son be capped and introduced to the Han-lin academicians for his education.

In the end Wan-li had to yield to public opinion, but grudgingly and most bitterly. When the eldest imperial son was finally designated his successor and the third son, Prince Fu, sent off to a provincial home, the wound thus inflicted did not heal—nor would it heal during the rest of His Majesty's long reign. Never again would the occupant of the throne consent to perform his duties as the bureaucrats wanted him to, in ways that only served their interests. He remained emperor, with the prerogatives due him, but he refused to do one more thing to satisfy the civil officials. For decades court rituals, if conducted at all, had to proceed without the ruler's presence. The emperor derived a malicious satisfaction from leaving numerous high-ranking positions inside and outside the capital unfilled, so that civil officials, with a few exceptions, were denied opportunities to be promoted to the very top of the hierarchy. He chose to ignore the bureaucrats' protests, because he knew that if he acted on their remonstrating papers, either coolly or heatedly, the petitions and his own rescripts would be turned over to the supervising secretaries' office for publication. This in fact would serve the purpose of the remonstrators, as they would earn a righteous reputation because of their criticism and defiance of the throne, while the throne would again be exposed in a bad light. So a better way of handling those irritating memorials was to bury them in a pile of wastepaper.

Under the circumstances, responsible officials with clear consciences were compelled to resign. But the emperor's reply to a request for resignation could also inadvertently give the petitioner a chance to air his grievance; so those requests were similarly pigeon-holed. A handful of officials, angry and desperate, left without authorization. Nor would the emperor follow the advice of the Ministry of Personnel to press charges against the deserters. During the later years of Wan-li, a position unoccupied became a position lost by default on the part of the bureaucrat concerned.

Classical canons, with which both the sovereign and his courtiers were of course familiar, sanctioned revolt against a ruler who was brutal and committed gross atrocities against his subjects. But neither ancient sages nor historical references offered guidance in a situation where a ruler selectively and quietly ignored some of his duties, and in doing so was literally following the Taoist doctrine of inaction.

Inasmuch as the Civil Service was a self-perpetuating body, most of its functions were carried on as usual. Palace examinations took place in the Years of the Ox, the Dragon, the Ram, and the Dog. It was also in those years that provincial officials were evaluated. The evaluation of capital officials in the Years of the Snake and the Pig completed the cycle. Starting from the reign of Wan-li, the appointment of officials to middle- and junior-grade positions, including those who were transferred, promoted, and demoted, was decided by drawing lots. The Ministry of Personnel listed all the vacant positions of the same rank and matched them with an equal number of eligible candidates. Except for the rulings that no one was to be appointed to serve in his native province or to become a superior or subordinate to his own kin, the details were left to chance. To those matters in which official personnel were handled in bulk the emperor gave his routine approval, generally allowing trusted eunuchs to wield the vermilion brushes for him.[1]

After reigning for forty-eight years, the Wan-li emperor died peacefully and was buried, along with his empress and Lady Wang, in the mausoleum that he himself had helped to design. The woman he loved, Lady Cheng, was left behind to outlive him for ten years. Accused of every sort of intrigue and considered a curse on the empire, she was forced to spend her old age in a desolate lodge within the Forbidden City, separated forever from her beloved son, Prince Fu, cause of all the controversy. The prince's land grant in excess of 600,000 acres remained another source of widespread irritation. None of the bureaucrats even bothered to explain to the public that the so-called fief existed only on paper, and that the bulk of reported acreage, grossly exaggerated, had actually been converted into an annual stipend of some 20,000 ounces of silver, in accordance with the dynasty's practice.[2]

Paradoxically, once the succession had become a settled issue, debate on the conditions that had led up to it, taking place after the emperor's death, paralyzed the court more than the issue itself had done. Now every reference to the past was bitterly debated and fought over. The court, already split into factions, had numerous accounts to be settled, most of them of merely the slightest significance. In several decades the Wan-li emperor had through his negligence and omissions done the bureaucracy irreparable damage.

His Majesty, being ruler, was expected to fulfill this role by presiding over the civil officials impartially. Even if Wan-li had worked earnestly he might still have had to face insurmountable difficulties. Fundamentally he had to cater to the dual character of the bureaucrats, to provide them with materialistic incentives as well as nurture their spiritual growth. Not only were these two objectives divergent in purpose, but the only means to achieve a balance between them that lay at the throne's disposal were abstract and indirect at best, limited as they were to personnel management and ceremonial proceedings. Moreover, after the controversial management of Chang Chü-cheng, the seeds of distrust had already been sown among the bureaucrats.

In practice, the emperor did precisely the opposite to what was required of him. Bent on being uncooperative, he virtually eliminated a number of prestigious government positions, dampening the hopes of many officials who had counted on their meritorious service to enable them to reach the highest rung of success, thereby enriching themselves and glorifying their ancestors. Skeptical as he was, the monarch did not even pretend to perform his duties according to moral law. Numerous individuals who remained loyal to the throne must have inwardly felt the futility of their own blind devotion.

So the outward tranquility of the Civil Service was indeed misleading. With no sense of cohesion it became a turbulent body. Unless its members could strive to equip themselves with some measure of mental alertness and voluntary exertion, their perfunctory and indirect writing of memorandums could not hope to dissolve the numerous discrepancies or bridge the many technical gaps within the gigantic network of bureaucratic offices. During a great part of His Majesty's reign of forty-eight years, when the top of the hierarchy, in despair, found that central leadership did not exist, cynicism and slack discipline spread through all the ranks. The diligent had less reason to maintain their diligence; the corrupt, on the other hand, had a better chance to indulge their corruption. The decline of the overall performance of the bureaucracy was steady and gradual. If the dynasty did not collapse at this point it was largely because no alternative to it existed. In an immense yet noncompetitive empire such as ours, the establishment continued to exist through mere inertia.

The atmosphere was depressing, to say the least. A group of bureaucrats, later known as Tung-lin partisans, nevertheless refused to give up. They believed that moral leadership could be established outside the monarchy. Cultured gentlemen, they were obliged to hold fast to what they had learned from the *Four Books* and Chu Hsi. Their classical education ordained them to be active and unyielding. Labeling themselves as "good elements," some of them managed to enter the Ministry of Personnel and the censorial-supervising branch of the government. They immediately put their moral perception to work by purging these offices of the "bad elements," including persons whom they regarded as acting apathetic and indolent during the scheduled personnel evaluations. As long as their program did not touch the emperor himself, it was routinely approved.

But this effort at moral reformation without the sovereign's active direction only rendered a disservice to the Civil Service as a whole. The ruler as a human being could not perform better than anyone else. But as the Son of Heaven he had at his command the mystique of the throne. As he was thought to be impartial, his human and technical errors could be overlooked. Even an act of injustice meted out by him would elicit protest but not retaliation. The Tung-lin partisans never held the advantage. In an age when 20,000 gentlemen dressed in service robes already found it difficult to reach a consensus as to what was right and what was wrong in conducting their affairs, the championing of an absolute standard no less ambiguous and abstract and set by some two dozen no less human individuals with their own petty aims and personal ties was not likely to win general approval. To counter the purges threatened by the Tung-lin, their rivals also formed blocs and cliques in the name of morality, until everyone had to take sides in order to survive.

The death of the emperor actually removed the last obstacle to open feud between the rival partisans. The question was now raised as to why, when Wan-li was still indecisive on the succession issue, the top bureaucrats had not spoken up more vigorously. Had Wang Hsi-chüeh, who later became first grand-secretary, agreed to some compromise that had actually encouraged the emperor to hold out? What about the story that Lady Cheng had made an attempt on the heir designate's life? And what about those two eunuchs who had master-minded the unsuccessful plot? Had her brother been involved? Emotionally loaded but factually vague and legally ambiguous, these questions were often asked without a genuine desire to find answers. In fact, none was ever offered. They were fired back and forth between opposing camps like accusations. The ultimate purpose was to advance partisan interests by conveniently putting the enemy camp on the defensive.

The dynasty was even less prepared for partisan politics. With a hopelessly undeveloped judiciary system, the machinery required to conduct arbitration over conflicting claims was wanting. Even technical problems brought before the emperor's court had to be reduced to moral archetypes of perfect good and absolute evil before they could be deliberated upon. Only when thousands of hidden motives and private interests had been restrained and neutralized by the teachings of the *Four Books* could the empire be held together. The moment the bureaucrats started to quote the text of the canon to wage a verbal civil war, the most vital organizational principle was abandoned. Clearly, when the bureaucracy began to disintegrate the empire became ungovernable. And this conclusion could have been drawn long before 1620 when the Wan-li emperor's body was carried to Ta-yü-shan for burial. A little over three decades before, in 1587, a year of no significance, his grand-secretary, Shen Shih-hsing, had already predicted that under such conditions the state could not long remain in peace and order.

But Grand-Secretary Shen had commanded little influence in shaping public opinion in his own day, let alone afterward. Because the succession issue began to emerge as a serious problem while he was master of the

Literary Depth Pavilion, the fact that he occupied that position for several crucial years was later much deplored. He was regarded as having been too weak and pliant. Also, he was accused of having encouraged Wan-li to put aside remonstrating papers unread and not acted upon.

When he was forced from office in 1591, the Year of the Rabbit, Shen carried no public sympathy with him. In early 1590, the Year of the Tiger, the first imperial son, Ch'ang-lo, had reached age ten by Chinese count, though his actual age was only eight-and-a-half. The fact that he had not yet been initiated for formal education under the tutorship of the Han-lin academicians caused the civil officials considerable anxiety, as they feared he would grow up without the ability to communicate with the court. But unless a princely title was conferred upon him, no ritualistic proceedings could provide for him to meet his tutors and no initiation could take place. In an attempt to right this situation, the civil officials exerted great pressure on the four grand-secretaries, who were required to urge Wan-li promptly to install Ch'ang-lo as imperial heir. They, Shen Shih-hsing included, duly submitted their resignations to the emperor and threatened to leave office unless this demand was met.[3]

Faced with this ultimatum, Wan-li replied that he had no desire to change the order of succession; yet the tactic of exerting pressure on him to act on a matter that lay within his own prerogative he must resist. He would, he promised, install his eldest son as imperial heir in early 1592, the Year of the Dragon, provided that in the interim no one would bother him about the matter of succession again. Should silence on the issue be violated, he warned, the installation would again be postponed. With this agreement the grand-secretaries had to return to their desks.

The following year was tense. There was a general suspicion that Shen Shih-hsing, who now enjoyed an intimate relationship with the throne, might be bribed by the emperor to use his influence to steer public opinion to favor Ch'ang-hsün over his elder brother, especially when, in the spring of 1591, Wan-li first offered to make Shen Grand Preceptor and then to confer on him the stipend due an earl—both rare honors far beyond ordinary awards and promotions.[4] Even though in each case Shen Shih-hsing declined vigorously and frantically until the offer was withdrawn, he was embarrassed and thrown into a state of consternation by it. Unknowingly, by his magnanimous gestures Wan-li had reduced Shen's effectiveness as a liaison between officials and the throne. Despite his mild and gentle disposition, Shen was feared as a potential king-maker as well as in his position as chief counsellor to the sovereign. Once again he was exposed to the criticisms of the censorial officials. In September 1591, even a provincial official from Fukien memorialized the throne to censure Shen Shih-hsing for suppressing a report that underground water was seeping from the floors of the emperor's mausoleum, the construction of which had been under Shen's supervision for six years.[5] Was it necessary for this minor functionary more than a thousand miles away to risk his position for such a small detail? The censure nevertheless served as a warning to the first grand-secretary that even though he enjoyed imperial trust he was by no means unaccountable to his fellow officials. In this particular case the memorialist was briefly dismissed from the Civil Service for his unwarranted accusation. Yet, his purpose already accomplished, he could expect to be recalled in the future, perhaps with added glory and prestige.

In October, with 1592 only months away, a secretary with the Ministry of Works, completely within his jurisdiction, submitted a budgetary request to the emperor for the pending installation of the heir designate. The imperial rescript on this petition turned out to be a shock to the courtiers. Wan-li seized upon the memorial as an infraction of his edict of silence on the succession issue and therefore felt justified in postponing the installation ceremony. How could someone who showed such lack of faith be the Ruler of All Men? Responsible officials in the court felt obliged to urge the emperor to honor his pledge. On the day they did so, Shen Shih-hsing was on sick leave. The joint petition of the grand-secretaries was drafted by Hsü Kuo, second in command, without his knowledge. Hsü nevertheless included Shen's name on the paper just before his own.[6]

When he learned of the petition, Shen Shih-hsing wrote a confidential note to the emperor, using a special kind of stationery. In his effort to soothe the sovereign, he pointed out that he himself had not even been consulted before the petition was submitted. Wan-li then rescripted that he appreciated Tutor Shen's kindness. The matter could have ended there. Standard practice demanded that a confidential note submitted by a grand-secretary, after being read by the emperor, should be returned to the writer and not be circulated. As it happened, this particular note was intercepted by Hsü Kuo, who routinely sent it to the supervising secretaries' office to be entered into the public record. Shen Shih-hsing was able to retrieve it from the file before copies had been made but not before its contents were known to many. To remove a document from the offices at the Meridian Gate, moreover, was in itself a violation of procedure, which constrained the supervising secretary in charge to impeach Shen. The first grand-secretary was said "to have openly supported public opinion in favor of the immediate installation of the imperial heir, yet privately to have maneuvered to impede action so that he could court personal favor." The impeachment then continued: "After using evasive words to betray his friends, he resorted to a confidential note to misguide his master. If Your Majesty should ever be so lenient as to spare his life, the spirit of our dynastic founder would assuredly deliver him to his deserved destruction."

These harsh words ended a splendid career of twenty-nine years that had started with the winning of first place at the Civil Service examinations and had endured hundreds of rounds of kowtowing on the granite yard outside the Literary Floral Hall.

Even at this point the Wan-li emperor did not grasp the serious nature of the case. He ordered that the supervising secretary who had submitted the impeachment order be demoted and transferred to a provincial post and urged Tutor Shen to return to office, which the latter consented to do. But a wave of protest engulfed the court and it became clear that the first grand-secretary's usefulness to the throne had already been destroyed. What defenses Shen Shih-hsing could rally for the confidential nature of his note and the factual truth it represented, both of a technical nature, could never provide him with immunity against the charge of duplicity, a fatal moral accusation that lay beyond procedural considerations. In a sense, the emperor's chief counsellor had already been tried by public opinion and found guilty. The consensus of the court was so clear that, having been given a vote of nonconfidence, Shen Shih-hsing could no longer even be retained by imperial authority. He had no alternative other than to tender the throne his resignation repeatedly until his involuntary retirement was finally authorized. If he stayed on, he would become another Chang Chü-cheng.

The discharging of the emperor's first grand-secretary was not unaccompanied by other dismissals. In his wrath Wan-li withdrew his order of demotion and transfer of the supervising secretary involved, stripped him of his Civil Service status, and made him a commoner—ostensibly because of his violation of the imperial demand for silence on the succession issue, but in reality because he had been openly praised by subsequent memorialists as their hero; they were now petitioning the throne to retain him in the capital. The next day His Majesty also accepted the resignation of Second Grand-Secretary Hsü Kuo. For many years Hsü had been thought to be close to Shen Shih-hsing; now it was revealed that intense rivalry and contention must have existed between them. His deliberate disclosure of Shen's confidential note could never escape the criticism of being malicious. It was evident that a person of such character should not be retained within the inner circle of the throne. Once his de facto dismissal went into effect, the emperor waited two more days to accept with sincere regret the request for retirement by his beloved Tutor Shen.[7]

The tragedy of the Year of the Rabbit was that nobody emerged a victor. The succession issue, which had kindled the round of controversy and produced casualties at the top level, could not for some time be comfortably brought up by the courtiers. Because of the woman he loved, the emperor was not ready to surrender his personal wish, which, in the light of the public opinion so unmistakably expressed during the recent confrontations, could not be attained without resorting to force — and that, for better or worse, could never be the sovereign's choice, as it contradicted his Buddhist inclinations.

In his handling of the succession issue Wan-li had blundered badly. The inevitable consequence of his making Lady Cheng imperial consort was that Ch'ang-hsün, his son by her, would rank higher than Ch'ang-lo, given birth by Lady Wang three and a half years earlier, since his second son had died prematurely. Yet Wan-li had no moral justification for favoring one son over another; so he resorted to procrastination. First he refused to designate Ch'ang-lo as his heir on the grounds that he was too young and delicate to fulfill the ceremonial requirements that would be expected of him. Then he said that he resented being pushed into action by his subjects. As a matter of principle he refused to do what he was told. In between times he himself came up with the proposal that he confer the title of prince on all three of his sons equally. When that was not endorsed by the civil officials, he retreated to the position that his empress was still young enough to give him another son, so that the entire business of designating an heir could be postponed. These inconsistencies exposed not only the sovereign's lack of good faith but also his lack of courage, which naturally strengthened the opposition.[8]

The deadlock soon became a constitutional crisis because no legal apparatus existed to break it. One little-known point was that the emperor's wish to make his third son his heir rather than his first was not without justification from the standpoint of statutory or customary law. Had the empire been governed by an independent judiciary and the throne submitted its proposal to the court, and had his wish been candidly presented and vigorously argued by jurists, chances are that the sovereign's case against the bureaucrats would have been won.

First of all, Ch'ang-lo could not be said to have a right to succession. Nobody had. Until an emperor's son had the title of prince conferred upon him, he was technically a commoner. If there had been such a thing as birthright, this rule would have been superfluous. Second, primogeniture was a social norm of ceremonial custom, not a binding rule on the imperial family. This fact was amply confirmed by the successful rebellion of Prince Yen, the dynasty's third emperor. As a fourth son he had not only dislodged a nephew born of his eldest brother, but also, by seizing the throne for himself, he had disregarded the priority of the heirs of his other two elder brothers. Third, the dynastic founder's instructions on the succession issue did declare that sons born of an emperor's secondary wives must follow age sequence. However, a son born of the empress was not bound by this restriction; he took priority over his half brothers, older or younger.[9] Since Ch'ang-hsün was born of an imperial consort, who ranked next only to the empress, his case could have been considered exceptional. And fourth, if Wan-li had wished it, there was nothing to prevent him from deposing Empress Hsiao-tuan and replacing her with Lady Cheng, thus raising Ch'ang-hsün's status. In the history of the dynasty, four emperors had deposed their empresses and elevated secondary wives of their choice to the vacated position. All that was necessary was the emperor's own order, which in none of these cases had been resisted.[10]

Why did Wan-li not clearly announce his intention from the beginning and firmly declare that the succession issue lay within the domain of his own prerogative and was therefore not a matter open for public discussion? No single answer will suffice. But fundamentally, His Majesty's realm had never been legally structured in such a way as to enable him to make such a claim. Rather, it was governed directly by the moral law proclaimed in the *Four Books*. From their classical education, including historical lessons, the entire population had learned that fathers must be impartial to their sons, that elder brothers were supposed to command and lead their younger brothers, and that men of rectitude should never be swayed by the influence of women to modify their public obligations because of private sentiments. These tenets had been repeatedly cited in every school in every village and even passed on to the illiterate to keep the empire in order. Had legal technicalities been permitted to override these tenets, the organizational logic of the empire would have been challenged and the magistrates would never again have been able to manage the affairs of their counties. The entire bureaucracy had simply never been educated or accustomed to accept that kind of government.

In short, Wan-li's desire to depart from custom was not so much illegal in terms of statutory law as it was unethical in the eyes of orthodox bureaucrats. The weight of public opinion nevertheless compelled him to deny what he actually had in mind, and at times even to pay lip service to the principle of primogeniture. But once he had recognized the succession as a moral issue, that recognition nullified all the legal arguments that would have been in his favor.

Continuing to cherish a personal wish that was now unmentionable, the sovereign also suffered from lack of counsel. Until the day he died, the Wan-li emperor was destined to be a lonely man. Undoubtedly he had hoped to draw Shen Shih-hsing to his side, the only individual over whom he might exert some personal influence. Yet, because even in private he could not admit his true intention and disclose his strategy, he had no way of advancing his cause. No counsellor of his, principled or unprincipled, could have taken a stand on his behalf. On the contrary, one first grand-secretary after another felt compelled to act not as an agent of the throne but as a spokesman for the bureaucrats, who were demanding that the sovereign clarify his position and rectify himself. When their efforts produced no results, one after another they had to leave office under public pressure. As a result, Wan-li had to deal with several first grand-secretaries of varying temperaments. His ad hoc maneuvers with these diverse personalities exposed his inconsistency more than ever.

Faced with such a hopeless situation, Wan-li's unwillingness to abandon his desire to place Ch'ang-hsün on the throne led to the widespread speculation that he might have been forced by Lady Cheng to act the way he did against his own better judgment. For some time the courtiers had also suspected that the sovereign and his favorite concubine were waiting for the death of the empress, who was then said to be in very poor health. At this point no one could have anticipated, of course, that Empress Hsiao-tuan was to live for many more decades, and eventually when her death did come, that it would be followed four months later by the emperor's.

But amid all the confusion and intrigue a most important development that was taking place went virtually unnoticed: the changing character of the monarchy as an institution prior to and during His Majesty's reign. Wan-li occupied the same dragon seat his ancestors had; however, he was required to rule with fewer human qualities and less personal passion. Unlike his ancestors who, with little or no accuracy, had been lavishly described by the literary-educational officials of their day as paragons of virtue, this latter-day emperor was carefully tutored by the corresponding officials to cast his life into the mold created for him. The difference was subtle, but the essence of it was that, when the dynasty was established, the emperors proceeded to build up the bureaucracy as an instrument of the state to carry out their ideas of administration, whereas two hundred years later, the bureaucracy, now firmly established, needed only a cloistered sovereign to act as its presiding officer, whose impartiality was deemed far more important than his ability to command.

With all their talk of the sovereign's responsibility to heaven, the sixteenth-century bureaucrats were actually preventing him from becoming actively involved in the matters brought to the throne for disposal. He was encouraged to be emotionally neutral and personally bland. There was little chance for him to become responsive to state affairs in any functional way. In short, an effort to dehumanize the monarchy was under way, against which the occupant of the throne had no defense. Evidently this milieu first caused the Wan-li emperor, who since childhood had been taught to take rather than give orders, to hesitate to assert himself on the succession issue, and later, when bitter experience enabled him to see the inner mechanism of his court, to feel totally alienated from it.

The trouble was that while the emperor chose to suspend the issue of the imperial heir, the bureaucrats were growing restless. Since 1587, the Year of the Pig, no other issue had attracted so much attention and rocked the court of Peking so profoundly as the matter of succession. Neither the rebellion of Yang Ying-lung in the southwest, nor the revolt of Pübei in the northwest, the invasion of Korea by Hideyoshi, or even the empire-building of Nurhaci had generated the degree of anger and concern on the part of the 2,000 silk-robed gentlemen in the capital as the question of who should succeed His Majesty on the dragon seat did.

Even after Ch'ang-lo was installed as heir designate and Ch'ang-hsün sent to Honan, the case was by no means settled. As long as the notorious Lady Cheng was keeping company with the sovereign day and night, alternating her allure with termagancy, what abominable act was she incapable of trapping him into? The angry officials ardently wished there was some way Lady Cheng could be impeached.[11] Without naming names, several memorials to the emperor in fact pointed out to His Majesty that an upright ruler should never subject himself to the spell of beautiful women. Historically they were the kind of temptation that ruined dynasties.[12]

There were rumors, rumors of all kinds, and rumors that contradicted one another. There were rumors suggesting palace intrigues that involved murder and sorcery, and rumors involving delightful stories of human interest. As always, men were predisposed to believe whatever reinforced their wishful thinking and to pass along whatever helped to relieve their fear and anxiety. Rumors therefore served useful purposes at this time.

Effigies were said to have been found in the palace. According to popular tradition, when an image of one's enemy was stabbed with a new pin on every seventh day by an expert specialized in the craft, the victim would be afflicted with an unknown ailment for which even the best physicians could find no cure. Was Lady Cheng trying to do this to Ch'ang-lo? Soon it was being said that the empress's effigy was found; and then, even more alarmingly, that of the emperor.

In those frantic days a certain grand-secretary was continuing his calm practice of bowing down before a wooden board fastened on the doorway to his office. He had posted that board inside the Literary Depth Pavilion as a reminder to himself not to do ten things that he believed would injure the population and therefore provoke the displeasure of heaven. Every morning he paused in front of his own ten commandments before attending to his desk. Though in the past the eccentric act had been ignored, now it was reported to the emperor that the grand-secretary was practicing witchcraft, as he had been observed cursing in front of a tablet with dubious writing on it. The emperor was concerned enough to have the board brought to the palace for his personal scrutiny before reprimanding the eunuch who had called this bit of hearsay to his attention.[13]

Some of these circulating stories in time became part of history. One of these related that when Lady Wang first met the emperor she was already past her most flourishing years, and subsequently she developed a cataract on one of her eyes. This was an explanation of why she had first infatuated the emperor yet in the end lost his favor. Another story had it that once Wan-li was ill and thought he was dying, only to wake up and find himself lying in Lady Wang's arms, her face streaked with tears.[14] Meanwhile Lady Cheng was nowhere to be found. Naturally, she was such a heartless woman! Still another story involved Empress Dowager Tz'u-sheng. It was said that she was dismayed by the emperor's intention of cutting off the right to succession of her eldest grandson, Ch'ang-lo. The following conversation was supposed to have taken place between her and Wan-li:

Empress dowager: Let's face it. What will people think about all this? What are you going to tell them?
Emperor: I'll just say, well, that he is only a son born of a chambermaid.
Empress dowager: How dare you! Don't you know that you yourself are only a son born of a chambermaid?!

According to the story, at this point the emperor had to kowtow and apologize to his mother.[15]

Most of these stories could not be verified. Despite this, all of them, including the one implying that Lady Wang was much older than the emperor, were eventually engraved on plates and printed for public distribution. Centuries later, Lady Wang's tombstone inscription nevertheless testified that she was born in early 1565; this would have made her sixteen years old when she first met the emperor, then only eighteen himself.

The fact that block printing was in wide public use during the Wan-li emperor's reign added a disturbing element to those decades of anxiety. Anonymous pamphlets and pseudonymous literature appeared in Peking to stir up and intensify the controversy. One of these pamphlets asserted that a movement to depose Ch'ang-lo as the designated heir and recall Ch'ang-hsün to replace him was imminent. The publication also named responsible officials of the court as belonging to the pro–Lady Cheng group that was supposed to carry out the impending coup. When the emperor ordered the Secret Police to arrest the author as well as the publisher of the pamphlet, the search threw the capital into turmoil, inflaming both those whose names appeared in the pamphlet and those whose names did not.[16]

Few of the people involved in the controversy at the time understood that although the succession issue had crossed the path of their lives by chance, their overreaction to it reflected their own sense of insecurity and the intense rivalries existing among themselves, which had nothing to do with primogeniture. Even without Lady Wang and Lady Cheng, even without the Tung-lin partisans, the bureaucracy had long been approaching an unmanageable state. The unidentified cause of the contention among the civil officials went deeper than any of them realized. It could be traced all the way back to the founding of the dynasty.

A fact often overlooked by contemporaries was that the dynasty's reliance on ideology as an instrument of government was in many respects unprecedented, both in intensity and in scope. Ideology worked well in the early years, especially after the dynastic founder, the Hung-wu emperor, systematically destroyed the empire's large landowners and wealthy households and imposed a stringently puritanical standard of living on the rest of the educated elite, insisting that they were civil servants of the general population in the literal sense of the word *servant*. In an atmosphere of rustic simplicity, the gap between an individual's inner urge for self-gain and his professed moral standards could be minimized, or at least prevented from appearing to be a cause of concern to the administration.[17]

By the time Chang Chü-cheng took over the reins of the government on behalf of the Wan-li emperor in 1572, the dynasty had already run a course of two hundred years. At this later date the civil officials were definitely not servants to the agrarian masses. Discrepancies between the earlier ideal and the present reality were many. Among them the most troublesome was that many problems could no longer be handled by practical means. Numerous business proceedings that should have been carried out according to organizational principles were actually handled by the personal touch. One of the reasons for this was that, at the outset, the state settled for a level of income too low to finance its operations throughout an immense empire. The salary scale of the Civil Service was set so low that many officials were virtually unpaid.

Although it recognized these undesirable conditions, the court in the later period was helpless to provide a fundamental cure for them. The dynasty had followed the vision of the *Four Books* too closely to consider other approaches. Adjudging simple living a permanent national characteristic, the bureaucratic apparatus had deliberately been constructed to avoid technical complexities. It was a huge web, centrally controlled and of enormous dimensions but with little depth and focus, and still less adaptability. No provision had been made within it to handle an expanding budget and adjustable incomes. The Civil Service had neither the administrative expertise nor the necessary service facilities to allow itself to keep pace with a national economy that was expanding in both size and degree of sophistication.[18]

Impelled by necessity, behind-the-scenes magistrates in many districts had started to collect supplementary payments from the populace in the name of customary fees, which varied in amount and nature from one county to another. Basically, the magistrate added a percentage on taxes collected in silver in the name of melting charges and demanded extras on those items collected in kind in the name of samples and wastages. The community also took care of the magistrate's housekeeping expenses, supplying him with food, wine, and even gifts to his superiors and colleagues. Connived at by the central authority but never given formal recognition, the twilight legality of such impositions naturally led to abuse. Tax quotas, furthermore, differed widely from region to region. A small percentage on the proceeds from a rich county kept the magistrate amply provided. The same sum would nevertheless be an extortionate drain on a poor county. The ambiguities had rendered the honor code irrelevant. Should a county magistrate, who by official order was entitled to an annual compensation of less than thirty ounces of silver, still be considered honest if he helped himself to 300 ounces, but not if he took 3,000? If he appropriated 5 percent of the district's gross tax proceeds, or 10 percent? At what point was honesty defined?[19]

Still more ambiguous was the integrity of the capital officials. Denied access to customary fees, many of them nevertheless received subsidies from provincial and local officials in the form of cash gifts. The inflow of silver to Peking was so routine that Hai Jui cynically called the years when the evaluation of provincial officials was due "the years when capital officials collected their mortgage payments."[20] What, then, was all this talk about honesty and corruption, when those who were making the character assessments were being paid by the subjects under evaluation? This institutional weakness helped to ruin the personal reputations of many an administrator, including Chang Chü-cheng.

Worse yet, from an organizational point of view, administrators at nearly all levels were not equipped to handle problems arising from changing circumstances. Nor, evidently, had they exercised sufficient control over their subordinates, when the latter had to pay themselves and the power of appointment and dismissal rested with the emperor's court. The system therefore forced officials to find remedies in personal exertion and moral value. Indeed, the appeal of self-sacrifice to a cultured gentleman produced many a heroic act in the dynasty's annals. There were officials who, although literati never militarily trained, commanded hastily organized defensive forces on city walls and fought fierce battles to the death. There were also officials who ate and slept with common laborers, refusing shelter and braving epidemics to secure river dikes in the face of threatening floods. But what efficiency they did demonstrate had to be drawn entirely from the spiritual lessons of the *Four Books* and was all they had at their command to apply to emergency situations. The demand for ideology thus tended to spiral upward in an age when technical and organizational solutions to problems should have been being sought and provided.

The result was polarization of the dual character of the bureaucracy. Because on the one hand it persistently pushed the scholar-officials toward the doctrine of compassion and seeking virtue as its own reward, yet on the other hand its organizational inadequacies offered them every opportunity for unearned self-gain, the Civil Service found it increasingly difficult to maintain its balance. The yin and the yang were moving farther away from each other on the spectrum.

This was a problem Chang Chü-cheng had been unable to solve. Though he worked in the Literary Depth Pavilion for a decade, he barely assessed the situation. In fiscal administration the best he could do was to demand the payment of the existing quotas; yet the pressure he applied to the bureaucracy to this end was felt to be unbearable. The silver bullion he accumulated, prodigious as it seemed, was insufficient to fill up the organizational vacuum or to enable him to plan for a major reform. He certainly would not have hoarded the cash deposits in the treasuries if means could have been found to invest them.

After Chang Chü-cheng failed, his successor, Shen Shih-hsing, had to lower his sights drastically. When Shen said that he wished to provide something for virtuous men to rely on and the evil-minded to be afraid of, he was trying to reconcile the two extremes: he would neither strictly enforce the honor code nor encourage abuses. The first grand-secretary never intended his personnel evaluation of 1587, the most lenient on record, to be aimed at relaxation of moral discipline for its own sake. As far as he could see, an extraordinary situation had now come to exist which demanded that he abandon the moral rule to respect his sister-in-law at a distance. The time had come for him to grab her in order to save her from drowning.[21]

There is no evidence that he succeeded. Shen himself was called a great compromiser who moved his head in one direction and his tail in another. The feebleness with which he conducted the evaluation program was challenged by a hard core of young officials, among them an inconspicuous figure, Ku Hsien-ch'eng by name. At that time Shen Shih-hsing had no difficulty transferring his critic to a remote provincial post. Ku Hsien-ch'eng was nevertheless to reemerge later as a prime organizer of the Tung-lin movement, which, with its singleminded drive toward purification, stopped at nothing short of tearing apart the very organization that Shen Shih-hsing had tried to patch up.[22]

So, around the Year of the Pig, before the full impact of the succession issue had been felt, the internal relationships of the bureaucracy were already seriously strained, as neither the application of pressure from the top nor the call for reconciliation from the middle had actually helped. Civil officials in Peking regarded one another with hostility and suspicion. Some were upstarts who wanted to achieve a life of luxury in a hurry. Others came from well-to-do families who, having chosen to forgo the materialistic gains from office, demanded that others do the same. The text of the *Four Books* could be taken literally and devoutly, or eclectically and skeptically. Still others, regardless of family background, were undecided and wavering, or else unconsciously motivated by personal ties. Once such individual differences were transformed into moral issues, the resulting conflicts became highly charged with emotion. There was a special kind of bigotry afoot that incited a bureaucrat to feel angry and ashamed of the silk-robed creature next to him, who seemed to have disgraced the mandarin square and the looplike service belt. Yet, prejudice could also come from the other direction. And such bigotry and prejudice were reinforced by the thousands of petty causes of bickering in daily life.

The succession issue, however, was by no means either petty or abstract. In a practical sense imperial succession became a problem only when two candidates were competing for the throne. But once the issue was settled and one of the contenders emerged as the next ruler, he would, in order to justify his position as the Son of Heaven and in the name of morality, be obliged to punish those who had either overtly or tacitly supported his rival in the past. Without such drastic actions the absolute authority of the throne, already lessened by the competition itself, would never be restored.

This situation had occurred twice before in the dynasty's history. The third Ming emperor, Yung-lo, had started a rebellion against his nephew and in the course of time was forced to challenge the latter's right to succession. After seizing the throne, he meted out the death penalty to many who had been unenthusiastic in acknowledging him as the heaven-mandated ruler.[23] The sixth emperor, Cheng-t'ung, had been captured by the Mongols during an ill-conceived military compaign. He was later released by his captors because the court of Peking, with the empress dowager's approval, during the interim had installed his half-brother as the Ching-t'ai emperor in order to nullify the Mongolian advantage in negotiation while they held the reigning emperor as hostage. Upon his return, Cheng-t'ung lived peacefully in a villa within the Imperial City for seven years; yet in the end his supporters staged a coup to restore him as the legitimate ruler. When this was accomplished, those who had previously been instrumental in Ching-t'ai's accession had to be sacrificed to make the restoration an act mandated by Heaven.[24]

In 1587 there was no assurance that the present uncertainty would not lead to atrocities of the same dimensions. Civil officials, in both red and blue service robes, realized from past experience that at this point an unintentional gesture or speech, or even silence on their part, could many years later be seized upon by their enemies as evidence of treason or giving aid and comfort to a usurper, incriminating them and their families. Yet the danger also offered opportunities for the bold and daring to demonstrate their righteousness, with full knowledge that their audacity could very well lead them to future martyrdom and its attendant fame. They delivered the most provocative memorials to the emperor and, when that was not enough, printed seditious pamphlets and circulated inflammatory handbills. The heavy moral content of the succession issue became firmly established only as a result of their efforts.

Toward the latter part of his reign, the Wan-li emperor must have been aware that because of his estrangement from his courtiers he would never escape history's judgment of him as a ruler who had failed in his imperial responsibilities. But he did not even try to avoid this ultimate condemnation. His immediate concern was to keep the annoying criticisms out of his hearing. He made no attempt to exert his influence as an active ruler; yet as a passive one he refused to be dehumanized, or if he was, it had to be on his terms. His tragedy was that although he rejected his role as an instrument of the bureaucracy, the imperial constitution dictated that he could not function otherwise.

Part of Wan-li's failure was that he was too intelligent and sensitive to occupy the dragon seat. The more he gained an insight into its apparatus the more skeptical he became. He began to realize that he was less the Ruler of All Men than a prisoner of the Forbidden City. His power was basically negative. He could remove or punish an official or a group of officials, but he could hardly promote a favorite or grant him an unusual honor. Above all, he could never employ a confidant who had public status. In response to the petitions of governors and ministers, he authorized exceptions to existing laws; but he could never revise a law directly from the throne. He was asked to arbitrate when the bureaucrats had a disagreement they could not resolve themselves; but he could not initiate more fundamental changes in order to avoid such an impasse. Moreover, in the case of Wan-li, his arbitration became progressively ineffective because as emperor he was recognized as neglecting his duties, and that recognition only encouraged the quarrelsome officials to counter his rulings with more protests and remonstrances. Every setback on the frontier was reported to His Majesty the Wan-li emperor; but he was restrained from issuing his own directives. Above all, he was not allowed to exercise personal command over the army. Unlike his ancestors, he was not free to leave the palace, let alone the capital. Was the benefit of occupying the imperial throne worth so many restrictions? He had no say in deciding that either. He had become the Son of Heaven by birth, not choice.[25]

The only way Wan-li could hope to exert some positive influence rested with his character, not his power. But to rely on his character meant reliving the days when he was manipulated by Chang Chü-cheng, remaining an abstract symbol of virtue and wisdom, and enduring all the ceremonial proceedings. The tedium of those proceedings was widely recognized. But few understood that to Wan-li the suffering went beyond the discomfort of the sessions themselves. These practices made no distinction between the monarchy as an institution and the emperor as a person. When he performed the rituals he was subjecting himself to the rule of moral law, and moral law as the diehard bureaucrats interpreted it! Unlike his bureaucrats, he could never shield his yin with his yang. His moral obligation was virtually limitless.

The day Wan-li's mother Tz'u-sheng died, the Ministry of Rites promptly worked out the detailed procedures for observing national mourning for twenty-seven days. During the period all imperial subjects had to wear white headgear in public. Capital officials and army officers wore robes of unbleached hemp, the fringes unstitched. Instead of boots they wore straw sandals. Their black hats were covered with hemp fabric. The wings on their hats were detached, and in their place two white ribbons hung down to their shoulders. Meatless diet and abstention from alcoholic beverages were decreed in Peking for thirteen days, during which time the temples and chapels in the city rang their bells 30,000 times. Twice a day three days in a row, all officials, in addition to the wives of those of rank 4b and above, were ushered into the Forbidden City in groups. They stopped in front of the Palace of Compassionate Tranquility to perform the ceremonial wailing. The proceedings involved "fifteen laments and groans," which were well coordinated. The sound had to be "suspended as soon as it was uttered."[26]

Clearly enough, in this instance the empress dowager was being mourned less as a person than as a symbol of universal motherhood. The proceedings were basically disciplinary and theatrical. The compulsory lamentation reaffirmed the participants' loyalty to the throne as well as underlining their subscription to filial piety. Conceivably, once the wailing was done, the mourners would be more than ever devoted to their own parents and would try harder to promote propriety and good feelings throughout the empire, so that His Majesty's reign would go down in history as one of the most enlightened. But there was no indication that His Majesty himself was at this point convinced of such a result. He knew only too well that rituals led to more rituals. In the end the question would arise as to how much sincerity he, as sovereign, put behind the performances. The crucial point was whether he was leading a simple and frugal life or not. He had had enough of all this before and most definitely had no more appetite for it now. With the excuse that his "lower body was still infected by dampness and poison," he called off the ceremony that would have required him to announce in public the honorary title of the deceased.[27] Nevertheless, as the Jesuit fathers then residing in Peking reported, he spent a great deal of time seeing to it that his mother's body was laid out comfortably in her coffin, taking care of all the details with his own hands.[28]

When Wan-li persistently refused to comply with the conventional requirements made of an emperor, his indolence became a legend—so much so that historians began to comment on his inborn laziness and to speculate on whether he had turned into an opium addict. None of these writers noted that of a sunny day Wan-li, having stayed away from ceremonial functions, often spent his time in the palace yard watching a game that he had organized for his eunuchs, where the players tossed silver pieces toward target areas marked on the ground, to have their bets doubled, tripled, or taken away by the dealer—a pastime that sadly reflected the state of the emperor's active but unused mind, which could find no better outlet amidst the deep boredom of his life.[29]

Why did he not attempt to reorganize the empire, to make the office of emperor more substantial instead of symbolic and abstract? Many obstacles stood in his way. But above all there was the precedent of his granduncle, the Cheng-te emperor.

During the reign of Wan-li, the succession controversy brought another fundamental conflict into the open. Behind the scenes there was the fact that the monarchy had become such a highly stylized institution that no thinking man could occupy the dragon seat with comfort. Before the present emperor, the same conditions had been contested by Cheng-te. Although Wan-li was separated from his granduncle by about a half-century, what destiny had in store for him had been very much conditioned by the life and deeds of his predecessor.

Cheng-te had ascended the throne in 1505 when he was not yet fourteen. Endowed with unusual physical courage and a great deal of energy and creative curiosity, he soon discovered that those gifts only made him a gross misfit for the latter-day monarchy cast in the dynasty's mold. Nevertheless, this unfortunate situation in no way deterred him from his own way of seeking happiness, which he pursued with all the authority at his command. To the chagrin of his courtiers, he also had the strength to defy and ignore their moral criticisms, and perhaps even to derive pleasure from doing so.[30]

A little over two years after his accession, Cheng-te moved out of his palace quarters. His new residence, designated the Leopard House, was constructed in the open space of the Imperial City, which consisted of clusters of apartments, hunting lodges, and club rooms.[31] Soon he was surrounded by eunuchs, courtesans, Lamaist monks, and magicians from other lands. Court audiences and public study sessions were held by the fun-loving emperor only when it suited his convenience.[32] His favorite pastimes were fishing and hunting. Once at least he was wounded by a tiger when he was learning to tame it, only to be rescued by his favorite army officer, Chiang Pin.

Chiang himself had attracted the emperor's attention because of his daring. One of the three arrow wounds he had sustained in battle had left a scar on his face stretching into his ear. Ever since his interview with Cheng-te in 1512, he had been with the imperial entourage. The palace army was organized into two camps. Chiang Pin was in charge of a battalion of soldiers selected from the northern frontier units, while the emperor commanded his own battalion of mounted archers consisting of eunuchs. Yellow capes worn over armor and hats with sun visors decorated with feathers gave this legion a gallant appearance.[33] Previously, Cheng-te had conducted field exercises with soldiers on the palace grounds.[34] With Chiang Pin his military training acquired a professional touch. Now field maneuvers inside the Imperial City became a daily routine, followed by evening entertainments in the Leopard House. About civil affairs the monarch allowed his courtiers to fight with his eunuchs. Apparently he considered such quarrels inevitable and in any case not his specialty.[35]

The greatest thrill for Cheng-te came in 1517. Batu Mengke, the Mongol leader, had made incursions into the empire's northern frontier several years in a row, inflicting heavy injuries. In October of that year, with 50,000 mounts, he again besieged a Ming general at a forward post. Leading the relief column, the emperor had the opportunity to test his own strategy as well as to see action.[36] Later he claimed that during the engagement he had personally slain a Mongol.[37]

All this was not accomplished without bureaucratic opposition. First an imperial censor overseeing the defense on the Great Wall refused to let the emperor go beyond the barrier, as he had no business there. Forced to return to the capital, Cheng-te simply issued a formal order to remove that particular official and put a eunuch in his place. Only then was he able to enter the combat zone. For the next four months the civil officials virtually lost contact with the sovereign. The couriers run by the eunuchs between the capital and the emperor's forward headquarters delivered many petitions but few rescripts.

Most comical was the emperor's triumphant return to Peking early the following year. The day before his arrival he ordered palace attendants to distribute to all officials silk fabrics of imperial design, with pythons and flying fish—up to this time reserved for rare honors—now to be handed out in large numbers. The badges of military and civil ranks were completely mixed up. The shape of the hats was designed by the emperor. That night the recipients of the textiles were told to have their costumes made in time for the welcoming assembly outside the city wall the next morning, which was to take place without a rehearsal. When the courtiers were further instructed to display banners and posters stating welcoming messages, they were in a dilemma as to how to find a proper way of addressing themselves; because His Majesty now chose to call himself "General of the Army of Greater Valor," it would have been inappropriate for the officials to sign themselves "Your loyal subjects." On the triumphal day it rained and snowed. The emperor, arriving on a chestnut-colored horse, stopped at the city gate for the ritual glass of wine handed him by the first grand-secretary, then galloped directly toward the Leopard House, leaving thousands of officials stumbling and slipping behind him in the muddy streets.[38]

As evidence of his victory the emperor displayed captured equipment before the palace.[39] The imperial mint turned out silver medallions to commemorate the campaign, complete with colored ribbons.[40] But Cheng-te's jubilation was not shared by his court. The entire Han-lin Academy refused to congratulate him. A number of censorial-supervising officials took the opportunity to impeach themselves and ask to be relieved from duty.[41] Even though the siege was broken by the relieving column and for the rest of Cheng-te's reign Mengke never again became a serious threat, skeptical civil officials simply denied that the emperor's campaign had been a success. According to them, only sixteen Mongols had been killed, at a disproportionate cost of six hundred Ming casualties.[42]

In the autumn of 1518, the emperor directed that a commission be granted to the General of the Army of Greater Valor for a visit to inspect the entire northern frontier. All four grand-secretaries refused to draft the commission. One of them, prostrating himself on the ground in tears, begged the emperor to execute him rather than force him into such impropriety.[43] Unmoved, Cheng-te proceeded to make the tour regardless. On the way he issued a personal order conferring on himself the title of Duke of Cheng-kuo in addition to that of General of the Army, at an annual stipend of 5,000 bushels of grain. Five months later he went on to proclaim himself (already a duke and generalissimo) Grand Preceptor, and thus the senior civil official of his own court, outranking all ministers and grand-secretaries.[44]

Cheng-te's second trip was uneventful; no enemy was encountered. But the emperor crossed the Yellow River and searched the edges of the Ordos before returning to Peking in the spring of 1519. During the nine months of his absence, remonstrating memorials submitted by capital officials first arrived by scores and then by the hundreds. In these papers the courtiers expressed their deep anxiety over the fact that the imperial capital had become an empty shell without the sovereign as its stabilizer. Two grand-secretaries argued that if the emperor demoted himself to a duke, by dynastic law the same title should be granted posthumously to his ancestors for three generations back. Would His Majesty be so unfilially pious as to demote his parents, grandparents, and great grandparents in addition to himself? The first grand-secretary was even more emphatic. He wanted to know who this person, the General of the Army of Greater Valor, was. He further suggested that whoever used that title in official documents be arrested and charged with falsifying the imperial order—a crime punishable by death.[45]

All these arguments fell on deaf ears. Cheng-te was too independent, too taken with his own nonconformity, and too confident of himself to be annoyed by such bookish disputations. He loved to drink and play games with his subordinates. He could not care less if a charming companion was a prostitute, was married, or even pregnant. During one of his tours of inspection he so mingled with his retinue that at the governor's dinner party he was seated at the table without chopsticks! Many was the time he waved aside carriages and sedan chairs bearing the imperial insignia to ride in an unmarked wagon. At his grandmother's funeral service he saw that the ground was soaked with water, so he ordered that the customary kowtow by the court be omitted. His kindness was not appreciated. One of the officials thus deprived of the privilege of floundering in puddles of water to show his devotion to the imperial family wrote a strong protest to Cheng-te. A discourse on filial piety quoting Confucius and Mencius, this

remonstrating memorial subsequently became a piece of oft-cited literature, thus securing its author his place in history.[46]

How competent Cheng-te was as a general cannot be ascertained, as he
excluded the literary-educational officials from his forward command
post. But in the 1517 campaign he was definitely with the front-line troops.
On his trip to the northwest during the winter of 1518–19, a snowstorm
brought low all those around him. The emperor alone rode along in good
spirits, carrying his own weapons. He never used his sedan chair.[47] All these
actions, however, became a prolonged nightmare to the civil officials. From
their point of view, the ruler had abandoned his position as the Son of
Heaven to take up a job that could have been relegated to any illiterate.
Little did they realize that they were really unhappy because the emperor
was sabotaging their brand of statecraft, based upon the mandarin square,
the kowtow, and the quoted verses from the *Four Books*.

Under the circumstances it was not surprising that in the spring of 1519,
when Cheng-te made known his plan for a still more extensive tour in the
southern provinces as generalissimo, all the censorial-supervising officials
in the capital delivered two joint petitions against the trip. When those
memorials were not rescripted, the petitioners knelt before the Meridian
Gate to demand a prompt reply from the throne. Before the case was
settled, officials from the literary-educational branch of government and
the ministries delivered their circulating petitions. No matter how humble
their words and sentences, they made it clear that they had every right to
demand satisfaction. The emperor's patience finally ran out. At the advice
of Chiang Pin, who was now in charge of the capital garrison, Cheng-te
retaliated by giving the order that the 146 demonstrators be beaten with
whipping clubs for thirty strokes each. Eleven of them subsequently died of
their injuries.[48] The resignations of grand-secretaries, however, were politely rejected. The emperor knew that if he let them go he might never be
able to find adequate replacements for them, as other bureaucrats would
be bound to think that they too must avoid an office the moral obligation of
which they had no hope of fulfilling.

Cheng-te delayed his tour until autumn. But he stayed in the south until
the end of 1520. During one of his fishing trips his boat capsized. Though
rescued from the water, he was said never to have fully recovered from the
incident.[49] Early the next year he died in the Leopard House without an
heir. The grand-secretaries conferred secretly with the empress dowager to
call in Wan-li's grandfather and installed him as the next emperor. These
events took place fifty-one years before Wan-li's own accession.

On the surface Cheng-te had succeeded in frustrating, ridiculing, and defeating his bureaucrats with ease; they were always outmaneuvered by the sovereign. Under the circumstances one might be led to wonder, if imperial supremacy could be so easily asserted by one occupant of the throne, what prevented succeeding occupants from redefining the throne's function to suit them? But the real story was far more complicated than this.

First of all, while it would be difficult to say that the civil officials' obedience was conditional, it could not be said that it was not without practical considerations. In fact, absolute monarchy of the dynasty's kind served a bureaucratic purpose. Repeatedly in the past matters brought by the civil officials to the throne for disposition had been thoroughly mingled with anomalies at every level. Imperial decisions on those matters became necessary, not because the word of the emperor was always just and rational, but because it was authoritative. This meant that the inviolability of the emperor had not been sought after as an end in itself. Together with the mystic quality of the throne, it was employed to sustain an administrative logic that the bureaucrats could not hope to maintain by themselves. It was essential that the sovereign, as the final arbiter of controversies, avoid personal entanglement in the issues. His character and personality must be hidden behind the image of the Son of Heaven. This requirement dictated that a latter-day emperor have virtually no chance to contribute his own creative energy to the functioning of his office.

By a stroke of genius Cheng-te evaded this process of dehumanization. He separated himself as an individual from the monarchy as an institution. But precisely because of this separation he failed in his assigned role and at the same time disrupted the standing practice of the bureaucracy.

The emperor's military operations, deviating from the contemporary institutional arrangement, tended to reopen the issue of civil supremacy over the military, a supremacy that had existed for about one hundred years.[50] His generalship notwithstanding, the ruler never stopped to think that his own realm could always provide a task-force strong enough to check Mengke's 50,000 cavalrymen if its commander-in-chief, like himself, were free to maneuver his battle formations and to draw services and supplies as he saw fit without being restrained by civil officials. In practice, however, this freedom of action was exactly what the empire wanted to deny its army commanders, who were restricted within their defense areas under the close supervision of frontier governors from the Civil Service and made accountable to them down to the last piece of equipment and the last man.

Without this stringent restriction, the 20,000 silk-robed officials could never have been able to deliberate on state affairs at their leisure, quoting Confucius and Mencius. Powerful generals not only had a tendency to emerge as domestic menaces, but also would have insisted on rapid practical solutions to problems, which would upset the doctrine of neutralizing opposites by means of undergoing ritualistic exercises and citing the *Four Books.*

What was the implication of the title General of the Army of Greater Valor? The emperor either intended to take over the operations of the entire military establishment or, at least, to set an example for his senior commanders. Whichever the case, the demand for dynamic responses to changing situations would have clashed with the sedentary nature of the Civil Service, which always operated by balancing compartmentalized responsibilities; this method had been consolidated by the dynasty's taxation system and personnel management procedures. Besides, the bureaucrats also believed that striving too hard toward technical perfection was a hindrance to virtue; on the other hand, they also believed that no organizational incapacity could not be compensated by moral strength.

As loyal subjects, these civil officials never threatened the emperor. But when they knelt in the palace yard demanding a reply from the throne, it was nothing short of a confrontation. Even when abused, they refrained from rebellion. It would have been unrealistic, however, to expect them to rally behind the throne with the same degree of devotion in any future crisis, after the emperor had so repeatedly acted against their wishes and thwarted their purposes. During Cheng-te's reign two imperial princes, the emperor's own cousins, raised standards to dethrone him, thinking that his alienation of the civil officials would lead to a transfer of the mandate of heaven. In fact they had miscalculated: their separate rebellions proved premature and were crushed. No one could predict, however, what might have happened if the Cheng-te emperor had lived longer and persisted in his concept of a free monarchy.

Cheng-te managed to reach his independent position for a number of reasons. He had no family ties. The influence the empress dowager had over him could be said to be less than marginal. None of the palace ladies did he hold in affection. And he died childless. At his accession all three grand-secretaries had been men of perfect virtue and great literary fame; but their pedantry made them helpless as far as court politics went.[51] Given only two options—the boredom and self-discipline inherent in the abstract and passive government on the one hand, and hawks, hounds, and live soldiers on the other—the fun-loving youth simply followed his natural aptitude and chose the latter. Since they controlled the capital garrison and the Secret Police, his eunuchs and army officers were able to chastise the civil officials and eliminate them as an effective opposing force.

Yet in the long run the emperor's rebellion against the established order produced only negative results. His temporary gain could not be institutionalized. He had no choice but to remain a playboy to the end of his career. Upon his death he was posthumously honored as the "martial emperor," a title not devoid of derogatory inferences. His adviser, Chiang Pin, still in command of the capital garrison, was lured into the palace, arrested, and later tortured to death. Charged with every conceivable crime, he was also said to have accumulated a personal fortune too enormous to be true.[52]

When Wan-li took over the reins of government after Chang Chü-cheng's death in 1582, his colorful granduncle had passed from the scene more than sixty years before. But his story was by no means forgotten. The bureaucrats, who had previously been caught by surprise, now felt that they must benefit from the experience of the sequence of events recorded in the annals. Outwardly the despotism of the throne remained as potent as ever, yet it would be grossly mistaken to assume that the courtiers, as before, would not even bother to find out how this power, which so affected their lives and limbs, was invested. When they brought up the issue of the "foundation of the state," they meant to deal with an entire range of questions involving the designation of an imperial heir, his family life, parental guidance, classical education under the supervision of the Han-lin academicians, and the possible influence upon him of the eunuchs and army officers. They felt free to debate these questions, and sometimes even to scrutinize the current emperor in light of them.

Wan-li lacked the physical courage, exuberance, and aggressiveness of his granduncle. For a young man who had never for a single day experienced the feeling of freedom, or at any stage in his life earned what was his due, it was extremely difficult to set his own rules for conducting his office, which, in an era of uncertainty, would inevitably have had to undergo lengthy contention, regardless of who was occupying the throne. Besides, having studied the records of his granduncle, Wan-li knew that when they stood together the civil officials could be a formidable body. Thus irresolute, the unadvised emperor again and again yielded to his courtiers. But he was neither gracious enough to forgive nor magnanimous enough to forget. His pride was hurt; his sensitivity drove him to seek revenge, not so much to recover the authority of the throne as to vent his anger. The actions he took were therefore often remote from the area of previous conflict, sometimes causing injury to those who had not had the slightest intention of offending him. Yet his most effective weapon remained inaction.

That is why, as the idle sovereign watched his eunuchs tossing silver pieces in the palace yard, his empire was sliding into an abyss. No matter how the succession issue was to be settled, the Civil Service had already lost its balance and would remain a turbulent body. That being the case, what difference did it really make if His Majesty the Wan-li emperor had become an opium addict,[53] or was inherently lazy, or was growing tired of being a passive and cloistered sovereign?

But to a handful of people who knew the emperor well, including former First Grand-Secretary Shen Shih-hsing, it did make a difference.[54] Given another set of environmental conditions, Wan-li could have acted differently. Since childhood he had been observed to be precocious. He was responsive. Tz'u-sheng's close supervision had given him a sense of purpose. At one time he was very much distressed by official corruption; he was sufficiently concerned about the problem to draft a decree personally forbidding the exchange of valuable gifts among governmental functionaries. He had once taken ceremonial rituals seriously. He had asked why so many officials absented themselves from his morning audience; and he had shown displeasure when the officials did not drill themselves to perform their part in ceremonies with flawless perfection.[55] In later years, when his critics grumbled about his permanent suspension of the public study sessions, few remembered that at one time the Wan-li emperor had insisted that his grand-secretaries supply him with the Veritable Records of all the reigns preceding his own, and had taken the initiative in discussing the content of the historical lessons.[56] Similarly, once his indolence became well known, it was difficult to recall that at one time his courtiers had been afraid he might be carried away by his enthusiasm, for instance, on the occasion when he conducted an archery contest on a hot summer day that lasted until evening and caused several eunuchs to faint from the intense heat.[57]

No one could say for sure exactly when and how the turning point was reached. But considering first the emergence of the succession issue and then a sequence of events that truly disturbed the Wan-li emperor, 1587 or thereabouts should not be overlooked as a line of demarcation. So the Year of the Pig, though seemingly insignificant, may, over the long course of history, have some significance after all.

4 THE LIVING ANCESTOR

In retirement former First Grand-Secretary Shen Shih-hsing lived several days beyond his seventy-ninth birthday. That birthday was a very special occasion; it marked his entrance into the eightieth year of life and was celebrated with due respect. The Wan-li emperor, whom Shen had not seen for twenty-three years, conveyed his greetings through a special envoy and sent his former tutor fifty ounces of silver, a crimson robe with a python embroidered on it, and four bolts of satin with imperial designs in assorted colors. Shen Shih-hsing had to struggle with the infirmity of age in order to kneel down facing the direction of Peking while reading the emperor's message. In his subsequent reply he indicated that this congratulatory note would be handed down to his descendants and preserved forever as a family treasure. But all the imperial gifts were returned unopened.[1] Not that Shen wished to offend the emperor, but he simply could not bring himself to accept such graciousness and generosity from Wan-li, because as tutor and chief counsellor to the throne he felt he had failed in his duties. If not, why was the eldest imperial son, now in direct line of succession, not being instructed by the Han-lin academicians? And how could it be that both inside and outside the capital numerous governmental positions remained unfilled? Upon receiving Shen's reply Wan-li was said to have been very disturbed. Yet, not ready to make amends, he ordered that the returned gifts be put aside in their original parcels.

Evidently, during those twenty-three years, although Shen Shih-hsing considered himself a man of leisure—spending a great deal of time on poetry, calligraphy, and travel, and watching the sunrise over T'ai Lake, marveling at the rolling waves pounding on rugged cliffs, and searching for rhymes to describe the misty rain over the wooded hills of his native Soochow—he had not completely detached himself from issues of public interest. He could not. In this span of time he produced copious writings, which were published posthumously by his sons.[2] In these pages the topic of court politics in Peking predominates. The composing of so many poems, essays, personal letters, as well as eulogies and tombstone inscriptions for former friends and colleagues, provided the author every opportunity to reflect on the days when he had been master of the Literary Depth Pavilion.

These reminiscences do not attest the absolute honesty of the writer. There are distortions and inconsistencies; the credibility gaps in and between certain passages are too obvious to be overlooked. Nevertheless, it would be unfair to say that Shen Shih-hsing was purposely deceitful. It seems that he was merely exercising his faith. As a high official of a latter-day empire, he had to face the fact that few problems which came his way could be institutionally or organizationally solved. There were simply no appropriate legislative or judicial tools for solving them. He had to rely on moral inducement and diplomacy. In the process, he had become habituated to rationalizing, and he was equally eager to accept the rationalizations of others. His occasional disregard of factual truth was consistent with his stance of continuing to hold himself responsible for the emperor's conduct twenty-three years after he was forced from office.

Yet in retrospect the ex-grand-secretary had neither qualms nor remorse. He remained serene to the end; he had a clear conscience. His office required him to apply the human touch to the business he handled; he had done so with sincerity. What the ultimate outcome might be was beyond his control.

He must have heard the criticism that Chang Chü-cheng, though ruthless, had at least accomplished something, while he himself, unquestionably a good-natured gentleman, had left a public record that was a total blank. This was not enough to disturb Shen, however. To him maintaining the moral tone of government meant preventive government. His type of statesman excelled not so much in the skill of solving problems as in preventing problems from developing. If little could be said about his management of his office, this meant that he had kept things as they should be. In fact, though, Shen Shih-hsing had to admit that he had never reached that ideal; as chief counsellor he had failed to help the emperor settle the matter of succession. But again this was a case in which he was no more at fault than anyone else, at least not more responsible than Hsü Kuo. As first grand-secretary he had tried to solve the problem behind the scenes; it was the second grand-secretary who had insisted on bringing it up for public debate.

With all his humility and meekness, Shen Shih-hsing would not take the blame for others. Nor did he accept the criticism that his public record was a total blank. If he had, why would he have left such a prodigious amount of writing behind him and bidden his sons to publish it after his death? After all, he wanted people to see that his commitment to his lines of action was not without design and purpose. His record, when thoughtfully examined, would be seen to be better than it appeared on the surface.

Shen Shih-hsing could not be said to have remained in the Literary Depth Pavilion for eight and a half years by doing nothing. His achievements were little publicized; what he wished to accomplish had to be accomplished through the subtle management of personnel. This was indirect and his approach was usually unaggressive. There is little truth to the statement that he was nothing more than a good-natured gentleman. If that had been the case, for one thing the flood problem with the Yellow River would certainly have taken a turn for the worse during the years when he was in office.

The Yellow River had always been a threat to the empire's security, in previous dynasties as well as in the present one. Flowing in and out of a large area covered by loess soil, its current carried an excessive amount of silt, which now and then choked its course and caused serious overflow. As Shen himself warned the emperor, "a wide stream could turn into flatland overnight, and thousands of miles of levee could be swept away in an instant." Under these circumstances many human lives and vast areas of farmland were at stake. But all the court of Peking could do was to delegate authority. Technical decisions had to be made in the field and the commissioner in charge of the rehabilitation project had to be empowered to mobilize materials and labor on the spot to carry out those decisions. Sometimes he had to demand serious sacrifices from the local districts.

It often happened that a major rehabilitation project called for the rerouting of the river, in fact, the modification of the terrain in several provinces. On such occasions there were always several possible solutions, even to the point of advocating that the river be turned in opposite directions, in accordance with different theories and inseparable from local interests. Court politics therefore could bring havoc to such undertakings. It had occurred in the past that a project director was impeached before his work had taken effect, only to be replaced by another specialist from a different school of thought. Meanwhile, lives and homes by the millions were endangered.

Grand-Secretary Shen's choice of commissioner was P'an Chi-hsün, the foremost promoter of the "channel contracting theory."[3] Instead of widening the channel of the river to facilitate the movement of silt, P'an argued in favor of narrowing sections of it to increase the velocity of the current. By diverting streams with less silt content into the main channel at strategic points, the combined effect was to make the river "self-scouring," so that without incessant dredging it could discharge its silt into the sea. P'an also argued that dikes should never be built as a continuous bulwark along each bank of the river. They should be built in several parallel rows, with outlets for floodwater in the first, and "distant dikes" behind them forming "retention basins" in case of overflow. Usually by the time the water reached the third or fourth dike, the power of inundation was reduced and the situation could more easily be brought under control.

To divert a water channel and plug gaps P'an used fascine bundles containing compacted earth and vegetation, the latter for its expanding effect. These bundles were rarely less than twenty feet in diameter and 150 feet long; each had to be maneuvered into place by several hundred workers. When these bundles were delivered to the designated points, ships loaded with rocks were scuttled alongside them to effect an immediate stoppage of water. On short notice, thousands of additional workers rushed earth fill to the site in order to secure it. Eventually dikes thus constructed would be lined, at places, with hewn stone surfaces miles long.[4]

In practice, to finance a project of such dimensions the central government could not afford more than a token appropriation, usually a grant-in-aid to enable the commissioner to work on his initial planning and organization. The necessary materials, manpower, tools, transportation, food supply, security, and medical service had to be procured locally, always in the form of additional levies from the surrounding population. All these had to be obtained in time from scores of counties and prefectures and coordinated to meet the seasonal demand of the project.[5] Thus the commissioner had to be a man of impeccable character who commanded the high regard of provincial as well as capital officials, and whose technical and organizational abilities were reinforced by moral strength. P'an Chi-hsün, having previously served with distinction as commissioner, was the ideal candidate. But P'an was none other than the minister of justice who, in 1584, had been accused by the emperor of taking sides with Chang Chü-cheng's family and subsequently discharged from the Civil Service.

When the river dikes burst in a number of places in 1587, Shen Shih-hsing first let a less distinguished official handle the emergency repairs, at the same time working for P'an's return. By several months later he had mobilized sufficient public opinion to recall the former commissioner. Luckily, during an interview with the Wan-li emperor the sovereign had brought up the topic of water control. Shen seized this opportunity to argue that for a major reconstruction program such as this, the commission had to be entrusted to experienced hands. Upon the emperor's approval, the dialogue was duly recorded and published; this was effective enough to silence P'an's critics, who otherwise might have turned a technical problem into a moral issue. In his correspondence with the recalled commissioner, and later in P'an's tombstone inscriptions, Shen Shih-hsing made it clear that he himself had given P'an all the support he needed in the capital. P'an Chi-hsün remained commissioner as long as Shen Shih-hsing was first grand-secretary, but was censured and forced to leave office soon after Shen's removal.[6]

The absence of major frontier wars during these eight and a half years was another record the first grand-secretary felt proud of, although in 1590 the empire had found itself on the brink of fighting Prince Cürüke and his all-Mongolian confederation. This situation was triggered when a Chinese deputy commander-in-chief near the Kansu-Kokonor border was ambushed and killed by the Mongols. The court in Peking was clamoring for war. Even the emperor, now rarely seen in public, personally demanded that stern measures be taken.

This is how the frontier problem appeared to Shen Shih-hsing: Some twenty years before, Altan Khan had organized an all-Mongolian confederation uniting the tribes on the Ming empire's northern frontier and had fought the Chinese on numerous occasions. In the winter of 1570–71, however, he pledged submission to the Chinese emperor in exchange for trading privileges and annual subsidies. Altan was made a Chinese prince and his chief vassals given appropriate titles along with stipends. Vowing never again to maraud the borderland, they also promised to discipline their subordinates if they should ever break the agreement.

As long as Altan was alive this covenant was observed to the minutest detail. But after his death and that of his son, his grandson Cürüke could hardly hold together the now defunct confederation. Among the newly rising Ordos leaders were Busuϒtu and Qulaci, who were active on the Kansu-Kokonor border, occasionally causing the Ming garrison trouble.[7] When questioned, they always insisted that they were raiding the Tibetans and Turkish peoples in Kokonor, and had no intention of disturbing the Celestial Empire. With this excuse they retained the material benefits of the peace settlement along with their own freedom of action.

In an incident that occurred in 1590, a Chinese battalion commander was informed by his soldiers that the Ordos hordes were looting the area under his jurisdiction. Whether at the time he was intoxicated or not was unclear, but he immediately jumped on his horse and dashed unescorted to the scene. The Mongols held their reins, awaiting his arrival. The commander, however, had no interest in diplomacy; instead he made a gallant charge with his sword, only to sustain fatal arrow wounds inflicted by the retreating Ordos and to die the next morning. Obliged to avenge his death, the deputy commander-in-chief in the defense area gave vigorous pursuit to the Ordos. He too lost his life in the ambush set up by Qulaci.[8]

In July it seemed that the Mongols were about to launch a coordinated attack against the empire's line of defense. Scores of tribes arrived in the area under dispute, including Prince Cürüke himself. The logical line of action open to Peking was, as many hawks cried out, to rescind the peace settlement in preparation for all-out war. Whoever countered the militant demand risked impeachment. During these exciting days the public never bothered to find out the details of what had happened; nor did they ponder the military consequences of the drastic action they were advocating. They could always quote historical works to accuse anyone who was willing to subject the empire to the humiliations meted out by the barbarians of being a traitor, thus ignoring the lesson that repeatedly appeared in the same historical records: the empire could score a hundred victories over the nomads in the borderland yet still see no end to the problem; neither could the deserts ever be occupied nor the nomads converted. But on the other hand, a serious setback during one of the campaigns could lead to the ruin of a dynasty. The demand for sufficient war supplies to sustain a prolonged struggle would virtually guarantee collapse.

As Shen Shih-hsing saw it, the situation was grave but by no means desperate. There was no evidence that Cürüke had formulated ambitious plans. Nor would the numerous tribes be willing to part with their lucrative trading privileges and subsidies if they had a choice. As long as peaceful solutions to the problem had not been exhausted, it would be unwise for the empire to consider itself at war with the entire Mongolian confederation. The frontier incident was indeed unfortunate; it exposed the empire's weakness, which must have emboldened the barbarians in the borderland. Yet the cure lay not merely in tactics and generalship. More basic was the need to improve services and supplies. Once the numerous vacancies among the ranks of the frontier garrison had been filled and empty space in the warehouses eliminated, the nomads would not dare to venture close to our defense line. Until then, a local victory could in no way safeguard the thousands of miles of frontier even for a short breathing period.

All reasoning pointed to the conclusion that the military establishment must be placed under civil control, that the latter must be centrally directed to serve the empire's long-term interests, and that the emperor, at the very top of the civil leadership, would do well to maintain the high morale of the bureaucracy as a whole rather than make ad hoc decisions. Because of the immensity of His Majesty's realm, particular and technical considerations in the various departments and areas were too diffused to be even ascertained. The sovereign therefore should refrain from aligning himself with any one proposed solution to the problems. He must personify the universal spirit, which was perfect but neutral.

Yet, in a crucial situation such as this, when the empire found itself at the crossroads of peace and war, the commitment of the throne was still indispensable. Without the emperor's backing, the first grand-secretary could never, in those summer months of 1590, have steered the court of Peking away from the war fever that had infected so many ardent young officials. In the last analysis, Shen Shih-hsing must have felt gratified by the arrangement of the dynasty, which required imperial princes to be tutored by academicians like himself. While the princes grew up to be emperors, the academicians, already assistants and understudies to the senior courtiers, in time became chief counsellors to the throne. In this way the continuity of the imperial court was maintained; at the same time, the instructor-disciple relationship tied the first grand-secretary to the sovereign by a degree of intimacy unreachable by others.

The interview between the Wan-li emperor and Shen Shih-hsing on August 25, 1590 (see Appendix B), was their last on record.[9] It put that intimate relationship to work. For some time the conversation seemed to be drifting without developing a central theme. Yet with humility and diplomacy Tutor Shen succeeded in prevailing over the young sovereign on several matters concerning the borderland crisis. None of the frontier governors and governors-general was to be removed or punished. Responsibility was delegated by His Majesty on a long-term basis, which for the sake of morale should avoid unexpected shake-ups. Nor was the principle of civil supremacy, part of the dynastic constitution, to be modified. The peace settlement reached with Altan twenty years earlier was still considered to be in force. As for strategy, the grand-secretary proposed to concentrate on defense. He nevertheless suggested that a high-ranking official be dispatched to the border region as imperial commissioner to coordinate the maneuvers of several defense areas; to this the emperor consented. On one item of business Tutor Shen's suggestion failed to carry. He urged the emperor to meet the court often. Wan-li replied that he was still not well enough for that. The conversation, duly recorded by Shen Shih-hsing and delivered to the Meridian Gate for publication, served as a declaration of policy by the throne that should have silenced the hawks.

Four days after the interview, Cheng Lo, who held the rank of minister of war, was made imperial commissioner to coordinate northern frontier defense. But even while the emperor was conferring with his first grand-secretary, the Kansu-Kokonor frontier had already been stabilized. The Chinese withheld punitive action. The much-feared nomadic penetration also failed to materialize. Cheng Lo's commission, however, did not tie his hands unconditionally. His victory came early the following year. He caught Busuytu on the move to join forces with Qulaci. Surprising the Ordos from the flank, he captured their supply train and a large number of cattle. Once having gained the advantage, the imperial army carried out Shen Shih-hsing's instruction "to clear the field." The Lamaist temples built by Altan in Kokonor were burned to the ground. Additional lumber accumulated by the Ordos Mongols for construction purposes was also destroyed. A wide area of grass was set ablaze. Various groups of Tibetans and Uighurs were forcibly relocated.[10] At this point Cürüke, seeing the absolute futility of Qulaci's endeavor, took his hordes back to the Yellow River bend to the north. The Mongols had yet to give the defenders of the Ming frontier problems, but the grand scheme of uniting all the nomadic tribes on the empire's northern frontier with those on the west to form a formidable confederation was permanently shelved.

In recording these events in his memoirs Shen Shih-hsing did not completely refrain from self-congratulation, although his claim for credit was so toned down that it could hardly offend anyone. He was equally complacent when he related how he had managed a frontier incident with the Burmese. But he never mentioned the case involving a Chien-chou chieftain in Liaotung in 1587.

During the Year of the Pig the governor in the northeast territory noticed that a certain ambitious tribal leader was well on his way toward building an empire by eliminating his rivals and annexing the adjacent domains. He tried to do away with this potentially dangerous nomadic warrior by sending imperial forces into a preemptive war against him, only to be turned back with losses. The governor then charged the district director, personally bent on placating the Chien-chou tribesmen, with failure to carry out his plan vigorously enough. When his complaint reached Peking, the governor himself was placed under enquiry by a number of censorial-supervising officials whose sympathy lay with the district director. In the belief that the setback was a minor matter not worth a split among the bureaucrats, Shen Shih-hsing advised the emperor to have both charges dismissed. The two officials supporting contradictory policies therefore retained their positions within the same channel of command, to the delight of the empire-builder in question, who would yet derive more profit from the dissension. His name was Nurhaci.[11]

But 1587 was a long way from 1644. Because Shen Shih-hsing kept quiet about the Liaotung incident, no one remembered that he had had anything to do with the founder of the Manchu dynasty. In history he is not known as the first grand-secretary who unwittingly gave Nurhaci full rein, but as the imperial tutor who failed to settle the succession issue. In the eyes of the bureaucrats, in the first moment the Wan-li emperor entertained the thought of depriving his eldest son of the right to succeed him, he had already committed an act of unrighteousness. It was up to Shen Shih-hsing, who maintained an intimate relationship with the throne, to extend his protest to the point of being willing to forgo his position, and if that was not enough, life and limb. Had he taken such a strong stand, whoever succeeded him would not have dared to be any less unyielding on the issue. Had the resoluteness of the bureaucracy been thus unmistakably conveyed to the emperor, the throne would have been saved the gross infamy and the court so many years of fruitless deadlock.[12]

In making this assertion the bureaucrats completely ignored the first grand-secretary's outlook and style of management. Nor did they realize that his close relationship with the throne could never be taken for granted; it was precisely because of his skill at mild persuasion that he continued to hold Wan-li's confidence. Moreover, for years Shen had been exercising his influence to induce the emperor to live up to bureaucratic expectations. He wanted the sovereign to wield his absolute power without exhibiting any trace of his own human attributes. But this was by no means easy.

It was ironic that many years later Shen should be accused of attempting to postpone the installation of the imperial heir. The record shows that he was the first person to speak out on the issue. He had advised Wan-li to declare Ch'ang-lo his heir almost as soon as Ch'ang-hsün was born.[13] In making the recommendation at that early stage he seemed to have foreseen the emperor's problem, partly because he had, at Wan-li's direction, acted as one of the envoys who conferred the title of Imperial Consort on Lady Cheng, Ch'ang-hsün's mother.[14] This duty befell Shen because he was the senior civil official in the court. Actually, he never even laid eyes on the lady so honored. Along with Hsü Wen-pi, duke of Ting-kuo, he received the emissary's scepter from the throne hall. They marched with guards and musicians to arrive at the Right Concord Gate, where the eunuchs were waiting. Silently they handed them the scepter as well as the regalia signifying the conferred title—a solid gold seal and a patent paper encased in a gold frame. The actual investiture was administered by the eunuchs inside the palace quarters.[15] The implications of the ceremonial arrangements were obvious: the position of imperial consort was not greatly different from a public office. The conferring of it on Lady Cheng was not only witnessed by the bureaucracy but also required its participation. With her new title she was inferior in rank only to the empress but ahead of all the other secondary wives of the emperor, including Lady Wang. Cast against such a background, the story that her son would become the next emperor could not be said to have been without substance.

But when the emperor insisted that the two issues were unrelated, it left Shen Shih-hsing with no justification for linking the question of succession with the women in His Majesty's life. In fact, later, when the subject of his private life with the palace ladies was brought up by the sovereign himself (see Appendix A), Tutor Shen scrupulously declined to comment. As the only courtier who saw Wan-li as a man of flesh and blood as well as emperor, the first grand-secretary must have realized his deep emotional distress over the dilemma. To say that the ruler must act without showing any sign of human attributes did not mean that he should have no inner feelings at all. Thus when the emperor resorted to delaying tactics regarding the succession issue, Shen Shih-hsing waited patiently. From experience he felt that Wan-li was a sensible person and that, given time, he should be able to work out the problem himself.[16]

Subsequent events proved that Shen had miscalculated. Time was not on his side. After eight and a half years as master of the Literary Depth Pavilion, he of course could not complain about short tenure or a premature retirement. But his misfortune arose from the bad timing of what took place during the period he was in office.

After his appointment as first grand-secretary in 1583, Shen Shih-hsing had to wait two years for the case of Chang Chü-cheng to be clarified. Until the Year of the Rooster, 1585, when the case finally came to rest, neither he nor the emperor could see where they actually stood. Yet the 1585 settlement marked only a brief respite. A few months later, in early 1586, upon giving birth to Ch'ang-hsün, Lady Cheng was made imperial consort. The issue of succession had started at this point. At the same time the emperor, thoroughly prevented from doing what he wished, began steadily to reverse his outgoing tendencies and to withdraw from public functions. Bureaucratic remonstrances requiring his attention now became louder and more acrimonious. Unless their suggestions were immediately adopted, the memorialists usually argued, the sovereign would surely sink into the vilest infamy, his ancestors would cry out in their graves, and the foundation of the state would crumble. No sooner would the emperor rule one petitioner out of order and demote him, than he would receive another memorial saying that the previous memorialist, by giving loyal advice, had actually performed a meritorious service to the throne. Thus His Majesty's decision was slightly in error; rather than a demotion, the person in question should have been given a promotion. Thus by 1587, if not earlier, the deadlock had already been reached.

A sensitive man, Shen Shih-hsing was gifted at reading other people's minds. His long association with Wan-li since the latter's childhood, now having survived the incident that arose from Kao Ch'i-yü's examination question, had provided him with the kind of assurance he needed. But still more of his political acumen came from his understanding that in the empire's special brand of statecraft, the monarchy and the bureaucracy had to coexist in a state of mutual deference. Should a confrontation between the two occur, it was bound to be a negative contest. The emperor, of course, had the power to punish; the civil officials would then be compelled to protest and withdraw in groups until banishment became a public honor. All this could start from mutual distrust, but the consequences were sure to be destructive. In 1587, when the first grand-secretary was worried about the possibility of such consequences, the emperor's court was actually moving in that direction. Before the Year of the Pig came to a close, the power of surveillance exercised by the throne through the Secret Service had become an issue of public concern.

The Eastern Depot, which commanded the Silk Robe Guard, had always reported to the emperor through its eunuch director. Its intelligence reports were indispensable to the ruler for managing his enormous realm. The depot's surveillance over the metropolitan area was considered especially vital to the administration. Some amount of constitutional ambiguity was involved; as the depot also functioned as a semijudicial body, it had always conducted trials of cases touching upon the interests of the throne, a tradition that could be traced to the early years of the dynasty. This operation could not avoid overlapping with the functionings of the censorial branch of the government, which was an integral part of the Civil Service. But the Eastern Depot regularly kept the sovereign informed of the prices of major commodities on the market, any unusual traffic observed at the city gates, fire and other incidents in the capital, and overheard conversations that for one reason or another were regarded as significant. The gathering of such intelligence could not be assigned to civil officials, since they all functioned in the public eye, and nobody was supposed to have direct access to the emperor lest he gain undue influence over him. Nor could ordinary judges arbitrate cases involving the emperor, who was the final arbiter himself.

The activities of the Eastern Depot and the Silk Robe Guard were by no means more detestable or more harassing to the populace under Wan-li than they had been in previous reigns.[17] But under Feng Pao's management during the Chang Chü-cheng era the depot had apparently enlarged its field of operation. Civil officials, resenting that their "petty household affairs such as food budget should be made the object of laughter at the palace,"[18] wanted to curb its influence but found no recourse.

As it happened, the issue had to be settled along with a most unexpected and freakish case in 1587. This particular issue involved a magistrate of Peking who had illegally beaten several ceremonial performers in service at the Court of Imperial Sacrifices, which constituted a criminal offense; it was possible to construe this as an offense to the throne as well.[19] The trial was to be handled by the metropolitan court, which, with top officials from the censorial-supervising branch of the government on the bench, normally served only as an appellate court. The case fell under its jurisdiction because there was no lower court except the district one presided over by the magistrate himself, but also because the civil officials did not wish to see the defendant magistrate abused for such a petty offense, which in reality was a technical quarrel with a service agency. But the Eastern Depot must have sensed that its jurisdiction was also involved, in accordance with the practice of two hundred years' standing. After some lengthy consideration, the eunuchs decided to dispatch two agents from the Silk Robe Guard to observe the trial proceedings and possibly to reserve the right of the Eastern Depot to intervene. It so happened that the Minister of Justice, Li Shih-ta, was very concerned about the integrity of the Civil Service and wished to have the case settled without involving the Secret Police.[20] Yet precedent favored the eunuchs and an outright rejection on the part of Minister Li seemed to be out of order. So, when the two agents called on him and asked for permission to be present at the trial, he used obstructive means to discourage them and ended by giving them a false promise rather than a flat refusal. On the day of the trial the two men were barred entrance to the courtroom by a ministerial official serving as sergeant-at-arms. In time the case was reported to the emperor.

From the sovereign's point of view, the exclusion of the agents constituted not only a contempt of the throne but also a curtailment of the imperial prerogative. Worse yet, the incident had turned into a confrontation between the bureaucrats on one hand and his personal staff on the other, and compelled him to take sides in order to uphold his authority. Wan-li must have been seriously disturbed. Sending word to the Literary Depth Pavilion to the effect that he was about to transfer the case to the Eastern Depot for retrial, he nevertheless refrained from carrying out the threat. The subsequent delay enabled Tutor Shen to assume his usual role of peacemaker. He managed to obtain an apology to the emperor from Minister Li Shih-ta. The official serving as sergeant-at-arms was fined two months' salary. The case was never transferred. What verdict was handed down to the offending magistrate by the metropolitan court was not a contested point as long as the throne had scored a moral victory over the bureaucrats. But this victory was short-lived. In less than a year the civil officials retaliated by demanding the dismissal of Chang Ching, eunuch director of the Eastern Depot.

The accusation that Chang was receiving money from official circles could be substantiated, but at the time few persons in the emperor's court would have been free from the same charge. More likely, as the eunuch himself later suggested, he had offended too many civil officials by disclosing some secret information that had passed through his hands. Perhaps by doing so he had already violated a cardinal rule of managing a secret service. Yet the Wan-li emperor, still unaware of the bureaucratic antagonism rapidly building up in the background, never thought that Chang's offense deserved dismissal. As he hesitated, the civil officials first threatened and then proceeded to impeach all the grand-secretaries and the minister of personnel. The idea was to rouse public opinion to demand the discharging of the emperor's senior advisers and assistants unless the hated Chang Ching was removed. Grudgingly Wan-li had to suffer another humiliation.[21] At this juncture a junior official, unaware of the consent already extracted from the throne, delivered a remonstrance in which he stated that the emperor himself must have been bribed by Chang Ching if he found him so difficult to part with. For this audacious accusation the remonstrator received sixty strokes of the whipping club at the Meridian Gate.

This unhappy incident plunged the young sovereign into a deeply downcast mood for a long time.[22] In court politics it marked a point of no return. Already tired of his morning audiences and study sessions, the Wan-li emperor was henceforth to suspend them permanently. He had lost all interest in seeing the civil officials as a group. He was growing cynical about being the figurehead of a dishonest organization in which everyone said one thing and meant something else. He drew closer to Lady Cheng. There were her emotional needs to be taken care of too. She was unhappy over the possibility that her infant son might be sent away to live as a residential prince in some remote corner of the empire when he grew up.

For Shen Shih-hsing, what took place in those two or three years was most unfortunate. The line of communication between the sovereign and himself was very flimsy. When the emperor suspended even his study sessions, little opportunity to have a dialogue with the throne remained.

Years later in retirement, when he reviewed the sequence of events, Shen made no complaint against the emperor; nor in his writings did he ever blame himself. He felt the fault was entirely that of the "young people" in the court, whose agitation had made the situation unmanageable.[23] In reality the only opportunity for him to assist his pupil and master to become an enlightened ruler presented itself in several months of 1585—that is, after Chang Chü-cheng's death and before the birth of Ch'ang-hsün. Once this opportunity had slipped away it was never to recur.

The Year of the Rooster stood out in the former grand-secretary's memory as a satisfying period in his life because at that time the Wan-li emperor was performing his duties as required, voluntarily and with enthusiasm. For a highly stylized government such as ours, form was substance. The sovereign's readiness to subject himself to his assigned role marked the extent of his prior commitment to a state of make-believe, which alone could inspire others and make them sincere and honest. It was a gratifying experience to see the emperor putting his heart and soul behind ceremonial proceedings, sometimes even enlivening them with an extra effort and a personal touch. If Shen Shih-hsing closed his eyes, he could reconstruct every detail surrounding Wan-li's prayer for rain, which also took place during that short period of great promise in 1585.

This was no ordinary ritualistic exercise. In late 1584 drought had set in around the capital district. As it stretched into the summer of the following year, rivers and wells began to dry up. The emperor was deeply worried by the knowledge that the daily life of the general population was threatened. He had already ordered local officials to pray for rain, but with no results. The emperor then decided to perform the ceremony himself in the presence of the entire court. A checking of the records yielded some guidelines for the proceedings, but the detailed arrangements of this 1585 event were made according to the emperor's own design; the sovereign had worked them out from the preliminary proposal submitted by the Ministry of Rites. It was Wan-li's own resolution that neither horses nor sedan chairs would be used; everybody was to be on foot.

Two days before the ceremony the emperor had already put himself on a vegetarian diet. The day before he reported his decision to his ancestors at the palace shrine as well as to his mother, Empress Dowager Tz'u-sheng. The written prayer was signed by himself and carried in advance to the Altar of Heaven.

At daybreak on May 16 the proceedings began. The emperor first went to the Imperial Polar Gate, where the master of ceremonies reported that the procession was in order. With his guards and personal staff forming a phalanx around him, he then walked to the Gate of Greater Brilliance to meet the large assembly of officials and army officers.

Never before had the residents of Peking seen so solemn a procession, yet one organized with such simplicity. From the emperor downward, including the army officers, all participants were dressed in blue robes with black bands around the necklines and hems. Their belts were all decorated with ox horn, not jade or gold or silver. Banners and music were noticeably absent. Walking on the left side of the street were close to 2,000 civil officials, matched by an equal number of army officers on the right side. They walked in single columns with about three feet between each man; it took close to a half-hour for the procession to clear any point.[24]

For many residents of Peking, this was the one time in their lives they ever saw the Son of Heaven in person. While street traffic was suspended, the normal procedure for the imperial presence, which demanded that all shops be closed and all pedestrians keep out of sight, was not followed on that day.[25] Some of the onlookers caught a glimpse of the emperor, a nice-looking young man though already growing stout. The trek was not at all easy for Wan-li, because the day was turning steadily warmer every minute and the Altar of Heaven was four miles away from the palace entrance—the longest distance that he had ever covered on foot.

The open-air altar in the southern suburbs of Peking had been built by the reigning emperor's grandfather in 1530.[26] On the lower tier of the circular stone terraces Wan-li performed his kowtow. Offerings were made and the prayer spoken. The assembled officials and army officers were arrayed outside the brick wall enclosing the altar. Their kneeling and standing up was synchronized with the movements of the emperor by commands relayed through the gate by ceremonial officials.

No less important than the service itself was a short lecture given by the sovereign in his tent immediately after the ritual and attended by courtiers of ministerial rank and above. The prolonged drought, the Wan-li emperor pointed out, undoubtedly reflected his own lack of virtue, but in part it was also caused by the corrupt and ruthless functionaries of the government. Their harassment of the general population must have reached a point where it was disturbing the celestial harmony. Now, even though the prayer was said and amends were being made, it was still essential that only righteous persons be appointed to office. He wanted everyone to take that seriously.

On behalf of the assembly, First Grand-Secretary Shen Shih-hsing replied that the emperor's sincerity must undoubtedly have touched the heart of Heaven. As for the present disaster, it was indeed the fault of the present officials, himself included, who had not discharged their responsibilities as expected. He promised that an effort would soon be made, especially to rectify the situation that numerous governmental functionaries were acting contrary to His Majesty's good intentions. At this point Wan-li interjected that a general declaration to that effect be made, of which the grand-secretary took note. Eventually the imperial decree of May 16, 1585, stood as a stern warning to all functionaries across the empire against practicing cruelty and excess toward the civil population, issued along with a general tax remission applicable to the disaster-affected areas.[27]

Before returning to the palace the eunuchs had already ordered the emperor's sedan chair brought forward, but Wan-li insisted on walking back. The movement of several thousand people naturally involved delays here and there. As a result the procession arrived at the palace entrance late in the afternoon. By that time it was so suffocatingly hot that as soon as the assembly was dismissed one impatient official drew a folding fan from his sleeve and started waving it. Following too closely upon the ceremony, this act was noted by the censors, and eventually cost that official six months' salary![28]

Shen Shih-hsing escorted the emperor to the Imperial Polar Gate before performing the long day's last round of kowtowing, this time to his youthful master.

"Great effort on your part, Your Majesty," he said. By then he was dead tired as well as hungry and thirsty.

"Honorable tutor," replied the emperor, "we are much obliged to have you come along and go through all this with us."[29]

And the first grand-secretary realized that while everyone else was able to retire at last, the emperor still had to report the event to his ancestors at the palace shrine and his mother in her living quarters.

According to the record, the first grand-secretary was never a believer in supernatural forces. He had at one time written to the emperor, "Your servant has never studied divination; he knows nothing about omens and portents."[30] He also recalled that the emperor himself, on an occasion when his courtiers were quarreling over the relative geomantic merits of his mausoleum, had blandly remarked: "When Ch'in Shih-huang-ti built his tomb at Li Shan, did he not study geomancy? What happened then?"[31] Wan-li could not bring himself to have unquestioning faith in the effectiveness of prayer.

Yet, the line separating make-believe from irrationality was thin. When desperate, man could not afford to exclude any possibility, illusory though it might be. In that sultry summer of 1585, when every day turned out to be rainless, one did not need to be reminded that the emperor's court could not sit forever in a parched capital. The sovereign's effort to alter the situation, make-believe or not, at least elicited a feeling that something could be done, and along with it a sense of direction and a gleam of hope. His personal struggle, his self-criticism, and his instructions to governmental officials to exercise restraint probably gave some comfort to his hard-pressed subjects.[32] In this sense, His Majesty had led a passive government to action, and the kind at which it was best.

When the rain finally did come, it came with a vengeance. First it was accompanied by hail; then followed more intermittent downpours that lasted into the next day. Relief was instant. The fact that this occurred on June 12, almost a whole month after the imperial procession to the Altar of Heaven, in no way deterred the emperor from claiming credit for himself. Joyfully he ordered a thanksgiving service in appreciation of Heaven's favorable response to his prayer.[33] Shen Shih-hsing was only too glad he did. At least on one such occasion Wan-li had derived some satisfaction from his office. But such opportunities were few and far between.

And Tutor Shen, while mindful of Wan-li's sensitivity, shared with his fellow bureaucrats the notion that the emperor's place was in the palace. Above all, his great achievement came from his forbearance. In no way should he swing into action aside from taking part in ceremonial proceedings. When during the Year of the Rooster the Wan-li emperor demonstrated great interest in horses and soldiers, therefore, Shen Shih-hsing was compelled to intervene. In this way the grand-secretary worked along with other officials to block the sovereign's creative energies. And denied the outlet of pursuing his interests, Wan-li became more and more emotionally dependent on the woman he loved.

When the civil officials tried to stop the Wan-li emperor from taking an interest in horses and soldiers, they were dealing with a sensitive area. Since the reign of Cheng-te no emperor had attempted to command the army personally. Even imperial travel had been severely restricted. The Chiaching emperor had revisited his birthplace in Hukwang in 1539, after which he did not leave the capital again for the next twenty-seven years of his life.[34] Throughout his reign the Lung-ch'ing emperor made only one trip to the imperial mausoleums in the suburbs of Peking, which lasted four days.[35] Wan-li's four visits to the same site in less than three years' time, extending from the spring of 1583 to the autumn of 1585, was already considered excessive.[36]

More alarming still was that, in the process of providing honor guards for the imperial procession, the sovereign had taken a personal interest in the division of the palace army. Wan-li's guard of 2,000 men had been organized in 1581 with Chang Chü-cheng's approval. Its barracks located immediately northeast of the city wall of Peking, the command was placed under the eunuch director in charge of the Imperial Stable.[37] The guard began to attract public notice when it doubled in size and intensified its training on the palace grounds. Peking residents now heard the cavalry trotting in the streets every day before dawn. Numerous eunuchs were commissioned as officers and enlisted as soldiers, followed by younger ones serving as valets. And then there was that hot summer day of 1584 when the emperor conducted an archery contest with a division of soldiers in the Imperial City that lasted until evening and during which several eunuchs fainted from the intense heat. Such displays of imperial energy were not at all encouraged by the civil officials, who watched these developments with increasing apprehension. Having delivered several ineffectual waves of memorials to the throne calling for a halt to the exercises, they eventually exerted great pressure on First Grand-Secretary Shen Shih-hsing to stop the drills.[38]

In legal terms, the position of the officials who made this demand was questionable at best. Despite the bad example of Cheng-te, constitutionally there had never been any injunction against the sovereign's keeping in touch with the armed forces. A most eloquent argument in favor of the throne was a lance once used in battle by the Yung-lo emperor and still preserved in the tower atop the Meridian Gate.[39] Palace guards under eunuch control had, moreover, always existed under previous reigns. Any polemics the bureaucrats might want to let fly had to be aimed in a moral direction. They could argue that, as a matter of principle, during peacetime the ruler should never play with swords and spears because of their inauspicious implications. But such arguments were too broad and nebulous to be made precisely binding.

In realistic terms, however, conditions favored the civil officials. Collectively far more the masters of the empire than the emperor himself, they knew that the imperial dynasty could not exist for a single day without their tacit consent. It was understandable that, having developed a special kind of statecraft based on literary skill and philosophical discourse, they resented an autonomous army that was the emperor's own, and that sooner or later would inevitably lead to military dominance. Yet as loyal subjects they could not even conceive of bargaining with the sovereign, still less of negotiating an advantage. And so once again a crucial contest was conducted without the interested parties expressing their true motives.

A great advantage Shen Shih-hsing held in a case like this was his insight into the interplay of the yin with the yang. As the problem could be solved by the human touch, why insist on organizational principles? Quietly he approached the eunuch commanders. He must have recounted many stories of palace intrigues and plots, the central message being that any one of the thousands of officers and men within the legion of guards could easily become involved in some conspiracy. It was a great risk for them to carry weapons into the sensitive areas near the emperor's living quarters. Who would take responsibility if an incident should occur? At this point the grand-secretary might have stressed the fact that in the dynasty's history no individual, not even the emperor's favorite, who had run counter to the general wishes of the civil officials had ever died peacefully. He could use

Chiang Pin to illustrate that in the short run the emperor's party might win but in the long run the bureaucracy always triumphed. His persuasion was effective. "They all shuddered in horror," Shen later wrote.[40]

Once the eunuchs had been disarmed by reason, it was a simple matter to rely on them to prevail over the sovereign to discontinue the drills and exercises on the palace grounds. His Majesty was a sensible person. Unprepared to follow the Cheng-te emperor all the way, he knew that he had to stop at a certain point. So he allowed the force of palace guards to fade into the background. It never regained status as a combat formation, and toward 1587, the Year of the Pig, it was gradually forgotten.[41] But Shen Shih-hsing did not forget. Even in retirement, he still relished the memory of this episode in which, as chief counsellor and imperial tutor, he had succeeded in conveying a general wish of the bureaucracy to the emperor without going through the usual confrontation. How he wished that his fellow officials had let him handle the succession problem the same way! Then it might have been accomplished without hard feelings.

After 1585 Wan-li also relinquished his annual sojourns in the suburbs. He had yet to make one more trip in 1588 to inspect his own mausoleum. With that one exception he was to remain in Peking for more than three decades until he was carried to the stone chamber for his permanent rest.[42] Partly because of His Majesty's long reign, his uninterrupted palace-bound life established a record for all time.

The ruler's trips to the countryside within fifty miles of the capital and never more than seven days long were the object of serious concern, not only because his granduncle's interest in travel had been sparked by similar short-distance journeys, but also because they touched the monarchy as an institution. Although in Wan-li's case his primary interest was to locate and inspect the site of his own future burial, homage and sacrifices at his ancestors' tombs nearby could by no means be neglected. Days before such a journey, the Ministry of Rites had already consulted earlier records in order to work out the ceremonial proceedings to take place at the nine imperial mausoleums, with details tailored to suit the itinerary.

On every trip Wan-li was accompanied by the two empresses dowager, his empress, and his secondary wives, but not his concubines. As a result, large contingents of eunuchs and palace women had to be included in the entourage, escorted by a whole regiment of armed guards. The imperial family was quartered at Buddhist temples during the trip; but bivouac and temporary shelters had to be provided for the accompanying officials and army officers. Additional tents were pitched in the countryside. En route local magistrates, elders, and outstanding teachers were ushered in to visit the sovereign. The emperor, in turn, declared the taxes in their districts remitted in appreciation of any services and supplies they rendered to his party.[43]

Left behind, the city of Peking was placed under curfew. Guards were reinforced. Each city gate was under the joint control of a high-ranking official and an army officer of noble title. Prince Lu, the emperor's younger brother, slept in the tower atop the western gate that led to the avenue on which the imperial party was traveling. In essence, the pyramid of the empire immediately lost its balance when its pinnacle was removed, even for a short period.

Toward 1585, when such inspection tours were considered to be too frequent, frontier army posts began to alert the capital to unusual movements of various nomadic tribes and pleaded caution. The ministerial officials haggled with the sovereign to reduce the length of time he spent on his journeys. Once there was a stampede of horses near the emperor's mounted guards. Another time several officials were censured for being out of order by appearing on a hillside where they were not supposed to be. In each case censorial investigation ensued, responsible officials were found to be at fault, and the details were reported to the emperor for disposition. In this way the civil officials succeeded in taking the joy out of the emperor's spring and autumn outings.[44] Nevertheless, before Wan-li's permanent confinement in the palace, he attempted one more trip, which never materialized because a group of censorial-supervising officials jointly petitioned that, since His Majesty had discontinued his morning audiences with the court in order to take care of the fire element within his body, he should be consistent by not exposing himself to wind and weather on the mountain roads. Was this argument enough to persuade him to cancel the contemplated journey? No hint of it is to be found in Shen Shih-hsing's papers.[45]

But by this time the emperor's mausoleum was being constructed in earnest, the ground having been broken in the summer of 1584.[46] The project could also be considered part of the effort to dehumanize the monarchy, except that the proposed construction was happily accepted by the monarch himself. The arrangement on the whole was nevertheless unfortunate. Not yet buried, Wan-li found it most difficult to keep his active and intelligent—albeit weak and irresolute—mind chained to the palace yard for decades. Furthermore, the burial chamber of the mausoleum contained not two burial places but three. Along with the emperor and the empress, the stone platform was to offer rest to the remains of the natural mother of the next emperor, whoever she might be. By tradition she would also be honored as an empress. This made it even more difficult for the present emperor to cast away the thought of saving that space for the woman he loved, the only person in the world to whom he could express his personal thoughts and reveal his true feelings. Thus the construction of the massive stone structure at Ta-yü-shan also became tightly interwoven with the question of succession, the only issue worth the attention of the imperial court these days.

The construction of an emperor's mausoleum in his own lifetime was by no means unprecedented, having been done during the reigns of Hung-wu, Yung-lo, and Chia-ching.[47] What made Wan-li's case unique was his youthfulness. According to Shen Shih-hsing, the idea had originated with Chang Ssu-wei, who preceded him as first grand-secretary in 1583, before the emperor had celebrated his twentieth birthday.[48] But Wan-li immediately seized upon the suggestion with joyful enthusiasm. Far from being offended by the insinuation that he might die soon, he was flattered that he was literally to be given a place, well ahead of his time, among his ancestors. By early 1583 the emperor was not yet twenty, but he had already become a father and been Ruler of All Men for over a decade. He undoubtedly considered himself deserving of the honor and therefore happily set out to investigate the sites and to decide on the design.

Unlike so many other imperial undertakings, the project aroused no objection from the court.[49] The only controversy it gave rise to concerned the geomantic merit of the selected site. Minister of Rites Hsü Hsüeh-mo, whose daughter was married to Shen Shih-hsing's second son, as governor of Chang Chü-cheng's home district had previously relied on private connections to rise to his present position. He was unpopular and the opposition seized the opportunity to impeach him on the ground that, not having consulted with enough specialists, he had selected a site with inadequate features. The forcing of Hsü's retirement did not settle the issue, however. Since the argument over geomancy had been so effective a weapon in removing a minister, why allow it to slip away without being used to get rid of more of one's enemies?[50] The quarrel ended only after the emperor said that he wanted Ta-yü-shan and that in any case he believed in the power of geomancy only in a relative sense.[51]

As the project was a state function, its execution was entrusted to a commission composed of three ministers, several army officers, and the

eunuch director of ceremony, and was placed under the joint superinten-
dence of the first grand-secretary and Hsü Wen-pi, the seventh duke of
Ting-kuo. The inclusion of the army officers was practical because military
manpower was indispensable to the construction project. The duke's participation, on the other hand, was merely symbolic. As holder of the highest
aristocratic court title, he always had his share of assignments to important
state functions in order to give the impression that the nobility was still a
component of the emperor's court, although its usefulness was no more
than ornamental. The overall responsibility for the work fell on Shen Shih-
hsing. By the end of 1587 he had made a half-dozen trips to Ta-yü-shan,
including one in bitterly cold winter and one in unbearable summer heat.[52]

The so-called mausoleum in reality involved three kinds of construction
work. Outside the tomb, there was to be a large ceremonial hall that also
stood as a permanent monument to the emperor, complete with entrance
hall and service facilities. An additional building leaning against the tomb
was to enshrine a large stone tablet. The tomb itself was eventually to
appear as a huge earth mound of about 700 feet in diameter and twenty to
fifty feet in height. The round tomb and the square layout enclosing the
outside buildings formed a gigantic form the shape of a keyhole.[53]

The most difficult part of the structure, to be executed first, was the
burial chamber. This was actually a cluster of five chambers, three on the
main axis and one on each side connected to the main axis by corridors
forming the shape of a cross. In all, the main axis covered a distance of 250
feet and the two side-chambers with connecting corridors a distance of 120
feet. Since the cross-shaped structure was buried under many tons of earth,
the entire chamber had to be built with stone blocks culminating in a
vaulted roof. The granite came from the neighboring county of Fang-shan
as well as Honan Province. Bricks, which lined the floors of the burial
chambers and the entrance tunnel, were transported over the Grand Canal
from Shantung. Lumber for the outside surfaces of the structures was
provided by provinces farther south.[54] As indicated in the accounts of
palace construction in Peking, the largest pieces of stone had to be loaded
on specially constructed carts pulled by 1,600 mules each. Even earth fill
had to be carted from miles away from the construction site.[55]

Called the "Mysterious Palace," the underground chambers in some ways
simulated palace living quarters and the throne hall.[56] The middle
chamber on the main axis was furnished with three dragon chairs carved
from marble, to be flanked at some distance away against the side walls by

two stone benches decorated with phoenixes in relief; all had footstools. The inner chamber contained a granite platform, which was to support the coffins of the emperor, the empress, and the natural mother of the succeeding emperor. This traditional combination thus evoked a controversial point that was to be felt increasingly as the work progressed.

Security and aesthetic touches were by no means ignored. Seven doors, possibly the most elaborate part of the work, separated chambers and corridors. Of those on the main axis, the openings for the doors were carved out of stone partitions that transected the tunnels. Above the door opening was a cornice that simulated those of gateways conventionally leading to free-standing buildings, complete with purlins, tiles, and animals on the ridges—all carved in marble. Each of the two door panels was a monolithic piece of stone measuring about ten by five feet. The pivot, built into the piece, was more than one foot thick so that it could sustain the entire weight of the door panel, while the other edge of the panel, like a razor blade, was only half that thick. The door head was a bronze beam behind the partition, two and a half feet wide and one foot deep. A mechanism had been devised so that when the door was being closed, a granite block would slide down diagonally, eventually buttressing the panels from inside along a track on the ground and serving as a permanent bolt, without the removal of which the door could never again be opened.[57]

The religious implications of the structure were too obvious to be dismissed. While the stone structure itself and its furnishings carried the imperial insignia of dragons and phoenixes, the bases of the stone furniture near the ground level were carved with designs of the lotus, the Buddhist icon.[58] In both 1584 and 1585, while construction was in progress, the death penalty was suspended.[59] Yet the afterlife which the Mysterious Palace tried to suggest was far from resurrection as an assured state, but one of make-believe. The presence of gold and silver utensils and porcelain water jars and wash basins gave the setting a sense of realism, only to be offset by the presence of wooden horses and servants carved in the size of toys. On the floor of one of the side chambers, which appeared to be servants' quarters, was a simulation of a well; but it had no sunken pit to reach water. The several lamps, of course, could not be kept burning once the entrance tunnel was sealed. When the light went out, the pots of oil would soon become encrusted and solidify, leaving a lingering odor in the subterranean hallway. All this was known to the architects, since imperial mausoleums had been sealed, reopened, and sealed again to deposit the remains of the empresses who had outlived their husbands. The exact conditions upon reopening could be found in the repair reports on file with the Ministry of Works.[60]

Centuries later, visitors to the underground palace were less impressed by its rich furnishings than chilled by the sobering thought of being close to a tragic life. Here was the resting-place of a youthful ruler who had been prematurely canonized and half-buried as a patron ancestor of an empire which, because of its organizational inadequacy, could make little use of his creative energies except by directing them toward make-believe—even to the extent of blurring the distinction between this life and the hereafter. The scores of artifacts on display only conveyed the misery of the Wan-li emperor, who would have much preferred to be buried with the woman he loved than with the two skeletons on either side of him. The poetic philosophy that life is a state of mind which can overcome all barriers could never enable an onlooker to dispel the presence of grim reality amid the soaked and rotten silks and half-burned wicks of gummy lamps.

Had not Shen Shih-hsing, the first grand-secretary in charge of the project, who had been so close to the Wan-li emperor, drawn away from him and then, drawn close again while watching the stone-carving, foundation-laying, and the final furnishing, had his sentimental moments about his master and pupil? It would be difficult to believe that, with his sensitivity, he had remained detached all the time. But his inner thoughts on the subject, inexpressible, were never expressed.

What the first grand-secretary put down in writing had nothing to do with sadness. Felicitously, the construction of this huge tomb tied the present emperor to his family tree, which, with all the blessings and the magic power of geomancy, had yet to produce enlightened rulers over many, many generations.

When the ground was broken for construction, Tutor Shen delivered his congratulatory note to the Wan-li emperor, in which he outlined what the project meant to the sovereign:

> To render to your forefathers
> Eternal comfort for their spirit;
> To plan on this auspicious land
> Myriad years of good life.[61]

In the late autumn of 1586, the work on the burial chamber had progressed well. The construction of the ceremonial hall had also begun. While the emperor absented himself, officials representing various departments and ministries were on hand to celebrate the event. Grand-Secretary Shen again reported to the emperor:

> The day we selected to put the ridge beam in place the weather turned out so fine that it was almost a return to springtime. The day before we had warm sunshine and a comfortable breeze. As the hours went on, the moon brightened and the stars twinkled. Now officials as well as artisans danced in joy for the good blessings, and commoners dashed to work cheering.[62]

Such rhetorical symmetry and balance achieved one purpose: it conveyed a state of make-believe. Shen Shih-hsing had yet to be censured for deceiving the emperor, but never on such a happy occasion when he slightly rearranged what he had seen in order to please the sovereign. Both of them must have known, however, that things at the constructional site could not have been so pleasant, because the long-term project was about to produce its draining effect on the Treasury as well as on the populace over a wide area. In 1587, the Year of the Pig, a state paper, which must have been read by both the emperor and his first grand-secretary before being published, acknowledged that among those working on the mausoleum were old people and young children who were wailing from hunger and cold. The sovereign directed that medicine be provided to the sick and some of them be sent home.[63] To what extent his order was carried out no one knows for sure.

5
HAI JUI,
THE ECCENTRIC MODEL OFFICIAL

On November 13, 1587, the censor-in-chief at Nanking, Hai Jui, died in office.[1] His demise eliminated one of the most exceptional personalities of the era, but not his legend. The name Hai Jui had yet to be associated with more controversies for centuries to come.[2]

Unlike most of his fellow bureaucrats, the late censor-in-chief did not accept the notion that government according to moral principle meant an ideal perfection conceived from above and the attempt to approximate it, insofar as was possible, on the part of the lower offices. Hai believed that laws should be enforced to the letter at all levels. Since the salaries for governmental functionaries were set at the subsistence level, he, without protest or manipulation, consented to live in extreme poverty. The day after his death his friends found among his personal effects less than twenty ounces of silver—not even enough to pay for a decent funeral.[3]

Moreover, Hai had also believed that officials should extend their functions to pursue the spirit of the law beyond statutory limits. As governor of Chihli, he had sparked one of his many controversies by demanding the return of landed properties to their previous owners who had mortgaged them and then, because of usurious interest rates, had lost them to their lenders.

Hai Jui's convictions and temperament dictated that he would be both a highly regarded and a lonely man. During a quarter of a century he often found himself fighting a one-man battle for one cause or another. Although he was widely admired, no one followed him in practice. He had thus simultaneously personified the best and the worst features of government by moral principle. His life demonstrated what contribution a cultivated gentleman could render to society through selfless spiritual sublimation. Yet the utilitarian value of his virtue was limited. More resembling that of a popular hero onstage, Hai's commitment to simplicity enabled him to arouse the emotions of a large audience. When the way in which he conducted his office was under scrutiny, however, opinions differed widely and violently. What could be readily concluded was that his approach could not be institutionally adopted as a standard.

As a model official yet an eccentric, Hai Jui derived his concept of civil governance from the idea that all patterns of human behavior could be instinctively classified into moral archetypes of good and evil. He felt that those standards could also be reinforced by social values. To illustrate this point he declared that, of all the civil suits brought to his attention as a local official, six or seven cases out of ten were ones in which right and wrong could be easily ascertained. There might be two or three in which verdicts could not be so easily arrived at. For dealing with cases of the latter category he outlined his principles:

I suggest that in returning verdicts to those cases it is better to rule against the younger brother rather than the older brother, against the nephew rather than the uncle, against the rich rather than the poor, and against the stubbornly cunning rather than against the clumsily honest. If the case involves a property dispute, it is better to rule against the member of the gentry rather than the commoner so as to provide relief to the weaker side. But if the case has to do with courtesy and status, it is better to rule against the commoner rather than against the gentry: the purpose is to maintain our order and system.[4]

Hai's directions closely paralleled the doctrines expounded by the *Four Books*. But alas, at the time when he composed this paragraph, nearly two thousand years had rolled by since the *Four Books* had been written. Also, the day Hai Jui was admitted to the Civil Service in 1553, close to two centuries had elapsed since the Hung-wu emperor had founded the present dynasty. Though not recognized by Hai's contemporaries, this passage on judiciary decisions in fact reflected the perennial dilemma of our empire: with a literary bureaucracy managing the affairs of the agrarian masses, no method had yet been invented to improve and refine the legal system. Lacking such a breakthrough, court decisions had to be in harmony with ancient social norms. The lack of dimension and depth of governmental operations in turn made it mandatory to stress the personal virtue of its functionaries.

More about this dilemma can be gleaned from the life story of Hai Jui, whose character in the end proved to offer no effective cure for the inadequacy of the bureaucratic management.

Personally, Hai could never have reached the degree of eminence he did without the element of luck. A civil official lacking the doctoral degree, he had to spend four years as the Confucian instructor attached to a local government in Fukien. By the time he was promoted to a county magistrate in Chekiang in 1558, he was already forty-five years old. The position he was to assume was one that many holders of a doctorate had relinquished in their early thirties or even late twenties. Shun-an County, however, was at the crossroads to three provinces, and its importance as a center of transit increased during the 1550s, when the campaign against the pirates on the eastern coast diverted a volume of seaboard traffic inland into its territory.

This placed considerable financial burden upon the local population. Part of the fiscal arrangement established by the founder of the dynasty was that the government budget had no provision for official travel. But the empire's 1,040 message-relaying stations, all locally manned and supported, provided transportation and hostelry to dignitaries in transit. Food, lodging, horses, boats, sedan chairs, and porter service were all furnished by the local populace as a part of their tax obligation. The official traveler was entitled to these services free of charge upon showing his travel document.[5] Hai Jui first made a name for himself because he succeeded in protecting his district from abuses of these privileges by governmental functionaries and their auxiliaries.

One story, seemingly exaggerated, described his confrontation with Hu Tsung-hsien, a civil official commissioned as supreme commander in charge of the campaign against the pirates. Hu's son, it was said, was passing through Shun-an with many pieces of luggage. Dissatisfied with the reception given him by the local station, he tied the station master up and insulted him. Magistrate Hai intervened, seized the young Hu, and, the story went, confiscated the large amount of silver found in his procession. When he turned Hu's son over to the supreme commander, he asserted that the arrested man must be an imposter, since His Excellency's son could never be so arrogant and savage, and the prodigious amount of cash carried by him was incompatible with His Excellency's life-style, which everyone knew was simple and unpretentious.[6]

If this tale was embellished, the story of Hai's challenge of Yen Mou-ch'ing was not. It is substantiated by published documents. In 1560 Yen received an imperial commission to tour the southern provinces for the purpose of reorganizing the salt gabelle so that additional funds could be raised to meet mounting military expenditures. Like Hu Tsung-hsien, he must have felt that local officials would not dare to extend to him anything less than the importance of his mission demanded. Nevertheless, conforming to the general practice of the time, he issued a circular letter to them in advance, which in part read: "By nature I always prefer simplicity to ostentation. Your courtesy extended to my party and myself must be modest—that includes food and lodging. Nothing should be excessively extravagant, since every item has to be contributed by local communities." Basically intending to publicize his own virtue, Yen probably never expected anyone to take the message literally. But Hai Jui did.

Before Commissioner Yen set foot in Shun-an, he received a reply that was by no means lacking in ordinary politeness. Its opening paragraph read: "The magistrate of Shun-an County, Yen-chou Prefecture, by surname Hai, begs to petition His Excellency. Your servant has now read your circular letter." After quoting the commissioner's own words, the paper went on: "As for Your Excellency's tour of duty in the south, all reports by the forward agents bear out this fact: 'Everywhere a lavish banquet is prepared, each feast costing three to four hundred ounces of silver. Gold and silk gifts are given at every course of the meal. Rare birds and animals are supplied to the quarters. The furnishings are splendid, including a urinal made of silver.' " In conclusion, Hai urged Yen to stop this kind of extravagance. Once having accepted the flattery and compliments of the local officials, Hai further warned, His Excellency might one day find it difficult to deal with them strictly according to law, and that could cause the failure of his mission.[7] Tradition has it that, after reading Hai's petition, Yen Mou-ch'ing made detours to avoid Shun-an County on all his remaining trips.[8]

Such confrontations might or might not have cost Hai Jui a subsequent promotion.[9] According to the record, he remained magistrate of Shun-an until 1562, when he was transferred to a similar post in Hsing-kuo County, Kiangsi. These facts attest that he must have conducted himself impeccably; otherwise he would certainly have been the recipient of serious charges, having offended the dignitaries who maintained connections with the court in Peking. The censorial officials who kept an eye on him certainly would not have let his slightest flaw go unquestioned. But possibly by this time he had already established his reputation for absolute frugality. Another story, also connecting him with Hu Tsung-hsien, alleged that once the supreme commander had exclaimed: "Sensational news! Magistrate Hai is providing a banquet to celebrate his mother's birthday! He has already bought two pounds of pork!"[10] This story might or might not be true; it is recorded that Hai Jui ate modestly and that his food usually came from his own garden in the yard behind his office.

Because the application of ground rules became uncertain, individuals tended to fall back on their own personal strength and resourcefulness.[11] As a result it was not unusual in this age for officials of the lower ranks to show their defiance toward their superiors when the moral code was at issue. But in most instances such episodes had only local repercussions and were soon forgotten. Good fortune intervened on behalf of Hai Jui, however, and saved his show of character from slipping from public memory. It became part of him. As it happened, Grand-Secretary Yen Sung, who had dominated the court of Peking for close to two decades, was dismissed in 1562 by the Chia-ching emperor (Wan-li's grandfather). Suddenly the position of his retainers in and out of court became untenable—among them Supreme Commander Hu Tsung-hsien and Imperial Commissioner of the Salt Gabelle, Yen Mou-ch'ing.[12] The moment the two were censured and recognized as immoral, Hai Jui's prestige was given an unexpected boost. Thus at age forty-nine, without a doctorate and still a holder of Civil Service rank 7a, Hai Jui was destined to become a popular hero of historical significance.

The next time Hai Jui demonstrated his daring was in 1565. He was then a secretary on duty with the Ministry of Revenue, rank 6a. He had been promoted and transferred to the capital a year earlier, a notable honor for a holder of the licentiate degree.

The atmosphere in Peking in the 1560s, however, was hardly inspiring. Pressed by the increasing military expenditures in the north and south, the government felt the urgency to raise revenue. Yet without an organizational change no adequate means were available. What fund-raising programs were in practice during the era featured manipulation of accounts at the top and addition of surtaxes at the bottom. The former did not increase revenue, nor did it effect forced savings; it merely arbitrarily intercepted certain incomes and rerouted them. The latter, on the other hand, made the tax system, already a hodgepodge, more complicated and its management more difficult. Yet the junior members within the ministry could do little to relieve these problems. Decisions were usually made by senior officials and carried out by clerical workers, who were the only ones familiar with the procedural details. In fact, when Hai Jui was secretary he was not required to report to the ministry daily. He was expected to hold his appointment only in order to accumulate seniority.[13]

The emperor, who by then had reigned for over four decades, was residing in a villa in the Imperial City. His main interest was seeking longevity through Taoist formulas. Yet Chia-ching could not be labeled as simply indolent in the ordinary sense. Despite his absence from public functions, he did make decisions about vital state affairs, sometimes meticulously.

But the sovereign's love of flattery and intolerance of criticism knew no bounds. Because he restricted his personal contact to a handful of sycophants, he was constantly fed false information. Only after something had gone drastically wrong would he try to make amends, usually by sending a formerly trusted lieutenant to his death. This made his personal rule seem more capricious and the officials more concerned with their own security than with the proper functioning of the court. By 1565, his favorite grand-secretary, Yen Sung, had been deposed for three years; but the emperor continued his style of governing, which was "harsh, obdurate, and lacked compassion." Chia-ching's tragedy was that, with all that he did, he fancied himself to be one of the greatest rulers in history.[14]

It took Hai Jui considerable soul-searching and resolution to write his famous memorial submitted in November. The paper held the emperor directly responsible for the sorry conditions of the state. The enumeration of Chia-ching's sins included his failure as a father, husband, and ruler. The monarch was described as vain, cruel, selfish, suspicious, and foolish. Excessive taxation, widespread governmental corruption, exorbitant palace spending, and rampant banditry were cited in detail to justify the charges. The caustic tone of the memorial culminated with the sentence, "It has already been some time since the people under Heaven started to regard Your Majesty as unworthy."[15]

Falling just short of inciting revolt, Hai Jui nevertheless bade the sovereign to reform. "All that is needed," he assured the throne, "is a change of heart on Your Majesty's part." Under the present circumstances, Heaven would not speak; longevity was unattainable. Chia-ching must rid himself of superstitious practices, which were as hopeless as "trying to stop the wind or catch a shadow." On the other hand, there was still time for the emperor to become a sage ruler, if he would adopt the proper approach and maintain it with determination and vigor.

The emperor's violent reaction to Hai's memorial was not a surprise. At one point he threw it on the ground and shouted: "Quickly arrest this man, don't let him get away!" A eunuch attendant, in an effort to calm the sovereign, said deliberately: "Myriad Years, you needn't worry about that. This man has the reputation of being silly. I heard that before he turned in this paper he bought himself a coffin and said goodbye to his family. All his house servants ran away. But he is not going to run, that is sure."[16] The emperor sighed, picked up the paper, read and reread it.

Up to that time Hai Jui's memorial was unprecedented. Remonstrances to the throne had been written by civil servants of the dynasty, but only to protest either a single policy or an act of impropriety, not to criticize the emperor's private and public life, attacking his character and describing his misrule over decades.

For several months the Chia-ching emperor had the paper on his mind, yet he did nothing to its writer and the memorial was kept in the palace. At one point he contemplated abdication. But that extreme act, implying abandonment of responsibility, was also against the dynasty's tradition. Already in poor health, Chia-ching must have been haunted by Hai's charges, which had so much truth in them yet had never before been leveled at him even in the mildest language. The accusations caused the emperor to call Hai, alternatively, his loyal subject and "that creature who has cursed me." When he got angry with his maids, they would say: "He was bawled out by Hai Jui and he's taking it out on us!" Very likely the strain caused by the whole disturbance contributed to Chia-ching's death about a year later.[17]

It was not until late February of 1566, in one of his most depressed moments, that the emperor finally ordered the arrest of the memorialist. The Ministry of Justice recommended Hai's death by strangulation, citing from the penal code a clause that demanded extreme penalty for a son guilty of cursing his own father. The emperor, who had ratified the death penalty before on less substantial charges, now hesitated. Both the prisoner and the ministry's recommendation were held in suspension for almost ten months.

In confinement one day, Hai Jui was served a big meal including rice wine. He was under the impression that this was the last meal customarily served to a prisoner before execution. As he was prepared to die, he consumed what was handed him in good spirits. Only then did the jail warden whisper to him, informing him of the death of the Chia-ching emperor and his consequent imminent release. Instead of rejoicing, Hai Jui wept—and vomited.[18]

So, on the enthronement of the Lung-ch'ing emperor in early 1567, Hai walked out of prison. His position caused considerable difficulty to the grand-secretaries. His prestige was now well established. Undoubtedly the most virtuous civil servant in the whole empire, he could be very honest and straightforward, but he could also be very rude, very brusque, and very demanding. On the whole he would not accept the dual character of the yin and yang; and he could be counted on to force his standards on his superiors as well as his subordinates. What could the grand-secretaries and the minister of personnel do with such a person? Kick him upstairs. Let him have the honor he deserved—but no official function of course.

In quick succession Hai found himself appointed a director in the Office of the Custodian of the Imperial Seal, transferred to Executive Officer at the Grand Court of Revision, and then again promoted to Commissioner for the Transmission of Official Documents in Nanking. Thus in the space of one year he had attained rank 4a.[19] His frustration was that there was little to do in the southern capital and still less in an ornamental post. The only compensation was that now he had his family with him, but that too was to give him painful experiences in time.

In early 1569, a year for personnel evaluation, Hai Jui followed the tradition of self-criticism by writing that he deserved to be discharged from the Civil Service. His memorial addressed to the Lung-ch'ing emperor argued: "Your Majesty first ordered my release from the death cell and gave me rebirth, and then promoted me by waiving normal procedural requirements. Among Your Majesty's servants no one else, I dare say, could be more motivated to express his gratitude through devoted service than myself." The petition was actually a very thinly disguised protest against his inconsequential assignment despite the fact that his merit had been recognized by the throne. After briefly indicating his lack of skill and wisdom, Hai went on to describe the position he was now occupying: "The commissioner checks and examines the incoming messages and dispatches them. He has neither fiscal responsibility nor a single decision to make. Since I cannot even fulfill this requirement, what else am I qualified for?"[20]

Rhetorically Hai was asking to be discharged on the ground of lack of talent; actually he was exerting great pressure on those in charge of personnel management in Peking to reconsider his case. As a matter of fact, his request for leave constituted a threat. Anyone who would have dared to accept his resignation on the emperor's behalf would have run into unmanageable difficulties with public opinion. Within the context of a government which disallowed individuals to make claims for themselves, convention had provided Hai Jui with a device of which he had not hesitated to take advantage. In this instance, at least, he was not completely unaware of the interplay of yin and yang.

His maneuver bore fruit in the summer. Hai Jui was appointed governor of South Chihli, with his office in Soochow, the richest and most developed prefecture of the empire. It was rather extraordinary for the governorship of such a territory, in fact any governorship, to be assigned to an individual who had no doctoral degree. But Soochow was a difficult post; those who had foresight could have predicted that Hai Jui was heading for trouble. Sure enough, eight months later he was impeached and discharged from the Civil Service.

When Hai Jui's new appointment was announced, a number of officials in South Chihli who anticipated his censure voluntarily and promptly left. The vermilion front doors of many of the city's mansions were repainted black to avoid ostentation. A eunuch commissioner stationed in Soochow reduced the number of his sedan-chair bearers from eight to four.[21] Governor Hai, on his part, issued to the prefects and magistrates in the province a "personal proclamation" consisting of thirty-six articles.[22] Besides interdicting graft and corruption, the document demanded that male adults marry, that widows who had not remained loyal to their deceased husbands find new homes, and that cremation and infanticide be prohibited. When he visited their districts, Hai cautioned his subordinates, they would not be permitted to come out from the city walls to welcome him; but the governor himself might interview the village elders to hear their grievances. When his tour of duty made it necessary for him to stay in a city for a short period, the responsible officials would be allowed to serve him food not exceeding the cost of 0.2 ounces of silver per day in those districts where food was cheap and 0.3 ounces of silver per day where it was more expensive. Chicken, pork, or fish was allowed, but no goose or yellow wine. As long as Hai Jui was governor, official documents originating in the province were to be written on cheap and simple paper. Spaces that had customarily been left blank at the end of each document were eliminated as a part of the austerity drive. With the publication of this personal proclamation, many luxurious items, including special kinds of textiles, headgear, stationery, and pastry, could no longer be manufactured within the territory.

The greatest contribution Hai made to his district during his short term as governor was the organization of the dredging of the Woosung and Paimao rivers in early 1570. But as soon as the project was under way, he was forced out of office.[23]

Hai's downfall was caused by his intervention in local land tenure, which for some time had been exploited by moneylenders. These were comprised of a number of well-to-do households that offered selective loans to the poor through intermediaries, usually neighborhood roughnecks. Under normal conditions the borrowers had great difficulty repaying these loans, so overburdened were they by the exorbitant interest rates. Their homesteads, pledged as collateral, were then swiftly taken over by the lenders. Even though there was a clause in the statute book limiting monthly interest rates to 3 percent and stating that accrued interest was never to exceed the principal regardless of the duration of the loan, these laws were now unenforceable and had never been seriously enforced in the past.[24] The government, in principle, also recognized the right of the dispossessed to redeem their lost properties within five years; that only made the problem more complicated.

Hai Jui was not interested in settling these cases for the sake of legality. Rather, he was fired by moral zeal. His concern, primarily for the poor and ignorant, was also intensified by his ambition to level social classes. Undoubtedly his stand encouraged many of those who had lost their property in the past to petition now for his intervention and redress.

The largest landowner in the territory, and the one who had received the most complaints, was Hsü Chieh. His "household men" were said to number several thousand and his holdings to consist of either 40,000 or 60,000 acres, although those figures could have been significantly exaggerated. Hsü nevertheless was the head of a large extended family whose members consistently practiced usury in the rural areas. The governor simply passed on to him all complaints against the family and ordered him to reduce their holdings by half.[25] Their exchange of correspondence indicated that this order was carried out, at least in part. It so happened that Hsü Chieh, previously a grand-secretary, had interceded in Hai Jui's favor when, as a remonstrator against the Chia-ching emperor, he still had a recommended death penalty hanging over his head. But the new governor by no means considered his present reproof of his former benefactor ungrateful. On the contrary, he regarded his action as a great service to him, because Hsü, now out of power, was under scrutiny. By allowing his family members to seize the property of the poor on a grand scale, he was subject to criminal prosecution. By asking him to return some of the land in question voluntarily, Hai Jui would help to mitigate the offense, thus in fact shielding Hsü from the worst penalty. At the same time, the governor's willingness to tackle a prominent figure who had such a close personal relationship with himself must have deeply impressed the public. If Hai Jui had only stopped at this point and allowed this case, or at most a few similar selected cases, to stand as a warning against the practice of dispossessing the poor, he probably would have fared better.

But he could not stop. His efforts toward just retribution were generated by a passion that could not be tempered. The governor now set aside two days each month to hear the complaints of dispossessed landowners. His own writings indicate that every day he received three to four thousand petitions.[26] From this point on Hai Jui was headed for trouble.

Fundamentally, in the rice-producing area, because of the conditions of the terrain and the water supply, agricultural land had to be carved into the

smallest plots in order to accommodate manpower from individual households. No single individual ever owned a very large continuous tract of
land. The affluent and the poor had their plots of land side by side, with
one's holdings sometimes separated by those of another person. Tenant
farmers and small independent farmers were next-door neighbors. Had
this not been the case, the complicated land-tenure problem would not
have arisen. Moreover, dispossession because of debt was not always a
situation created by professional moneylenders and tough operators. It was
also closely connected with property transactions in the rural areas. Since
credit institutions did not exist, any small cultivator who managed to accumulate a saving would lend it to his neighbor or a relative and hold the
right to use a portion of the latter's land as lien.[27] As the fortunes of the two
families followed the upward and downward trends, the eventual takeover
of the assets by the stronger one was only a matter of time. But until that
time, not all the creditors were from an upper class. Many of them, as
reported for the same period as the Hai Jui episode but apart from it, were
in fact illiterate.[28] Therefore, when Hai accepted all unresolved cases, he
simply put himself in an impossible position.

In practice, the governor made no survey of the field conditions existing
before he launched his one-man campaign. No new legislation was proclaimed. No apparatus was set up for investigating cases, returning verdicts, or reviewing appeals. By handling the cases himself Hai enabled the
petitioners to bypass his prefects and magistrates. Furthermore, he even
permitted the reopening of cases beyond the five-year statutory limit, on
the ground that when a takeover was not specified by written contract the
statutory limit did not apply. Even though he held that in only one case out
of every twenty he had ruled in favor of the original owner,[29] this fact
hardly made his administering of justice more defensible from a procedural point of view.

Before the land-tenure problem ever came up, Hai Jui had already been
censured by a censorial-supervising official for his personal proclamation
dealing with such petty matters as blank spaces on official documents.[30]
The subsequent impeachment petition by Supervising-Secretary Tai Feng-
hsiang said that Hai Jui had encouraged hordes of riffraff to make false
charges against men of substance and then presided over the cases indulg-
ing his own whims; his misgovernment was such that in South Chihli the
peasants were hindered from delivering their rents and repaying their
loans.[31] Tai, by making such exaggerated accusations, encouraged the
speculation that he himself was connected with the moneylending in-

terests. But further censure of the governor was initiated by others. Along with his other charges, Supervising-Secretary Tai also brought to the emperor's attention the fact that only seven months before, Hai's wife and concubine had died the same night and that circumstances suggested murder and suicide. In Hai's reply he admitted his concubine's suicide by hanging on August 14 but insisted that his wife had died a natural death on August 25, after a lapse of eleven days.[32] This disclosure did little to remove the cloud of suspicion darkening the governor's character. No matter what the circumstances, the minister of personnel who acted on the charges concurred with them and reported to the Lung-ch'ing emperor that Hai Jui indeed had "enormous ambition but diffuse talent."[33] This was a drastic reversal from the situation a year before, when no one would have dared to use such words to describe the most impeccably moral and fearless civil servant of the empire. Profoundly bitter, Hai in the spring of 1570 submitted his last memorial to the throne before leaving office. In the paper he reminded His Majesty that the court of Peking was composed of "a bunch of women."[34]

Two years later, after the accession of the Wan-li emperor and the rise of Chang Chü-cheng, Hai made contact with Chang, apparently in the hope that the master of the Literary Depth Pavilion would reopen his case, since Chang himself at the time stood for law and order and discipline. But the first grand-secretary's reply read:

> The Soochow district had not been law-abiding for quite some time. All of a sudden your lordship tried to cut and shear it. Not surprisingly, the district could not bear it. When rumors were circulating, they caused a great deal of fear and panic. Your humble servant, unworthily occupying a position within the central administration that permits him to make a few minor suggestions only, must in this instance say that he is deeply ashamed that he is unable to encourage on behalf of His Majesty's court a law-enforcing administrator, or to check the abusive criticisms against him.[35]

As a result of Chang's refusal to intervene, Hai Jui's forced retirement was to last for fifteen years. But the controversy over him by no means ended there.

Chang Chü-cheng was charged by his critics with being cruel, false, and self-seeking. Hai Jui, on the other hand, was regarded as eccentric, unbalanced, and obstinate. Few had given thought to the fact that both men, in their distinctive ways, were seeking directions in which the empire could be led. Strangely enough, Hai Jui's approach was constitutionally closer to and more logically consistent with the system originally established by the Hung-wu emperor. Indeed, his story would make little sense outside the context of the founding of the dynasty.

When Hung-wu had organized the dynasty two hundred years before, he had seen to it that every aspect of his establishment accentuated the rustic simplicity of an agrarian society. The entire civil bureaucracy had fewer than eight thousand positions. The clerical workers were organized into a sub-bureaucracy. Called "lesser functionaries," many of them were drafted into service and not paid. For those who were paid, the salary amounted to no more than a food ration for their families.[36]

The most unusual feature of the governmental operation was that all local officials were permanently restricted within their respective city walls. They entered the rural areas on pain of the death penalty. They could, however, summon any imperial subject to their offices. Only after the same subpoena had been disregarded three times could a warrant for arrest be issued. Further to protect the commoners from being abused by the governmental functionaries, the emperor promised that he would take up their grievances himself. His discourse on sound government and the justification of severe penalties for wrong-doing was published in a pamphlet called *Grand Monitions*, of which each household must retain a copy. In the case of any serious grievance, a copy of *Grand Monitions* was as good as a passport for the imperial subject's journey to reach the sovereign.[37]

Under the Hung-wu emperor villages were organized into self-governing communities, each drawing up its own charter to be patterned after the model specified by an imperial decree.[38] In every community two pavilions were constructed, one to commend the good deeds of the residents and the other to reprove evil-doers. In these pavilions the village elders arbitrated disputes over inheritance, marriage, property holdings, and cases of assault and battery. The good and bad deeds of the villagers were also posted at those pavilions.

Twice a year, in the first and tenth lunar months, every community held its local banquet. Attendance by all households was compulsory. Before food and drink were served there were chants, lectures, the reading of imperial laws, and the reprimanding of individuals who had committed misdeeds in the village. A person who had committed an offense yet chose to absent himself from the public denunciation was declared an "incorrigible subject," whom the village community must then recommend to the civil government for a sentence of exile to the frontier.

Along with these guidelines the founding emperor also conducted a series of purges that affected the entire social elite, from His Majesty's own court down to the rural communities. Some historians have estimated that more than 100,000 persons perished during these waves of persecution.[39] Because of the resultant confiscations and expropriations of the landed properties of the victims, the empire was converted into a nation of small independent farmers. In 1397, however, the Ministry of Revenue reported that there were still 14,341 households across the empire that possessed 120 acres of land or more.[40] The emperor allowed them to remain as they were. But those wealthy and middle-class households were harnessed with many service obligations during the reign of the dynastic founder, who personally kept a list of their names.

This arrangement had many profound consequences. The direct application of moral law at the village level prevented the judiciary system from maturing and attaining technical sophistication. The reliance on moral archetypes of "good" and "evil" in their most simplistic sense must have significantly obstructed the entire populace as well as officialdom from distinguishing whether a matter was "legal" or "illegal."

Given the difficulty of managing the affairs of millions of peasants residing in a wide area, the dynasty was operating under a severe handicap to begin with. Yet its rigid commitment to simplicity severely restricted its competence in dealing with a wide range of problems. This is best illustrated by the way it handled public finance.

Under the Hung-wu emperor, the dynasty proclaimed a very light landtax on all landowners in each district. In addition, service obligations were imposed on taxpayers according to the principle of progressive taxation, with heavy burdens falling on the more affluent. The horses, sedan chairs, and food needed by the message-relaying stations, for instance, were provided by the large and wealthy households, whose fiscal responsibility was virtually unlimited. They had to contribute more when official travel increased.

For expenditures involving variable amounts such as official travel, which were taken care of by designated taxpayers, most governmental offices could operate with a fixed budget consisting basically of grain quotas disbursed as pay and salaries. Because of the low level of fiscal activity, most districts attained financial self-sufficiency. For those exceptional cases where transferral of revenue was involved, the revenue-surplus units were matched with the disbursing agencies and were ordered to carry out lateral transactions at the lowest possible level. In this way, income and expenditure canceled each other out item by item, and the empire was thickly covered with short, interlocking supply lines. The Ministry of Revenue ceased to be an operating agency; it had become a huge accounting office. Without the necessity to reroute supplies at the intermediate level, most of the services, including transportation, communication, bookkeeping, and warehouse storage, were eliminated. In the short run this master plan seemed to have effected considerable saving.

But in the long run the dynasty had permanently restricted its own ability to make fiscal readjustments. In a few generations the tax quotas in numerous districts had become rigid. Local land tenure, leasing, sharecropping arrangements, and interest rates had combined to create circumstances which made future attempts to upgrade the quotas most difficult, if feasible at all. When not taxed, profit from land utilization had already been parceled out by too many interested parties to provide additional revenue to latter-day administrators.[41]

Even income from industrial and commercial sources, never a significant factor in the dynasty's financial history, followed the same pattern and stagnated at the earlier stages. The overriding factor was bureaucratic practice, which required all members of the Civil Service to act on generally recognized principles. Having accepted the Hung-wu concept of agrarian simplicity, the bureaucrats could no longer actively stimulate and develop the more volatile sectors of the national economy, which would have produced not only a different kind of managerial system, but also a different political philosophy, a different set of laws, and different office organizations. The two approaches would inevitably clash. As it was, when an economic activity produced a social consequence that the government could not handle, it had to be abandoned. Hai Jui's order forbidding the manufacture of certain consumer goods reflected this kind of restraint.

Unable to modernize its fiscal operations, the dynasty thus did the populace a disservice. Their surplus capital, lacking other outlets for investment, usually returned to landholding in order to exploit the prime producers. Thus, while the major part of governmental income had to be extracted from agrarian sources, nowhere were the peasants protected from debt and exploitation by usurers, sometimes their own neighbors and relatives. Governmental orders limiting interest rates could not be effectively enforced because opportunities to borrow on generous terms did not exist. At the time when Governor Hai was applying laws on interest rates and mortgages strictly to moneylenders, the only thing resembling a credit institution in his province was the pawnshop. In fact, by that time there were 20,000 pawnshops across our empire.[42]

Within the two hundred years between the founding of the dynasty and Hai Jui's governorship, significant changes had taken place. The wealthy households to whom Hung-wu had assigned heavy public duties no longer existed. The affluent, as a group, were now tied to the official circles and were thus able to claim exemption from service. The clerical positions within the government had now become lucrative. Owing to its peculiar type of financial administration, the empire consisted of numerous administrative pockets, whose inner workings were familiar only to the lesser functionaries. The clerical workers naturally took advantage of this situation.[43] The Civil Service had also matured. The original eight thousand positions that existed during the reign of Hung-wu had more than doubled. The imperial order forbidding governmental functionaries to enter rural areas had long been disregarded, even though, because of the nature of their work, most officials never needed to go outside the city walls. Yet the most striking difference from the Hung-wu period was that the 20,000 households of civil servants virtually composed the empire's upper middle class and above. Far from being civil servants in the literal sense, they were the masters.

In this new setting a large-estate owner like Hsü Chieh could be dealt with easily. His family holding clearly recognized as a threat to the functioning of the bureaucracy and his case well publicized, he could have been arrested and punished by order of the emperor on any of the numerous misdemeanor charges the civil officials might choose to level against him. There was practically no defense for an individual who had so alienated himself from public opinion. It actually happened, shortly after Hai Jui's dismissal, that Hsü's family holdings, now said to be close to 10,000 acres, were confiscated by the throne, his eldest son exiled to the frontier, and two younger sons reduced to commoner status.[44]

Agrarian exploitation of the poor, however, was far from limited to such isolated incidents. It affected all walks of life and was carried out on a large and small scale without surcease generation after generation.[45] Essentially, such exploitation was the economic basis of the bureaucracy as an institution. Official families, who collected rents from landholdings and interest from the moneylending business, were an integral part of the rural economy. As individual households moved in and out of officialdom, the rise and fall in their family fortunes gave impetus to social mobility. By keeping membership in the social classes mobile but the social structure itself intact, these practices perpetuated a system.[46] Hai Jui's intervention in all those cases concerning ownership and lending interests, whether legally questionable or not, tended to disrupt the whole operation. Regardless of his intent, it was one man's effort to check the normal workings of a society. On this ground the Minister of Personnel was justified in declaring that Hai's talents did not measure up to his ambition.

Beyond the power of the conscientious governor to apprehend lay the fact that the agrarian problem he was facing could not be solved locally. What the empire needed most was a better monetary system and more workable business laws. Without such changes the interest rates would never come down.

The origin of the monetary problem could also be traced to the founding of the dynasty. Basically, the Hung-wu emperor had attempted to create a national currency completely separate from his fiscal administration. Paper notes, issued in large quantities, were neither redeemable nor acceptable as tax payment. They were released outside commercial channels, largely as grants to officials and soldiers and as payments for the relief of famine. The imperial government thus gave away the negotiable notes without securing any credit for them and remained unaccountable. Had this scheme succeeded, it would have been the simplest way to redistribute wealth on a grand scale, since the liability of the paper currency fell squarely on those who traded their goods for it, or the ultimate recipients of those notes. In practice, the confiscatory aspect of the paper money was quickly recognized. Despite threatened penalties, the use of precious metals in private transactions continued. In the markets where government policy was effective, the currency was accepted but discounted. Its depreciation in value proceeded rapidly and progressively until it became virtually worthless.

Unwilling to create competition with its own paper notes, at first the government had refrained from minting bronze coins. By the time it realized the necessity to do so, the project was hampered by many factors. To mint money for private persons for a fee was out of the question, yet the government itself had only a meager cash income to invest in the coinage. The minting, small in quantity and lacking uniformity, was obliged to make a profit, thus creating a situation of which counterfeiters lost no time in taking advantage. The market was soon inundated with debased money of various kinds, which the recipients accepted at their own risk. Retail trade was adversely affected by the chaotic coinage. When ensuing unemployment in the cities presented a threat to general security, the court of Peking had to admit its failure. Its effort to establish the bronze coin as the legal tender also came to an end. Unminted silver in chunks and bits was accepted as the monetary standard in private and public transactions, its weight and purity to be verified by the users on each occasion: this was now the only alternative left.

But this was to subject the populace to the tyranny of the hardest currency of all, a precious metal not adequately backed up by bronze coins. The government had no idea how much money was in circulation; still less had it the ability to adjust the amount. What did wealthy families do when they had surplus capital not yet invested in landholding and moneylending? Most likely they buried the bullion underground for safekeeping, and loaded themselves down with silver jewelry and utensils, knowing that these articles could be quickly converted back into ready cash when needed. This, however, withdrew a significant portion of money from circulation and made borrowing more difficult. In short, whether the existing capital was or was not utilized, the lack of cheap money and easy credit put heavy pressure on the indebted peasants. The dispossession of their homesteads was in fact accelerated by the incompetence of the government—an error that could not be corrected, as Hai Jui had tried but failed to do, by manipulating court proceedings to avoid foreclosures.[47]

Still, had elaborate business laws been put into practice, abstract money could have been created to supplement the volume of bullion in circulation, thereby easing the pressure on the credit market. But as it was, the dynasty's codified law, designed to facilitate a literary bureaucracy's management of the affairs of agrarian masses, had few provisions for business transactions, leaving immense areas uncovered, especially those concerning debts, bankruptcy, nonfulfillment of contract, and the forming of corporations.[48]

In the context of bureaucratic procedure, this void was by no means surprising. The empire's logistical system, still in the Hung-wu mode of lateral transactions at the lowest possible level, required practically no commercial assistance in order to run. With few exceptions, there was no need to enlist mercantile interests in order to manage the finances of the state. Local officials, assigned to territorial posts for three-year terms, were too preoccupied with matters immediately affecting their records of performance (such as tax collection and public security) to think of promoting private business—not to mention that in order to do so, it would have been necessary to accept property rights as supreme and therefore above immediate administrative and moralistic considerations. That would have run counter to everything the bureaucrats had learned from the *Four Books*.

Ironically, property rights were honored and contractual obligations were enforced in our empire, not in large-scale business transactions in the cities, but in rental and mortgage agreements in the rural areas. To honor these agreements had become a general practice of customary law, and as such rarely required official intervention; the informal exercising of power and leadership by the gentry in the villages was sufficient to assure its continuance. Had this not been so, the financing of food production would have faced serious problems. Under the circumstances, Governor Hai Jui's unilateral rulings over litigations became even more unforgivable, as was explained by Supervising Secretary Tai Feng-hsiang in his impeachment paper. Hai's major fault, again it can be said, rested in his disregard of the dual character of the bureaucracy, which embraced the yin as well as the yang.

In retirement Hai Jui published the memoirs of his career as a local official. His admirers usually relished the sections in these volumes that had to do with fiscal administration, which established the author as a man of uncompromising integrity and meticulousness.[49] But Hai's life story proved that such commendable personal characteristics contributed little to the public welfare. The recollections actually provided a true picture of a reprehensible case of local government extracting an inadequate budgetary income from an impoverished populace. The writer offered no explanation of the cause of the dilemma; nor were his advocacy of frugality and his prohibition of unscheduled tax collections effective remedies.

Often neglected by readers, the portions of Hai's writing dealing with judiciary practices at the local governmental level should have been given more attention; they throw light on the special polity of our empire. The passages testify that the bureaucracy could never adequately dispense justice to millions of peasants; that fact might well be recognized as an intrinsic weakness of the system. To define and safeguard individual rights, the civil officials would have had to involve themselves in such small issues as brothers taking alternate years to use the same fishpond, and the right of way on flagstone bridges over ditches.[50] Obviously, that would have been impractical. Yet by dismissing those matters as petty and irrelevant, the officials would never again find an adequate point of reference to the context of village life. Nor could the local government, whose source of tax revenue was the peasantry, afford the court proceedings and litigations that would arise from the complexities of dispensing equity. The demand for imperial uniformity further reduced all legal actions by the government to those essential to maintaining the orderly conduct of the populace. This meant that the dynasty's judiciary structure was technically limited from the start.

Ignoring the concept of intrinsic justice, the court system remained indifferent to ordinary disputes, which the officials regarded as being of little social consequence.[51] Because the court withheld its jurisdiction, the issues were expected to be settled in families and clans by village and community leaders. The delegation of authority required continuing adherence to the social guidelines set down in the *Four Books:* the older generation was requested to set an example for the younger, the male to command the female, and the educated elite to lead the unlettered. This mode of governance was closely tied to the ancient cultural tradition and leaned on it for support. For all its moral tone, the system could never free itself of its authoritarian cast, for social pressure as a substitute for justice was always exerted from the top down. It was taken for granted that whoever could recite verses from the *Four Books* was more enlightened than an individual motivated by self-interest.

But there were areas where no delegation of authority was possible. Especially when the penal code was invoked the official position was absolutely uncompromising. Any case involving loss of life always called for lengthy investigation, with the magistrate himself sometimes acting as coroner. Men guilty of manslaughter were treated essentially the same as murderers; they were condemned to death by strangulation. By holding life sacred yet meting out an eye for an eye punishment, the legal system in this instance was following the mentality of the peasantry. At the same time, the summary reprisal offered a form of abbreviated justice that suited the handling capacity of the bureaucrats. When the penal code classified offenses in broad categories and made the moral law directly applicable, court proceedings lacked sophistication. Jurists were unnecessary; the magistrates and their assistants, even without professional training, confidently served as district judges. The government retained a unitary outlook. Judicial independence was unheard of, as it was not required.

The final results of these practices could be appalling. Since the government took drastic action in enforcing the penal code but showed no interest in upholding the civil law, and village leaders were preoccupied with decorum and social status, the villagers in reality were denied legal services of any kind. They were never given a clear indication of what they were entitled to. Despite the official sanction of morals, the peasants never lost sight of their self-interest in the use of fishponds and the right of way on flagstone bridges. In Hai Jui's writings they were described as being driven by their animal instincts—crafty, ruthless, and impulsive.[52] Plagued by poverty and ignorance, they were unaffected by the culture above them, which was too absorbed in its own sense of elitism to be of any use to the lower social strata. Even Hai Jui never spoke of the unruly villagers in an affectionate tone.

Petty quarrels were very common among the peasants. Cursing and fist-fights leading to serious injuries were not infrequent. The embittered antagonists could always choose to commit suicide in order to criminally implicate their adversaries. Sometimes family members abused the bodies of persons who had died of natural causes to make it appear that they had been beaten to death. Aside from framing enemies from old feuds, such machinations might also aim at deriving pecuniary gain from the settlement of the case. Magistrate Hai mentioned that he himself had discovered a case in which red paint was used to simulate dry blood.[53]

The rigidity of the legal practice could also put a great amount of pressure on the county magistrate as the presiding judge. All the crucial cases that came to him had to be settled, and settled decisively. Inevitably, at times the process required him to supplement evidence with logical deduction, thus subjecting human lives to guesswork. Most revealing in this connection is one of the actual cases cited in Hai Jui's papers.

It involved a husband and wife who let a friend stay in their home overnight. The latter had just been accepted by a local government as a clerk and was running errands in the vicinity. When food and wine were provided for his visit, the wife's brother also came by. It so happened that the husband owed his brother-in-law three ounces of silver and the repayment was long overdue. An argument flared up about it that led to a fight. During the excitement the husband was pushed into a pond, where he drowned. Aware of the mandatory death penalty that faced her brother if the case were duly reported, the wife and the guest remained silent and sank the body of the dead man into deep water by weighing it down with rocks.

When the case came to light, the presiding judge sentenced all three defendants to death: the brother-in-law by strangulation, the guest by beheading, and the wife by torture. What seemed to be a case of manslaughter had now been turned into one of adultery and murder. The killing must have been premeditated so that the wife could marry the clerk. Otherwise, why were celebratory wine and a house guest with his own servant mixed up in such a tragic incident? After being tried three times and referred to the Court of Grand Revision in Peking, the case remained unsettled, although the last trial, presided over by three magistrates of the adjacent counties, sustained the original verdict and sentence. At the intervention of a censorial official, the case was given one more review by Hai Jui, who was another magistrate close to the location of the death by drowning.

Hai maintained that this was a simple case of manslaughter. The charges of adultery and premeditated murder must be dismissed on the grounds that the wife, having borne the husband's two sons and one daughter, could have not taken such steps. The guest, having just been appointed a novice clerk, was not much richer than the husband. Since he already had a wife, concubinage would be all he could offer a partner in adultery. These trains of thought pointed to the profitless nature of premeditated murder as far as the victim's wife was concerned. Nor should an attempt at murder have required so many accomplices, who, according to the testimony, included the servant of the newly appointed clerk.

What about all those testimonies? They should be tossed out, Review Judge Hai concluded. The witnesses had been intimidated into making false statements.[54]

Fifteen years of forced retirement would be difficult for anyone to endure, and even more so for an individual as used to plain speaking and abrupt action as Hai Jui. Being a Confucian scholar, the ex-governor was at a serious disadvantage. Because almost all his creative energies had been devoted to public service, when his career came to an end he was unable to find any other activity to fill the emptiness of his life.

His home locale, on the edge of the South Sea, bore no comparison to the metropolitan districts where the literati, after leaving office, could hobnob with poets and painters, if not pursue such arts themselves. Many of them even organized classical seminars for moral betterment. But tropical Hai-nan Island, the shores of which were lined with palm trees and inhabited by crocodiles, provided no such salonlike atmosphere. In the mountains there the aborigines were still at war with the Han Chinese. Occasionally appearing in the straits between the island and the mainland were so-called pirates—actually amphibious bandits who plundered on land and then took refuge on the water.

Apart from the humiliation of being labeled as a man of enormous ambition but diffuse talents, Hai Jui's loneliness was intensified by the fact that he lacked a male heir. He had married three times and taken two concubines. His first wife, after bearing two daughters, was divorced by him when she quarreled with his mother. His second marriage lasted for only a month; it was annulled on the same ground. The wife who died in 1569 under suspicious circumstances was his third. She, and one concubine, had given birth to his three sons, none of whom lived to maturity. Even though all of his three daughters survived, Hai could never have the satisfaction of educating them to excel in Civil Service examinations and thus to carry on his campaign for righteousness. In fact the girls are never mentioned in his papers.[55]

It is conceivable that the story of his mother added a note of sadness to Hai's life. Widowed when he was three, she had endured great hardships in raising him. She taught him elements of the classics orally even before he had learned to read. His uprightness therefore was inseparable from her character. When he relinquished his office as governor, she was already eighty-one years old. Yet the authorities, after consenting to recommend her for the title of Ladyship of the Fourth Grade, persistently refused his request to name her a model mother with an imperial patent exemplifying her virtue. Had not she, like himself, carried that moralistic character too far, eventually causing him to divorce twice? Had she had anything to do with the unhappy event of 1569, directly or indirectly? Whatever the reasons, the refusal of his petition must have been a bitter disappointment to Hai.[56]

But the retired governor had long passed his point of no return. Defeat and frustration must be put aside; loneliness and bitterness must be overcome. As Confucius had taught him, the moral burdens of a cultured gentleman were endless. In retirement, Hai Jui hung on his house a banner that read *Loyalty and Filial Piety*.[57] At fifty-seven, having served in the highest office, one to which most licentiates would not even have dared to aspire, he still needed to be reminded to practice those basic virtues he had been taught since childhood. His official career had convinced him that to be loyal to the emperor was by no means a simple matter. Likewise, his family history suggested that it could be complicated and troublesome to be devoted to even one parent unconditionally. In both cases living up to the ideal was a lifetime struggle. Yet as a cultured gentleman he had no choice. The alternative to bearing the moral burden was to give in to the animal instincts of "lesser men." This uncompromising morality could make a single individual's life miserable. Yet it could also make our civilization splendidly enduring. Hai Jui, who traced his ancestry to non-Chinese origins in the northern borderlands, was to carry this cultural tradition down to the southern tip of the empire.

Poverty, which understandably contributed to his many domestic problems and tragedies, had not weakened the will of Hai Jui in the past and never would in the future. He was content to live on the rents from some sixteen acres of land he had inherited from his ancestors. Indeed, in the fifteen years of his retirement he benefited from the gifts of his many admirers and visitors. Yet he continued to live modestly, turning most of this extra income over to charity and the publication of his books.

As his writing attested, Hai's singlemindedness was less a natural instinct than the result of continual spiritual effort. Enlightenment brought him the burden of morality, which in turn could only be borne by enlightenment. If this had not been so, the writing and publication of so many essays would have made little sense.

Any official, essayist Hai Jui argued, must be prepared for destitution.[58] Why should he choose to enter public service? Because of compassion and anger. He must feel sympathetic with those who had to suffer hunger, cold, and illness. He must be indignant at seeing the weak and inarticulate unfairly treated. A silk-robed position provided an opportunity for him to rectify and to give aid. He should have no desire whatsoever for self-gain. Had he been motivated by greed, moralist Hai charged, he would have chosen to be a farmer or an artisan or a merchant. In arriving at this conclusion the ex-governor was in perfect agreement with the dynastic founder, the Hung-wu emperor, who had laid down the principle that a public servant must literally be a servant.

Hai Jui's recall to active service in 1585 was neither a climax nor an anticlimax. Unfortunately for him, it brought him to the lowest point of his life. By this time Chang Chü-cheng had been posthumously disgraced, and anyone who had fallen from the deceased grand-secretary's favor automatically gained some degree of eminence. Yet the court action that reappointed him reflected a reluctant compliance with public opinion rather than an enthusiastic endorsement.[59] Hai, now seventy-two years old, no longer had his earlier confidence that all the evils in the world could be overcome by "a change of heart." Before leaving home he expressed his doubt that the Wan-li emperor would ever put aside his interest in horses and women.[60] Nevertheless, it would have been contrary to his character to decline an opportunity for public service.

His assignment as assistant head of the censorate in Nanking fell short of a responsible position. Nominally the southern capital, the city had not, with the exception of the Cheng-te emperor's pleasure trip, seen any imperial functioning in the past 160 years. The official circles there represented a leisure club of the semi-unemployed. Inadequately paid, all the governmental functionaries stretched their powers of requisition to demand services and goods from the shopkeepers in the metropolitan area in predatory proportions, shocking even by contemporary standards. The atmosphere must have been extremely distressing to someone whose sense of integrity exceeded normal expectations.[61]

Hai Jui was promoted to Censor-in-Chief of Nanking in 1586, the Year of the Dog.[62] But before the order of promotion arrived, he had submitted his most controversial memorial to the throne, in which he urged the Wan-li emperor to institutionalize the severest penalty to stop official corruption. During the reign of the dynastic founder, the Hung-wu emperor, Hai pointed out, officials found guilty of embezzling eight *kuan* of public funds were put to death. Those who were charged with committing more serious offenses suffered the fate of having their skins peeled off and made into balloons filled with grass for public exhibit.[63] However, before the bureaucrats had had the opportunity to digest his message, Hai himself had already been censured by the superintendent of public schools in the Nanking district.[64]

The impeachment paper accused Hai of being the "greatest hypocrite," who made a saint of himself and down-graded Confucius and Mencius as compromising characters and the reigning emperor as a mediocre ruler. His eccentricity was such that when recalled to governmental service he did not even humbly decline. Subsequently he made an issue out of the fact that he had to sell household goods in order to equip himself with a belt and robe. In his own responsible position of overseeing the school system, the petitioning official said, he would not hesitate for a moment to lash any government student and suspend his scholarship if he should ever be so debased as to follow the example of the censor-in-chief. That being so, he would prefer to see Hai Jui dismissed first.

The censure elicited a wave of protest by young scholars in Hai's favor.[65] But at about the same time his own memorial was publicized. The situation was getting out of hand. The emperor personally decided that the censor-in-chief in the southern capital should remain in office. Nevertheless, to his rescript he added the paragraph: "His suggestion for cruel punishment contradicts our sense of good government. Furthermore, he has made some personal criticisms of myself; the wording is silly and inept, even though I have decided to ignore it."[66] The minister of personnel agreed. In his subsequent report to the throne, he said that Hai Jui should never be appointed to an office of any substance, yet he should be retained, as he stood for an abstract standard of official integrity.[67]

These statements, published by the office at the Meridian Gate, actually acknowledged the divergence between theory and practice in governance and, more seriously, exposed the government's inability to reach a consensus between yin and yang. These declarations also destroyed Hai Jui's usefulness. Where was the place for a censor-in-chief whose words could never again be taken seriously? He must have been in the depths of despair during the last months of his life, which extended from the Year of the Dog to the Year of the Pig. During this period he submitted his resignation seven times—and each time was told to stay.[68] His death toward the end of the year must have given the court of Peking a sense of relief. Now no one had to be held responsible for removing a popular hero who was worshipped by the public even though, in the eyes of his fellow bureaucrats and the emperor, he was silly and inept.

6

CH'I CHI-KUANG,
THE LONELY GENERAL

Ch'i Chi-kuang's death on January 17, 1588, also fell in the Year of the Pig, as by the lunar calendar it was the twentieth day of the twelfth month of the previous year. The event was not taken notice of by the court. If it was ever reported to the emperor, it was presumably by the Secret Police. The dispatch therefore never turned up in the palace archives.

Three months before his death, Ch'i's name was mentioned to the Wan-li emperor for the last time by an investigating censor who wanted the throne to consider the general's reappointment. That suggestion cost the censor three months' salary.[1] The imperial rescript on his memorial reminded him that he was endorsing an officer who had recently been impeached. In reality almost three years had lapsed since Ch'i's censure and dismissal. If the emperor had been willing to forgive the general, one of the most capable for many centuries, he could have let the reinstatement take effect without referring to the past. Since in this case he did refer to the past, this meant that Ch'i Chi-kuang had not been forgiven. His close association with Chang Chü-cheng had made him unforgivable—at least throughout Wan-li's reign.

But even without a state burial or a posthumous restoration of honor many decades later, Ch'i Chi-kuang still fared better than other generals. His senior officer and close friend, Yü Ta-yu, was subject to all kinds of criticism and never allowed to hold a responsible position for long, even though he had repeatedly distinguished himself on the battlefield and his effort at reviving the dynasty's military power could be matched only by Ch'i's. Another general, Lu T'ang, was detained before being dismissed.[2] T'ang K'o-ku'an was likewise arrested but was told to redeem himself in combat, which eventually led to his death in an ambush set by the Mongols on the steppes. Ch'i's own lieutenants, including Hu Shou-jen, Wang Yü-lung, Chu Yü, and Chin K'o, were either abruptly discharged from service or exiled to the frontier.[3] Only Liu Hsien, also Ch'i's contemporary, managed to weather many rounds of impeachment and censure. He did so largely because he was directing a protracted campaign against the aborigines in Szechuan and his service was indispensable. After his death his son Liu T'ing inherited his position with reduced rank. He, too, survived many censuring actions and career crises as he gained prominence, only to perish in the ill-directed campaign against Nurhaci in 1619.[4]

The unhappy experiences of these generals could not have been entirely coincidental. There were basic incompatibilities between military operations and the dynasty's style of bureaucratic rule. In essence, the army had to deal with a situation arising from an imbalance. Wars and battles resulted from the uneven growth of socioeconomic forces which had gone beyond the point where they could be politically reconciled. Or sometimes armed conflict was necessary because of a peculiar and extremely distressing situation requiring immediate relief that could not be secured by usual and peaceful means. These military solutions challenged the primary purpose of the bureaucracy of our empire, which had been geared to the principles of stability and balance. In the minds of the bureaucrats strength was not power, regional interests should be minimized rather than freely championed, and there was no distress that could not be relieved by the spirit of sharing.[5]

Although in practice the moral objectives of the government were often compromised, its approach still presented a serious technical handicap to the armed forces. Military commanders, in order to be successful, had to habituate themselves to maintaining a selective vision and be willing to take extreme measures. When facing the enemy they must deliver concentrated and lethal blows; when on the defensive they had to concern themselves with vital points only, generally considering life expendable that could be traded for time and space; and when victorious, they could spare no effort to widen the path of success. None of these strategies could have met with the approval of civil officials preoccupied with the dogmas of restraint and moderation, and whose sense of history, virtually timeless as it was, made them most reluctant to accept the merit of any drastic action based on physical force, which to them led only to temporary and localized gains.[6]

Even the maintenance of army installations in peacetime had to an extent conflicted with the style of civil administration peculiar to the dynasty. A separate system of army logistics which lay outside the control of the civil bureaucracy would have been out of order. Yet to set up a network of supply depots with strategic emphasis and geographical preference also ran counter to the homogeneous development that the Civil Service was determined to encourage. The presence of soldiery was never favorably regarded by a large agrarian population governed in the spirit of simplicity, as both recruitment and discharge tended to create social problems. In numerous cases a soldier entering the service was a farm laborer leaving the productive force. And his eventual return to his village usually added an undesirable element to the local community, as his newly acquired skills and living habits hardly enabled him to resume his former life with ease and comfort. Such problems were compounded in the case of army officers. Unlike other societies where a retired officer could reappear as a man of proven ability entitled to leadership roles in the local community, or become a civil administrator backed by prestige and expertise, the empire offered no such advantages to a commander discharged from our armed forces. Trained to deal with technical precision, he would soon find that elsewhere value was placed on serenity, literary accomplishment, the powers of moral persuasion, and skill in subtle maneuvers—all qualities diametrically opposed to his own talents.

These fundamental incompatibilities were too profound to be overlooked. Not only did civil officials react to army officers with feelings of rivalry and disdain, but also they could, in matters of high-level command, raise questions as to the latters' wisdom. There was room for controversy in every individual case: one outlaw should have been persuaded to lay down arms rather than fight; another, however, should have been quickly crushed with incessant blows rather than being allowed to rest and gain breathing space. Logistical problems could also add to the complexities. A commander could, of course, be punished when his soldiers mutinied and looted the general population. Yet a continual cause of uprising was pay arrearage, which could be completely out of the commanding officer's control.

The dynasty's Civil Service had gained maturity roughly within the hundred years from the mid-fifteenth century to the mid-sixteenth century.[7] During the same period the prestige of army officers had sunk to the lowest level, extreme even by our own standards. The technical difficulty of raising sufficient funds to maintain the military units cannot be ignored as a cause of the decline. But on the other hand, the unitary structure of the government, with its emphasis on ideological cohesion, could never have reached such a final stage of development had it not constantly advanced at the expense of the armed forces. The differences between the two branches of service were too great to allow them to coexist as equals. Yet, before there was any contest for hegemony, the military bureaucracy had been destined to defeat. For a settled empire such as ours, an accomplishment of the most valiant general had to be temporary and localized. And of course army officers were no match for civil officials in gaining influence through rhetoric.

In 1555, when Ch'i Chi-kuang was transferred to Chekiang, the coastal province that was being scourged by Japanese pirates, on the northern frontier the Mongol leader Altan Khan was penetrating Chinese defense lines at will and, when he left, taking the captured population and its movable goods along with him. The decline of the dynasty's military power was not a surprise, but the extent of it was. While despair and confusion reigned along the east coast, a band of pirates, reportedly fifty or seventy men, was bold enough to maraud inland on a route that encircled the southern capital, which—unbelievably—had a garrison boasting, at least on paper, 120,000 men.[8]

A general conclusion could be drawn that the defense installations of the empire, along with their logistical framework, had largely vanished. Ch'i Chi-kuang's contribution was not only the defeat of the pirates. Before the pirates could effectively be dealt with, he had virtually to organize a new army. His book, *Chi-hsiao Hsin-shu*,[9] reveals that Ch'i himself settled the recruiting procedure, decided the pay scale, devised general rules governing personnel assignment, standardized the organization of combat formations, selected weapons, outlined the duties of individual soldiers and their officers, designed his own banners and coordinating signals, invented his own tactics and schemes of maneuver, prescribed military etiquette, and issued his own orders of court martial, which, based on the principle of group responsibility, compelled both officers and men to guarantee one another's performance in combat on threat of the death penalty. He even handed out a recipe for making field rations! But other aspects of army logistics remained under the control of civil officials. The fact that Ch'i had to take responsibility for these details revealed that, until then, the empire had failed to institutionalize its military establishment. There were no military handbooks or field manuals, no schools that specialized in the martial arts, not even an effective ordnance department. If there had been any organizational tables, maintenance charts, and articles of war, they must have been inoperative for a long time.

These historical facts made Ch'i Chi-kuang's remarkable creation nothing less than a personal command, regardless of what he might have wished it to be. Significantly, thirty years later his command still appeared to be more personal than institutional—in fact, to many stability-minded civil officials a potential threat to the dynasty rather than a safeguard of it.

Ch'i's long-term association with Chang Chü-cheng only made his impeachment easier to carry out.

It was extremely paradoxical that in the middle of the sixteenth century the Japanese could violate China's security on the eastern seaboard. In many respects it seemed that the invasion should have been reversed. Not only was Japan much smaller and less populous than China, but also for decades its home islands had been in a state of anarchy. Law and order had completely broken down; the territorial lords were embroiled in warfare with one another, at times even betrayed and dislodged by their own lieutenants. China, on the other hand, was governed by a highly integrated civil bureaucracy; the emperor's orders extended to the remotest corners of his realm. Moreover, the centralized state was supposed to maintain the largest army in the world, backed up by close to two million hereditary military households, each of which was required by law to furnish a soldier for active service at all times.[10]

But there was a huge gulf between theory and practice, and in the case of Ming China between reality and the projected ideal. The registration of hereditary military households had not been put on a sound basis even at the founding of the dynasty, although it was designed to shield the general population from the disturbance of conscription. At the very beginning, large numbers of households were pressed into service; desertion and absconding started as soon as the military colonies were organized.[11] In later centuries the tax-exempt land assigned to these households was sold and mortgaged by the users at will.[12] Increased mobility of the population had made the original concept unworkable. It was not unusual for a colony to be reduced to a skeleton, in some extreme cases a tiny fraction of its former self, such as 2 to 3 percent of its originally recorded strength.[13] As the dwindling manpower could not be advantageously deployed, it was more likely for soldiers to be used by their commanders as construction workers and porters, and no less frequently as domestic servants.[14]

Also responsible was the supply system. Army logistics was integrated with the civil administration, which operated on the principle of lateral transmission of supplies at the lowest possible level.[15] The Ministry of Revenue was really a huge accounting office, which supervised the scheduled and automatic deliveries of revenue-collecting agencies directly to the corresponding disbursing agencies. The services and supplies were by no means assembled and routed at intermediate depots. They were channeled into numerous short and interlinking supply lines which covered the empire like a closely woven net. The number of intermediate agencies must have been greatly reduced as a result. But the lowest civil office, that of county magistrate, could be required to make deliveries at a score of disbursing agencies, each of which would in turn receive consignments from a score of suppliers. This system permanently deprived the higher echelon of the opportunity to develop a logistical capacity to keep pace with changing conditions, at the same time ensuring the likelihood of shortage in all units, as apparently some of the many delivering agencies for one reason or another would become delinquent, while others were neither able nor required to make up the deficiencies. After the system had been in operation for over two hundred years, the accounts also drifted away from reality.

This way of managing supplies, with its centralized direction but decentralized execution, had a more profound effect than was generally realized. The annual moving of grain to Peking was a good example. The foodstuff was collected from the land-tax quotas of a large number of counties and prefectures in the southern provinces. Nominally, a special transportation corps within the army was organized to haul the supplies on the Grand Canal; this comprised 120,000 officers and men operating close to 12,000 grain boats. Yet, no supporting services were ever set up within the transportation corps. Army captains and lieutenants commanding individual ships, who had received the quantities of grain from the tax-paying communities, were held directly responsible to the imperial government.[16] More illustrative was the construction of grain boats, due to be rebuilt every ten years. A "dockyard" was established on the Huai River, which in its heyday had an annual capacity of over 700 craft. But inasmuch as the services and supplies that were to contribute to the ship construction program had never been fiscally organized, the divided resources could not be pulled together under a central administering body. The so-called dockyard had to be divided into eighty-two separate units—in effect eighty-two boat-yards. Its site on the riverbank was a long strip of land only thirty yards wide. But the adjacent constructional units with their individual housing facilities extended over two and a half miles.[17]

Needless to say, such an organization had little sophistication, linked as it was to the technological level of the village. A case in point was the turning out of high-quality shirts of mail by palace artisans for the emperor's bodyguards;[18] the armor used by field troops generally consisted of quilted cotton garments, some reinforced with iron strips, others stuffed with wastepaper.[19] This was a situation that even Ch'i Chi-kuang could not correct. Toward the end of his career the basic equipment at his command was still submitted by numerous communities as a part of their tax quotas.[20] The crude manufacture and lack of standardization of gear must have accounted for the quality of the field army. It could not be significantly different from a large force of militia.

Furthermore, army officers, including high commanders, were not required to be profound thinking men. In them, gallantry in action was much more highly valued. Liu T'ing, who had yet to die in Liaotung, was famous for the long-handled sword he wielded, which weighed no less than 160 pounds.[21] Tu Sung, another general who laid down his life in the same campaign, was even more brutish and unschooled. Never lacking dash when at the head of charging troops, in times of defeat and humiliation he would not hesitate to destroy his own weapons, armor, and saddle, threaten to commit suicide, or shave his head, declaring himself an ordained Buddhist abbot.[22]

Almost all officers had inherited their positions from their forefathers.[23] By a complicated procedure, men of junior grade received their commissions without diminution; but descendants of general officers inherited reduced ranks. The military service examination, intended to open army commissions to all qualified candidates, fell short of this goal, as commanders originating outside of hereditary circles were rare. The examination itself emphasized archery and horsemanship. The written portion, given by civil officials, never really dealt with military science. The so-called military school also offered a curriculum that gave preponderant attention to the Confucian canon. Its primary concern, furthermore, was "to teach the student to write 100 characters daily."[24]

In order to compensate for the lack of generalship among the generals, the court of Peking empowered governors and governors-general to give orders to army commanders. Under them, censorial officials commissioned as military circuit intendants extended their power of surveillance to take full charge of operations.[25] This setup merged well with the bureaucratic structure of the government, as both logistics and communication had to be integrated under civil leadership. Territorial control had to be stressed. After all, the army was organized with the principal aim of pacifying provincial districts, not meeting or launching full-scale invasions. This preconsideration held especially true in the southern provinces, the coastline hitherto having been regarded as an insulated barrier.

Civil officials, nevertheless, lacked intrinsic and professional interest in the affairs of the army. In those territories where the military colonies were in a state of decline they let them fall into further inactivity. It was the mid-century Japanese invasion that changed the picture: it dramatized the risk of an undefended coastline and showed that, in order to mend the situation, general officers had to be selected from groups of individuals who possessed qualities more sophisticated than those expected of the best sergeants and platoon leaders.

The marauders who rampaged on the eastern seaboard in the sixteenth century were not exactly pirates. Onshore they built inland bases and besieged walled cities. Their incessant raids lasted for at least two decades. Nor were they exclusively Japanese. Most of the time they cooperated with mixed bands of Chinese; on many occasions the latter predominated. Their leadership was even supplied by Chinese adventurers. But within the fighting element, the role played by the natives could not be more than auxiliary. The invasion was based in Japan; and the Japanese furnished all the military skill and military equipment.[26]

The problem of piracy was inseparable from international trade, which, even though proscribed by law, had been flourishing on the eastern coast for some time, engaging adventurers of different nationalities. The most impressive junks in the traffic measured 100 feet in length and 30 feet in width, with shells 7 inches thick, and were therefore unmatched by the government's warships. It was said that on a busy day during the trading season as many as 1,200 large and small ships hugged China's coastline, extending their trade routes on a huge arc that ran from the Japanese islands to the Gulf of Siam.[27] Ports of call were designated on the desolate offshore islands not covered by official patrols. In the absence of a court system to enforce contractual obligations and settle cases of indebtedness, a score of sea captains, most of them Chinese but some of them undoubtedly of mixed parentage, acted as armed arbiters in an attempt to fill the legal vacuum. They eventually rose to be pirate leaders.[28]

Before the officials moved in to confiscate their ships and seal off their harbors, some of the pirate leaders had already extended their influence inland by marrying into families of the gentry and inducing the latter to join in their adventures. But when they began to service their ships inland and, as de facto authorities on the seaboard, summoned villagers to their "courts" for questioning, the imperial government was forced to act. Such a maritime power, however embryonic, threatened the agrarian-based dynasty in theory as well as in practice.[29]

Yet, when the showdown came, the weakness of the imperial government was thoroughly exposed: its formidableness appeared only on paper. Senior commanders had no inkling of the number of soldiers at their service, or the number of ships. Regional commanders demanded cash payments from the general population before they would consent to function. Soldiers characteristically started to flee at the first glimpse of the enemy. Combat units had not had a field maneuver for so long that they marched in close formation. "When one man was lost, ten thousand stampeded." The distressing situation soon became universal.[30] The most heroic resistance to the invading pirates was put up by civilians hastily organized on city walls.

On the other hand, the Japanese, comprised of fighting men from Yamaguchi, Bungo, Ozumi, Satsuma, Hakata Bay, and Tsushima and Gotto islands, were noted for their lack of a unified command.[31] Unable to develop a war aim, in the early stages of the campaign they followed their Chinese leaders in the vague hope that the devastation they wrought would force the court of Peking to open trade, perhaps granting army and naval commissions to those leaders. Once this hope was dashed by Governor-General Hu Tsung-hsien, who trapped the traitors at negotiations and delivered their heads to the capital, the subsequent waves of invasion from Japan gradually developed into a senseless affair, serving no purpose other than to satisfy the predatory urge of the warriors.[32]

But China's weakness was Japan's strength. While lacking unity at the top, the Japanese demonstrated remarkable organizational ability on the battleground, indicating that, however warlike, there was a certain solidarity within their social order which, in contrast to China's, was rooted at the bottom. Chinese writers were unanimously impressed by the stern discipline the invaders were able to impose on their fighting men, in action and in camp.[33] Uniformity of military skill marked the pirates more than the temporarily recruited mercenaries. Unlike rebelling Chinese peasants, they repeatedly defeated the government forces, which were overwhelmingly superior in number.

The invaders arrived on the Chinese coast in ships carrying about a hundred men each. Though small landing parties were reported, a major wave involved scores of such ships, and therefore several thousand men. At the high point of their marauding, the pirates were said to be able to set up an enclave of 20,000 men. Natives were either enticed or forced to join the ranks. But subsequently some of those captured were sold in Japan's slave market.[34] The pirates maintained their mobility by seizing inland shipping. Their loot included not only valuables but also bulky cargo. At least one source indicates that they collected silk cocoons in quantity and assigned village women to work on them, thus showing themselves enterprising enough to enter the area of manufacture.[35] When the ships could not be conveniently moored they were burned on the beaches. In all events, the invaders made the systematic pillage of the coastal provinces a long-term project, and with the profits they reaped, were ready to quarter in China for the winter. In the spring they would be relieved by new waves of invaders. There were also instances where the Japanese constructed their ships for the return voyage on Chinese shores.

The invincibility of the Japanese was based on the skillful handling of contact weapons and close teamwork within small units the size of platoons and squads. Infantry tactics, in fact, accounted for most of their field performance. The twin swords, in particular, were wielded with such dexterity that onlookers "could see only the flash of the weapon, not the man." Squad leaders gave commands with folding fans. Usually they directed the swordsmen to lift their weapons upward, and as soon as the attention of the enemy was distracted, they would signal the lowering of the blades, the sharpness of which exceeded anything of Chinese make. Since each swordsman in action could cover as large an area as eighteen feet in diameter, this skill gave the invaders an advantage in close combat. Chinese observers also noted that the Japanese used bows eight feet long and arrowheads two inches wide, and that their javelins "were thrown before they could be seen." Firearms had never been considered vital by the pirates. Ch'i Chi-kuang himself mentioned that the Japanese had introduced the musket to China, but there is no evidence that they themselves used it effectively. Scattered evidence indicates that the heavier guns in their possession had been captured from the Chinese.[36]

In the early phase of the campaign Chinese officials persistently overlooked the importance of teamwork. As the Japanese were recognized as being superior in soldiery, an effort was made by those officials to recruit Chinese individuals capable of acrobatic performance—including boxing instructors, Buddhist monks, salt smugglers, and aborigines from the southwest—as an answer to the challenge. Only after their troops were repeatedly ambushed and annihilated by the enemy did the organizers for the defense come to the conclusion that the problem was far more fundamental than they had thought.[37]

Although the Japanese usually entered the field in bands of no more than thirty men each, such platoons were well coordinated, even when they were operating at a distance from each other. Signals were given by blowing seashells. The invaders were experienced at using native guides, sending out patrols, deploying in depth, creating deception, and driving refugees in front of them to harass and confuse the defenders.[38] Ironically, the government forces were not versed in such basic tactics. At best, the stout-minded would dash toward the enemy unaided, only to fall victim to the better trained pirates, who would then proceed to encircle and mop up the remaining government troops. The numerous rivers, creeks, and lakes in the territory were the source of yet more woe for the routed units. Once the men started to flee, many of them eventually died in water—an infamous fate that Supreme Commander Hu Tsung-hsien himself once narrowly escaped.[39]

Holding the advantage, the pirates usually assumed defensive positions if they had the choice. They preferred to wait for the Chinese to make mistakes. Ch'i Chi-kuang made the following observation:

> The numerous battles I have fought over the past several years give me the impression that the pirates always manage to sit on the heights waiting for us. Usually they hold on until evening, when our soldiers become tired. Then they dash out. Or else, when we start to withdraw, they will catch us out of step to launch their counterattack. It seems that they always manage to send forth their units when they are fresh and spirited. They adorn their helmets with colored strings and animal horns of metallic colors and ghostly shapes to frighten our soldiers. Many of them carry mirrors. Their spears and swords are polished to a shine and look dazzling under the sun. Our soldiers, therefore, are awed by them during the hours of delay before contact.[40]

Thus, despite what official circles called the "campaign by government forces to suppress the pirates," in terms of military proficiency such a phrase was misleading. At least until Ch'i Chi-kuang perfected his tactical command, the engagement could better be described as a contest between Japanese professionals and Chinese amateurs.

When organizing his command, Ch'i Chi-kuang turned his back on the hereditary families and military colonies. His volunteers were recruited from the inland districts in Chekiang.[41] This was possible because the government, facing a protracted campaign, had authorized a surtax on all existing revenues to finance it.[42] Ch'i exhorted his soldiers:

> Any day you are in the service, even a rainy and windy day when you are sitting there with folded arms, no one can do away with the three cents of silver due you. But every bit of this silver comes from the tax money turned in by the general population, some from your own local districts. At home you are farmers yourselves. Who of you is not? You

must now think of the toil and trouble of working in the field to raise the tax money, and be glad to have the present easy time of receiving silver payments. The taxpayers feed you for a whole year without asking you to work. All they expect is that you beat off the pirates in one engagement or two. If you do not even try to kill the pirates to give those people protection, what are they feeding you for? You might get by with a court martial, but even then, Heaven would let someone somewhere put you to death.[43]

With this combination of moral suasion and the threats of popular religion Ch'i established combat discipline among his recruits. He declared that he would execute an officer if his entire unit ran away from the enemy, or his subordinate commanders if the stampede occurred and the officer perished in his effort to halt the retreat. If a squad leader should die without the support of his men, the death penalty would be applied to all the soldiers in the squad.[44] Although such extreme measures could not be put into effect in more than a few selected cases, its intimidating effect achieved the purpose and Ch'i's command became most difficult to beat. To keep conditions this way he had frequently to invoke this article of war. He pointed out that even in the midst of disastrous defeat there had to be some deserving individuals whose merit must be recognized. Conversely, even after an overwhelming victory the few officers and men who had failed to perform their duties should never be allowed to go unpunished.[45] In a memorial to the emperor, Ch'i recounted the battle of 1562, when his troops tried to recapture a stone bridge from the Japanese. The first attempt failed and all thirty-six men in the platoon died. The second platoon, following it up, also lost half of its men. At this time the survivors began to fall back. Ch'i, on the spot, personally cut down the retreating platoon leader in order to renew the attack. Eventually the enemy was overpowered and the battle ended with one of the most satisfying victories of Ch'i's career.[46]

Ch'i's discipline was sometimes terrifying. He left many instructions to cut off the ears of his own soldiers for a number of offenses.[47] An unconfirmed story held that he actually ordered the execution of his second son. But brutal or not, with his persistence and constant personal supervision he built up an army that was truly invincible. He could assemble a whole division of troops in the rain and they would stay in the drizzle for hours without shirking their duty.[48]

Discipline, especially discipline in combat, nevertheless went hand in hand with pride and self-confidence, which cannot be sustained without skill and proficiency. Ch'i Chi-kuang had to work hard with his men on the training ground. Like the Japanese, he focused his attention on contact weapons. All these weapons, he further stressed, could be mastered through learning the technique of wielding a simple wooden pole—the basic of basics.[49]

The techniques adopted by Ch'i had been handed down through oral tradition by individuals, some of them working as army instructors. Yü Ta-yu had made some effort to narrate the techniques; but it was Ch'i who put the instructions together in the form of a technical manual. The fundamental principle could be said to take a "dialectic approach" to the art.[50] Every posture had its duality: the static and kinetic aspects, the guarded and unguarded portions of the body, the frontal and lateral alignment, the defensive and offensive potentials—in short, the yin and yang. One could also maneuver a contact weapon consonantly with the techniques used in dancing and boxing, since every motion involved three phases: the start, the pause or reversal, and the continuation until the recess. Whether for effectiveness or gracefulness, the mastery of the art depended upon proper rhythm—or perfect timing in transforming the yin to the yang.[51] The general emphatically reminded his officers and men that in dueling with an enemy with a contact weapon, the cardinal rule was to maneuver the opponent into a false move before delivering the fatal blow.[52] In more detailed analysis he gave fancy designations to different poses and gestures, such as "riding the tiger," "a hermit fishing," "the maiden's embroidery needle," "an iron buffalo plowing the land," and so on. Each case was a study of motion at the instant of equilibrium before reversal.

The more creative part of his tactics had to do with teamwork, embodied in the concept that each infantry squad must coordinate the use of long and short, offensive and defensive weapons. In dealing with the pirates, the most effective weapon of all was the lance, which had an overall length of twelve feet or even longer. Ideal for making deceptive movements, it nevertheless had to be manipulated at some distance from the enemy. Once the lancer missed his target and came within striking distance of the opposing swordsman he was virtually disarmed.[53] In order to provide a protective screen for the four lancers in the squad, Ch'i assigned four soldiers to walk ahead of them, one carrying an elongated pentagon shield on the right and one carrying a small round shield on the left, to be followed by two carrying bamboo trees complete with upper branches. Behind the lancers were two rearguard men with three-pronged, fork-shaped weapons, from which arrows propelled by firecrackers could also be fired. Including a corporal and a cook-porter, a squad consisted of twelve men.[54]

The symmetry of the squad earned it the name of the "mandarin duck formation." Yet, though both shield-men carried swords, the one on the right with the longer shield was supposed to dig in to hold the advance position of the squad. The man on the left with the round shield must throw javelins, crawl on the ground until he reached the enemy, and lure him out into the open. That done, the bamboo-tree carriers would pin the opposing pirates down at a distance to permit the lancers to throw more easily. The last two soldiers guarded the flanks and rear, and when needed, supplied a second line of striking power. Their fork-shaped weapons, however, could not be maneuvered to create deception.[55]

Obviously, the success of this operation depended upon the cooperation of the soldiers; there was little opportunity for individual heroism.[56] Instructions were repeatedly given by Ch'i Chi-kuang that soldiers in each squad must be rewarded or punished collectively and that under no circumstances should the lancers be separated from their protective screen. But when the terrain and position of the enemy justified it, the squad might split itself into two identical sections and proceed abreast; or leaving the fork carriers behind, it could line up the eight soldiers in a continuous front line, with the lancers alternating with those carrying shields and bamboo trees.[57]

The use of rattan shields, pitchforks, and bamboo trees as standard weapons suggests that Ch'i's command had never separated itself from its peasant outlook. Later the bamboo tree was replaced in some instances by an antler-shaped metal weapon; but its function was still to obstruct the opponent rather than to inflict wounds.[58] Using two soldiers to perform the work of one, his tactics could never earn a high efficiency rating by any objective standard.

It would be inexplicable if Ch'i Chi-kuang had been unaware of the significance of firearms. He used them satisfactorily in engagements, lectured on their importance before his officers and men, and brought them to the attention of the emperor. Yet he never abandoned the formation and fighting methods of his infantry squad, which, compared with contemporary uses of weapons, seemed to be lagging a hundred years behind. This incongruity was a very complicated matter, however.

The issue of bringing the conducting of warfare up-to-date had arisen before. Yü Ta-yu, who had repeatedly defeated the Japanese offshore, had pointed out that the so-called pirates were skillful at land warfare but inexperienced in sea battle. He had continually argued in favor of equipping more warships with heavy artillery and intercepting the intruders before they reached the shore. "In sea battle," he went on, "there is no special trick. Larger ships defeat smaller ships. Larger guns defeat smaller guns. The side that has more ships defeats the side that has fewer. The side that has more guns defeats the side that has less." In a message submitted to the governor-general, he bluntly declared that if half the funds supporting the ground forces had been diverted for sea operations the problem with the pirates would have come to an end. Yet, despite his prestige and performance record, Yü's agitation in no way changed the course of the war or the government policy on equipment.[59]

Unknown to Yü himself, his suggestion involved more than modernizing weapon systems. In order to follow his advice the fiscal authorities in the provinces would have had to be integrated, and centralized treasuries and large arsenals set up. Not only would additional personnel have to be recruited to manage these offices, but also their functions, more responsive to modern technology, would differ from all lines of duty hitherto known to the bureaucrats. Still, the greatest difficulty lay in the question of where to draw a line to limit the reform. Functional specialization of a handful of officials would not be enough. Their operations, in order to be successful, required the support of other bureaus and departments, which must also be rendered in the same businesslike manner.

But our empire was a large conglomeration of village communities. State affairs had always been conducted through symbolism and ritual; justice had sometimes been sacrificed in the name of morality; and numerous irregularities had been tolerated in order to evade insolvable problems. It was from devotion to abstract principles that the bureaucracy drew its strength. Many internal business links had never been established; the government was incapable of being precise at details. Thus, although he was unaware of it, Yü Ta-yu had already touched on the dilemma that China had yet to face for many centuries to come. A large agrarian nation which had been settled with a common ideology in pursuit of uniformity and stability could find no easy way to avail itself of modern technology, which could never be employed to serve such a loose organization and preserve its status quo.

Ch'i Chi-kuang's command started in 1559 with 3,000 men. Two years later its authorized strength doubled. In 1562 it was further expanded to 10,000 men.[60] But Ch'i never had a supply officer, a quartermaster general, or a commisariat's office within the civil government with which he could deal. As the maintenance of his troops was contributed to by many counties and prefectures, no unified or permanent factory capable of producing advanced types of weapons was ever created.[61] The normal procurement procedure called for the assigning of quotas to the local districts by provincial officials. As commanding general Ch'i produced samples; the local officials then copied these models using whatever resources they had at their disposal. The muskets thus manufactured had a tendency to explode, as Ch'i related. Soldiers therefore did not dare hold them with both hands to steady their aim. It often occurred that lead shot did not suit the gun barrels they were made for and fuses would not ignite.[62] Given the loading time of the muskets, Ch'i Chi-kuang could not help but see their limitations. Even in the later years of his career, he authorized only two muskets for each infantry squad and maintained that each company of musketeers must be accompanied by a company of soldiers carrying contact weapons. Any ratio that favored firearms would be unrealistic and might endanger the army as a whole.[63]

The composition of Ch'i's infantry squad also reflected social influences. When recruiting, he deliberately turned away volunteers from the cities and accepted only peasants. It was with more than prejudice that he classified the former as crafty and roguish. It would be illogical for a man of a steady trade in the city to join the army as a soldier, whose pay was never abundant and possibility for career advancement even less promising. The recruitment, therefore, usually attracted only urban misfits who looked at enlistment as a temporary solution to the food and lodging problem until something else turned up. Such undesirables, singled out by Ch'i for rejection, were those "whose countenance was fair, whose eyes were shiny, and whose movements were light and nimble." Did his army have no use for nimbleness? His experience had taught him that a man fulfilling this description would, "before facing the enemy, work out a method of self-preservation, and at the critical moment not only desert but also instigate others to do so in order to provide cover for himself." All things considered, Ch'i Chi-kuang had to turn to the rural population for his supply of soldiers whose characteristics were "sturdiness and dependability."[64] Consequently, his tactics had been partly designed to suit the traits of his recruits. The two soldiers who wielded bamboo trees, for instance, were required to have muscle power; maneuverability was not expected from them. The inclusion of bamboo trees as weapons was frankly acknowledged to embolden the peasant soldiers.

Unlike Yü Ta-yu, who continued to agitate for better equipment and higher proficiency of the armed forces,[65] to be achieved by supporting one soldier by the allowances now allocated for two, Ch'i Chi-kuang generally accepted conditions as they were. Considering the social milieu, the proposal to upgrade the quality of the army with fewer and better soldiers had its impractical side. Fundamentally the imperial army was an all-purpose army; as a permanent institution it was expected to coordinate with other state institutions and, above all, to be integrated with Chinese society. Among its many missions the most important in the interior was to crush peasant rebellions, and sometimes to overpower the minority groups in the mountain regions.[66] Local overpopulation, rural unemployment, natural disasters, and misgovernment often caused uprisings of this type, whose fluid and unpredictable nature made them beyond the handling capacity of mobile task forces. Often the rebels were able to tie down contingents of the imperial army and compel them to operate under the living conditions in the rural areas. With the advantages of military quality neutralized or greatly reduced, numbers more than ever remained a decisive factor. On the other hand, the establishment of an elite corps with highly selected and better-paid personnel could create more social problems than it could solve. Such a force would forever remain a foreign body in the social order. In fact, the impracticality of Yü Ta-yu's proposal could be compared to the policy of building a modern navy in order to discourage foreign trade.

Aligning himself with traditional statecraft and its agrarian emphasis, Ch'i Chi-kuang quietly built up his corps of volunteers. His men sometimes fought alongside soldiers from hereditary military families. They were paid at the rate of day laborers. But an additional incentive was provided by the "rewards" following the campaign, the established rate being thirty ounces of silver for each enemy head cut off and turned in.[67]

The record of Ch'i's tactical command accredited it, from the time of its inception in 1559, with having attacked heavily defended positions, fought in confrontations, relieved sieges, and pursued the pirates to offshore islands without losing a battle.[68] Ch'i Chi-kuang never attempted anything overly ambitious or even truly innovative; but when he was committed to anything he thought it over well. His handbook went into such practical details as that on the march he anticipated that some soldiers would use the need to urinate as an excuse to leave their units, and that under enemy attack some of the men's "faces would turn yellow and throats run dry," and they would "forget everything they had ever learned about combat." He predicted the percentage of firearms that would never fire, and the number of shots that would be fired but do no damage to the enemy. On the battlefield, he candidly pointed out, few could put more than 20 percent of their skill to work. "Whoever could put out 50 percent would have no rival."[69] All this, however, was not intended to be pessimistic. The grim realities only called for more intensive drilling and deliberate planning before contact with the enemy.

Two or three days before a battle, Ch'i Chi-kuang demanded up-to-date intelligence reports every two hours. He maintained a reconnaissance company under his own control. Maps sketched in red and black ink were prepared for briefing his officers, whenever possible along with clay models to simulate the terrain.[70] His units carried charts showing the hours of sunrise and sunset on specific days of the year. A string of 740 beads was used as a timepiece, to be counted in synchronization with an ordinary walking pace.[71] In these ways Ch'i prepared himself for the engagement from every conceivable angle before jump-off, in which on many occasions he personally took part.[72] As commanding general Ch'i knew his men and knew them well. Many years later he could still reel off the names of individuals who led the first waves of assault in his major and minor battles.[73]

Even though Ch'i Chi-kuang became commander-in-chief in Fukien Province in 1563, his operations involved little strategic planning. His corps of volunteers remained essentially a tactical command. With firearms not playing any significant role in the fighting and cavalry charges also unfeasible in the rice-paddy-covered south, there was no chance to develop the kind of variety characteristic of combined arms in action. Field maneuvers were generally restricted. Ch'i's own favorite tactic was to storm the strongholds of the enemy line. The risk of attacking the more substantial portion of the opponent's entrenchment was greatly reduced by selecting unexpected avenues of approach and striking with high speed.[74] Ch'i's men had the endurance to suffer the hardships of rough terrain in order to employ the element of surprise. Ambushes were laid by them whenever possible. Their simple equipment enabled them to move briskly.

Again and again, the commanding general was willing to sustain the initial loss of a battle. His experience had convinced him that once the hardest fighting was over, the lines held by the pirates would disintegrate. Many of their followers, especially Chinese natives, would lose the will to resist and would lay down their arms. Its continual success established the reputation of Ch'i's command of being able to annihilate in a matter of hours divisions of pirates that other government troops had been unable to subdue in months. In these operations Ch'i usually employed numerical superiority to achieve his swift and sweeping victories, with the obvious exception of the winter of 1563–64, when he was seriously outnumbered and the battle dragged on for fifty days.[75]

Yet, when the siege of Hsien-yu was lifted in the spring of 1564, the campaign against the pirates changed its complexion. The Japanese, realizing that armed raids on the coast were no longer profitable, gradually withdrew from the adventure.[76] Those that continued were made largely by Chinese bands who now drifted to Kwangtung, away from the region where Sino-Japanese trade had once flourished. Without a formal declaration, the empire had finally achieved its military objective. Now the amphibious bandits could be dealt with strictly as internal insurgents.

In the course of events, Ch'i Chi-kuang had established himself as the most successful Ming general. Although not the most straightforward, he must be recognized as the most adaptable general. As such, he saw warfare first as a contest of will power and second as an application of military science and technology. For an agrarian nation managed by a civil bureaucracy whose object was to resist international trade, the use of technology should never be allowed to upset the empire's constitution and therefore to defeat its purpose.

Three years later Ch'i Chi-kuang was transferred to the north. Although his rise to prominence had been the result of the peculiar situation in the middle of the century, he nevertheless owed a great deal of his success to the unreserved support and patronage of a civil official. Among the bureaucrats T'an Lun himself was a man of unusual aptitudes and accomplishments. A doctoral degree holder, he followed his offices on the seaboard, culminating in the governorship of Fukien, with the achievement of becoming a specialist in military affairs. His love of action was such that often, under the pretense of observing the fighting, he would accompany the combat troops to the front, and before officers and men were aware of it, would have moved to the forward position. Once he became so involved in fighting that he was covered with blood up to his elbows. Eventually he accumulated a lifetime record of 21,500 enemy heads submitted by the troops who had in one way or another been placed under his leadership.[77] When Ch'i Chi-kuang made the suggestion to train volunteers, T'an gave the plan his hearty approval. Afterward he had seen to it that this corps of volunteers was properly supplied and not overtaxed in field operations, and above all, that its merit was recognized. He had also been instrumental in working for Ch'i's promotion to commander-in-chief.[78] In 1567, when T'an

Lun was appointed governor-general of North Chihli in charge of defense installations around Peking, it was only natural that he should suggest to the throne that Ch'i Chi-kuang be transferred to his defense command to take charge of troop training.[79]

Arriving in early 1568, Ch'i was later to become commander-in-chief at Chichou, the principal garrison city in North Chihli, for a period of fifteen years. During those years T'an Lun was promoted to minister of war and died in office, but not before he and Ch'i Chi-kuang had given the Chichou command a new surge of life.

The problems they had to deal with were numerous. Immediately after his arrival Ch'i discovered that even his own status was an unsettled issue. Beneath the awkward situation lay the fact that the military had been subject to civil dominance for so long that there were no channels through which senior officers could exercise their administrative functions. Many of the generals were semi-illiterate at best. Their subordinates, on garrison duty in local districts, were at the beck and call of the Civil Service magistrates and prefects. With army logistics out of their hands, these field commanders had been forced to limit their performance to leading battle formations in combat.[80] Ch'i Chi-kuang's elevation to a position that required him to supervise and direct all elements falling under his command in peacetime actually created a situation that deviated from standard practice.

By nature a northern command had little in common with conditions in the south. The Mongolian borderland harbored a constant threat. Periodic droughts compelled the nomadic hordes to make attacks on the Chinese frontier, where military unpreparedness invited deeper and more frequent incursions. The Mongols' greatest advantage resided in their mobility and concentrated striking power. Cavalry charges remained their dominant mode of fighting, even though they also sometimes laid siege. An onslaught organized by them could involve 100,000 mounts on the rampage. When Altan united the tribes in the steppes extending over one thousand miles from east to west, the Ming frontier forces, trapped in their defense positions and hopelessly scattered, never found a way to stop his annual raids.[81]

The Chichou command was one of nine defense areas on the northern frontier. With its associated garrison towns, it formed a buffer zone around Peking; but it was separate from the capital garrison. According to the order of battle, it should have had 80,000 men bearing arms plus 22,000 combat horses.[82] Its actual strength was unknown. Among the soldiers organic to the command were conscripts from military colonies in the territory. Referred to as "host soldiers," they were in principle locally supported. Additional personnel were furnished by districts outside the defense area and were known as "guest soldiers." Although their transfer was in fact permanent, the districts from which they originated were never free of their residual responsibility to support them. The central government also subsidized the command. Still, there were soldiers from hereditary military families in the interior provinces whose frontier duty was limited to the spring and autumn months. In practice few of them came in person; they paid hired substitutes, whose numbers usually did not correspond to those originally prescribed. The supply system dictated that the command was to consist of bodies of fighting men deriving their pay from a variety of sources, some of which existed only on paper. The quality of these men was also an unknown quantity.[83]

The loose organization and lack of integration in service support had not been completely unintentional. Behind it lay the apprehension that any efficient general would eventually make himself the final answer to all political questions. History had provided many illustrations that the installation of such a general in the capital district could mark the beginning of the end of a dynasty.[84] Ch'i Chi-kuang's ambition to build up the fighting efficiency of the Chichou command, therefore, was destined to encounter obstacles of many kinds, some of them having the sanctions of the Civil Service and the force of tradition.

Fortunately for Ch'i, his design and purpose had been shared by an important figure in the court, Chang Chü-cheng. Chang himself had been appointed grand-secretary only months before Ch'i's arrival. He had yet to machinate to make himself the number one statesman of the empire. But he had already set his sights on rejuvenating the armed forces, with the Chichou command looming large in his schemes. Ch'i Chi-kuang was soon to discover that he did not need to deal with the political issues himself. What needed to be done had already been arranged by Governor-General T'an Lun and Grand-Secretary Chang Chü-cheng. What they failed to deliver was beyond anyone's reach.

As grand-secretary, Chang had no authority to issue formal instructions. He was not even free to discuss institutional reform in the court. What he did was to write personal letters to his associates, urging them to memorialize the throne with proposals of his own; then in his official capacity he drafted rescripts for the emperor approving those proposals. Serving first one emperor who had no genuine interest in state affairs and then another who was a minor, he was able gradually to make his influence felt within officialdom. The bureaucratic rule of the empire had reached such an advanced stage that all the hidden needs and wants of thousands of individuals, along with their personal aspirations, were irreversibly linked to the gigantic status quo; now even an urgently needed technical reform could not be overtly attempted to disturb the delicate balance. Only when a suggestion was made by the functionary who had jurisdiction over the issue and it was approved by the emperor could it be implemented. Sometimes the entire process was a matter of pretense; but as long as Chang Chü-cheng was alive the opposition found it difficult to challenge him.[85]

The changes within the Chichou command were introduced in the following manner. Ch'i's original proposal, which would have placed 100,000 selected recruits under his command for intensive training for three years, was too ambitious to be put into effect.[86] No effort was subsequently made even to integrate the contingents of northern soldiers. But Ch'i was permitted to bring into the defense area the volunteers he had recruited in the south, along with their officers. The first group comprised 3,000 men; the authorized strength was continually increased until it reached 20,000 men.[87] In order to stress Ch'i's unusual function, Chang Chü-cheng had hoped, and for a short period managed, to confer on him the title of "Superintendent of Military Affairs at Chichou." No such title had ever been granted an army officer in the dynasty's history. After considerable criticism, the grand-secretary bowed to public opinion and later changed the title to "Commander-in-Chief." But other senior officers in the defense area were removed to give Ch'i undivided authority.[88] On T'an Lun's recommendation, all civil officials in the district were explicitly instructed not to interfere with Ch'i's management. T'an further suggested that for a three-year period Ch'i Chi-kuang should be free from censorial criticisms; to this the censors furiously objected.[89] The rescript from the throne finally called for a compromise. No such immunity was granted; yet the censors were reminded of the paramount importance of Ch'i's training program and told to accommodate themselves to it. Their tour of duty to the Chichou command was now limited to once a year. Those who tried to obstruct the general's administration were quietly removed by the grand-secretary.[90]

At the outset the Chichou command received an extra allocation of combat horses and funds for manufacturing firearms and wagons.[91] Though not prodigious in quantity, the appropriation nevertheless caused jealousy and contention. There was also rivalry between northerners and southerners, between local conscripts and recruits, and between officers of the old school and those of the new training program. In his private correspondence to T'an Lun and Ch'i Chi-kuang, Grand-Secretary Chang Chü-cheng urged them to practice humility.[92] The critics, he warned, were "searching for your faults and determined to degrade and discredit you." But one argument only led to another. The best way to handle the situation was to make peace with the critics in order to ease the tension. One time Altan's hordes were about to attack the empire's defense line but at the last moment turned away without giving battle. Personally Chang regarded this retreat as the result of the prompt mobilization of the Chichou command and therefore labeled the efforts of two other defense areas to claim the credit as "shameful," "absurd," and "ridiculous." Yet he confided to Governor-General T'an that he had already accepted their claims on behalf of the emperor. The matter was not even sent to the Ministry of War for evaluation as it normally would have been, because the opening of a debate "would have ended with more controversies." On the contrary, Chang instructed the governor-general to submit a memorial to the throne also paying tribute to the other commands but refraining from mentioning the merit of Chichou. This was the only way to silence the jealous rumblings and force the malicious rivals to "chew their tongues in disgrace."[93]

Outwardly the grand-secretary had achieved statesmanship by his unusual move of turning yang to yin. By pretending that the balance was maintained, he should have promoted good feelings. But in doing so he actually made his management more personal than ever. Inasmuch as the charge of favoritism could never be sufficiently silenced by appeasement, he had to continue to keep his entrusted lieutenants within a confidential circle. The Chichou command appeared more and more as a petty project of his, and his attitude toward Ch'i Chi-kuang appeared to be more patronizing after T'an Lun's death in 1577. The following year the grand-secretary had to leave Peking to bury his father. He was so concerned about Ch'i's sense of security during his absence that he wrote the general to inform him that the next governor-general of North Chihli was to be Liang Meng-lung, "a disciple of mine, who will not do you any harm." Ch'i Chi-kuang had furnished a company of soldiers to serve as Chang's bodyguards. The grand-secretary selected half-a-dozen musketeers from it and included them in his retinue, but sent back the rest. By special courier he also sent the general copies of his personal correspondence with Liang Meng-lung.[94] With messengers running between Chang's residence and the command headquarters at Chichou, sometimes at night, the public, and especially Chang Chü-cheng's enemies, had good reason to believe that the grand-secretary's power monopoly in the court of Peking and Ch'i's long-term command of army installations in the suburbs were actually insepa-rable. One must have led to the other.

The tactics that Ch'i Chi-kuang developed in Chichou could be most adequately described as an infantryman's concept of combined arms. Any criticism as such, however, must be made within the context of his techni-cal limitations. The modern firearms available to him were still in their infancy; and he had to take a defensive position. Since most of the northern troops were below combat standards, he had to rely on his southern re-cruits. This in turn meant that he was expected to check the advances of large troops of Mongolian cavalry with battle formations only the size of a brigade.

Essential to his fighting method was the "battle wagon," basically a huge two-wheeled mule cart; but in place of the raised sides was a wooden screen made of eight sections which could be folded flat to rest on the vehicle's platform. In combat the mules were unhitched. The wagon was turned on its side with one wheel facing the enemy, and the screen opened and raised behind the wheel to cover an area of fifteen feet. The wagons in battle position were lined up next to each other to form a continuous wall. The end sections of the screens served as swinging doors, permitting foot soldiers to enter and exit.[95]

Each battle wagon carried two pieces of light artillery called *fo-lang-chi*, presumably of European origin.[96] More a large-calibre rifle than a cannon by latter-day standards, the *fo-lang-chi* was cast in bronze or iron. Its length varied from 3 to 7 feet, its calibre not larger than two inches. The lead bullet was loaded from the muzzle. The cartridge containing propel-ling charges, made of the same material and strength as the gun barrel but in the shape of a flask, was inserted into the cut-open rear end of the weapon. An iron rod inserted in holes on either side of the gun barrel served as a bolt. The most formidable type had a range of 2,000 feet. The *fo-lang-chi*, as well as muskets, were fired from the battle wagon, through holes in the screens provided for the purpose.[97]

Ch'i assigned twenty soldiers to each battle wagon.[98] Ten of them were never to leave the vehicle; they maneuvered it into place and manned the *fo-lang-chi* guns. The other ten formed an assault team around the wagon. Even though four soldiers of the latter squad also carried muskets, when the enemy came close they all changed to contact weapons, including rat-tan shields, fork spears, and long-handled swords, to engage them in hand-to-hand combat. Teamwork was still stressed, however. The assault team was never to venture twenty-five feet away from the wagon. When it advanced, the combat wagon must follow. At times additional infantry squads took part in the fighting. They followed essentially the same tactics as Ch'i had developed in the south against the pirates, except that now the soldiers who carried shields and swords concentrated on slashing the knees and hooves of enemy horses, while those with lances stabbed the men riding them. The bamboo tree was still regarded as useful in obstructing the opponent.[99]

In a paper submitted to the emperor, Ch'i described further details of his tactics. A mixed brigade should have 3,000 cavalrymen, 4,000 infantrymen, 128 heavy battle wagons, and 216 light wagons. Facing the enemy, the cavalry first provided a screen behind which the vehicles were positioned. The wagons were arrayed either in a square or a circle. To allow horses to go through, spaces were left between the wagons; but abatises and other removable obstacles filled the gaps. When the Mongolian mounts approached, the cavalry withdrew, taking cover inside. An enemy formation of fewer than a hundred mounts would be ignored. Otherwise the soldiers would open fire when the Mongols were within 250 feet.[100] In addition to *fo-lang-chi* and muskets, the army also had firecracker-propelled arrows ignited by fork spears. Sometimes heavy guns accompanied combat units in the field. One type, known by its nickname, the "generalissimo," operated according to the principle of a shotgun. Its juglike cartridge, similar to that of the *fo-lang chi* in appearance, was slotted into place. But it contained explosives, pebbles, and tiny iron balls stacked in layers; its front was closed with a wooden plug sealed with mud. The generalissimo was used as a point-blank weapon. Even though it was loaded on a wagon for transport, it weighed over 1,300 pounds and required wooden ties to be piled on the ground for its emplacement before firing. A light mortar 2 feet long was also used.[101] Ch'i Chi-kuang did not have guns that fired exploding shells.

Infantry counterattack was always regarded as important to Ch'i's tactical plan. He had the foot soldiers rush out from the sides of battle wagons and from underneath them in waves signaled by bugle calls.[102] As soon as the momentum of the enemy charge was checked and its formation broken, the cavalry would give chase. But Ch'i's cavalry was little more than infantrymen on horseback. Individual soldiers within the same squad were also equipped with various contact weapons and were expected to maintain "mandarin duck formation" in combat.[103] No effort was made to imitate the Mongolian hordes, who wielded sabres en masse and capitalized on the initial impact of their forward movement.

It was ironic that such a carefully worked out scheme was never put to a serious test on the battlefield and allowed to become a standard operating procedure of the imperial army.[104] Less than three years after Ch'i Chi-kuang took over the command of Chichou, Altan Khan pledged his submission to the Ming court in exchange for annual subsidies and trading privileges. His confederation was no longer militarily active.[105] Remaining outside this agreement were the eastern Tümed Mongols, who made their raids in Liaotung, far away from Ch'i Chi-kuang's territory. The several local engagements against some of the tribes in which the Chichou command took part were of no great significance.

At the same time, the empire was too overburdened with problems of its own to launch an offensive war as T'an Lun had advocated. The fundamental problem was that imperial uniformity was only skin deep. Things called by the same name were not alike. There was always a discrepancy between theory and practice. In a major operation the overall performance was often determined by the strength of the weakest member of the team. These conditions were sufficient to discourage enterprises of any magnitude. When T'an Lun suggested dispatching an expeditionary force to the steppes, Chang Chü-cheng was unreceptive.[106] To deal with the nomads who continued to cause trouble on the frontier, the grand-secretary chose cajolery and intimidation, considering the use of force a last resort. He wrote to Ch'i Chi-kuang, "The number of soldiers under your command who can really fight is not great." He then explicitly told his trusted general: "Our main concern is defense. It is already a great achievement if the nomads are contained. As long as you are keeping Chichou peaceful your mission has been accomplished."[107]

The greatest liability within the Chichou command, of course, was the coexistence of northern conscripts and southern recruits. The latter Ch'i Chi-kuang could count on and discipline. The former he could neither rely on nor dismiss. Thus, although he had so scrupulously recruited his volunteers on the foundation of peasantry, in the eyes of others he had still established an elite corps, with selected personnel, preferential appropriations, and steadier supplies.

Originally Ch'i had proposed to use his better trained units to give instructions to the bulk of the army.[108] But in view of the large number of southerners he had to bring into Chichou and the letter Chang Chü-cheng wrote him, it is evident that this goal was never attained. In order to utilize the otherwise wasted manpower to strengthen the defense permanently, Ch'i suggested the construction of castlelike watchtowers along the Great Wall, the first of their kind.

As outlined in his proposal, every 250 men were organized into a construction battalion, each of which was expected to complete seventy towers a year.[109] This crash program must later have been drastically revised, as in fact the imperial government authorized only some 1,200 towers for Chichou out of the 3,000 that Ch'i had proposed.[110] The time limit for construction was extended to at least 1581, well over a decade later.[111]

A typical tower of Ch'i's design had three levels and a minimum of 12 feet for each dimension on the top, and was intended to house thirty to fifty soldiers with their equipment. The construction materials, including stones, bricks, and cement, were produced by the labor force itself, most of them northern soldiers enlisted in the program. The grant-in-aid appropriated by the civil government for purchases, again small amounts of silver paid directly to the working units, was held to the minimum. This entire project had been strongly opposed by the northern officers. But with Chang Chü-cheng's powerful personal influence behind it, the fortification was built, and in fact became the only lasting gift the grand-secretary left to our empire.[112]

Though rarely noted, the construction of the towers and the defense strategy tied to it also had a great deal to do with army logistics. Ch'i's own writings pointed out that while each one of the keeps could accommodate a platoon of foot soldiers, only five to ten of these were his southern recruits, the only ones required to be stationed inside all the time.[113] The rest, being northerners and thus inadequately paid and in principle partially self-supporting, were allowed to find ways of seeking their livelihood when their active service was not required.[114] This arrangement was made official and remained so for some time after Ch'i Chi-kuang had relinquished his position as commander-in-chief. Having himself advocated the scattered commitment of his troops to these forts, Ch'i had no reason to complain about it. But his writings persistently suggested that if he had had the choice, he would have much preferred attack and mobile warfare.[115]

Ch'i Chi-kuang's fifteen years as commander-in-chief at Chichou were equal to the entire length of the combined tenure of his ten predecessors.[116] The office kept him amply occupied. He loved drills, inspections, ceremonies, and giving lectures. There were opportunities for him to demonstrate his personal vigor and agility, such as the occasion when, discussing the relative advantages of different types of contact weapons with his sub- ordinate commanders, he on the spur of the moment had a mounted officer charge him with a sabre while he defended himself on foot with a spear.[117] On his inspection trips he occasionally rode outside the Chinese barricades, once unescorted for ten miles.[118] He took pride in the fact that as commanding general he had ascended the highest peak occupied by a forward sentry, accessible only by a rope dangling over the cliff. Yet, with all these activities he still managed to produce literary works. His second treatise on troop training, *Lien-ping Shih-chi*, was published in 1571. Nine years later came the collection of his belles lettres, entitled *Chih-chih-t'ang-chi*.[119]

Ch'i's military licentiate degree could not have been a substantial asset impressive to the civil officials. Nor did his poetry show great literary quality. It produced neither the kind of intriguing sensitivity that emerges from deep emotional traumas lightly and casually presented, nor the angu- lar naturalism conveyed by powerful staccato rhythms inevitably repeating themselves and inviting echo—two major techniques in which most Chinese poets excelled. As an artist Ch'i Chi-kuang had yet to learn to exercise restraint for the sake of subtlety; yet he was too concerned with the art form to be his true self. Fortunately, his publications never have to be judged on literary merit alone. His ability to wield the writing brush so effectively already distinguished him from other general officers, with the obvious exception of Yü Ta-yu. Because he could quote Confucian classics and cite historical events along with his Civil Service counterparts, Ch'i Chi-kuang was able at first to dispel the fear that he was the type of general who would sack the capital; and as both his own reputation and his rapport with the bureaucrats continued to grow, he became accepted by them as a peer, drank with them and exchanged complimentary compositions and poems. He must have gotten along well with Wang Shih-chen, historian, poet, and above all the greatest prose-writer of a century. Wang wrote two birthday greetings praising Ch'i's virtue and also composed introductions to his *Chi-hsiao Hsin-shu* and *Chih-chih-t'ang-chi*.[120]

Did Ch'i Chi-kuang find his sense of fulfillment? Few persons in his time could even hope to accomplish what he had accomplished. He had never done anything that seemed impossible; but within the bounds of what was possible he usually did well. His resolution was rarely the best for all circumstances, but it was the best under the *given* circumstances. He had earned every honor due an army officer except an earldom. It was only because of the dynasty's standard practices that he could not advance further in his career. A general officer had reached the highest rung when he became commander-in-chief of a defense district.[121] Further promotions were only titular and honorific. An earldom could be earned only on the battlefield or by marrying a daughter of the emperor.

But seven months after Chang Chü-cheng's death Ch'i was transferred to the post of commander-in-chief of Kwangtung and was thus deprived of the honor and prestige of guarding the gates of the capital with the most formidable battle formations of the empire. A year later he was under still more pressure, as the purge of Chang Chü-cheng's associates had reached the high point. Already in poor health and low spirits, Ch'i turned in his resignation. The general was not even granted the courtesy of being allowed to leave with a clean record. Officially the decree from Peking confirmed that he had been censured and dismissed by the throne.[122] Similar pressure had been brought to bear upon Li Ch'eng-liang in Liaotung, another commander who had earned Chang Chü-cheng's trust and was considered to be one of the grand-secretary's inside circle.[123] The emperor, however, regarded Li as less of an offender and permitted him to stay.

Ch'i Chi-kuang's death in the Year of the Pig was noted only by a few of his unwavering friends. For some time the prose writer of the century, Wang Shih-chen must be considered one of those few, as he had sent to the general, a year before his death, when he was in disgrace, his last birthday greetings, a splendid essay in itself.[124] Yet subsequently Wang also published a biography of Chang Chü-cheng in which he implicated Ch'i.

The biography itself was controversial. The only full-length account of the grand-secretary's life and times written by a contemporary, it included intriguing details described at great length, among them many anecdotes that were later verified. Its claim to authenticity was strong, since in private life the author had been well acquainted with Chang and knew most of his associates and even antagonists. Wang made no effort to withhold praise from the statesman when it was deserved, and this included acknowledgment of his wisdom in entrusting the empire's key defense areas to capable men like Ch'i Chi-kuang and Li Ch'eng-liang. Nevertheless, the overall tone of the portrait is derogatory. To complicate matters, in this piece of literature Wang also frankly admitted his dispute with Chang Chü-cheng, using in that passage the third rather than the first person singular when referring to himself.[125]

The grand-secretary's death, Wang went on to assert, was traceable to his sexual indulgence. His carnal excesses had in reality been started by

T'an Lun, who offered Chang secret formulas to enhance his libidinous adventures. The role played by Ch'i Chi-kuang was that of procurer. "Using enormous funds," the commander-in-chief at Chichou was said to have, from time to time, provided his patron the grand-secretary with "a young lady who was worth one thousand ounces of silver."[126] This provocative charge, right in the middle of an otherwise serious piece of historical work, created a troublesome problem for later scholars. Every biographer of Ch'i Chi-kuang's chose to ignore it.

Before Ch'i Chi-kuang died in the Year of the Pig his wife deserted him. He was reported to have sunk to the level where he could no longer afford medical care.[127] Previously, when he was in office, he had been known for his generosity to his friends. The way he was dismissed, his final destitution, and the denial of any official notice of his death completed the acts of injustice that fate had in store for a deserving hero. The lingering sadness of the story touched his admirers, who had ample reason to lavish kind words on him, sometimes portraying him as an infallible character.

But those who tried to claim traditional virtue for Ch'i Chi-kuang constantly put themselves in an embarrassing situation. Ch'i's outlook was too complex to suit their stereotyped framework. There was no adequate way to explain the inexplicable—for example, that Ch'i Chi-kuang had five sons born of three concubines yet kept their existence from his wife's knowledge until they reached their adulthood.[128] Ch'i Chi-kuang could shed tears without shame in front of his generals when they discussed the hardships of the soldiers. Having himself put an end to the arrangement of having soldiers deliver firewood to his household, he once complained that because of a shortage of fuel his family could not have dinner on New Year's Eve.[129] Yet it was general knowledge that he often dispatched mounted messengers all the way to Peking, fifty miles distant, to fetch food from his favorite restaurants.[130] At Chichou he revived the ancient ritual of drinking with his officers from a common cup containing animal blood in wine. During this ceremony he and his subordinate commanders pledged to each other never to do a number of things: among these were increasing troop strength within the units in order to intercept the extra pay, withholding allowances due to soldiers, misappropriating public funds, and providing cash gifts to superiors. On several occasions the participants swore that whoever violated the pledge should die instantly and violently, be condemned to hell, and spread the suffering from retribution for sin to his descendants for ten generations, until the family became "endlessly involved in banditry and prostitution."[131] Later events, however, suggested that the commander-in-chief who had initiated these admirable ideals might himself have been a violator of them. While the handing over of a woman or women "worth one thousand ounces of silver" to Chang Chü-cheng could not be substantiated, it was on record that Ch'i Chi-kuang had let his younger brother call on the grand-secretary and deliver gifts of substantial value.[132] The *Ming-shih* concluded that Ch'i's personal integrity "fell short of that of Yü Ta-yu."[133] One of the charges for which Ch'i was censured after he had relinquished the command of Chichou was that all the financial records there "had vanished."[134]

Along with the solemn oaths to which Ch'i subscribed, he also introduced into his command mysterious practices reminiscent of popular religion. He designed battalion and company flags identifying their commanders with constellations in the sky and legendary animal-soldiers. He designated propitious and unpropitious days for public ceremonies, instructed his officers to check their own astrology on various occasions, and lectured both officers and men on heavenly rewards and hell-bound punishments.[135] Was the greatest soldier of the dynasty a scholar of the supernatural? Or was he merely taking advantage of mass psychology as he was taking advantage of everything else? Even the *Ssu-k'u Ch'üan-shu* editors who later handled his writings felt uncomfortable about including the superstitious passages in Ch'i's works.[136]

But the omission of such details only obscures the inner workings of history. Nor would the cause of justice be served by forcing a deserving hero to appear to be a person he was not. Because of his social milieu, Ch'i Chi-kuang could never have been a man of single-minded virtue like Hai Jui. It would have been unrealistic to expect him to remain naively innocent. With due respect to the soldier of indomitable will who had made himself a top administrator, organizer, military engineer, and writer of field manuals in addition to becoming a successful commander in battle, admirers of Ch'i must recognize that their hero had to be a political animal to achieve what he did. After all, Ch'i gained prominence in an era when the hereditary military families should have been completely abolished for the sake of establishing a recruited army, and the interlocking supply lines should have been swept away by an integrated system of finance. Inasmuch as our sedentary empire and its literary bureaucracy could never make these changes, the way to boost the fighting strength of the army had to come through compromise, mainly the blending of the yin with the yang.

Ch'i Chi-kuang's virtue rested in his perception of this inevitable necessity and in his willingness to work with tools that were far from ideal. In the age of gunpowder, he went back to brick fortifications. Within his mixed brigade, modern artillery was deployed along with rattan shields. His methodical observance of the sunrise and sunset hours contrasted with his backward practice of cutting off recalcitrant soldiers' ears. The simultaneous incorporation into Ch'i's command of elements of civilization which in other lands would have been separated by centuries, however, created the difficulty of integrating them at the higher level. In practice, the new elements had to slow down to keep pace with the old. When institutional means to achieve coordination had been exhausted, then the personal touch had to take over. Just as the Chichou command by its very nature required manipulation by its commanding general, so his link with the master of the Literary Depth Pavilion also became inevitable.

Was Ch'i Chi-kuang a student of the supernatural? In a way he was, as were many of his contemporaries. But, like them, he sometimes showed strains of fatalism and agnosticism in addition to his commitment to the doctrine of karma.[137] Furthermore, his indoctrination of his troops in legends, folklore, and popular religion had a specific reason in view of the audience to whom these messages were addressed. In a memorial to the emperor, he pointed out that within the northern command only one or two officers in every ten had attained the minimum level of literacy.[138] It was understandable that when talking to the peasant-soldiers, whose cultural level was even lower, he merely used the kind of vocabulary that made sense to them.

Before a different audience, the commander-in-chief at Chichou was completely prepared to reorient himself to speak a different language. For one thing, he designated his office-residence Chih-chih-t'ang.[139] Taken from *Chuang-tzu* and meaning the "Hall of a Felicitous Conclusion," it served to publicize that he had already taken the last step in his army career and had no further personal ambition. He first gave his collection of essays the title *Yü-yü-kao*. Equivalent to *A Fool's Foolish Draft*, it achieved the same purpose of advertising its author's humility.

Sympathy, when guided by proper historical perspective, should enable Ch'i's admirers to stop short of presenting him as a completely impeccable hero. But they should also stress that the general never pursued self-gain as an end. He was adapted himself yet at the same time served a purpose. Realizing that the affairs of the army, including military technology, were in no state to exert the influence needed to reconstruct Chinese society but, rather, would continue to be restrained by it, Ch'i Chi-kuang searched for viable ways to build up the best fighting forces under this restriction, and while doing so he still strove to lead a good life. Because he had worked with T'an Lun and Chang Chü-cheng for so long, his role as a politician-general was sometimes obscured; but this fact never escaped the attention of the bureaucrats and the emperor. To them he was still a monster lurking in the hallway, unable to be controlled by any institution. Why did Chang Chü-cheng have to be regarded as a near-usurper after his death? The indictment was made not on evidence but on logic. Whether or not Chang had had the intention of taking over the throne was not the most crucial issue. What was disturbing was that he had built up the *capacity* to do so. His power base at Chichou was too ominous to be ignored. It was from this logical deduction that the trial judge who interrogated Chang's sons wanted to know why in their father's lifetime it was necessary for messengers from Chichou to approach the house at night.[140] In an organizational sense, Ch'i Chi-kuang's limited innovations had already violated the bureaucratic principle of balance. For this sin he had to pay the price of dying alone and destitute.

A friend who did not waver wrote on Ch'i's tombstone how the lonely general had died at dawn: "When the cock crowed the third time, the star of the valiant soldier fell from the sky."[141] But Wang Tao-k'un[142] never realized that on that early morning of January 17, 1588—still the Year of the Pig by the Chinese calendar but already the year of the Spanish Armada in Western chronology—gone with Ch'i Chi-kuang was our empire's last opportunity to give its armed forces the minimal modernization needed to survive a new era. Three decades later its army was to fight Nurhaci without benefit of the tactics of Ch'i's mixed brigade, and once its inadequacy was exposed, the barricades of the Great Wall, also inadequately manned, were torn down here and there to make way for the invading Manchus. In the absence of the necessary reforms on the part of our empire, the Manchu Bannermen, who were able to adapt to China's agrarian base and bureaucratic management, proved to be a better replacement of the corrupt system of hereditary military households than anything that could be found on the south side of the wall.

7
LI CHIH,
A DIVIDED CONSCIENCE

The historical classification of Li Chih as a "martyr" is at best dubious. When he cut his throat with a razor blade in prison in 1602 he left no perceivable course for his admirers to follow. However, despite repeated proscriptions by the court, Li's writings were again and again reprinted. But nowhere in his copious publications is there any clear sense of release. The infectious elation typical of a person who has found a noble cause to die for is notably absent from both his essays and his private letters, even though he was not a man without courage.

Similarly, the categorization of Li Chih as a spokesman for the peasantry against the exploiting classes is completely out of proportion to the truth.[1] After relinquishing his official post as the prefect of Yao-an in 1580, he was supported by his gentry-official friends until his death. Never did he question the impropriety of this arrangement. Nor did he even remotely suggest that the social order from which he drew his sustenance should be reconstructed in any way. Whenever he indicted his gentry-official friends, he made it clear that the same indictment applied to himself. In fact, he sometimes spoke of himself with unconcealed self-pity mingled with self-criticism. In a letter to Vice-Minister Chou Ssu-ching, Li wrote: "I am not dying this year and may not even die next year. Waiting for death year in and year out, I am growing restless. While death does not come, woes are approaching. Yet those woes are not approaching fast enough!"[2] This is not the tone of a martyr who had a definite vision of what he was doing, or even the voice of a rebel who had diagnosed a social evil and was willing to perish in order to eliminate it.

Li Chih's main concern was related to intellectual honesty; it also had to do with freedom of conscience. Behind this concern lay an economic cause, and it was also particular to the interests of his social group. But taking all this into account, it would still be wrong to ignore the philosophical and psychological subtlety of his dilemma and to see it as arising from issues reminiscent of Western prototypes.[3]

Li Chih was reared as a Confucian and died one. Until the Year of the Pig he believed that he had discharged all the responsibilities of a family man as the Confucian code of behavior required. Only in 1588 did he shave his head and thenceforce lead a life halfway between those of a Buddhist monk and a Confucian scholar. In the same year his wife died and his only daughter had already been placed under his son-in-law's care. Li felt that now he could detach himself from his mundane obligations to his kin and lead his life as he wished. Yet, intellectually and even socially, this was by no means to flee from worldly affairs. Whether intentionally or not, from this time until his death Li Chih practically appointed himself the group conscience of all the literati. His own defense during his trial, "the accused has written many books, which should benefit the propagation of the teaching of the sages rather than damaging it,"[4] is similar to the position held by Martin Luther. His practice of reinterpreting classics and history as he saw fit runs parallel to the doctrine of a priesthood of believers. But Li Chih was never as self-assertive as Luther. He lacked even the self-confidence of Erasmus. When he was bleeding from his fatal self-inflicted wound, his jailer asked Li why he had to take such a dramatic step. His last words were: "What else could a man over seventy do?"[5]

This despondent tone reflected the frustration of an era. The traditional statecraft could not be replaced, and as long as this was the case China would not experience Reformation. In this social climate intellectual freedom and even personal honesty could hardly be expected to thrive. Li Chih's criticism of Censor-in-Chief Keng Ting-hsiang was really an intrapersonal conflict, unresolved by the accuser himself. Those who could sense his righteousness in his letter to his friend, antagonist, and former benefactor should also have noticed that on other occasions Li portrayed himself as a nongiver pointing his finger at other nongivers, and as "a peddler in mind and practice" who cloaked himself in the robe of Buddha in order "to deceive the world and earn for himself a false reputation" of being a man of benevolence.[6]

Li Chih was born in Ch'üan-chou, Fukien Province, in 1527. His sixth generation ancestor, Lin Nu, was a merchant engaged in trade on the Persian Gulf who married a woman of central Asian origin. Upon the rise of the Ming dynasty, Ch'üan-chou ceased to be a seaport of significance. For some time the family continued to maintain marital ties with those of mixed ancestry and the Islamic faith. But by the time of Li Chih's great-grandfather, if not earlier, this cosmopolitan outlook within the family had completely vanished. From childhood Li Chih was deeply imbued with traditional Chinese culture.

Poverty played a significant role in shaping Li's life; so did his own stubbornness, which would not permit him to bow down to anyone he considered his intellectual inferior. His early years were full of sorrow and misfortune. After receiving his licentiate's degree in 1552, he elected to enter officialdom rather than waiting for success in the metropolitan examinations. But this decision subjected him to long years of low-ranking appointments that paid hardly anything. His tenure was also interrupted by the mourning for his father and grandfather and by the waiting for a vacancy when he reported back to service, on one occasion for twenty months.[7] Li Chih had four sons and three daughters. All except the eldest daughter died when they were young, one son by accidental drowning and two daughters from malnutrition.[8] Li Chih himself related that once there had been seven days during which he did not have much to eat. When he was finally fed he did not recognize whether the food was rice or sorghum.[9]

Li Chih served as a director of Confucian studies at the county level for three years, as an instructor at the Imperial University in Nanking for two years, as manager of the business office of the Ministry of Rites for five years, and as vice director at the Ministry of Justice at Nanking for close to another five years before his assignment as prefect of Yao-an in Yunnan in 1577.[10] Except for the last assignment, which as the post of a local district provided customary fees and a quasi-legal income to the officeholder, all the positions he occupied yielded salaries that enabled him to live only in extreme to relative poverty. From his writings it may be seen that he had realized at least a modest saving from his three-year term as prefect, which he later turned over to his wife.[11] The nature of the office's compensation in itself, however, did not constitute for him a moral problem. Li Chih never imposed on himself, or on others, the rigid standard of Hai Jui, who saw anything beyond the officially allotted salary as a form of theft.[12] Li, rather, followed the conventional standard: high official posts should be not only prestigious but also lucrative. The moral conviction he did have centered on his belief that if a person was trying to exploit the fame and fortune inherent in public office, he should at least have the decency to admit that he was self-seeking. Why pretend to be completely selfless, wishing only to serve and to give? This led to a fundamental question: should not everyone admit his self-interest as he acted on it, instead of engaging in the duplicity of yin and yang?[13]

Equally burdensome was Li's memory of his wife. She had endured the great depths of sorrow, deprivation, inconvenience, and hardship demanded by his career. In the end she had given him everything except the understanding that, as a man with an insatiable urge to assert himself, Li was entitled to his own kind of fulfillment. It must have been a severe blow to her when, after a lifetime struggle, he decided to retire from the Civil

Service in 1580 at the age of fifty-three, thereby forfeiting a possible promotion. Yet she bowed to his decision and went along with him to become houseguests of his friends, the Keng brothers in Hukwang, for three years. His wish was also hers.[14] But the final break became inevitable when Li went to live in a Buddhist temple. His wife was escorted by their daughter and son-in-law back to Ch'üan-chou, the native district she had not seen for two decades. Up until 1587, she had often pleaded with Li to return home. Did shaving his head and thus declaring himself a Buddhist monk in any way hasten his wife's death? When the news of it came, Li composed a poem mourning her and expressing sorrow over the fact that after forty years of mutual devotion, she was unable to reach an ultimate understanding with him.[15] In a letter to their son-in-law he disclosed that ever since he had heard of her death he had not spent a single night without dreaming of her.[16] Many years later he was still advising his friends not to take up the tonsure lightly, especially those who had immediate family.

Li Chih's wish to be left alone must be appreciated in the light of the social practices of his time. If he had ever returned to Ch'üan-chou, he could never have confined his attention to his immediate family. As a man of distinction who had served as a prefect, he would have been bombarded with pleas and requests.

Even as a holder of the lowest Civil Service rank residing in his home district while mourning his father in the 1550s, Li Chih had been compelled to take care of his kinfolk, which included the impossible task of providing food for some thirty persons at the height of the pirate invasions, when "grain could not even be bought."[17] This experience was common among members of the gentry-official class. Ho Liang-chün, who lived in Nanking, received swarms of relatives from his native district. Kuei Yu-kuang wrote to a friend saying that he could not take refuge elsewhere because if he moved he would have to take "more than one hundred mouths" along with him.[18] Such a moral obligation, easily referred to as "Confucianism at work," was more than a temporary detour from one's own path for the sake of ideology; it had the force of socioeconomic necessity behind it and as such brought constant pressure to bear on the individual.

The fact was that, even though our empire was not a closed society, the vocational options it could offer were extremely limited. For families who wished to enjoy stability and respectability, there was little choice besides farming and officeholding. Usually the two were interconnected; success in one area led to success in the other. But it was most unlikely that both could be attained by a newcomer in his own lifetime. The common pattern was that a family persistently worked toward its common interest until the labor and self-denial of the fathers bore fruit in the time of their children, who benefited from clear titles to their land, sometimes from the liens they held over the properties of others, and above all from free time for education. Sacrifices on the part of mothers and wives were an integral part of the process. Thus, while sudden advances were possible at the time of the governmental examinations, the triumphs and satisfactions thus attained had in reality been shared, transmitted, and deferred.[19] The motivation to succeed required individuals within the household to maintain a collective personality, so to speak. Corresponding to the emotional need, the imperial conferring of honorary titles upon meritorious officials as a rule covered three generations in retrospect and their wives, often posthumously.[20] Li Chih's own life story shows traces of this general pattern, even though the early deaths of his sons and his own premature resignation prevented it from developing into a typical case.

The strong kinship bond could not logically stop at the limit of the conjugal family, since there was no reason why the common destiny that one shared with one's ancestors could not also be shared with one's uncles, brothers, nephews, and cousins. Besides, the benefits of mutual aid were reciprocal. One could never be certain when one's own children might need help from those relatives. The cult of ancestor-worship therefore had a strong rationale on its side. But along with its semireligious trappings and ethical values, the practice also became a relentless coercive force. The demands it made upon individuals were by no means limited to intermittent flashes of devotion to the common cause, nor were the obligations merely financial. In the main, it committed people to a definite pattern of life, characterized by the obsessive acquisition of land, the compulsive choice of official careers, the promotion of education for the sole purpose of perpetuating the system, and, in pursuing all these goals, the subjection of themselves to the pressures and expectations of the nearest kin, who felt justifed in inducing them to chart their course for the common good.[21]

In a situation where alternatives were few and the communal spirit had become a sort of custom, most people in Li Chih's position would have surrendered to the custom without a struggle. As a prominent member of the clan he undoubtedly had the obligation to occupy a strategic position in order to benefit the entire group. But in the 1580s he became deeply involved in Buddhist and Taoist studies.[22] The sorrows and misfortunes of his life had led him to question the very meaning of existence. Once he emerged from his soul-searching, he could not help but loathe the conventional standards. Consequently, his reaction to the pressure for conformity was violent.

Before his tonsure in 1588, Li related, without identifying the persons involved, that he had been repeatedly pressed by "people of no importance from home" to do "something against my wish."[23] It was about this time that his clan compiled what seemed to be the first genealogy of a Confucian type, citing the appropriate official rank and gentry status of each member of the clan after his dates of birth and marriage.[24] The incessant urgings from his relatives to return home and Li's hardened will to resist developed into a deadlock, which was not broken even after he had declared himself a Buddhist monk. Evidently, to the end his family designated a nephew of his to be his "adopted son" against his own wish. Li Chih, in turn, set down in writing that should this unwanted "heir" ever attend his funeral, he must be enjoined not to cry.[25] This was in 1596, eight years after Li had shaved his head.

Li Chih's retreat in the suburbs of Ma-ch'eng was called the "Hall of Buddha in Fragrant Iris." According to his own description, it was neither a temple nor a monastery. But as a private chapel its enormous size was disproportionate.[26] The main building consisted of two wings. There were also dormitories and guest houses. Built on a cliff overlooking a lake, Li's own cottage was on a most imposing height behind the complex. Normally the "hall" had more than forty monks under the direction of an abbot, who was also Li Chih's friend. These monks introduced to the establishment their disciples, who could also have their own novices.[27]

Though remaining tax-free, the Hall of Buddha in Fragrant Iris, however, was not licensed. It belonged to no specific sect and had no governing body, which made Li Chih its only trustee and elder. Its construction and maintenance relied largely on contributions to Li's cause, most of which were openly solicited. He often wrote to his official friends asking them to give him "a whole year's salary" or "half of your salary." Some of his best sponsors supported him continually for twenty years.[28] Li seemed never to have accumulated any cash assets; but neither did he run out of funds after his retirement in 1580.

Even before Li Chih's last appointment with the governmental service in Yunnan he had already earned the reputation of being an outstanding thinker well regarded in learned circles.[29] Many of his early admirers and later acquaintances eventually rose to be distinguished civil servants, holding positions as vice-ministers an ministers, governors and governors-general.[30] The way that Li lived off his own reputation was somewhat unusual but by no means unique according to the customs of those days. His friend Chiao Hung, for instance, was described by Li as having maintained a home that was an empty shell, "with only four walls standing by themselves," and Chiao was said to be entirely unconcerned for his own well-being. Yet when he traveled on the Grand Canal two ships carried his library. His father's eightieth birthday was celebrated with a party that lasted for ten days, with friends coming from hundreds of miles away. Li Chih, on his part, often urged his visitors to bring "as much rice and firewood as possible."[31]

Financial transactions between donors and recipients as such were not charity in the ordinary sense; the contributions were actually made for common interests if not a common cause. This peculiar development could be said to have arisen from the doctrine of government by moral principles. The ultimate rationale behind those principles was the unity of the universe. Since everything that functions depends upon its interaction with other objects, which in turn enables the world to make sense, the very meaning of existence must be to share and to cooperate. But why are individuals by nature selfish? This problem was seriously disturbing to the bureaucrats, especially those who occupied high-level positions.[32] Their lifetime education taught them selflessly to pursue the public good, yet in practice they repeatedly had to violate this principle, sometimes becoming involved to a certain degree in the moral decadence of the illiterate. Conversation with friends and other learned men could help to lighten the moral burden. Social gatherings often turned into philosophical discussions, followed by correspondence and even publication. These seminars and symposia therefore served a useful purpose: they enlightened the participants, or at least eased their inner conflict. During his retirement Li Chih traveled often. In those days it would have been inappropriate to discuss expenses and lecture fees. But because of Li's status, these matters were taken care of and finances were never a problem.[33]

Li's debate with Keng Ting-hsiang undoubtedly helped him to develop his creed of individualism, as he acknowledged many years later, albeit cast against the social background of his time it was destined to be a lost cause.[34] On terminating his official career, Li had taken his family to the Keng house and lived there for three years. Of the four Keng brothers, who were then at home mourning the death of their father, the two younger ones were rarely mentioned.[35] Li Chih developed a strong liking for the second brother, Ting-li. Contrary to general belief, the intellectual gap between him and Li was wider than that between Li and the eldest of the four, Keng Ting-hsiang. As a young man Keng Ting-li was unusually brilliant yet also possessed a deep sense of intellectual honesty, which would not permit him to accept the classical works until he became convinced of their truth. This unresolved conflict often led him into deep solitary meditation, sometimes as he wandered in desolate ravines. His final conclusion was that Confucian benevolence was self-negation. To him wisdom was a state of detachment, "odorless and soundless." Like other extreme idealists, Ting-li could never translate his uncommitted mind, really a state of mental emancipation from the physical self, into a standard of public morality. In real life he never took a Civil Service degree and never occupied public office.[36] His doctrine would have set him far apart from the opposite extreme position taken by Li Chih, who held that "ethics and morals are no more than food and clothing," or the livelihood of the common people.[37] What made Keng Ting-li affable was not his doctrinal flexibility but his temperament. True to his Ch'an Buddhist outlook, he could air his disagreement by making a pungent remark seemingly irrelevant to the topic under discussion. Since for him truth rested in universal breadth, he could not spoil it by engaging in any specific argument. As long as he lived, Ting-li managed to keep peace between his elder brother and Li Chih.[38]

The elder brother, Keng Ting-hsiang, is unfairly presented by historians. His own position as a serious thinker and a man of integrity in accordance with the norms of his day has been largely obscured—partly because of Li Chih's accusation, which portrayed him as the personification of bureaucratic hypocrisy, and partly because of Huang Tsung-hsi's account, in which he again appears as lacking in intellectual consistency.[39] Keng Ting-hsiang followed the Taoists and Ch'an Buddhists in believing that the ultimate reality is void. He also argued that any teaching that cannot be explained to ignorant men and women is worthless. Consequently he came up with the proposition that reason can be deep and shallow, fine and coarse, concentrated and diffused. Statecraft differs from agriculture, which differs from commerce. In his final analysis he came close to the realization that ethics differs from practical knowledge and politics may deviate from philosophy, facts which most of his contemporaries were not ready to accept. His clash with Li Chih was inevitable because both men immediately put their ideas to work, exhibiting them in their social behavior. In Li's eyes, Keng maintained a double standard, while Keng saw Li as a nonconformist for nonconformity's sake, who on occasion indulged in wanton debauchery in order to satisfy his love of exhibitionism.

In 1584 Keng Ting-li died. About the same time Keng Ting-hsiang was recalled to Peking to become the left assistant censor-in-chief. In his letters he expressed displeasure that Li Chih had misled his sons and nephews, which prompted Li's decision to send his family home and relocate himself in Ma-ch'eng, relying for a while on the hospitality of several local friends until he constructed the Hall of Buddha in Fragrant Iris.[40] For a long time he took Keng Ting-hsiang's accusation as a personal insult aside from their ideological differences.

By nature Li Chih was contentious and unyielding.[41] By his own account, when he was a governmental official he always clashed with his superiors, including his last encounter with the governor and the circuit intendant while serving as prefect under them. After his break with Keng Ting-hsiang, Li became more concerned about his independence. According to the standard practice of the dynasty, even as a retired official Li was still under the jurisdiction of the local functionaries. They could call on him, deliver visiting cards and token gifts, and expect him to return the courtesy, to be drawn into their circles, and to be present at all social and public ceremonial functions. The pressure for conformity was great: "A slight indiscretion causing them displeasure could lead to imminent disaster."[42] Becoming a monk was one way of excusing himself from such obligations.

Although he declared himself a Buddhist monk, Li Chih took no religious vows. Nor did he take part in the prayers and services that the assembly at the Fragrant Iris performed for the establishment's patrons. He did not even adhere to a vegetarian diet. Although his head was shaven, he still kept a long beard. His garments were meticulously laundered. His obsession with cleanliness was such that both inside and outside his cottage the floor and the ground were swept so often that "several servants assigned to make brooms could not keep up." On the whole, Li Chih maintained the life-style of a gentry official. Even when traveling short distances he rode in a sedan chair. He composed his own works by hand, but books were read to him by attendants.[43]

For a dozen or so years Li's main occupation was writing and publishing. He had a storage room in which to deposit the plates of his own books. His publications embraced expositions of classical works, comments on history and fictional writing, philosophical essays, miscellaneous notes, poetry, and personal correspondence.[44] But though the scope seemed to be wide, Li Chih was not a man of versatile talents. His historical works had nothing to do with historiography or historical research; they were composed in the form of marginalia, with long passages reproduced from earlier chronicles but rearranged under new headings with his own comments appended. In a similar way he studied fiction, but not in the interest of literary criticism. He ignored the author's plot, character portrayal, underlying psychology, dialogue, accuracy in social history, and prose style. Without dealing with creative writing as an art, he evaluated the heroes and heroines on the printed page as though they were real people, analyzing each individual's virtue or lack of it. The novel was examined for political implications, however. Even though he discussed philosophy, ethics, and theology in his essays, at no time did Li attempt to produce a treatise. His passing thoughts therefore remained unintegrated. It would be most difficult for an uninitiated reader to understand his appeal. It seems unbelievable that in Li Chih's time almost "everybody had on hand a volume of his work, which was highly prized."[45]

The fact is, Li Chih had a single purpose: how to coordinate the personal needs and wants of a member of the scholar-gentry class with public morality. He ventured into different disciplines as if to play the same tune on different instruments. If through this effort he did not provide a satisfactory answer, at least he asked the right questions, which had been and were disturbing most of those within the educated elite of the empire. Li's own life story added a new dimension to his inquiries and made them even more convincing. Thus his poems and private letters, all containing autobiographical elements, aroused a great deal of popular interest despite their lack of artistic value. A passage of one of his letters written to Keng Ting-hsiang immediately after their break crystallized his conviction:

> The way you conduct yourself does not make me believe that you differ a great deal from others. We are all doing exactly the same thing. This applies to Your Excellency, myself, and everybody else. From dawn to dusk, since the day we gained knowledge until today, we are occupied with how to work the land so that we can eat, to buy real estate so that we can become gentlemen-farmers, to build homes so that we can live in comfort, to study so that we can pass government examinations, to become officials so that we can have honor and prestige, to investigate geomancy so that we can pass our fortunes on to our children. In doing all these things everyone is absorbed in his own interests and those of his family; not the slightest thought is given to anyone else's benefit.

> Only when doctrinal polemics begin would you say: "Look, you only think of yourself, but don't you see that I am keeping others in mind?

So you are just as selfish as I am altruistic! Here am I, worried about the household to the east which is starving and thinking about the family to the west which is shivering with cold!"

When such-and-such a person consents to come and give lectures, you may say, "Splendid, he is carrying on the work of Confucius and Mencius!" Another person may decline to meet you. You will immediately jump on him and call him selfish. You admit that one person does not behave himself too well yet he is doing good things with others. Another person may be absolutely discreet; but as far as you are concerned he is ruining everyone with his Buddhist doctrine.

Put in the proper perspective, you often preach what you do not practice. At the same time you are doing things about which you keep your mouth shut. Why must there be such differences between your words and your deeds? Do you really believe that this is the teaching of Confucius?

I would say that all these practices make a person inferior to the little fellows in the field and market, who would not hesitate to discuss aspects of their own experience. Hustlers talk about their business; farmhands talk about field work. Really, theirs are the voices of virtue, lively with interest, and never tiring and boring to listeners.[46]

Li Chih's dilemma was that, despite such eloquence, he himself still relied on the patronage of the very gentry-official class he condemned, Keng Ting-hsiang having only been singled out to exemplify their falsity. The resultant ambivalence led him to varying degrees of self-criticism and occasional voluntary retractions.[47] Only when he was cornered would he become assertive and vindictive. It could not be said that Li had found the independence he was seeking, although he had more freedom than his contemporaries. Because of his unresolved conflict he felt compelled to write and rewrite on essentially the same theme. It seemed a wonder, as Yüan Chung-tao, a sympathetic observer, pointed out, that after resigning from the Civil Service because of his alienation from bureaucratic practices Li Chih never turned into a hermit.[48] Instead he further entangled himself in matters concerning officialdom, and in doing so was forced to give up his own life.

The controversy between Li Chih and Keng Ting-hsiang was rooted in the basic question of man's nature. While neither of them openly acknowledged it, the issue, because of its many implications, could never be decided by philosophers alone. Its origin could be traced all the way back to the days of Confucius. The great sage did not clearly state whether man's nature is good or evil. He spoke only of the perfectability of man. A cultured gentleman could strive to perfect himself by attaining *jen*.

What is jen? In the *Analects of Confucius* this term is used sixty-six times, and on no two occasions is it referred to as having exactly the same meaning. It may be said that the essence of jen is "not to do to others what you do not wish done to yourself," a simple matter of self-restraint indeed. But jen is also identified with benevolence, love, tenderness, and altruism. At one point the text of the *Analects* suggests that jen is reflected in cautious speech. To discipline oneself to observe strict ritual is also jen. Yet at times, to fulfill the requirement of jen one may need to surrender one's own life.

The quality of jen is both easy and hard to attain. Anyone who sets his mind to it can achieve jen. But even sages, Confucius himself included, found it difficult to live up to it constantly. A reader needed to recite the verses over and over again to grasp the central message: to achieve jen involves gradualism. Being gentle, responsive, and charitable marks the beginning of jen but not its end. To pursue it further an individual must discipline his mind, speech, and behavior to this single purpose, which supersedes his personal wants and needs. To be unselfish is not enough; one must be selfless. In this way jen becomes a dictum, an absolute, the only relevance in life, "transcendental perfection," and "a mystic quality . . . practically identical with the *tao* of the quietists."[49]

With the *Analects* and the sixty-six mentions of jen, Confucius provided a foundation for the metaphysical reconstruction now known as Confucianism. What better way to illustrate the organic view of the universe than this matter-of-fact presentation, where at the beginning a person is told to be thoughtful toward his fellowmen, is gradually induced to exercise self-denial, and finally is indoctrinated with the idea that in the interest of the mystic quality called jen he has yet to forgo his own right to self-preservation? This concept implies that it is irrational to be selfish because what we call "self" can never be preserved. In the end, the value of life consists in no more than an opportunity to demonstrate one's sensitivity toward others, which is the only reality.

This Confucian concept closely parallels the Hindu-Buddhist idea that the individual as such is merely an illusion, and what makes him seem real is the chain of cause and effect. Unless a person involves himself with his fellowmen and his external environment he is nonexistent. The question of man's nature, however, was left open by Confucius. It might be considered evil inasmuch as man has to engage in a lifetime struggle with himself to achieve goodness; yet as long as man is perfectible, there must be some good in him.

About 150 years after Confucius, man's nature was firmly asserted to be good. Mencius wrote: "Man's inclination toward goodness is like the tendency of water to flow downward. There is nothing but goodness, just as water always flows downward."[50] Immense changes had taken place between the eras of the two great sages. While Confucius merely attempted to replace the aristocratic administrators of petty kingdoms with philosopher-statesmen like himself, Mencius lived in a far more violent era, when territorial lords controlling areas larger than modern European states contended with one another for the position of universal ruler, waging total wars by the standards of those days. Mencius no longer carried on leisurely dialogues with his close disciples; he had to convert the rulers-to-be and their advisers to his way of thinking. The positiveness of his tone was matched only by his vigor in debate. Just as water must be channeled downward to solve the flood problem, so must man revert to his natural instinct to do good. In either case, the urgency of the problem required that no time be wasted.

The doctrine of jen, with its accompanying devotion to kinship relationships and to ritual, grew progressively overburdened as a unifying force in Chinese society as the latter advanced in cultural level. Its development over a long period must be viewed in light of the fact that, because of the early unification of the empire, which followed almost immediately upon the Bronze Age, local institutions and customary practices never had a chance to mature into civil law. With a judiciary system that was only rudimentary and any parliamentary procedure totally unknown to us, reliance on the principles of self-restraint and mutual deference had to be stressed more than ever; and to ensure that they would be universally observed, it was essential that those moral precepts be supported by a firm philosophical base.

During the early centuries of the present millennium, China experienced significant changes. The center of population shifted from the dry-cereal-producing north to the rice-paddy-dominated south. As a result, internal diversity became more pronounced. The bureaucracy no longer represented an agrarian plutocracy. Now maintaining close ties with the gentry, its social range broadened as social mobility increased. Civil leadership of the military became more clearcut. Once free from the domination of scores of the most influential clans and from regional military power, the centralized state was compelled to find a new way of unifying its social elite, comprised of many thousands of households. Confucianism as a loosely constructed body of ideas was not enough. It had to be developed into a system of thought with sufficient intellectual appeal to satisfy the scholar-gentry class, whose horizons had been broadened and whose exchange of ideas had been facilitated by the invention of printing.

The great scholar who synthesized all previous contributions to knowledge in order to fill this void was Chu Hsi. His method is sometimes referred to as "rational," "objective," "inductive," and even "scientific."[51] Working from a huge body of writing, including philosophy and history, and supplementing it with what he considered to be scientific inquiry, Chu came to the conclusion that Confucian morality, the way in which history unfolds, and numerous phenomena of the physical world are all mutually consistent. In fact, according to him all "things" in the universe are essentially made of the same material substance, which he called "ether." In accordance with different principles, this substance consolidates and integrates to appear as different things. By "things" Chu meant not only concrete objects, but also social relationships, personal virtues, events, and phenomena.[52]

The refusal to separate the spiritual from the materialistic is typical of Neo-Confucian thinkers and consistent with their organic view of the universe. When they refer to a form of physical matter, they do not conceive of it as an isolated, static entity but focus on its function. Like an occurrence or a personal trait, an object can be said to have a property only when it interacts with other objects. The whiteness of a white object is a quality transmissible by light and perceivable by the human eye; therefore, it involves a form of dynamics implying ether in motion. In the same way, Chu Hsi saw a similarity between thunder and firecrackers, as both represent "compressed ether seeking expansion."

The Confucian jen and the Mencian doctrine that man's nature is innately good were both upheld by Chu Hsi; so were a number of related social institutions and social values. These he designated "heavenly principles." But man could deviate from them because his ether could be pure or impure. When ether is impure, the heavenly principles are obstructed and "human desires" take over. As a remedy, man should proceed to the "investigation of things," or an assiduous effort to study and reflect, carry on discussions with others, and handle worldly affairs in order to gain firsthand experience.

In actual fact, Chu Hsi's method was less inductive and objective than it was aesthetic and poetic. In many instances he used figures of speech to convey his ideas, like the equating of man's natural goodness with the downward tendency of water described by Mencius. Chu's investigation of things usually concentrated on the study of classical texts; but since "every blade of grass and every tree possesses a principle," natural phenomena were included in his inquiry.[53] As a result of his investigation, the physical always confirmed the spiritual rather than challenging or revising moral doctrines. Physical reality, cited by him along with ethical maxims demonstrating the constancy of natural law, actually appears only as a parable for the critical reader. Chu Hsi nevertheless deemed his randomly constructed analogues as effective as logic. Like many of his contemporaries, he mistook the culturally conditioned patterns of man's behavior for his inner nature, and so his conclusions had already been drawn before he started, not by the investigator himself but by Confucius and Mencius.[54]

Shortly after his death in 1200, Chu Hsi was canonized by the imperial court. His commentaries on Confucian classics, especially the general summary of them later known as the *Four Books*, had from that point been accepted as the standard at the Civil Service examinations. It remained so under the Ming dynasty.

Yet, Chu Hsi's main weakness rests not so much in the fact that he was inaccurate as that he was wasteful and unproductive. Broad generalization always has a tendency to be hypothetical; the essence is not what it is but what it is assumed to be. In this Chu Hsi did not differ a great deal from other political thinkers. The organic view of the universe that he tried to purvey could in fact better be aesthetically appreciated than logically discussed. But by investigating things he led his followers in and out of the fields of botany, geology, geography, and history without making the slightest attempt to seek knowledge for its own sake. Since he already had an answer to every question, his study, basically a method of demonstration, did not need to do more than skim the surface. The question is whether the accomplishment was worth the effort or the effort was necessary?

Chu's system can be questioned from different angles. If one assumes that the fall of man is due to impure ether, a physical flaw, then the remedy should be physically applied independent of man's intellect, or at least the cure had to lie within genetic improvement.[55] The philosopher, however, had no patience with such a literal interpretation. As a matter of fact, he did not even want to hear that a man of unbalanced ether could be "cured." Such a person, he asserted, should get himself educated; and the best way was to put himself in touch with fundamental principles.[56] That being the case, Chu Hsi possibly could have declared that all he said about ether, including its clearness, coarseness, and principle-conductive and principle-obstructing effects, was no more than metaphor. But such a declaration would have placed his organic universe in jeopardy, as it was to acknowledge that physical reality is one thing and moral value another.

As it was, Chu's body of thought could never compensate for its most restrictive feature: it committed every literate person within the empire to a lifetime of study whose only purpose was to affirm that the world is organic and that he was bound by law of nature to perform his assigned duties in society.[57] Could there be a better way of achieving the same purpose? Indeed, one could designate his own mind as the unifying agent of this organic view.[58] While the moral perfection of an immutable universe would be most difficult to prove, it could be felt by the human heart. Could not the marvel and beauty of the world, without being analyzed, instill in man's mind his own sense of perfection? Or sometimes, even without the visual image, would not this feeling of perfection rise naturally from a person's mind, especially when he was at peace with himself, unhampered by the burdens and worries of daily life?

From the viewpoint of an orthodox follower of Chu Hsi's philosophy, the school of the mind tended to endanger Confucianism as an established institution for a number of reasons.[59] First of all, once the supremacy of the mind was accepted, the great unity of the universe could be turned on and off within the mind. It ceased to be objective truth. Individuals could now attain the universal feeling intuitively through meditation. This in fact would make the Great Unity indistinguishable from the *tao* of the Taoists and the void of the Buddhists. If this absolute quality could be effortlessly realized within an individual's own mind, he would be too elated over his own enlightenment and too relieved of care to fulfill his moral and social obligations, as in the case of Keng Ting-li. Furthermore, the huge body of the Confucian canon, so carefully prepared to coordinate the manners and social norms of the scholar-gentry-official class and to enable its members to remain conversant with one another, could be tossed out. Individuals could be their own masters. Li Chih fell into this category.

Such consequences must be regarded as a serious threat to our empire, the integration of which relied to a large degree upon the general acceptance of orthodox teachings by the educated elite, who, as middle-class landowners and above, were not only the masters of the government but provided it with all its administrators. Even though Li Chih was later arrested on charges of immoral and disorderly conduct, during his trial those alleged offenses, fundamentally personal and therefore less damaging to the public, were never seriously considered. The trial judge was more concerned with his publications.[60] Curiously enough, Li Chih himself had not been unaware of the implications those works might have for his future. He had entitled his commentaries on history *The Book to Be Stored Away* and his collection of personal papers, letters, and miscellaneous notes *The Book to Be Burned.* He had foreseen the futility of his own campaign.

When Li Chih broke off relations with Keng Ting-hsiang and publicized his letter to him charging his former friend with hypocrisy, Keng retaliated in a more subtle manner. He wrote to a mutual friend and allowed the contents of the letter to be circulated: "One time Yen Shan-nung was giving a public lecture. In the middle of the session he suddenly fell to the ground, rolled over and over, and shouted, 'Watch, my innate knowledge is at work!' To this day his friends think that this is a good joke."[61] After this opening he went on to argue that many eccentric things Li Chih did were no more than "rolling over and over on the ground." His purpose was to "seize the opportune moment of instant enlightenment."

The accusation, however, was not without malicious implications. Li Chih was said to have forced his younger brother to consort with prostitutes. At one time he was said to have led a group of Buddhist monks into a widow's inner chamber begging alms. "To this day this lady is suffering from the shame that she had not guarded her doorway with more care; and the gentry is annoyed by the incident. But again, this is the kind of opportune moment in which he can realize instant enlightenment."

When Li Chih composed his reply in 1587, the Year of the Pig, he defended the reputation of the lady in question but otherwise did not deny his own indiscretion.[62] More amusing is his elaboration on the "rolling over and over on the ground." In the first place, he stated, he had never before heard about the incident involving Yen Shan-nung. But if Yen had really done it, it only proved that he had a complete grasp of the meaning of innate knowledge. He then asked: "In daily life who is not rolling on the ground? And when has he ceased to do it?" Every time a person courted a superior's favor by flattering him in public, or kneeled while visiting him in private, he was indeed rolling on the ground.

Yet, in a way "rolling on the ground" was not too bad. "When a person is rolling," Li went on, "he cannot possibly turn inward to see himself, or turn outward to see others. Thus he no longer needs to glorify the internal and belittle the external. He can remain independent without turning his back on others. He can even move across the ground without being seen. The differences between self and surroundings become blurred at the moment when the body and soul merge into one. Isn't that a wonder! Isn't that a blessing!"

Still speaking of Yen Shan-nung rolling on the ground, Li Chih declared: "Those who wish to laugh may laugh; but those who appreciate him will appreciate him." His conclusion was emphatically defiant: "Buddhism, after all, is not supposed to be taught to a mediocre crowd, nor to be discussed with those incapable of the highest level of understanding, nor to be withheld from discussion because of the fear that someone may laugh."

Both the name Yen Shan-nung and the reference to rolling on the ground were symbolic of an intellectual movement to break away from Chu Hsi's philosophy, of which the terms "instant enlightenment" and "innate knowledge" were an integral part. The exchange of insults and satirical notes between Li Chih and Keng Ting-hsiang, regardless of the two men's differences in temperament, was less a clash of personalities than an indication of the controversy rising from this movement. It was very ironic that, in terms of the "academic genealogy" of various Neo-Confucian schools, Keng was not affiliated with Chu Hsi's orthodoxy.[63] Like Li Chih, he belonged to the T'ai-chou branch of the School of the Mind. Yet when he attacked the doctrine of "spontaneity," his tone was orthodox. Likewise, Li Chih could have been less radical; his rebellious spirit intensified when he found himself under attack.

The School of the Mind itself had reached maturity during the dynasty, due largely to the contribution of Wang Yang-ming, who was generally regarded as the foremost Ming thinker. Wang had tried to proceed from Chu Hsi's methodology. The oft repeated story that he sat under a bamboo tree for several days in pursuit of the "investigation of things" until he fell sick suggests that he had refused to accept poetic analogues as natural law, yet like other Neo-Confucians insisted on the great unity between physical reality and moral value.[64] He finally came to the conclusion that the universe exists entirely in the mind of the perceiver. He considered heavenly principles as no more than what the mind holds in high regard. Since devotion to the emperor and love of parents were states of mind, loyalty and filial piety emerged as universal principles, similar to the phenomenon of flowers blooming, but only in the mind of appreciative observers. Unless perceived by the mind, "grass, trees, tiles, and stones ceased to be grass, trees, tiles, and stones." In other words, there is no such thing as objective reality.

Wang believed that moral judgments are made according to "innate knowledge." Nature has endowed every individual with this vital faculty. Similar to "conscience," innate knowledge does not perform all the detailed tasks of knowing; those are the work of "volitional ideas" and "inclinations." Rather, as if located on a higher plane, innate knowledge presides over the latter and can tell instantly whether they are right or wrong. Wang was apparently influenced by the Buddhist doctrine of causation. His world was also organically constructed. While putting emphasis on the mind, his entire teaching could also be said to stress the inseparability of cause and effect.[65] As Wang saw it, the whiteness of a white object could never be considered real because merely as a cause it is in itself incomplete. It becomes real only when its effect is felt by the perceiver. This belief makes his theory of the unity of knowledge and action understandable. Knowledge, Wang argued, means commitment.[66] It can never be passive and indifferent, nor is it complete without accompanying actions. When a person encounters a foul smell, the notice of its disagreeable odor and the action of loathing it are simultaneous. Thus the attainment of innate knowledge can be simple; it is instant and spontaneous. One can in fact follow his own nature to be good and rational; in a way, this idea does not basically differ from what Confucius said about jen.

There is no indication that Wang Yang-ming ever entertained the thought of seeking truth as he could find it regardless of its consequences. Like Chu Hsi, he merely used his philosophy as a way of confirming ideas to which he already subscribed. In order to sustain the moral doctrines and values that he had learned by rote since childhood, his theorizing showed considerably more economy than Chu Hsi's system. Nevertheless, should anyone have put his theory ahead of the Confucian canon, he could easily take the road of pantheism, romanticism, individualism, utilitarianism, or even anarchism, depending on his predisposition, because the theory of innate knowledge includes the message that every individual may take his conscience as his guide to the exclusion of all other standards.[67] In 1587 Li Chih seems to have arrived at this crossroad.

Li Chih's family background has led to speculation about whether his nonconformist attitude had anything to do with the disposition of the marginal gentry.[68] Those who make this suggestion have also theorized that Keng Ting-hsiang, who was more inclined to favor the status quo, might have reflected the mentality of more settled landlords.

Such speculations are most difficult to verify. The evidence, if any, points to the contrary. The Kengs at Huang-an were indeed an established gentry family. But when Li Chih broke with Keng Ting-hsiang he was hosted by the two Chous—Chou Ssu-ching and Chou Liu-t'ang of Ma-ch'eng—who were no less socially prominent than the Keng brothers. Furthermore, the two families were connected by multiple marital ties.[69] In Ma-ch'eng, Li also befriended Mei Kuo-chen, who subsequently contributed a preface to Li Chih's commentaries on history. According to Li's description, the Mei clan undoubtedly exceeded all families in the district in wealth and social esteem.[70] In later years Li Chih became a close friend of Liu Tung-hsing, the canal commissioner. A man of distinction himself, Liu also married his daughter to a relative of Wang Kuo-kuang, one-time minister of revenue, whose extended family was the most affluent in Yang-ch'eng, Shansi Province. When Li Chih's publications became well received, he was invited to be the houseguest of an imperial prince.[71] His last patron was Ma Ching-lun at T'ung-chou in North Chihli. Ma was affluent enough to provide Li not only with a specially constructed cottage but also a piece of farmland to rent out.[72] Among his close associates Li singled out Chiao Hung as being poor. Yet Chiao's household was a joint family of more than sixty people.[73] In sum, throughout the years when Li studied and published, his social contact and patronage came exclusively from the top strata of the scholar-gentry-official class.

Those who claim that Li was associated with the "populist wing" of the Wang Yang-ming school would be hard put to find in his writings and his biographical data any trace of involvement with the populist movement. Far from differing from traditional historians, Li shared their opinions in many instances, such as when he denounced Wang Mang as a usurper and referred to the peasants who started rebellions by rallying behind popular religion as "satanic bandits."[74] Similarly, Li's attitude toward women was often misunderstood. Li Chih denied that women were inferior to men in native intelligence. Many outstanding women of historical fame, he pointed out, were actually superior. In his commentaries on history he praised Empress Wu at great length as a brilliant ruler.[75] But his enumeration of exceptional cases in no way constituted a campaign for women's emancipation. At times he also echoed the traditionalists by commending widows who chose suicide over remarriage.[76] Perhaps most disturbing to his present-day admirers was Li Chih's total support of absolute monarchy. He declared that if the Wan-li emperor should choose to be oppressive, the imperial subjects had no alternative but to bear it.[77]

Li's reputation as an individualist had already been marred by Yüan Chung-tao's remarks, related earlier. His position as an iconoclast was likewise unstable. Although he scorned blind devotion to Confucius, he did not abandon his own reverence for the ancient sage. A portrait of Confucius hung in the Hall of Buddha in Fragrant Iris. Li Chih also made a pilgrimage to the Confucian temple at the sage's birthplace.[78]

How could these inconsistencies be accounted for?

Many centuries later, Li Chih was not likely to be exposed to criticism for having gone too far than for having not gone far enough, and less for his destructive effects than for his failure to provide a constructive program in working order. Li's inability to offer an alternative to orthodoxy, however, had little to do with his indecisiveness. For the most part it was the result of the peculiar character of the social order, whose unadaptability restricted the opportunity for innovation. When an imaginative thinker found that his own philosophy had no relevance to real life, he was likely to turn toward the mystical and become an aesthete.

Had Li Chih lived in a time of a rising urban bourgeoisie, there is little doubt that he would have championed liberty and personal freedom without reservation, as he had already recognized the universal urge for self-gain, which in itself he did not consider immoral. But as it happened, destiny miscast him in the role of political thinker.

The fact is that our empire was a community of many, many millions of peasants who could not read or write or even comprehend tax regulations without the guidance of their local gentry and village elders. Although theoretically equal under the law, these villagers were often given the death penalty or set free, not on the strength of the evidence against them but by the logical deductions of the officials conducting the trial (see p. 151). China was a nation whose maritime trade had to be restrained lest it cause problems that the court system was not equipped to handle, and the development of commercial laws based on regional usage was not encouraged because it might impair the uniformity of the realm (p. 163). Even within the bureaucracy itself the consensus of its 20,000 members could not be easily assessed. The mixing of the public spiritedness of yang with the private aims of yin had to be camouflaged by puns and other innocuous devices in order to test public acceptance (p. 68). Was it possible to give everyone his due? The composite picture already answers the question.

Freedom, after all, must have a social context; it is invaluable to the individual only when it is publicly guaranteed. Would not "life, liberty, and the pursuit of happiness" become a meaningless phrase when a nation's judicial system had been lagging behind for centuries? Unconventional as Li Chih was, he was too realistic to misjudge this situation. Under the circumstances, direct subscription to moral laws, along with general acceptance of the Confucian jen, bound into a compulsory creed, had been designed to fill a technical void. Together they managed to destroy all possibility of administering justice with precision.

Although the principle of morality was immutable, the implementation of moral laws as an intervening factor in public affairs should still have involved skill, depth, and variation. The problem faced by Li Chih and his contemporaries in 1587 was that the application of moral laws to the workings of the state as well as to the personal conduct of the individual had been too close and direct, or too literal and narrow, and therefore too crude and simple. Official reliance on the *Four Books* as the legal guide and code of ethics for at least two hundred years had resulted in the absence of any effort to develop an intermediate zone of legality, which, capable of adjusting to changing circumstances, would have increased the flexibility of the government and broadened what was socially acceptable in the conduct of an individual, thus extending the range of creativity of both. The practice of passing moral judgment on every line of conduct, public or private—more characteristic of the Ming dynasty than any other period in our history—had excluded such a possibility.

The result was that the body of tenets that Confucius and Mencius had intended some two thousand years earlier to inspire and lead, became an instrument for repressive conformity. To the chagrin of Li Chih, mediocrity was encouraged in the name of morality and intellectual dishonesty remained a fixed characteristic of bureaucratic life, to the point where "benevolence and righteousness became the yang and the accumulation of wealth and scrambling for rank the yin."[79]

If Li Chih's life showed any consistent direction, it was in his continual struggle to free himself from this pressure to conform without abandoning his fundamental position as a moralist and positivist. This struggle had prompted him to resign from the Civil Service; to cut himself off from his family in Ch'üan-chou; first to become the houseguest of Keng Ting-hsiang and then to break away from him; to build his Buddhist chapel; to devote himself to publications that attracted the interest and earned the patronage of the scholar-gentry-official class; and, during his trial, to assert that his writings were useful in propagating the teaching of ancient sages. Yet, in carrying on the struggle Li never abandoned either his rascality or his elitism.[80] Freedom to him was not a right to which every individual was entitled but a privilege of the enlightened. The latter, being their own masters, could even defy the sex taboo. In this way he ended by creating a radical image for himself, and for that had to forfeit his own life.

Part of the difficulty in evaluating Li Chih's thought arises from the fact that the tragic philosopher never sat down and developed a coherent theme. Not all of his disjointed statements can be coordinated. But at least his commentaries on history, a work of sixty-eight chapters, were composed according to a general plan that can give the reader a sense of direction.

Li's theory of history was cyclic and dialectic. Rulers who brought cultural accomplishments to the summit of perfection, he pointed out, usually marked the end of peaceful reigns and the beginnings of disorder. On the other hand, emperors who created order out of chaos dealt only with the essence of things, and their governance was noted for its simplicity. Though Li was unaware of it, the converse relationship between cultural refinement and public security was a corollary of bureaucratic management; the broad commitment of its members to large areas and the derivation of administrative skills from the principles of homogeneity and uniformity restricted the government's own potential to grow and to diversify.[81] As society advanced, it usually created problems which lay beyond the capacities of a literary bureaucracy so preoccupied with stability and balance to handle. No escape from this pattern was anticipated by Li Chih, as anything outside of the dynastic cycle was also outside his experience of history. Nevertheless, in accepting the dynastic cycle as the result of some kind of recurring mystic element within the cosmic order, Li Chih had already acknowledged the existence of an objective reality independent of the human mind.

On this basis the role of emperors was played down by the commentator; their places in history, with few exceptions, were determined by the cycle. In his analysis Li placed more emphasis on the chief counsellors. At this point he departed from historians of the orthodox school by declaring that what the public expected from these statesmen was deeds, not words. A talented man capable of making outstanding contributions to the public welfare, he stressed, should never be overconcerned with his own personal reputation. In fact, he should take insult and humiliation in stride if it enabled him to accomplish anything at all.[82] He was justified in using flattery and temporarily dishonest means to secure his position, provided it served the public interest. This statement contained a dual thesis: there is a difference between private morals and public morals; and the end justifies the means. Not only is this idea materialistic, on this point Li's resemblance to Machiavelli is striking.

Li Chih accorded high positions in history to innovative fiscal administrators of previous dynasties, including Li K'uei of the Warring States period, Sang Hung-yang of the Han, and Liu Yen of the T'ang; but he took a dim view of Wang An-shih of the Sung, not because of his lack of virtue, but because his talent did not measure up to his spirit of enterprise.[83] The commentator further shocked his readers by making the statement that "a corrupt official might do small damage; an upright official could do even greater damage."[84]

Even though Li Chih showed a certain amount of respect for Hai Jui compared to other of his contemporaries, in his writings Hai and others who fell captive to a strict honor code were "evergreen shrubs," whose ability to withstand severe weather was basically a private virtue, which did not equip them to "become pillars and roofbeams."[85] On the other hand, Yü Ta-yu and Ch'i Chi-kuang were great men, "personalities of a thousand generations."[86] The most brilliant man of his day, whom Li Chih worshipped without reservation, was Chang Chü-cheng, whose courage he described "as magnificent as the sky."[87]

It is unclear whether Li ever met the grand-secretary he so admired. However, they did have many mutual friends and contacts. Both Keng Ting-hsiang and Chou Ssu-ching, Li Chih's hosts, had been active members of Chang Chü-cheng's inner circle.[88] Keng, in particular, during his term as governor in 1578, had been instrumental to the provincial land survey in Fukien[89] that provided the basis for Chang's national land survey two years later—generally regarded as the foremost attempt the grand-secretary ever made to organize the empire's public finances.

Thus Li's admiration of Chang extended far beyond the ordinary bounds of hero-worship. Moreover, when Chang Chü-cheng was still in his teens, his schoolwork had been supervised by a provincial official named Li Yüan-yang.[90] This man's outlook was very similar to Li Chih's. Like Li Chih retired in middle age, he had also led a life halfway between those of a Buddhist monk and a Confucian scholar. The two Li met at least once.[91]

It was owing to Li Yüan-yang's influence that Chang Chü-cheng developed his early interest in Ch'an Buddhism. The interest led him, as a Han-lin academician, to make contact with the T'ai-chou branch of the School of the Mind. He had even examined the papers of Wang Ken, its founder, for possible adaptation to practical politics.[92] But somewhere along the line Chang must have come to the conclusion that his patronage of a specific school of thought would inevitably establish a bad precedent. Ironically, he was later accused of being a persecutor of its adherents, having caused the death of Ho Hsin-yin, one of the school's renowned members, although Li Chih emphatically defended the grand-secretary against the charge.[93]

But what could Chang Chü-cheng do? The organizational principles of the state were restraint and inhibition on a theoretical foundation that aimed to neutralize all individual differences and bring everything into balance. His own method of governing, even on its limited scale, called for readjustment and expansion. Caught in the discrepancy, no matter what he did he could never free himself from accusations of abuse and usurpation of power. Chang's solution, which must have impressed and inspired Li, was to force himself to bear the consequences of the inconsistency.[94] When he said that his own body was "no longer his possession" and that he offered himself as "a mat on which others were welcome to lie down, tread, or urinate," Chang of course was prepared to be called the vilest names by his critics. In the end he communicated with his early mentor, Li Yüan-yang, pledging "to enter into the burning pyre in order to reach the gateway of soothing coolness." These words crystallized the tragedy of a large empire which elected to govern itself by moral principle rather than by statutory law.

Chang Chü-cheng's frustration was also Li Chih's. In an age when creative talent found so few outlets, and still fewer in public service, Li in his lifetime witnessed the public failures of the Wan-li emperor, Grand-Secretary Shen Shih-hsing, Censor-in-Chief Hai Jui, and Regional Commander Ch'i Chi-kuang. But it was Chang Chü-cheng's posthumous downfall that distressed him most. He had expected Vice-Minister Chou Ssuching to sacrifice himself in order to right Chang's wrong. When Chou refused to act, Li wrote him, his own patron and supporter, and told him in no uncertain terms that he lacked chivalry.[95]

Li Chih's life story does not suggest that he would have turned Wang Yang-ming's philosophy into a justification for senseless debauchery; at the same time, it is most unlikely that he would have been far enough ahead of his time to work for social justice. His philosophy nevertheless encompassed both idealistic and materialistic elements. It seems that, as a divided thinker, he aimed at both transcendental emancipation and earthly accomplishment.

In fact, his adherence to Wang Yang-ming's School of the Mind showed such a dual approach. Wang, while invigorating his followers and boosting their self-sufficiency by stressing the importance of will power, suffered from the opposite extreme of Chu Hsi's thoroughness with his over-simplified view of things. The nature of innate knowledge, sometimes referred to as inborn intuition, was never clearly defined; this opened the door to a variety of elaborations and articulations.[96] That the many branches ramifying from the School of the Mind all claimed to be academic descendants of the master was hardly a surprise. But Li Chih's position of extreme idealism and extreme materialism both rooted in the teachings of the same thinker was rather unusual.

When Li said that "morals and ethics are no more than matters connected with food and clothing," he was actually echoing Wang Ken of T'ai-chou, a close associate of Wang Yang-ming. This second Wang was an activist who had popular appeal. Like Thomas Hobbes, he based his political philosophy on the doctrine of self-preservation. But once this concept was established he immediately diverged from Western thinkers. His 'self' was not the animal self who was at war with others, but essentially a social being capable of moral perfection. Seeing his own biological needs, the self could not help realizing that others had the same needs and desires. In other words, Wang Ken's mind was not one that could turn the world of phenomena on and off, but more closely resembled the universal mind of Mencius, ready to share, compassionate, and basically guided by common sense. To dispense such good will in reality served one's self-interest, as one could never survive without the similar good will of others.[97] With the precept "*tao* means the daily necessity of the common people," Wang Ken brought Wang Yang-ming's teaching down to the level of the common man. One could indeed follow his natural instinct, perhaps slightly modified by reasoning, to attain wisdom. Li Chih, a man of passion, found this appeal too inviting to resist. He eventually emerged, more than anything else, as a spiritual descendant of Wang Ken.

At the time when this strain of thought took hold of him, Li Chih was materialistic and positivistic. He dismissed a profusion of virtuous utterances as hypocritical and devotion to ritual as a great waste. Yet his "utilitarianism" never progressed beyond the theoretical state. Li showed no interest in industrial technology, business management, or the science of agriculture. Moreover, he aligned himself behind the top bureaucrats who wished to benefit the population on practical issues through their leadership and statecraft. Under the circumstances, Li Chih the critic and theoretician had no intention of becoming a food producer or industrialist himself.

But it was precisely in the domain of the top bureaucrats that the limitations of Wang Ken's philosophy became apparent. Indeed, by applying the principle of reciprocity one could immediately determine whether one's own intention behind private conduct was good or evil; it was not so easy to pass judgment on a public decision arrived at by a statesman. Fundamentally this touched upon one basic fact: ethics is one thing and its application another. But the bureaucracy, operating as an homogeneous body and lacking the services of an independent judiciary, rarely made the distinction on a number of issues. The traditional standard was that a gentleman must let his virtue exceed his talent, never allowing the latter to eclipse the former. And what was it that defined the two? It had to be convention and past standards. This discouraged personal initiative. What had not been done before should never be attempted. Not infrequently a technical innovation simply incited charges of immorality. In Chang Chü-cheng's case Li Chih clearly saw the ring of conformity closing in, if he had not already sufficiently experienced it firsthand.

Not a revolutionary, Li never proposed reorganizing the empire. The limited change in governmental operation that he had in mind called for more freedom of action on the part of top administrators. Unable to find a legal means of enfranchising the privileged few, he found a way residing in Wang Yang-ming's theory of the mind, which he highlighted in his commentaries on history.

When Wang Yang-ming said that volitional ideas have the specific function of knowing while innate knowledge decides whether it is right or wrong, he made it clear that volitional ideas are no more than one's random thoughts but never specified the nature of innate knowledge. Possibly he might have said that it, like conscience or the perfectibility of man, is a natural endowment but in itself is undefinable, as it has no content of its own. Instead he went on to say that volitional ideas can be good or evil, while innate knowledge is beyond good and evil.[98] This prompted Wang Chi, another associate, to feel justified in driving home the theory that in order to attain innate knowledge one has to put aside volitional ideas. His reasoning was that man's sensual, physical self, together with his random thought, being transitory and always in a state of flux, has no claim to absolute reality. On this ground, volitional ideas are a distraction from the search for truth and must be banished. Innate knowledge, which alone is real, transcends all physical characteristics, properties, and inclinations. It is not nonbeing yet it exists without a trace. When the argument had reached this point, the displacement of Confucian ethics by Buddhist metaphysics was apparent. Li Chih's interest in the works of this third Wang started from the days when he was a junior member of the bureaucracy in Peking. Later he visited Wang Chi and was instrumental in publishing his *Selected Works.*[99]

Logically, to put Wang Chi's idea to work one would have to muster one's will to negate the sensual and physical aspects of life in order to reach the transcendental feeling of what is beyond and above good and evil. Yet, since ultimate reality exists only in the mind, when the mind is set to rights no work is left undone. In other words, this means that the purgation does not need to go beyond what was essentially an intellectual exercise. When a person wills no evil he sees no evil and, as far as he is concerned, no evil exists in the world—an extreme form of idealism. It was from this position that Li Chih defied Keng Ting-hsiang's criticism. When the latter accused him of consorting with prostitutes, Li admitted that he had indeed visited "the streets of flowers and markets of willows" in Ma-ch'eng. But in reality, Li Chih had his individual sense of purity. It was doubtful that he would have been comfortable with ladies of easy virtue. Nevertheless, he continued to argue by citing the Buddhist doctrine that "enlightenment can be reached while one remains playful"; this was also in accord with Lao-tzu's doctrine that one way to settle worldly affairs is not to try to cleanse the world, but to submit oneself to the dust of the crowd so as to share its outlook. In this way no ground rule is inviolable, provided the violator is of "a superior mind."[100]

It was now easy for Li Chih to exonerate a number of historical figures from their transgressions of moral law as moral law was understood in his day. This exception was justified, he reasoned, because the temporary suspension of morals brought public security of a more endurable nature. His elitism continued to grip him. Without rewriting history, Li Chih thus made exceptions for the heroes and heroines whom he considered to be superior. He himself, who granted moral pardon, must be "super-superior."[101] The writer vaguely hoped that his written judgments, although lacking legal authority and theoretical consistency, would "after centuries or even millennia become the basis for the Civil Service examinations and the emperor's public study sessions."[102] What reforms the highly stylized society would have to undergo before replacing the *Four Books* with Li's own erratic writings the author neglected to elaborate. Understandably such a transformation would be difficult; that was why it might take centuries and millennia. Yet, foreseeing that the Civil Service examinations and the emperor's study sessions would continue to remain in existence, the avant-garde and Li's forward-looking society continued to remain highly stylized.

Shortly after the beginning of 1601, the Hall of Buddha in Fragrant Iris was burned to the ground by hoodlums hired by local officials and members of the gentry.[103] The details of this case were never disclosed. But a major controversy surrounded the fact that Li Chih maintained contact with Mei Kuo-chen's widowed daughter and several other ladies in the family. In an age when sexual segregation was an iron rule for the upper class, Mei Tan-jan's pledging to be Li's disciple had already raised eyebrows. Either carried away by her unusual intelligence or in a mood to express himself, Li Chih, now over seventy, continued to mention her in his papers: "Mei Tan-jan is a wonder," "man is inferior to her," "truly intelligent, truly making bold progress, and truly magnificent!" In one published paper he compared her to the Goddess of Mercy.[104]

Li Chih's past record of consorting with prostitutes and visiting an unnamed lady, already confessed by him in writing, undoubtedly worked against him even though a dozen years had elapsed since that episode during his verbal battle with Keng Ting-hsiang. As a matter of fact, later Li made peace with his old friend, and when the incident of 1601 occurred Keng had already been dead for five years. In the mind of the public, nevertheless, the image of Li Chih as a notorious heretic had not faded with time.

It was paradoxical that while the top bureaucrats regarded Li's nonconformity as a more or less personal matter and therefore academic, the local gentry and the lower echelons of the government were unable to treat him with such indifference and leniency. In practice, it was the latter groups who were expected to carry out the orthodoxy and translate its abstractions into reality. The local gentry was morally obliged to see to it that within their districts the younger generation honored the old, women obeyed their menfolk, and the illiterate followed the educated elite. Personnel evaluation of local officials also took these matters into account, citing the numbers of virtuous men and women in their districts and the absence of disputes as a measure of their moral leadership. In this sense, Li Chih's arguments in favor of the fulfillment and expansion of the individual personality was tantamount to condoning licentiousness. Moreover, many of those whose anger he provoked had never read his publications or understood his real argument. To them Li Chih the madman stood for everything contrary to law and order and decency.

So it was doubly ironic that Li Chih's publications were what antagonized them most. In fact, periodic deviations from the moral code on the part of the gentry themselves must have been common. Nevertheless, it was an entirely different matter to justify such nonconformity on the printed page. Thus Li Chih was trapped by his own renown. The more widely read his books were, the less forgivable he became.[105] Otherwise his antagonists would never have waited for over fifteen years to destroy his fortress. Oblivious to their own misplaced self-righteousness, the gentry and local officials believed that they were avenging Confucius and Mencius.

In 1596, Li Chih and his religious establishment had already faced a crisis. A circuit intendant by surname Shih threatened to arrest him, hoping that the threat would intimidate him to run away. When the plan failed, Shih then spread word that he would dismantle the Hall of Buddha in Fragrant Iris on the ground that it had never been licensed as a religious establishment. Li Chih put up a stiff fight, claiming that it was a private chapel, endowed by top officials in the capital. Mediators maneuvering behind the scenes forced Shih to drop the case.[106] Li Chih, on his part, took a long trip that lasted for four years. He visited Liu Tung-hsing's home region in Shansi, toured the Great Wall, took a boatride the entire length of the Grand Canal, stopped at Nanking, which precipitated the publication of his *Book to Be Stored Away*, and returned to Ma-ch'eng in 1600.[107] By thus attracting more attention, Li was even less welcomed by local circles. To make matters worse, at this time he wrote to Mei Tan-jan, the controversial lady, that Ma-ch'eng was his everlasting resting place and that he would like to have a Buddhist burial on the hills behind the Fragrant Iris.[108] Still not having found a way to deal with this unwanted heretic, the local leaders resorted to violence.

When this happened, his good friend Ma Ching-lun came all the way from T'ung-chou to take Li north. Ma, previously a censor who had offended the Wan-li emperor, was studying and writing in forced retirement. His generosity enabled Li Chih once again to live in modest comfort, with a cottage, orchards, and vegetable gardens, and a piece of land the income from which provided support for a number of monks who served as his personal attendants. Most important, the necessary intellectual setting was provided; here Li had his friends, visitors, and admirers among the younger generation.[109]

Li spent the last year of his life revising a manuscript on the *Book of Changes* — traditionally the kind of work that marked a Confucian scholar's last effort.[110] As an intellectual Buddhist, Li had long accepted the idea that the self is no more than a phantom around which a number of causes and effects fluctuate. As a Confucian scholar he had also espoused the cyclic interpretation of history: when a society has exhausted its possibilities for cultural refinement, peaceful reigns will end; rebirth will occur after a period of disorder.[111] Yet, the nascent dynasty has to proceed from childlike simplicity, so that room for growth and ostentation will exist. It was appropriate that this theory be given such timely emphasis in 1601, the year when Nurhaci created his "Banner System," through which he converted the tribal organization of the Manchu into more adaptable units in order to conquer our empire, a settled civilization of three millennia. Barely two years earlier the Manchu had devised their own system of writing, thus reaching the minimum level of sophistication while still remaining qualified for unspoiled simplicity.

Under the circumstances what could Li Chih do? For all his insatiable drive toward personal emancipation, he could never escape the doctrine of jen. After the Year of the Pig he had become a monk. Yet the Buddhist doctrine of emptiness failed to dispel his concern for the material security of his fellowmen.

Li did not need to resolve the dilemma. A decision was made for him when he was censured by Chang Wen-ta, a supervising-secretary. In his memorial to the Wan-li emperor, Chang accused Li Chih of many crimes and misdeeds — past and present, real and imaginary, by quotations, established fact, and implication. Li's interpretation of history was said to be "deceiving, perverted, and seditious." Li's consorting with prostitutes and "bathing with them in daytime" was mentioned, along with the charge that he held theological seminars with the wives and daughters of the local gentry. Some of his female guests were alleged to have often stayed in the Ma-ch'eng chapel overnight. Chang then urged the emperor to consider that in recent years many young people had openly seized the properties of others and taken possession of their wives, and that many governmental officials, rosaries in hand, had worshipped Buddhist idols instead of following Confucian teachings. All these infractions supposedly could be traced to Li Chih's heresy. "Now I have heard," the supervising-secretary concluded, "that Li Chih has moved to T'ung-chou, less than twenty miles from the capital. If he should enter the capital, he would mislead and poison the urban population just as he did in Ma-ch'eng." The imperial rescript authorized the arrest of Li by the Silk Robe Guard and the proscription of his books.[112]

The case created a momentarily awkward situation in Peking. While the proscription of heterodoxy could be said to be an assumed stance of our empire, it had never been persistently carried out as a general policy. When Li Chih was imprisoned, Matteo Ricci, whom Li had encountered earlier, had made a successful entry into the emperor's court. The Jesuit priest had yet to convert some of the top officials to Catholicism. Indeed, in 1587, the Year of the Pig, the Wan-li emperor had accepted the suggestion of the Ministry of Rites to issue a general order enjoining the use of quotations and phraseology taken from Buddhist and Taoist literatures in schoolwork and examinations within the public school system.[113] Yet, in 1599, he wrote to his grand-secretaries indicating that he himself was absorbed in reading the *Treasuries of Buddhist Literature* and *Treasuries of Taoist Literature.*[114] His Majesty had also contributed generously to Buddhist temples, sent eunuchs to Buddhist shrines to pay homage, and declared amnesties in the Buddhist spirit. On the other hand, the many charges against Li Chih, either impossible to substantiate or not exactly crimes when closely examined, under Chang Wen-ta's influence loomed large enough as serious offenses that they could not be dismissed. At least Li Chih was not abused; he was permitted to read and write during his imprisonment.

At the end of the trial the judge recommended no harsher penalty than that the accused be escorted back to his district of origin, in this case Ch'üan-chou of Fukien. Customarily such a recommendation meant a suspended sentence, with the offender placed under the surveillance of local officials for life. For unknown reasons these papers were held in the emperor's office.

One day the prisoner asked the jailer to give him a razor so he could shave. The jailer complied, and after he left Li Chih slashed his throat with it. When he returned the man was horrified to see Li apparently in agony but still very much alive. "Is it painful?"

Unable to talk, Li traced his answer with his finger on the jailer's palm: "No pain."

"Monk, why did you cut yourself like that?"

"What else could a man over seventy do?"

According to the only surviving account, Li Chih lingered on for two days before he died.[115]

Li Chih should have died sooner. If he had slipped from the picture in 1587, the year before his tonsure, he would have remained historically obscure yet at the same time would most definitely have saved himself immeasurable agony. As it happened, his subsequent fifteen years of toil and trouble proved to be only futile. Despite the fact that his books were repeatedly issued, they never came close to becoming the standard for the Civil Service examinations and the emperor's public study sessions. From our vantage point, suffice it to say that they never will.

Yet, those fifteen years of Li Chih's life had not been a total waste. He provided us with an invaluable record, without which we would perhaps never be able to fathom the depth of intellectual frustration that characterized this era. A highly stylized society wherein the roles of individuals were thoroughly restricted by a body of simple yet ill-defined moral precepts, the empire was seriously hampered in its development, regardless of the noble intention behind those precepts. The year 1587 may seem to be insignificant; nevertheless, it is evident that by that time the limit for the Ming dynasty had already been reached. It no longer mattered whether the ruler was conscientious or irresponsible, whether his chief counsellor was enterprising or conformist, whether the generals were resourceful or incompetent, whether the civil officials were honest or corrupt, or whether the leading thinkers were radical or conservative—in the end they all failed to reach fulfillment. Thus our story has a sad conclusion. The annals of the Year of the Pig must go down in history as a chronicle of failure.

APPENDIX A:
AUDIENCE ON FEBRUARY 5, 1590

On the lunar New Year's Day, which fell on February 5, the Wan-li emperor absented himself from public celebrations. As had been done before, the grand-secretaries, including First Grand-Secretary Shen Shih-hsing, Second Grand-Secretary Hsü Kuo, Third Grand-Secretary Wang Hsi-chüeh, and Fourth Grand-Secretary Wang Chia-p'ing, went to the Polar Convergence Gate to kowtow to the throne. At the end of the ceremony they were surprised to be told that the emperor wanted to see them in his living quarters. In the western chamber of the Yü-te Hall the four secretaries saw the sovereign sitting on a couch. When they knelt at his side, Shen Shih-hsing was closest to the emperor. So the day's conversation was mainly carried on between Wan-li and the first grand-secretary, who recorded the dialogue as follows. Aside from my bracketed interpolations, the statements in parentheses appear in the original text, but italicization is mine.

Emperor: I am afraid that my illness has become incurable.

Shen: Please don't say that, Your Majesty! You are in the prime of your life, full of pep and vitality. All Your Majesty needs is a good rest and some good care. In no time you will get over it.

Emperor: Last year, because the fire element rose from the heart and liver, I constantly had this congestion in the chest and dizziness in my head. After resting for a while I was on the verge of getting well—but then came the memorial of Lo Yü-jen—and his wild accusations! It makes me mad. The fire from my liver is flaring up again. That's how I am today.

Shen: Your Majesty, your health comes first. You should never allow the silliness of an ignorant minor official to bother you.

(*At this point the emperor handed the memorial under discussion to the first grand-secretary.*)

Emperor: Dear tutors, take a look at this. He says that I'm drunken, lustful, greedy, and have a terribly bad temper. Now I ask you to judge——.

(*Shen Shih-hsing had barely opened the memorial and was trying to read it, not yet knowing what to say. The emperor continued.*)

Emperor: He says that I'm an alcoholic. I do drink—who doesn't? But have I ever after the cup got into a fuss unfitting to the emperor, such as dragging around a sword or wielding a sabre?

He also says that I am under the spell of women; in particular, that I favor Lady Cheng too much and side with her. This is because Lady Cheng is always with me whenever I retire to the palace quarters. She takes good care of me, day and night. As for Lady Wang—Consort Kung—she has my eldest son. I want her to take care of him. Mother and son are always together, so she cannot be with me all the time. What has this to do with partiality and impartiality?

Well, he accuses me of being greedy, saying Chang Ching has bribed me so I retain him in my service. Last year Li Yi said the same thing. I'm the Son of Heaven, supposed to own all that is within the Four Seas, am I not? If I covet Chang Ching's fortune, why don't I simply confiscate it?

He goes on to say that I have a terribly bad temper. An ancient proverb says: "When you are young, be careful about your lust. When you are mature, beware of your contention." Here the word *contention* means temper. Don't I know it? But, then, who doesn't have a temper?

You, my tutors, also have your own household servants. Can you go on forever without punishing them? It is true, some palace maids and eunuchs have been beaten. They have either made errors or committed offenses. Some of them may have [subsequently] died of illness. How can he say that I have beaten every one of them to death?

Gentlemen, take this paper back to your office, draft a rescript for me, let us give him a severe punishment.

Shen: It seems to me that he is a small official, ignorant, misinformed. He simply picked up the wrong things that he heard and hastily wrote a memorial.

Emperor: But he is trying to invite attention, and he goes way beyond his station to do it.

Shen: If that is the case, Your Majesty's severe punishment would exactly serve his purpose. At the same time it may damage your imperial virtue. The best way is to ignore him, that would truly show Your Majesty's greatness.

(*The first grand-secretary carefully put the memorial on the stand in front of the emperor. The latter contemplated for a moment.*)

Emperor: There is something in your way of thinking. But this has nothing to do with my virtue. However, it might make me look less tolerant.

Shen: Your Majesty's tolerance is as high as heaven and as wide as the earth. It accommodates everything.

(*The emperor once again handed the memorial to the grand-secretary so that the latter could read it more carefully. But Shen grasped only the general ideas.*)

Emperor: (*Repeatedly*) I can't get rid of this anger. He must be given a severe punishment.

Shen: This paper is full of falsehood. If we dignify it with a rescript along with a severe punishment, soon word would spread. People would think that what is said here is true. If Your Majesty will listen to me, I would say that the best way is to ignore it, just put it aside. Let us record what is taking place here today in history. Let's pass it on to posterity, so that thousands of generations later people may praise you as a ruler of the stature of Yao and Shun.

(*He once again placed the memorial before the emperor.*)

Emperor: But what about this man?

Shen: If we put aside the memorial, there's not much we can do about him in terms of a penalty. But if Your Majesty will be lenient enough to let us, we shall pass word to his superiors—we'll just say, well, that he may leave.

(*The emperor nodded his consent. He looked calmer.*)

Emperor: Dear tutors, you are part of my close circle. You know better. Whatever I do, you gentlemen know. How could have I done all these things that he said?

Shen: Even we cannot say that we know it all, Your Majesty. Palace life, with so many gates, involves privacy. But of course neither can a minor official so remote from us [know it all].

Emperor: When a subject serves a sovereign, there must be principles. Nowadays everything is disregarded. There is no difference between the superior and the inferior; everyone simply says what comes into his mind. Some time ago that Tang Chieh—he scorned me. I let him go. And now Lo Yü-jen does exactly the same thing. It happens because they can get away with it; they are not punished.

Shen: When a subject offers advice to the throne, even though his motive is loyalty and devotion, he must tone down the words, it must be gently persuasive. Even we ourselves, unless there is a matter compelling us to speak up, wouldn't dare to. We wouldn't dare to disagree with Your Majesty.

Now, here is a minor official. How dare we take sides with him? We are concerned only with Your Majesty's health and reputation. Those are more important.

Emperor: All right, even you, my own tutors, recognize that there is a superior above and subordinates below. But those junior graders are so out of control! They have so many opinions! Right is wrong; and wrong is right! I have not finished reading one paper when another comes along contending it. I just don't have the time to deal with them all. I have to read these papers under an oil lamp, to struggle with the blurred images of the writing. This is not a court; we have no discipline. You tutors are my limbs; you should do something about it.

Shen: Your Majesty, we have very little talent, and we command so little influence. Seeing the mistakes of our predecessors, we wouldn't dare to take matters into our own hands, so everything is reported to Your Majesty for decision, and referred to the outer court for consensus.

Emperor: No, no, that is not the way it should be! You are my arms and thighs. I am the heart. How can the heart make a move without the limbs? I have delegated the responsibility to you, what do you tutors have to be afraid of? You must take charge for me, do all the work and bear all the criticisms. Never should you find an excuse to avoid that.

(*The four grand-secretaries kowtowed to express their gratitude [to the emperor for the confidence he had in them].*)

Shen: Since Your Majesty has so graciously entrusted us as limbs to the heart, how dare we not try to do our very best? Indeed, we should write "Do all the work and bear all the criticisms" down, put it on our desks, and be reminded by it every morning and every evening.

Now, excuse me, may I ask, is Your Majesty taking medicine?

Emperor: Twice a day.

Shen: Your Majesty still needs to be careful, though. Must take the right kind of medicine.

Emperor: That I know. I'm reading medical books and am quite familiar with the principles of pulsation.

Shen: Take good care of yourself, Your Majesty. The thing to do is to maintain a pure mind, get rid of distractions. Don't let yourself get angry. When your emotions are tranquil, recovery will come naturally.

(*After a pause and some similar remarks by others, Shen Shih-hsing continued.*)

Shen: We have missed Your Majesty for so long. Today we have the privilege of having been called in for a visit; what humble opinions we have we wouldn't dare keep to ourselves.

Recently Your Majesty has not attended the morning audience and study sessions very often. The outer court is eager to see you. Well, since Your Majesty needs to rest quietly, we wouldn't dare to bother you too much. But would it be possible to have an audience with your court, say, just three or four times a month? That will give comfort to the public which wants to see Your Majesty so very much.

Emperor: Only when I get well. When I feel well, don't I also like to get out? I would like to preside over the sacrificial ceremonies to our ancestors and go to the imperial shrine. And the empress dowager, my own mother—who has given me this life—I should visit with her regularly, too. But this aching is right here in my waist. My feet are simply too feeble to walk.

Shen: One more thing. The issue of the heir apparent is a matter of public concern. Your Majesty had better settle it, the sooner the better.

Emperor: I am aware of it. The empress does not have a son. The matter of succession is settled by the date of birth. This has been repeatedly brought up by Lady Cheng; she is afraid that outsiders may cast suspicion on her. But my eldest son is very delicate. I would like to wait until he becomes just a bit more sturdy before I let him out. Only then can I feel at ease.

Shen: But the eldest imperial son is already nine *sui* [actual count seven and a half years old]. Now is the time for schooling.

Emperor: There is the matter of individual difference. Some people find their own way without being taught. Others have to take lessons. There are still others. Unless they are troubled they will never learn. A lot comes from natural endowment. When a person has it he has it. You can't expect education to change everything.

Shen: Your Majesty, endowment is a natural gift. But learning is a human effort. Even a genius cannot get along without education. Time is an important factor. In order to develop his full capacity, his education has to start on time.

Emperor: All right, I have heard you. Now, dear tutors, you may go back to your offices.

(*The emperor also ordered that food and wine be served them at their offices. Shen Shih-hsing and his colleagues kowtowed to the sovereign before leaving.*

They left the palace. But when they were not more than a hundred paces away a eunuch from the Directory of Ceremonies ran and caught up with them. He asked the four grand-secretaries to return to the palace, as the emperor had ordered the eldest imperial son to meet them. The four turned back. They stood on the avenue inside the palace gate for a long time. Then another eunuch came. This one had actually been dispatched by the emperor to observe whether or not Grand-Secretary Shen was showing any sign of delight upon being told that he was to meet the eldest imperial son. [The errand was so unusual that the runner was not sure what kind of report he was supposed to bring back to the emperor, so he simply conferred with Shen Shih-hsing.] He subsequently reported back to the emperor that the first grand-secretary was overwhelmed with joy. This caused the sovereign to grin [as Shen Shih-hsing learned afterward].

Yet there was more waiting. Still standing on the pavement, the grand-secretaries met two more eunuchs from the Directory of Ceremonies who came to tell them that the emperor had now ordered Chang Ching to report to them on the spot, and that when he came Shen Shih-hsing should scold him. [Chang Ching, a senior eunuch previously in charge of the Secret Police, had been impeached by the civil officials and removed from office one and a half years earlier. By this time the Wan-li emperor had recalled him and secretly retained him on the palace staff. When this was discovered by the civil officials it caused considerable tension. The emperor had now arranged to have Chang do public penance before the grand-secretaries, pledging, in particular, not to reveal derogatory information about the civil officials. The arrangement seems to have been effective. After the event the agitation over Chang Ching no longer appeared in state papers.]

But at this Shen Shih-hsing and his colleagues balked: Chang Ching was a member of the emperor's personal staff, how could they exercise the prerogative to rebuke a person so close to the throne? Their argument was again relayed to the emperor; but the messengers brought back the stern instruction that what had been said earlier was an order and must be carried out.

When Chang Ching came, he bowed his head in humility. On the pavement he knelt down facing the Yü-te Hall, where the emperor was resting. Shen Shih-hsing's lecture placed more emphasis on the future than on the past. In gratitude for the imperial trust placed in him, the eunuch should give loyal and dedicated service, bound by law and serving the public interest. Chang in turn murmured that he had been too talkative and thus offensive to others. Before all this was concluded, Chang also said three times, "Long Live His Myriad Years!" The entire proceedings were again reported to the emperor, who was said to be very pleased.

At long last the eldest imperial son came. But simultaneously the third imperial son also arrived, accompanied by a nursing mother. Once again the grand-secretaries filed into the chamber and knelt alongside the emperor's couch.

Still reclining on the couch, the emperor stretched his arm out to grasp the hand of the eldest imperial son. Next to him stood the third imperial son, with the nursing mother behind him. The dialogue between the sovereign and the first grand-secretary continued.)

Shen: Isn't His Highness the Eldest Imperial Son good-looking! With such a dragon poise and such phoenix eyes! There is not the slightest doubt about it: Your Majesty's kind-heartedness is bringing you the strongest posterity ever! Your fulfillment is to reach the top of the sky!

Emperor: If that is the case, it is due to the virtue of our ancestors and the goodness of Her Majesty the Empress Dowager. How would I dare to take the credit?

Shen: Your Majesty, please allow me to say [that] His Highness is growing fast; this is the time for schooling.

Emperor: I have already let eunuchs teach him to read.

Shen: When Your Majesty was formally installed as heir apparent, you were nine *sui.* You had already started your public study sessions. If His Highness were to start right now, it would already be late.

Emperor: I could read when I was five *sui.* Look at this boy (pointing a finger at the third imperial son), he is also five *sui.* Always sick, he cannot even leave the nurse.

(*The emperor then had the eldest imperial son face the light so that the grand-secretaries could have a good look at him.*)

Shen: Your Majesty, you have the finest piece of jade here. All you need to do is a little polishing, the sooner the better. For the sake of your family temple and the imperial shrine, the sooner the better.

(*The grand-secretaries kowtowed before leaving. As soon as they returned to their offices each of them composed a note of thanks to the emperor.*)

APPENDIX B: AUDIENCE ON AUGUST 25, 1590

That day the emperor held his morning audience with the court at the Imperial Polar Gate. After the ceremonial proceedings, he called the grand-secretaries into the inner chamber under the gate-tower and handed Shen Shih-hsing a report by the governor of Shensi on the latest frontier situation.

Emperor: Take a look at this. The report of the governor-general also says that Cürüke has crossed the Yellow River with his hordes. He is planning an invasion, isn't he?

Shen: This is tied to our recent humiliation at T'ao-chou. We lost a general there. I am sorry, Your Majesty. It causes Your Majesty so much concern and worry. But let me very briefly explain the background.

Around the entire T'ao River region are what we call *Fan* tribes [Tibetans and Uighurs]. They may be divided into two groups. The sinicized Fan trade their horses for our tea. The others are barbarian Fan. Our defense installations have been set up to deal with these people. Until recently the Mongols have not entered the picture. That is why our defenses, which could not be very substantial, are unable to check the advance in such an unexpected situation.

As for Cürüke, we have some idea that he crossed the Yellow River at the urging of Qulaci. The purpose is to plunder the Fan people. They are afraid we may intervene, so they spread word that they are going to invade our interior. Of course, Mongols are tricky; I wouldn't say that we should remain unprepared.

Emperor: But the Fan people are also my subjects. Our ancestors had to work hard to bring their territory under our control. What happened to the governor and the governor-general? With our commission, our trust, have they done anything in the past? Have they exercised precaution? Only after the Mongol chieftain crossed the river would they write memoranda! Obviously, there is serious negligence here. In the days of His Majesty our grandfather, frontier governors who suffered defeats such as this were always arrested and severely punished. There must be some consistent way to handle these cases.

Shen: You are absolutely correct, Your Majesty. Your criticism of the failure of frontier defense is amply justified; it is so incisive. The officials on the scene must concede to it, no argument about that. But, Your Majesty, we may take this opportunity to demand that they do better, tighten the command and drill the soldiers more. Still time to mend the fence.

Emperor: The thing is, the governors and governors-general nowadays treat army officers with nothing but disdain! Ordinarily they put them under restriction, will not permit them to do a thing. Only in a time of emergency would they push them forward. It happens in all defense areas. Whenever there is a victory, the civil officials are awarded and promoted; all the credit is theirs. In case of defeat and failure, some army officers are named as scapegoats. All excuses and empty words!

Shen: But Your Majesty, either in civil or military service, every individual has his duties and functions. A governor or a governor-general can only formulate policies and exercise high-level supervision. On the battlefield it is up to the army officers. Our system provides a commander-in-chief; he has a deputy and a chief-of-staff. There is a commander in charge of the defense unit and one in charge of the mobile column. Everyone's responsibility is clearly defined. Whenever there is a setback, the charge of responsibility must follow these lines.

Emperor: That is no reason for saying that when a person is not an army officer he therefore can never achieve merit on the battlefield. Look at the civil officials in ancient times. Tu Yü never rode a horse: if you let him practice archery, his arrow would not even penetrate a letter envelope. And look at Chu-ko Liang: he wore a silken kerchief and wielded a feather fan. Both of them commanded troops and led armies to victory.

Shen: But Your Majesty, those are among the rarest talented men since time immemorial. Such talent cannot be easily found. Well, I just hate to see the problem bother you so much. I must immediately get in touch with the Ministry of War. We should instruct all governors and governors-general to do their utmost to relieve your worry.

Emperor: A good general officer must combine courage with ingenuity. Actually, he should have battle experience.

Shen: That would be difficult, I dare say. Ever since we had this peace settlement [with Altan Khan] few of our commanders are battle seasoned.

Emperor: Let us make our rewards generous. There is the saying, "When the prize is high, people will be brave." If we had not known how to promote it, even the bravery of Chang Fei and Kuan Yü would have been laid waste.

Shen: We are looking into it. A few days ago the censorial-supervising officials suggested open nomination of general officers. I told the Ministry of War to give it a quick response. We should have an extended Nine Ministers' Conference including the censorial-supervising officials to make the nominations.

Emperor: Haven't the censors already recommended two persons?

Shen: They did. One is Wang Hua-hsi. Used to be metropolitan police chief. I have seen him: mediocre at best. He could be commander-in-chief in an interior province, not much else. The other man is Yin Ping-heng. Used to be a good officer, now much too old.

Emperor: Don't take age too seriously. If he knows how to maneuver, an old general will do. Look at Chao Ch'ung-kuo. Wasn't he an old general?

Shen: True, Your Majesty. A general officer's strategic maneuver counts more than his personal agility. Your wisdom is far ahead of ours.

Emperor: I'm confined within the palace and cannot be expected to know everything about frontier defense. You are my limbs; all is up to you. But we know very well that the recent decline in frontier defense is not limited to Shensi. We shall dispatch some energetic censors or even ministers to go to the various places to take a good look. If the army is really weak or supplies are inadequate, ways and means must be found to correct the situation. If we did the groundwork beforehand, we would not need to face emergencies. This is exactly what the *Classic of Records* says. Now is the time. If the situation continues to deteriorate, it will be more difficult to deal with later on.

Shen: Indeed, Your Majesty. Originally when we went along with the tributary trade of Mongols the idea was to provide an external means of pacification while increasing our armaments inside [the frontier]. But this is universal: when there is a let-down, everybody takes the easy way out. That's why we have instituted the general inspection once every three years. Either we dispatch supervising-secretaries to the defense installations or we let the surveillance commissioners in the provinces do it.

Emperor: That once-every-three-years affair is a matter of routine. Now we need to dispatch a special commissioner.

Shen: I have just discussed it with my colleagues. The idea is to send a high-ranking official there and give him all the power he needs, so that he can exercise discretion to coordinate the defenses in several frontier districts. I will submit a name and draft the commission for Your Majesty's approval as soon as I can.

Emperor: Submit two names [so that the emperor might select one for the commission].

(*At this point the discussion drifted toward the peace settlement with Altan. The emperor said that this had been a wise decision made by His Majesty his father.*)

Shen: Since Altan turned his defiance into subordination, indeed, because of the wise decision made by His Majesty, Your Majesty's own father, to permit tributary trade, this peace settlement has been in force for twenty years. Just as a rough guess, one million lives must have been saved in those twenty years.

Emperor: That is true. But we cannot permanently rely on this settlement. Look at the Sung dynasty——.

Shen: I would say that there is a fundamental difference between the Sung dynasty and our present day. In Sung times China was weak and the barbarians strong; the two sides were rivals. Today the Mongols are calling themselves subjects and presenting us tribute; China's overlordship is acknowledged. This, of course, does not mean that we should sit here complacently.

Emperor: Granted, there is this fundamental difference. We still shouldn't try to appease the nomads. They could be very ambitious and arrogant; there is no way to satisfy their appetite. It is still essential to build up our own strength so that the borderland is alertly safeguarded.

Shen: This means that we cannot rely entirely on pacification, nor can we rush into war. In order to keep the borderland in our hands, we have to defend its strategic points, the mountain passes and so forth. We have to clear the field so that the nomads have no way to forage and their marauding would not pay off. All this, I would say, requires Your Majesty to mastermind the situation for our long-term interests. Only then will frontier administrators feel secure to do the work. As for setbacks, there are major and minor cases of them. If the case is not so serious and we give the man on the scene a heavy penalty, soon all frontier officials will not dare to do a thing. They will all sit on the sidelines. On the other hand, the nomads are led to believe that they have leverage over our officials. I am not so sure that this is the way to keep up morale. That is why when it comes to meting out rewards and punishments, I must beg Your Majesty to be lenient.

Emperor: But I do not feel that the present setback is not serious.

Shen: Even so, Your Majesty, I still plead for leniency. Please allow me to convey your kindness to the frontier officials, so that they will do their utmost, with devotion and in gratitude.

(*The emperor now asked about the condition of Wang Hsi-chüeh, the third grand-secretary.*)

Shen: He is truly sick. He has repeatedly turned in his resignation out of desperation.

Emperor: Now that we have both hands full and need his help. How can he leave?

Shen: Since Your Majesty asks about him, it shows Your Majesty's concern for your secretaries. I, for one, feel gratified. But Hsi-chüeh's illness has been going on for some time. I went to his bedside the other day. He looks terribly thin. Must be in lots of pain. It may not be easy to force him to stay.

Emperor: Let him take a sick leave. Take time to get well. Come back whenever he is recovered.

Shen: Absolutely.

(*The grand-secretary kowtowed to the emperor* [*to express gratitude*]; *then he continued*):

Again we have not seen Your Majesty for a fortnight. Today we heard that Your Majesty was to meet your court. You must feel well now; we are so delighted.

Emperor: Not quite. I still feel dizziness in my head and aching of the limbs. I still walk with discomfort. Only because of this frontier business have I come out to confer with you.

(*The first grand-secretary again kowtowed.*)

Shen: Your Majesty must take good care of yourself.

Emperor: I have heard that on Wu-t'ai mountain of Shansi there are mining brigands. Aren't the local officials withholding information? Why not a single report from them?

Shen: There were such brigands in Sung-hsien, Honan. After the governor sent troops there, they abandoned the mines and dispersed.

Emperor: I'm talking about Wu-t'ai mountain in Shansi. Because we dispatched someone there to present incense to the Buddhist monastery, I heard about them.

Shen: If that is the case, then the local officials are not only guilty of negligence; they are actually withholding information. I shall immediately ask the Ministry of War to find out.

(*The grand-secretaries kowtowed and left.*)

NOTES

Chapter 1: The Wan-li Emperor

1. *Shen-tsung Shih-lu*, 3398. The wording of the emperor's verbal order differs slightly from *Wan-li Ti-ch'ao*, 1.349. *Ta-Ming Hui-Tien*, 44.9–10 has a passage about the noon audience, but it refers to a small conference between the emperor and the top officials. Cf. *Shen-tsung Shih-lu*, 1568.

2. *Ta-Ming Hui-tien*, 39.1–7; *Ch'un-ming Meng-yü-lu*, 27.5; Ray Huang, *Taxation and Governmental Finance in Sixteenth-Century Ming China*, pp. 48, 184.

3. *Mu-tsung Shih-lu*, 1537–43, 1585–86.

4. Summarized from the sources cited above. On the execution of prisoners, see *Yung-ch'uang Hsiao-p'in*, 1.18–19, although the event described took place later.

5. *Shen-tsung Shih-lu*, 1432–34, 3399.

6. *Cho-chung-chih*, 16.112; *Shen-tsung Shih-lu*, 0095–96, 2990, 4948.

7. *Ming-shih*, 49.555–56; *Ta-Ming Hui-tien*, 51.1–6; *Ch'un-ming Meng-yü-lu*, 15.16–18; *Wan-shu Tsa-chi*, 116.

8. Aside from the general references cited above, specific events and incidents are found in: *Ta-Ming Hui-tien*, 44.11–12, 22–32; *Hsiao-tsung Shih-lu*, 2449; *Wu-tsung Shih-lu*, 3689, *Mu-tsung Shih-lu*, 0246; *Shen-tsung Shih-lu*, 3369; *Chung-hua Erh-ch'ien-nien-shih*, 5A.114.

9. See Goodrich and Fang, *Dictionary of Ming Biography* (hereafter referred to as *Dictionary*), s.v. "Chu Tsai-hou." Also, *Mu-tsung Shih-lu*, 0245; *Ch'un-ming Meng-yü-lu*, 23.27; *Ping t'a I-yen*, 1, 14, 19.

10. *Shen-tsung Shih-lu*, 0145–46.

11. Ibid., 0341, 3375, 3455.

12. See below, Appendix A, translated from *Shen-tsung Shih-lu*, 4104.

13. *Ming-shih*, 213.2479, quoted from *Kuo-ch'ao Hsien-cheng-lu*, 17.60.

14. *Shen-tsung Shih-lu*, 0151–53, 1009, 1040, 1465; *Ta-Ming Hui-tien*, 52.5–6.

15. *Ming-shih*, 114.1483; *Ming-shih Chi-shih Pen-mo*, 61.668; *Shen-tsung Shih-lu*, 1398, 1529; *Cho-chung-chih*, 5.29, 22.195.

16. *Shen-tsung Shih-lu*, 0229–30; Joseph Needham, *Science and Civilisation in China*, 3.425–26.

17. *Shen-tsung Shih-lu*, 0002, 0279, 0606, 0774, 1737; *Cho-chung-chih*, 7.39; *Ch'un-ming Meng-yü-lu*, 6.13; *Wan-shu Tsa-chi*, 179.

18. *Shen-tsung Shih-lu*, 0520, 0778–79, 1399; Ku Ying-t'ai, *Ming-shih Chi-shih Pen-mo*, 61.661.

19. For the palace layout, see *Ch'un-ming Meng-yü-lu*, especially chaps. 6, 7, and 8, and Huang, *Taxation and Governmental Finance*, pp. 8–9, and 256, 359n. Note that the names of buildings sometimes change with subsequent reconstruction and modifications. The acreages of the Imperial City and the Forbidden City are calcu-

lated from *Ch'un-ming Meng-yü-lu*, 6.16–17. For palace life, *Cho-chung-chih* is referred to, although *Wan-shu Tsa-chi* has many passages describing it. *Shu-yüan Tsa-chi* also provides some information about palace life, but of an earlier period. Ritualistic proceedings with anecdotes appear in *Ch'un-ming Meng-yü-lu*. A more systematic description, along with details about costumes, may be found in *Ta-Ming Hui-tien*, chaps. 42–67.

20. See Charles O. Hucker, *The Traditional Chinese State in Ming Times, 1368–1644*, pp. 11, 31, 56; and idem, "Governmental Organization of the Ming Dynasty," pp. 24–25. Also see *Shen-tsung Shih-lu*, 0186, 0392, 4172, 3415.

21. *Ch'un-ming Meng-yü-lu*, 6.60; *Cho-chung-chih*, 16.98, 22.198. Also quoted in *Ming-tai T'e-wu Cheng-chih*.

22. *Ming-shih*, 300.3367; *Shen-tsung Shih-lu*, 0838, 1449; and Chang Chü-cheng, *Shu-tu*, 4.18. Summarized in Huang, *Taxation and Governmental Finance*, pp. 153, 296. The combined evidence suggests strongly that Chang engineered the showdown.

23. *Shen-tsung Shih-lu*, 0618, 0628, 0685–86, 0726, 1461–62, 1753, 1761, 1784.

24. *Ch'un-ming Meng-yü-lu*, 13.2, 23.28–30, 25.1, 49.1-4. *Cho-chung-chih*, 16.97; *Yeh-huo-pien*, 2.46.

25. See *Ming-shih*, 93.973; *Shen-tsung Shih-lu*, 0810–11, 0814–15, 1017, 1023, 1043–44, 1051–53. The entries should be compared with *Ming-shih*, chap. 229, and entries under "Liu T'ai" in the *Dictionary*.

26. See *Ch'un-ming Meng-yü-lu*, 6.51; Hucker, *Traditional Chinese State*, pp. 8–9, 13; idem, "Governmental Organization," p. 28.

27. See Hucker, "Governmental Organization," p. 29, especially the footnote. Cf. Tu Nai-chi, *Nei-ko Chih-tu*, 197–98; and *Chung-hua Erh-ch'ien-nien-shih*, 5A.164–70.

28. See *Shen-tsung Shih-lu*, 0933. The arrangement was criticized by Wang Shih-chen in *Chia-ching I-lai Nei-ko Shou-fu-chuan*.

29. Chou Lung, *Ming-tai Chih Huan-kuan* (not seen by me) reports that the emperor dispatched eunuchs to tributary states as envoys eight times; the passage is quoted in *Ming-shih*, 304.3417–18. Also see *T'ai-tsu Shih-lu*, 1848; *Shen-tsung Shih-lu*, 2821. For the appointment of eunuchs as tax administrators in the early period, see Huang, *Taxation and Governmental Finance*, p. 47.

30. See *Cho-chung-chih*, 13.67–68, 16.97, 101, 19.161, 22.193, 23.301.

31. *Ming-shih*, 213.2479, 304.3422, 305.3427; *Kuo-ch'ao Hsien-cheng-lu*, 17.65; *Cho-chung-chih*, 5.29.

32. Specified in *Ta-Ming Hui-tien*, 11.2.

33. *Shen-tsung Shih-lu*, 1473–76, 1524–25, 1506; *Ming-shih*, 213.2480, 225.2595; *Kuo-ch'ao Hsien-cheng-lu*, 17.77–78; *Ming-shih Chi-shih Pen-mo*, 61.622.

34. *Shen-tsung Shih-lu*, 1480–84, 1485–86, 1490–91, 1501–02, 1506–07; *Ming-shih*, chap. 243.

35. *Shen-tsung Shih-lu*, 1476, 1555, 1586, 1640; *Kuo-ch'ao Hsien-cheng-lu*, 17.85. Chang's reference to his white hair actually appears in his letter to Kao before the pending reunion (see Chang Chü-cheng, *Shu-tu*, 6.17). For musketeers as bodyguards, see *Shu-tu*, 4.16.

36. *Ming-shih*, 213.2481; *Shen-tsung Shih-lu*, 1051, 1586, 1631–32, 1640;

Kuo-ch'ao Hsien-cheng-lu, 17.88. Summarized by Chu Tung-jun, *Chang Chü-cheng Ta-chuan.*

37. *Shen-tsung Shih-lu,* 1430, 1528, 1556; *Ming-shih,* 114.1483; *Cho-chung-chih,* 22.196. That the emperor took two concubines immediately after his wedding is mentioned in *Shen-tsung Shih-lu,* 1575. Empress Hsiao-tuan's death in 1620 is recorded in *Shen-tsung Shih-lu,* 11368.

38. It is described somewhat differently in the various sources. See *Shen-tsung Shih-lu,* 2052; *Ming-shih,* 114.1483, 305.3428; *Cho-chung-chih,* 5.29: Ku, *Ming-shih Chi-shih Pen-mo,* 61.666. But the most reliable account is that revealed in two memorials written by Chang Chü-cheng days after the incident, included in *Chang Wen-chung-kung Wen-chi* and reproduced in *Huang-Ming Ching-shih Wen-pien,* 326.1–5. For the assignment of Han-lin academicians to keep the emperor's company, see *Shen-tsung Shih-lu,* 2052–54, 2081–83.

39. See *Ta-Ming Hui-tien,* 46.26–36; *Shen-tsung Shih-lu,* 2276. Cf. Hucker, "Governmental Organization," p. 10.

40. *Ming-shih,* 114.1483; *Hsien-po Chih-shih,* 1; *Shen-tsung Shih-lu,* 2332, 2364, 2373, 2384, 2397; *Kuang-tsung Shih-lu,* 0001. She was granted the title Consort Kung on July 3, and gave birth to Ch'ang-lo on August 28, 1582.

41. *Shen-tsung Shih-lu,* 2321, 2329, 2334–35; *Kuo-ch'ao Hsien-cheng-lu,* 17.100–01; *Ming-shih,* 213.2482.

42. *Shen-tsung Shih-lu,* 2797; *Cho-chung-chih,* 22.186–87, 196.

43. *Cho-chung-chih,* 1.1–2; *Shen-tsung Shih-lu,* 3683–84, 4101.

44. *Hsien-po Chih-shih,* 2, 17; *Yeh-huo-pien,* 3.39. For her advancement in rank, see *Shen-tsung Shih-lu,* 2276, 2607, 2676, 2805, 2815, 3117.

45. *Shen-tsung Shih-lu,* 2404; *Cho-chung-chih,* 16.112.

46. *Ming-shih* 219.2534; *Kuo-ch'ao Hsien-cheng-lu,* 17.104; see also Chang Ssu-wei's biography in *Dictionary.*

47. *Shen-tsung Shih-lu,* 2378, 2530, 2732; Huang, *Taxation and Governmental Finance,* p. 301; *Ching-lin Hsü-chi,* 30.

48. *Shen-tsung Shih-lu,* 2435, 2436, 2438, 2440, 2454, 2460; see also Chang Ssu-wei in *Dictionary.*

49. See pp. 125–29 above.

50. *Shen-tsung Shih-lu,* 2520–22.

51. *Shen-tsung Shih-lu,* 2442, 2451, 2471, 2489. Cf. ibid., 2393.

52. Originated in *Cho-chung-chih,* 5.29–30; quoted in *Ming-shih,* 305.3428.

53. *Shen-tsung Shih-lu,* 2436, 2438, 2473; *Ming-shih,* 305.3428. That Feng had accumulated great wealth was substantiated by Wang Shih-chen, in *Yen-chou Shih-liao Hou-chi,* chap. 36, quoted by Fu I-ling in *Ming-Ch'ing Shih-tai Shang-jen chi Shang-yeh Tzu-pen,* 23–24.

54. *Kuo-ch'ao Hsien-cheng-lu,* 17.89.

55. *Ming-shih,* 305.3428.

56. The Chinese title is *Ping-t'a I-yen,* reproduced in *Chi-lu Hui-pien.* The standard bibliography, *Ssu-k'u Ch'üan-shu Tsung-mu T'i-yao,* summarizes the book thus: "When checked against other established facts in history, it is not always reliable" (27.2979).

57. *Ping-t'a I-yen,* 32. Different versions appear in *Kuo-ch'ao Hsien-cheng-lu,*

17.23, *Ming-shih*, 213, 2478–79, and Ku, *Ming-shih Chi-shih Pen-mo*, 61.654. Kao's dismissal is recorded in *Shen-tsung Shih-lu*, 0034. Shen Shih-hsing, an eye-witness, recorded Kao's arrogance and Feng Pao's malicious distortion but in this case did not involve Chang Chü-cheng. See *Tz'u-hsien-t'ang Chi*, 40.22.

58. Entries appear in *Shen-tsung Shih-lu*, 0332, 0338, 0356, 2494. Kao Kung's account is in *Ping-t'a I-yen*, 37–42. See also *Kuo-ch'ao Hsien-cheng-lu*, 17.24, 39; *Ming-shih*, 213.2478, 214.2487, 305.3428; *Tz'u-hsien-t'ang Chi*, 40.23. Circumstances suggest that Chang Chü-cheng was indirectly involved. Kao Kung's tombstone inscription was written by Kuo Cheng-yü and is reproduced in *Kuo-ch'ao Hsien-cheng-lu*, 17.26–40.

59. It proceeded in several steps, as indicated in the text. For the sequence of events, see *Shen-tsung Shih-lu*, 2440, 2460, 2509, 2610, 2713–14, 2756–59, 2771, 2778–79, 2797–98, 2802, 2805, 2816–17, 2819.

60. It was suggested by Wang Shih-chen in *Kuo-ch'ao Hsien-cheng-lu*, 17.92, 107. That Ch'i Chi-kuang was conspiring with Chang Chü-cheng was brought up during the trial of Chang's sons. See the note appended by Chang Mou-hsiu to Chang Chü-cheng, *Shu-tu*, 5.19; also quoted in Huang, *Taxation and Governmental Finance*, p. 362n. For more about the controversial examination question, see text, pp. 69–70, and *Dictionary*, 1188, s.v. Kao Ch'i-yü and Ting Tz'u-lü. Some sources, however, believe that the emperor was motivated by greed, having been swayed by the rumors of Chang's fabulous wealth. See *Ming-shih*, 213.2482; *Kuo-ch'ao Hsien-cheng-lu*, 17.104; Ku, *Ming-shih Chi-shih Pen-mo*, 61.668.

61. *Kuo-ch'ao Hsien-cheng-lu*, 17.92. In one of the memorials to the emperor, Chang did mention I Yin and the Duke of Chou, although the reference bears no direct connection to himself. See *Huang-Ming Ching-shih Wen-pien*, 326.6.

62. *Shen-tsung Shih-lu*, 2756–59, 2771, 2819.

63. Ibid., 2693–94, 2768.

64. Ibid., 2778, 2796, 2801, 2859, 2975. See also *Dictionary*, pp. 1109–10.

65. *Shen-tsung Shih-lu*, 3144–46.

66. Ibid., 3491.

Chapter 2: Shen Shih-hsing, First Grand-Secretary

1. *Shen-tsung Shih-lu*, 0611.

2. For Shen's longest term as imperial tutor, see *Mu-tsung Shih-lu*, 1597–98; *Shen-tsung Shih-lu*, 0153, 0927, 1435, 9877; *Kuo-ch'ao Hsien-cheng-lu*, 17.145. Since the tutorship continued along with his appointment at the Han-lin Academy, it is not noted in *Ming-shih*, chapter 218, where his biography appears, nor in *Dictionary*, which cites his early career as a Han-lin academician on page 1188.

3. For example, see *Shen-tsung Shih-lu*, 3458, 3473, 3549, 3565.

4. *Ta-Ming Hui-tien*, 52.1–5; Sun Ch'eng-tse, *Ch'un-ming Meng-yü-lu*, 9.1–22, 32.11–18.

5. Sun, *Ch'un-ming Meng-yü-lu*, chap. 9. The incident involving an emperor crossing his legs actually happened after Wan-li's time, but here the text refers to the practice in general.

6. *Shen-tsung Shih-lu*, 0336–37, 0342, 3669; Cheng Hsiao, *Chin-yen*, 147.14; Sun, *Ch'un-ming Meng-yü-lu*, 9.8–9; Ni Hui-ting, *Ni-wen-cheng-kung Nien-p'u*, 4.25–26, translated in W. T. de Bary, ed., *Self and Society in Ming Thought*, p. 441. On the fact that Cheng-te transferred critical lecturers to remote posts, see Ch'en Hung-mo, *Chi-shih Chi-wen*, 91.10.

7. Sun, *Ch'un-ming Meng-yü-lu*, 9.2, 23.1; Wang Ao, *Chen-tse Ch'ang-yü*, 125.10; P'eng, *Pi-chi*, 126.8; Charles O. Hucker, *The Censorial System of Ming China*, p. 109; idem, "Governmental Organization," p. 22. Its function is also summarized in Huang, *Taxation and Governmental Finance*, p. 7.

8. Found in Huang Tsung-hsi, *Ming-ju Hsüeh-an*, chap. 35. The fact that on cold mornings a participant's white complexion turned red and red complexion turned black was commonly referred to. See, for instance, Chu Kuo-chen, *Yung-ch'uang Hsiao-p'in*, 1.19.

9. Shen stated so himself in a memorial to emperor. See *Shen-tsung Shih-lu*, 3718.

10. Ibid., 2449.

11. Ibid., 3328, 3418, 3460, 3572.

12. Ibid., 3333–36.

13. Ibid., 3369, 3376, 3441.

14. Ibid., 3418.

15. They appear in his writing. See Hsü Fu-yüan et al., *Huang-Ming Ching-shih Wen-pien*, 380.11.

16. Shen Shih-hsing, *Tz'u-hsien-t'ang Chi*, 4.8, 35.13.

17. It was not mentioned at this time but was formally suggested later in 1588 (see *Shen-tsung Shih-lu*, 3634). The suggestion was not accepted. For new librarian assistants, see ibid., 3527.

18. Hsü et al., *Huang-Ming Ching-shih Wen-pien*, 380.10.

19. *Shen-tsung Shih-lu*, 2531, 3032; *Ming-shih*, 219.2534. The two other grand-secretaries, besides Chang Chü-cheng, who were senior to Shen were Lü T'iao-yang and Ma Tzu-ch'iang.

20. First stated by Wang Shih-chen; see Chiao Hung, *Kuo-ch'ao Hsien-cheng-lu*, 17.83–107. Also accepted by *Ming-shih*, 218.2525–26. Shen himself acknowledged that he was easy to get along with. See *Tz'u-hsien-t'ang Chi*, 19.5.

21. See *Shih-tsung Shih-lu*, 8366, 8369. By then Shen Shih-hsing was known as Hsü Shih-hsing.

22. See *Ta-Ming Hui-tien*, chaps. 12 and 13: Sun, *Ch'un-ming Meng-yü-lu*, chap. 34; Hucker, "Governmental Organization," pp. 15–16.

23. T'ung-tsu Ch'ü's *Local Government* is still a useful reference, as the Ch'ing retained many of the general features of the Ming. But constant exposure to the local gazetteers and biographies of local officials should convey those conditions to the reader.

24. Chiao, *Kuo-ch'ao Hsien-cheng-lu*, 17.83, 145. Also see Ch'ien Mu, *Kuo-shih Ta-kang*, 2:493, for the role of the Han-lin academicians.

25. *Shen-tsung Shih-lu*, 3392–93.

26. Hucker, "Governmental Organization," p. 19; idem, *Censorial System*, pp. 34–35.

27. Based on Cheng Hsiao's report in the early sixteenth century (see *Chin-yen*, 145.41). The number of capital officials is my estimate.

28. *Ta-Ming Hui-tien*, 61.12– 23.

29. See Ping-ti Ho, *The Ladder of Success in Imperial China*, and refer to Hucker's "Governmental Organization," pp. 13– 15, and *Traditional Chinese State*, pp. 15– 16.

30. *Shen-tsung Shih-lu*, 3296– 98.

31. *Shen-tsung Shih-lu*, 2871; Ch'en Hung-mo, *Chih-shih Yü-wen*, 89.2, 7.

32. This was quite common. Shen's reference appears in Hsü et al., *Huang-Ming Ching-shih Wen-pien*, 380.10– 11. The quotation comes from the same passage.

33. Ho Liang-chün, *Ssu-yu-chai Ts'ung-shuo Tse-ch'ao*, 178.42. On professional moneylenders, see *Hsien-tsung Shih-lu*, 1499; Ku Yen-wu, *Jih-chih-lu Chi-shih*, 3.85.

34. Huang, *Taxation and Governmental Finance*, pp. 60– 64.

35. *Shen-tsung Shih-lu*, 2645– 46, 2711; *Ming-shih*, 243.2764. (The quotation appears in the latter source.) Tsou's biography in *Dictionary* indicates that his dismissal in 1584 was partly because he offended Shen Shih-hsing; this is confirmed in *Ming-shih*, chap. 243. But other sources point to the contrary (see *Shen-tsung Shih-lu*, 2712).

36. *Shen-tsung Shih-lu*, 3435.

37. See Hsieh Kuo-chen, *Ming-Ch'ing Chih-chi Tang-she Yün-tung-k'ao*, 28; the statement also appears in Shen's *Tz'u-hsien-t'ang Chi*.

38. Probably initiated by Wang Shih-chen and directly applied to Chang Ssu-wei; but in his writing Wang also treated Shen as Chang Chü-cheng's lackey. See Chiao, *Kuo-ch'ao Hsien-cheng-lu*, 17.72; *Ming-shih*, 213.2480.

39. See Chiao, *Kuo-ch'ao Hsien-cheng-lu*, 17.67; Shen, *Tz'u-hsien-t'ang Chi*, 40.21; *Ming-shih*, 213.2479.

40. See his biography in *Dictionary*; *Ming-shih*, chap. 213: Ku, *Ming-shih Chi-shih Pen-mo*, chap. 61; the two modern biographies by Chu Tung-jün and T'ang Hsin; and Robert Crawford, "The Life and Thought of Chang Chü-cheng, 1525– 1582" (Ph.D. diss., University of Washington, Seattle). Also, summarized in Huang, *Taxation and Governmental Finance*, pp. 294– 305.

41. Chang, *Shu-tu*, 3.21.

42. *Shen-tsung Shih-lu*, 0442.

43. See Chang, *Shu-tu*, 2.5, 27, 3.2, 4.15, 5.7, 17. The same source mentions his servants in 1.9, 11, 5.7.

44. Ibid., 6.21– 23.

45. Ibid., 2.17.

46. Ibid., 2.16.

47. Best illustrated in his letters. See Hsü et al., *Huang-Ming Ching-shih Wen-pien*, 380.10– 11, and 381.9.

48. See *Ming-shih*, 110.1376– 79.

49. See *Shen-tsung Shih-lu*, 2511, 2514, 2517, 2618, 2653, 2747– 48, 2751– 54, 2806– 07, 2986– 89.

50. *Kuo-ch'ao Hsien-cheng-lu*, 17.69, 75, 87, 94. See also Huang, *Taxation and Governmental Finance*, p. 299.

51. See Hsü et al., *Huang-Ming Ching-shih Wen-pien*, 324.22–24; *Shen-tsung Shih-lu*, 3084–85.

52. *Shen-tsung Shih-lu*, 3395, 3456; *Ming-shih*, 225.2597; Hsieh Kuo-chen, *Tang-she Yün-tung-k'ao*, 29–30. Cf. Sun, *Ch'un-ming Meng-yü-lu*, 34.55.

Chapter 3: A World without Chang Chü-cheng

1. Wan-li's alienation from his court is described in most standard Chinese works on dynastic history. Typical is Meng Shen's *Ming-tai Shih*, of which chapter 5 is entitled "The Irresponsibility and Indolence of Wan-li." Ch'ien Mu, while assigning more blame to institutions than to individuals, quotes Ku Yen-wu to stress that in the later Wan-li period there was a serious moral decline. See *Kuo-shih Ta-kang*, 2:501–02. See also "Chu I-chün" in *Dictionary*.

2. No adequate account is available, but it is clear that the inflated acreage was no more than the basis for a modest expense account. See *Shen-tsung Shih-lu*, 9771, 9773, 9825, 9881, 9901, 9920, 9924, 9942, 9946, 9957, 10089, 10339, 10526, 10611. Cf. Huang, *Taxation and Governmental Finance*, pp. 108, 254.

3. *Shen-tsung Shih-lu*, 4212, 4216, 4219, 4225, 4227, 4228, 4231, 4232, 4233, 4236–37, 4238–43.

4. Ibid., 4274, 4319.

5. Ibid., 4419–20.

6. Ibid., 4440–41.

7. Ibid., 4451–53, 4454, 4457–58, 4461–63. The summary in *Ming-shih*, 218.2526, is essentially correct. For Shen's own account, see *Tz'u-hsien-t'ang Chi*, 40.9.

8. Aside from entries cited above, see also *Shen-tsung Shih-lu*, 4757–70, 4777–78, 4780–81, 4787–88, 4949–53, 4957–59, 4963–65, 4967–68, 4982–85, 6765, 6772, 6787, 6789.

9. *Huang-Ming Tsu-hsün*, 28.

10. The emperors were Hsüan-te, Ching-t'ai, Ch'eng-hua, and Chia-ching. See *Ming-shih*, 113.1472, 1475, 114.1481.

11. On subtle attempts to impeach Lady Cheng, see Hsieh Kuo-chen, *Tang-she Yün-tung-k'ao*, 21. Grand-secretary Wang Hsi-chüeh, in a memorial, also held Lady Cheng responsible (*Shen-tsung Shih-lu*, 4957).

12. Typical is Lo Yü-jen's memorial of 1590. See *Shen-tsung Shih-lu*, 4086, 4098.

13. See Ku, *Ming-shih Chi-shih Pen-mo*, 67.743–46. A grand-secretary, Shen Li, was accused of practicing witchcraft (ibid., 66.718).

14. See ibid., 67.745. Whether unreliable or false, these tales were nevertheless widely accepted.

15. Also appearing in *Hsien-po Chih-shih*, 2, this conversation is quoted in *Ming-shih*, 114.1483; Hsieh Kuo-chen, *Ming-Ch'ing Chih-chi Tang-she Yün-tung-k'ao*, 17, 19; Meng Shen, *Ming-tai-shih*, 292.

16. Ku, *Ming-shih Chi-shih Pen-mo*, 67.743; Hsieh, *Tang-she Yün-tung-k'ao*, 21; Meng, *Ming-tai-shih*, 293; *Dictionary*, p. 210.

17. Best presented in Wu Han's *Chu Yüan-chang Chuan*. See also s.v. "Chu Yüan-chang" in *Dictionary*.

18. See Huang, *Taxation and Governmental Finance*, pp. 315–16. The Ming's emphasis was on stability, ibid., p. 321.

19. See ibid., pp. 152, 185, 219, 235. They were institutionalized under the Ch'ing. See Ch'ü T'ung-tsu, *Local Government in China under the Ch'ing*, p. 26.

20. Hai Jui, *Hai Jui Chi*, 40.

21. See Chiao Hung's account in *Kuo-ch'ao Hsien-cheng-lu*, 17.155–56; idem, *Tan-yüan-chi*, 18.4–6. A characteristic observation is: "His [Shen Shih-hsing's] planning of state affairs dealt with substance, not making a good name for himself. As a great statesman his talent was turning the skills of the world into his own skills" (*Tan-yüan-chi*, 18.6).

22. Ku Hsien-ch'eng's dissatisfaction with the personnel evaluation of 1587 motivated him to spend the rest of his life trying everything possible to purify officialdom. See Sun, *Ch'un-ming Meng-yü-lu*, 34.55; Hsieh, *Tang-she Yün-tung-k'ao*, 31; *Ming-shih*, 220.2546, 231.2647. For Ku Hsien-ch'eng's protest, see *Shen-tsung Shih-lu*, 3432–35. See also Ku's biography in *Dictionary*, especially p. 739.

23. See s.v. "Chu Ti" in *Dictionary*, especially p. 360.

24. See s.v. "Chu Ch'i-chen" in *Dictionary*, especially p. 292, also "Chu Ch'i-yü," especially p. 296.

25. In trying to assess the negative nature of the imperial prerogative from the entire body of *Shen-tsung Shih-lu*, I find Wan-li's conversation with Shen Shih-hsing most revealing (see Appendix B). The only exception was the dispatching of mining superintendents to the provinces, which is not included in this study.

26. *Shen-tsung Shih-lu*, 9746; C. Alvarez Samedo, *The History of That Great and Renowned Monarchy of China*, pp. 78–84; Gouveia's account, chap. 17.

27. *Shen-tsung Shih-lu*, 9758.

28. Two Jesuits, Diego de Pantoja and Sabatino de Ursis, sent memorials of condolence (Gouveia's account, topic 203). Specialists believe that both Samedo and Gouveia worked on the same original, probably the "Carta Annua" of the year 1614. Scholars deeply interested in this Jesuit contact should consult the transcript at the Ajuda Library in Portugal or the original in the Jesuit archives in Rome.

29. Liu Jo-yü, *Cho-chung-chih*, 16.115.

30. This can be summarized after reading *Ming-shih*, 16.113; Hsü et al., *Huang-Ming Ching-shih Wen-pien*, 53.5; Li Tung-fang, *Hsi-shuo Ming-ch'ao*, 2: 293.

31. *Wu-tsung Shih-lu*, 0742, 1981, 2807; *Ming-shih*, 307.3471.

32. *Wu-tsung Shih-lu*, 2348, 2807, 3471, 3473, 3960.

33. *Ming-shih*, 307.3471; *Wu-tsung Shih-lu*, 2027.

34. *Ming-shih*, 186.2172.

35. Ku, *Ming-shih Chi-shih Pen-mo*, chap. 43; *Ming-shih*, chap. 304; Hsü et al., *Huang-Ming Ching-shih Wen-pien*, 97.7–8, 113.9–11.

36. *Ming-shih*, 16.114, 215.3762; *Wu-tsung Shih-lu*, 2937, 2951, 2968, 2970. The date of the engagement was October 18, 1517.

37. *Wu-tsung Shih-lu*, 3030. In *Dictionary*, where Cheng-te's biography appears under his personal name, Chu Hou-chao, the emperor is described from an orthodox Confucian point of view. In the biography of Batu Möngke in *Dictionary*, Cheng-te is said to have directed the battle "from a distance" (p. 19). This disagrees with *Wu-tsung Shih-lu*, 2969–70.

38. *Wu-tsung Shih-lu*, 3028–30.

39. Ibid., 3042.

40. Ibid., 3035.

41. Ibid., 3035–42.

42. The casualties of the Ming army, are reported in *Wu-tsung Shih-lu*, 2970, as "fifty-two dead, 563 seriously wounded," and in *Ming-shih*, 307.3471, as "several hundred dead."

43. *Wu-tsung Shih-lu*, 3151, 3463. *Ming-shih*, 190.2220; Chiao, *Kuo-ch'ao Hsien-cheng-lu*, 15.10, 51.

44. *Wu-tsung Shih-lu*, 3215, 3305.

45. *Wu-tsung Shih-lu*, 3160–61, 3198, 3208; *Ming-shih*, 190.2220.

46. *Wu-tsung Shih-lu*, 3271, 3404, 3471; *Ming-shih*, 307.3472; Hsü et al., *Huang-Ming Ching-shih Wen-pien*, 171. 1–9. For the biography of the remonstrator Shu Feng, see *Ming-shih*, 179, 2102. Also Ch'en Hung-mo, *Chi-shih Chi-wen*, 95.2.

47. *Wu-tsung Shih-lu*, 3285; *Ming-shih*, 307.3472. See also Ch'en Hung-mo, *Chih-shih Chi-wen*, 95.2.

48. *Wu-tsung Shih-lu*, 3318–22, 3324–26, 3329–30, 3332–44, 3347, 3352–54, 3363; *Ming-shih*, 16.114–15. The number of persons who died after being beaten is recorded differently in the sources. Note that Chiang Pin controlled both the capital garrison and the Secret Police. See Ch'en Hung-mo, *Chi-shih Chi-wen*, 96.1–2.

49. *Wu-tsung Shih-lu*, 3602, 3606; *Ming-shih*, 16.115.

50. This civil dominance could be dated from the second quarter of the fifteenth century. In this connection, see Wan-li's protest (*Shen-tsung Shih-lu*, 4187) and the comments by a modern historian: Ch'ien Mu, *Kuo-shih Ta-kang*, 2: 502. More sympathy toward Cheng-te and appreciation of his talent come from Li Tung-fang (see his *Hsi-shuo Ming-ch'ao*, 293).

51. The three grand-secretaries at Cheng-te's accession were Liu Chien, Li Tung-yang, and Hsieh Ch'ien (see *Ming-shih*, 109.1372). Their biographies all appear in *Dictionary*.

52. See *Ming-shih*, 190.2217, 307.3472; *Shih-tsung Shih-lu*, 0122–23. That 100,000 ounces of gold and more than four million ounces of silver were found in his house seems too exaggerated to be true for those times.

53. That Wan-li might have been addicted to opium has been suggested by Teng Chih-ch'eng and Li Tung-fang. So far I have not found any contemporary writer who corroborates it. It is clear, however, that in his middle years Wan-li found his escape in reading religious and philosophical works (see *Shen-tsung Shih-lu*, 6107-08). One more character appraisal of Wan-li was made by a contemporary, Lu Shien-chi, whose own defiance of the emperor cost him demotion and transfer. He wrote, "His weakness is being overly lenient" (*Jen-jen-ts'ao*, 1.10).

54. Shen's regrets are amply expressed in his essays, especially *Tz'u-hsien T'ang-chi*, 40.7.

55. See *Shen-tsung Shih-lu*, 2402, 2795, 2870, 2929, 2981, 3147, 3215, 3241, and 3463.

56. Ibid., 3664–68, 3680, 3690–91.

57. *Shen-tsung Shih-lu*, 2772.

Chapter 4: The Living Ancestor

1. See *Shen-tsung Shih-lu*, 9805, 9863– 64. Shen wrote a poem to commemorate the event (*Tz'u-hsien T'ang-chi*, 6.30– 31). He died very shortly thereafter; see *Shen-tsung Shih-lu*, 9877. Note that *Ming-shih*, 218.2526 indicates: "He died after the imperial message had barely arrived at his door."

2. Revealed by Shen in *Tz'u-hsien T'ang-chi*. Poems on 2.1, 4, 5, 5.1 of this work are very expressive.

3. *Shen-tsung Shih-lu*, 3799. For the different theories on how to tame the river, see Ts'en Chung-mien, *Huang-ho Pien-ch'ien-shih*, and *Ming-shih*, chaps. 83, 84, 223. Interesting observations may be found in Needham, *Science and Civilisation in China*, vol. 4, pt. 3, pp. 229, 237, 325, 344. P'an Chi-hsün's biography is included in *Dictionary*. It can be compared with the biography of Liu Ta-hsia in the same work.

4. *Shen-tsung Shih-lu*, 3706, 3722, 3798; Hsü et al., *Huang-Ming Ching-shih Wen-pien*, chap. 375; P'an's own *Ho-fang I-lan*.

5. Huang, *Taxation and Governmental Finance*, pp. 279– 281.

6. See Shen, *Tz'u-hsien T'ang-chi*, 18.6.

7. *Ming-shih*, 327.3767.

8. Ibid., 327.3767; *Shen-tsung Shih-lu*, 4173– 74; Hsü et al., *Huang-Ming Ching-shih Wen-pien*, 381.21.

9. *Shen-tsung Shih-lu*, 4186– 4191. See Appendix B for English translation.

10. *Shen-tsung Shih-lu*, 4193, 4197-99, 4253– 54, 4281– 83; *Ming-shih*, 20.139; Hsü et al., *Huang-Ming Ching-shih Wen-pien*, 381.21.

11. *Shen-tsung Shih-lu*, 3611– 12.

12. *Ming-shih*, 218.2526; Hsieh Kuo-chen, *Tang-she Yün-tung-k'ao*, 16, 28; *Dictionary*, p. 1189.

13. *Shen-tsung Shih-lu*, 3094– 95.

14. Ibid., 3117; see also 2607 and 2814.

15. As disclosed in *Ta-ming Hui-tien*, 46.26– 33; see also details of the 1584 proceedings, *Shen-tsung Shih-lu*, 2805– 11.

16. This may be observed from Shen's poetry (*Tz'u-hsien T'ang-chi*, 1.12).

17. See Ting I, *Ming-tai T'e-wu Cheng-chih*; *Ming-shih*, 95.993– 95; Liu, *Cho-chung-chih*, 16.104; Hucker, "Governmental Organization," p. 60. But ironically, the Wan-li emperor was more disinclined to use the Secret Police than his predecessors had been and as his successors were. See Meng, *Ming-tai-shih*, 287.

18. It appears in *Ming-shih*, 95.995.

19. *Shen-tsung Shih-lu*, 3613– 14.

20. This is not the artist in *Dictionary*, but he is referred to there on pp. 463 and 738. A more complete biography appears in *Ming-shih*, chap. 220.

21. *Shen-tsung Shih-lu*, 3828, 3833– 37, 3840– 44, 3846, 4103; *Ming-shih*, 305.3427. For more about bureaucratic involvement, see Chang's biography in *Dictionary*, especially p. 50.

22. Li Yi was the junior official. That Wan-li was very much disturbed by his memorial is stated in *Shen-tsung Shih-lu*, 3848, 3971.

23. In some instances Shen referred to them also as "junior officials" (see *Tz'u-hsien T'ang-chi*, 14.5, 38.17, 40.7).

24. *Shen-tsung Shih-lu*, 2933–35; *Ta-Ming Hui-tien*, 84.17, 20–22.

25. *Ta-Ming Hui-tien*, 84.21.

26. Ibid., 82.22–24; Sun, *Ch'un-ming Meng-yü-lu*, 14.1–2. It was modified in 1588 (see *Shen-tsung Shih-lu*, 3799). The 1587 woodcut plan shows triple arches on the south side only; on the other three sides there were only single-arched gateways. Recent air-photos show triple arches on all four sides. Otherwise the structure has remained virtually unchanged from its original design for nearly 400 years.

27. Quoted from *Shen-tsung Shih-lu*, 2935.

28. Ibid., 2935.

29. Ibid., 2935.

30. Ibid., 3171.

31. Ibid., 3012.

32. Matteo Ricci objected to this practice, writing: "They really believe that they are practicing a high form of religion if they are tolerant of falsehood and do not openly spurn or disapprove an untruth." On another occasion he commented: "Most of them openly admitted that they have no religion, and so by deceiving themselves in pretending to believe, they generally fall into the deepest depth of utter atheism." These passages appear in Ricci, *China in the Sixteenth Century*, pp. 98–99, 105. This English version, produced by Gallagher, has not been kindly treated by reviewers, partly because it is translated from the Latin version of 1615. I have asked my colleague Professor Gianni Azzi to check the several passages referred to in this manuscript against the Italian version, and as far as I am concerned there are no fundamental errors. But a more discriminating reader may consult Pasquale M. D'Elia, *Fonti Ricciane*, the Italian original. The passages appear in vol. 1, on pp. 120, 132.

Ricci apparently did not approve of the Hua-yen doctrine that all beliefs could be accommodated within its own concept of universal causation. The so-called tolerance of falsehood, nevertheless, must have had its utilitarian value, as shown on the occasion of Wan-li's prayer for rain, and also in the oaths taken by Ch'i Chi-kuang and his officers, related in chapter 6.

33. *Shen-tsung Shih-lu*, 2948–49, 2954.

34. Ibid., 4598–4630.

35. *Mu-tsung Shih-lu*, 0489–91.

36. Five times prior to 1587: two visits in 1583, one time each in 1580, 1584, and 1585. See *Shen-tsung Shih-lu*, 2498–2501, 2624–27, 2835–37, 3010–11.

37. See Shen Shih-hsing's narratives, Hsü et al., *Huang-Ming Ching-shih Wen-pien*, 381.10–11.

38. *Shen-tsung Shih-lu*, 2772, 2774, 2794, 2882, 2918, 2937.

39. Yung-lo's lance was examined by Wan-li (see ibid., 0942).

40. See Shen's recollections, Hsü et al., *Huang-Ming Ching-shih Wen-pien*, 381.22; Chiao, *Kuo-ch'ao Hsien-cheng-lu*, 17.148.

41. *Shen-tsung Shih-lu*, 2919.

42. Ibid., 3796–98.

43. Ibid., 2493, 2498–2501.

44. Ibid., 2499, 2614, 2625, 2835, 2837.

45. Ibid., 3893–94.

46. Ibid., 2841.

47. Ibid., 2462.

48. Shen, *Tz'u-hsien T'ang-chi*, 40.17; *Shen-tsung Shih-lu*, 2462. Wan-li's own enthusiasm is indicated in *Shen-tsung Shih-lu*, 2847.

49. The only exception was one petition from a censor in 1585 to postpone the work on account of drought (see *Shen-tsung Shih-lu*, 2917). But it was mildly expressed and gathered no following.

50. The critics were also noted for their anti– Chang Chü-cheng stand (see *Shen-tsung Shih-lu*, 2540, 2594, 2616– 18, 2669; *Ming-shih*, chaps. 218, 225, 236, 243). The political implications behind these geomantic polemics are noted by a modern scholar: see Hsieh, *Tang-she Yun-tung-k'ao*, 15. Cf. Hsü's biography in *Dictionary*.

51. *Shen-tsung Shih-lu*, 2983, 3013. The emperor's decision about the site marked the failure of the anti-Chang faction to advance further.

52. Ibid., 2847. Ten persons were included.

53. See *K'ao-ku T'ung-hsin* [Archaeological Bulletin] no. 7 (1958), pp. 36– 47.

54. Ibid., p. 37.

55. Hsiang Meng-yüan, *Tung-kuan Chi-shih*, 2; Ho Chung-shih, *Liang-Kung Ting-chien-chi*, 12.

56. *K'ao-ku T'ung-hsin*, no. 7 (1958), pp. 39– 44.

57. Ibid., pp. 42– 43; see also *Hsin Chung-kuo K'ao-ku ti Shou-huo*, plate 129.

58. *K'ao-ku T'ung-hsin*, no. 7 (1958), pp. 39– 44. Also, a Buddhist doxology embroidered on a sheet wrapped around the body of Lady Wang was found inside her coffin. See *K'ao-ku T'ung-hsiu*, no. 7 (1959), p. 358.

59. *Shen-tsung Shih-lu*, 2851, 3016.

60. Lung-ch'ing's mausoleum was reopened in 1614 for the burial of Empress Dowager Tz'u-sheng (*Shen-tsung Shih-lu*, 9832). Wan-li's own mausoleum was presealed and then reopened for the burial of Empress Hsiao-tuan, who died shortly before the emperor in 1620. The Ministry of Works was instructed to make repairs on that occasion. See ibid., 11377– 78, 11380, 11381– 82, 11390– 91. Inside the earth fill, a stone inscription gives instructions for digging. See *K'ao-ku T'ung-hsin*, no. 7 (1958), p. 39.

61. *Shen-tsung Shih-lu*, 2837.

62. Ibid., 3343.

63. Ibid., 3474.

Chapter 5: Hai Jui, the Eccentric Model Official

1. Noted in Hai, *Hai Jui Chi*, 599; *Dictionary*, p. 474. *Shen-tsung Shih-lu*, 3590, carried the entry on November 15, 1587.

2. Literary criticism of historian Wu Han's presentation of Hai Jui in the People's Republic of China prior to 1966 is generally regarded as a prelude to the Great Proletarian Cultural Revolution.

3. Hai, *Hai Jui Chi*, 599; *Shen-tsung Shih-lu*, 3591; *Ming-shih*, 226.2604.

4. Hai, *Hai Jui Chi*, 117.

5. See Su T'ung-ping, *Ming-tai I-ti Chih-tu*; Huang, *Taxation and Governmental Finance*, p. 38. A list of those stations is included in *Ta-Ming Hui-tien*, chaps. 145–46.

6. *Ming-shih*, 226.2602; Hai, *Hai Jui Chi*, 584 (cf. 553). Not included in Hai's biography in *Dictionary*.

7. The complete text is reproduced in *Hai Jui Chi*, 168–69, 552–53.

8. Ibid., 585.

9. *Ming-shih*, 226.2602, in disagreement with *Hai Jui Chi*, 587.

10. *Ming-shih*, 226.2602; *Hai Jui Chi*, 586; Chiao, *Kuo-ch'ao Hsien-cheng-lu*, 64.28.

11. In some respects, this circumstance resembles an aspect of the American Western frontier. When a gap occurred between the law and law enforcement, individuals tended to take the administration of justice into their own hands. In such an environment a person's rugged character was highly valued.

12. *Ming-shih*, 205.2381, 308.3490.

13. *Ming-shih*, 72.743, 225.2595; *Ta-Ming Hui-tien*, 14.1; Huang, *Taxation and Governmental Finance*, pp. 16, 266–67, 292–93.

14. See his biography, under his personal name, Chu Hou-ts'ung, in *Dictionary*.

15. Full text in Hai, *Hai Jui Chi*, 217–21; Hsü et al., *Huang-Ming Ching-shih Wen-pien*, 309.1–9. Abridged text in *Ming-shih*, 226.2602–03; *Shih-tsung Shih-lu*, 8919–25.

16. The eunuch was identified as Huang Ching. See the passage in *Ming-shih*, 226.2603; Hai, *Hai Jui Chi*, 528, 558 (cf. 539, 649). The latter entries establish that Hai's family was then on Hai-nan Island. Either the eunuch falsely reported to the emperor or the entire conversation was fabricated.

17. *Ming-shih*, 226.2603; *Hai Jui Chi*, 558, 588; Chiao, *Kuo-ch'ao Hsien-cheng-lu*, 64.29, 33.

18. *Ming-shih*, 226.2603; *Hai Jui Chi*, 558, 589, 646–47.

19. *Mu-tsung Shih-lu*, 0215, 0285, 0381.

20. The paper is reproduced in *Hai Jui Chi*, 228–29. The same source (590) dates the memorial in 1568; it should have been submitted for the personnel evaluation in early 1569.

21. Chiao, *Kuo-ch'ao Hsien-cheng-lu*, 64.29–30.

22. Complete text appears in *Hai Jui Chi*, 242–54.

23. *Mu-tsung Shih-lu*, 1051; *Hai Jui Chi*, 422–23.

24. *Ta-Ming Hui-tien*, 163.14, 164.25.

25. *Ming-shih*, 213.2476, 226.2603; Hsü's biography in *Dictionary*; Huang, *Taxation and Governmental Finance*, p. 157n.; *Hai Jui Chi*, 431–32, 592.

26. Ibid., p. 237.

27. Huang, *Taxation and Governmental Finance*, pp. 99, 158, 313.

28. Ku Yen-wu, *T'ien-hsia Chün-kuo Li-ping-shu*, 6.14, 15, 24–26, 35, 61. That the rural population had no knowledge of codified law was admitted by the governor, see *Hai Jui Chi*, pp. 115–16.

29. *Hai Jui Chi*, p. 237.

30. *Mu-tsung Shih-lu*, 1023.

31. Ibid., 1055; *Hai Jui Chi*, 648–49.

32. *Hai Jui Chi*, 239.

33. *Mu-tsung Shih-lu*, 1055.

34. *Hai Jui Chi*, 242.

35. Chang Chü-cheng, *Shu-tu*, 1.16.

36. See *T'ai-tsu Shih-lu*, 1176; *Ying-tsung Shih-lu*, 5417; Wu Han, *Chu Yüan-chang Chuan*, 194, 198. During the Hung-wu period, references to individuals being drafted as lesser functionaries appeared often in official documents. See also *Ta-Ming Hui-tien*, 39.22.

37. See *Ta-kao* [Grand monitions]. That government officials were not permitted to go to rural areas was still entered into the 1587 edition of *Ta-Ming Hui-tien*, 173.3, 6.

38. *T'ai-tsu Shih-lu*, 2436–38; *Hsüan-tsung Shih-lu*, 1990–91; *Ming-shih*, 56.617–18; *Ta-Ming Hui-tien*, 79.3; Hucker, *Traditional Chinese State*, p. 26.

39. *Ming-shih*, 94.987–88; Wu, *Chu Yüan-chang Chuan*, 159–70; *Ming-tai Shih*, 57–59; and s.v. "Chu Yüan-chang" in *Dictionary*.

40. *T'ai-tsu Shih-lu*, 3643. In Joseph Needham and Ray Huang, "The Nature of Chinese Society," the number of households is misquoted as "14,241."

41. Summarized from Huang, *Taxation and Governmental Finance*.

42. P'eng Hsin-wei, *Chung-kuo Huo-pi-shih*, 603.

43. This practice was very much criticized by Ku Yen-wu. See Ku Yen-wu, *Jih-chih-lu Chi-shih*, 3.78–79.

44. See *Dictionary*, p. 575.

45. This can be seen from the numerous lawsuits mentioned in contemporary writings such as Ku, *T'ien-hsia Chün-kuo Li-ping-shu* and *Hai Jui Chi*.

46. See Ping-ti Ho, *The Ladder of Success in Imperial China*.

47. Huang, *Taxation and Governmental Finance*, pp. 69–81.

48. This was an inevitable consequence when the emphasis of statutes was on moral conduct rather than on property rights. See *Ta-Ming Hui-tien*, chap. 164.

49. For details, see the "Single Whip Reform" in Huang, *Taxation and Governmental Finance*, p. 119.

50. These issues required Magistrate Hai's attention only because quarrels over them resulted in loss of life. See *Hai Jui Chi*, 171, 173.

51. This attitude was repeatedly revealed in Hai's writing. See ibid., 114–15, 251.

52. They were best presented in eight criminal cases brought to his attention. Ibid., 169–78, 215–16.

53. Ibid., 172–73. False charges of manslaughter must have been common in those days. See Kuei Yu-Kuang, *Kuei Yu-kuang Ch'üan-chi*, 491.

54. *Hai Jui Chi*, 175–76.

55. Ibid., 544.

56. Ibid., 578, 589–90.

57. Ibid., 570.

58. Ibid., 310, 554.

59. Ibid., 472, 597; Shen Shih-hsing, *Tz'u-hsien-t'ang Chi*, 36.13. Cf. *Ming-shih*, 226.2604.

60. *Hai Jui Chi*, 467.
61. See Ho Liang-chün, *Ssu-yu-chai Ts'ung-shuo Tse-ch'ao*, 176.3–4.
62. *Hai Jui Chi*, 597.
63. Ibid., 598, 648; *Shen-tsung Shih-lu*, 3128; *Ming-shih*, 226.2604.
64. *Hai Jui Chi*, 630.
65. *Shen-tsung Shih-lu*, 3254–56. 3293–94.
66. Ibid., 3128.
67. Ibid., 3188–89.
68. Ibid., 3254–56, 3568.

Chapter 6: Ch'i Chi-kuang, the Lonely General

1. *Shen-tsung Shih-lu*, 3565.
2. *Ming-shih*, 212.2463–64.
3. Hsieh Ch'eng-jen and Ning K'o, *Ch'i Chi-kuang*, 145–46, *Ming-shih*, 227.2613.
4. *Ming-shih*, 212.2467–68, 247.2804–06; and Liu T'ing's biography in *Dictionary*.
5. This has been expressed in different terms by John K. Fairbank. See Frank A. Kierman and John K. Fairbank, eds., *Chinese Ways in Warfare*, pp. 3–4.
6. During the Ming, this system was partly in effect prior to 1435; thereafter the Civil Service took over. See *Ying-tsung Shih-lu*, 0135; *Ta-Ming Hui-tien*, 22.29; *Ming-shih*, 79.834; Huang, *Taxation and Governmental Finance*, pp. 29–30.
7. Charles O. Hucker, *The Censorial System of Ming China*, p. 35, "from the 1440's to the end of the dynasty."
8. *Ming-shih*, 322.3692; Ku, *Ming-shih Chi-shih Pen-mo*, 55.597; Hsü et al., *Huang-Ming Ching-shih Wen-pien*, 204.3; Ts'ai Chiu-te, *Wo-pien Shih-lüeh*, 96; Kuei, *Kuei Yu-kuang Ch'üan-chi*, 95. Knowledge of this event circulated so widely that it even appears in a standard college textbook. See Edwin O. Reischauer and John K. Fairbank, *East Asia: The Great Tradition*, p. 332.
9. First printed in 1562. See Ch'i's biography in *Dictionary*, p. 223.
10. *T'ai-tsung Shih-lu*, 0589; *Hsiao-tsung Shih-lu*, 3322.
11. *T'ai-tsu Shih-lu*, 1292, 1331, 2533, 2735, 2788, 3192, 3225, 3264, 3592; *T'ai-tsung Shih-lu*, 2172; Wei Ch'ing-yüan, *Ming-tai Huang-ts'e Chih-tu*, 55.
12. *Hsi-tsung Shih-lu*, 1557–60; *Shun-te Hsien-chih*, 3.12–14; Wei, *Huang-Ming Chiu-pien-k'ao*, 1.25–26; Ku Yen Wu, *T'ien-hsia Chün-kuo Li-ping-shu*, 13.71, 26.106; Huang, *Taxation and Governmental Finance*, p. 288.
13. *Hsiao-tsung Shih-lu*, 1261, 3424; *Chin-hua Fu-chih*, 21.5; Wu Han, "Ming-tai ti Chün-ping," 169; Ray Huang, "Military Expenditures in Sixteenth-Century Ming China," p. 40.
14. *Shen-tsung Shih-lu*, 9573; Hucker, "Governmental Organization of the Ming Dynasty," p. 61.
15. Shen Pang, *Wan-shu Tsa-chi*, 49–50; Huang, *Taxation and Governmental Finance*, pp. 45, 131.
16. *Hsien-tsung Shih-lu*, 2178; Huang Shün, ed., *Huang-Ming Ming-ch'en Ching-chi-lu*, 22.22; Huang, *Taxation and Governmental Finance*, p. 55.

17. Hsi Shu and Chu Chia-hsiang, *Ts'ao-ch'uan-chih*, 1, 5–9.

18. See illustration in Chou Wei, *Chung kuo Ping-ch'i Shih-kao* and the description in *Ta-Ming Hui-tien*, 192.2, 9.

19. This expedient had originated many centuries earlier but became widely practiced in the later Wan-li period (see *Hsi-tsung Shih-lu*, 0761; Chu Kuo-chen, *Yung-ch'uang Hsiao-p'in*, 1, 266. Its use in the antipirate campaign is cited in Ch'en Wen-shih, *Ming Hung-wu Chia-ching Chien-ti Hai-ching Cheng-ts'e*, 166.

20. Hsü et al., *Huang-Ming Ching-shih Wen-pien*, 347.17.

21. *Ming-shih*, 247.2806.

22. *Ming-shih*, 239.2727. See also his biography in A. W. Hummel, ed., *Eminent Chinese of the Ch'ing Period*.

23. Hucker, "Governmental Organization," p. 19.

24. See *Ming-shih*, 70.727; *Ta-Ming Hui-tien*, 135.4–9; and *Ming-shih*, 69.721, 70.728; *Ta-Ming Hui-tien*, 156.1. For samples of questions asked at military examinations, see Kuei, *Kuei Yu-kuang Ch'üan-chi*, 422–24; Yü Ta-yu, *Cheng-ch'i-t'ang Chi*, 1.1–9. Note that the last cited places emphasis on "forbearance."

25. See Hucker, "Governmental Organization," pp. 41, 54.

26. *Ming-shih*, 205.2380; Ch'en Wen-shih, *Hai-ching Cheng-ts'e*, p. 160.

27. Hsü et al., *Huang-Ming Ching-shih Wen-pien*, 205.22, 206.10.

28. See *Shih-tsung Shih-lu*, 6325–26; Ku Ying-T'ai, *Ming-shih Chi-shih Pen-mo*, 55.589; Ch'en, *Hai-ching Cheng-ts'e*, 137–39.

29. *Ming-shih*, 205.2377; Hsü et al., *Huang-Ming Ching-shih Wen-pien*, 205.5–10; Ch'en, *Hai-ching Cheng-ts'e*, 142–44. See also the biography of Chu Wan in *Dictionary*.

30. Hsü et al., *Huang-Ming Ching-shih Wen-pien*, 204.3, 205.6; Kuei, *Kuei Yu-kuang Ch'üan-chi*, 97–99; Ku, *Ming-shih Chi-shih Pen-mo*, 55.591; Yü, *Cheng-ch'i-t'ang Chi*, 7.2, 9.4; biography of Chang Ching in *Dictionary*.

31. *Ming-shih*, 205.2380, 322.3692; Y. S. Kuno, *Japanese Expansion on the Asiatic Continent*, 1: 7.

32. *Ming-shih*, 205.2380–81; Kierman and Fairbank, *Chinese Ways in Warfare*, pp. 273–307.

33. Hsü et al., *Huang-Ming Ching-shih Wen-pien*, 200.6; Ch'en, *Hai-ching Cheng-ts'e*, 167; Cheng Mo, *Ching-hai Chi-lüeh*, 121; Hsieh and Ning, *Ch'i Chi-kuang*, 15–16; Ch'i Chi-Kuang, *Chi-hsiao Hsin-shu*, prelim. 10.

34. Yü, *Cheng-ch'i t'ang Chi*, 7.2; Hsü Hsüeh-chü, ed., *Chia-ching Tung-nan P'ing-wo T'ung-lu*, 8, 10, 16, 17, 27, 31; G. B. Sansom, *A History of Japan*, 2: 267, 270; Ts'ai Chiu-te, *Wo-pien Shih-lüeh*, 108; Ch'en Wen-shih, *Hai-ching Cheng-ts'e*, 160, 166.

35. Ts'ai, *Wo-pien Shih-lüeh*, 86, 99.

36. Ch'en Wen-shih, *Hai-ching Cheng-ts'e*, 167–68; Ch'i Chi-kuang, *Lien-ping Shih-chi*, 239. That the Japanese captured Chinese firearms is mentioned in Kuei, *Kuei Yu-kuang Ch'üan-chi*, 97; Cheng Mo, *Ching-hai Chi-lüeh*, 121.

37. Hsü, ed., *Chia-ching Tung-nan P'ing-wo T'ung-lu*, 31; Ts'ai, *Wo-pien Shih-lüeh*, 105. For a complete list of these troops, see Li Kuang-ming, *Chia-ching Yü-wo Chiang-Che Chu-k'e-chün-k'ao*.

38. Ch'en Wen-shih, *Hai-ching Cheng-ts'e*, 167. This is quoted from *Wu-pei-chih* and is essentially in agreement with other sources.

39. Ts'ai, *Wo-pien Shih-lüeh*, 95.

40. Ch'i, *Chi-hsiao Hsin-shu*, prelim. 10.

41. Ibid., prelim. 23; *Dictionary*, p. 221.

42. Huang, *Taxation and Governmental Finance*, pp. 134–35, 293; idem, "Military Expenditures," pp. 48–51.

43. Ch'i, *Lien-ping Shih-chi*, 2.66, and *Chi-hsiao Hsin-shu*, 4.7.

44. Ch'i, *Lien-ping Shih-chi*, 128–29; Ch'i, *Chi-hsiao Hsin-shu*, 3.3–5; Hsü et al., *Huang-Ming Ching-shih Wen-pien*, 348.6.

45. Ch'i, *Chi-hsiao Hsin-shu*, prelim. 28.

46. Hsü et al., *Huang-Ming Ching-shih Wen-pien*, 347.7; Hsieh and Ning, *Ch'i Chi-kuang*, 65. According to the latter source, fourteen persons were executed.

47. Ch'i, *Lien-ping Shih-chi*, 178; *Chi-hsiao Hsin-shu*, 3.6, 4.2.

48. *Ming-shih*, 212.2466.

49. Ch'i, *Chi-hsiao Hsin-shu*, 12.2.

50. Ibid., 10.2, 31, 12.1–2. The technique was said to have been developed by such great masters as Li Liang-ch'in, Liu Pang-hsieh, and Lin Yen.

51. This is my summary, based on the illustrations in Ch'i, *Chi-hsiao Hsin-shu*, 12.21–23.

52. Ch'i, *Chi-hsiao Hsin-shu*, 12.23, 31.

53. Ibid., 10.1, 12.1–2.

54. Ch'i, *Lien-ping Shih-chi*, 23, and *Chi-hsiao Hsin-shu*, 1.6–7.

55. Ch'i, *Chi-hsiao Hsin-shu*, 6.5, 12.30.

56. Ibid., 1.8, 2.5, 6.5, 8.7.

57. Ibid., 2.6–7.

58. Ch'i, *Lien-ping Shih-chi*, 221.

59. Yü, *Cheng-ch'i-t'ang Chi*, 5.2, 7.19.

60. *Ming-shih*, 212.2465; Chiao, *Kuo-ch'ao Hsien-cheng-lu*, 106.58; Hsieh and Ning, *Ch'i Chi-kuang*, 53, 68.

61. Ch'i, *Lien-ping Shih-chi*, 210; Ch'i, *Chi-hsiao Hsin-shu*, prelim. 17; Hsü et al., *Huang-Ming Ching-shih Wen-pien*, 346.4, 8, 13.

62. Ch'i, *Lien-ping Shih-chi*, 199, 239; Hsieh and Ning, *Ch'i Chi-kuang*, 142.

63. Ch'i, *Lien-ping Shih-chi*, 23, 275; Hsü et al., *Huang-Ming Ching-shih Wen-pien*, 347.21; *Mu-tsung Shih-lu*, 0741.

64. Ch'i, *Chi-hsiao Hsin-shu*, 1.1–3, 7.

65. Ch'i, *Cheng-ch'i-t'ang Chi*, 7.2, 17, 23, 8.13, 11.2, 4.

66. Note that both Yü Ta-yu and Ch'i Chi-kuang had to deal with internal rebellions apart from the pirate problem. See *Ming-shih*, 212.2462, 2465.

67. It started at ten ounces of silver a year in the south and later increased to eighteen ounces when the soldiers were on duty at the Great Wall. Combat rewards were set at thirty ounces of silver for each head submitted, in principle to be shared by the entire squad. See Ch'i, *Chi-hsiao Hsin-shu*, 3.1–2; Hsü et al., *Huang-Ming Ching-shih Wen-pien*, 346.22, 347.10.

68. Hsü et al., *Huang-Ming Ching-shih Wen-pien*, 349.3.

69. Ch'i, *Lien-ping Shih-chi*, 116, 179, 199.

70. Based on Ch'i, *Chi-hsiao Hsin-shu*, prelim. 27.

71. Ibid., 7.6–7.

72. Hsieh and Ning, *Ch'i Chi-kuang*, 23, 36, 37, 41, 42.

73. Hsü et al., *Huang-Ming Ching-shih Wen-pien*, 347.1–13.

74. *Ming-shih*, 212.2465; Hsieh and Ning, *Ch'i Chi-kuang*, 60–61, 65–66; Ch'eng K'uan-cheng, *Ch'i Chi-kuang*, 27–29; Jen Ts'ang-ch'ang, *Ch'i Chi-kuang*, 66–67.

75. *Ming-shih*, 212.2465; Hsieh and Ning, *Ch'i Chi-kuang*, 74.

76. *Ming-shih*, 322.3693. A different view is expressed by Y. S. Kuno: "The suppression of the pirates was only partly owing to the military success of the Ming. It is only to be accounted for by the national unification and the establishment of a strong central government in Japan." See his *Japanese Expansion*, 1: 295–96.

77. Ch'i Chi-kuang, *Chih-chih-t'ang Chi*, "heng-so-kao hsia," 33; *Ming-shih*, 222.2560; s.v. "T'an Lun" in *Dictionary*.

78. Ou-yang Tsu-ching, *T'an-hsiang-min-Kung Nien-p'u*, 21, 30, 37, 57, 58, 72.

79. *Mu-tsung Shih-lu*, 0545, 0548; Ou-yang, *Nien-p'u*, 103.

80. See Hucker, *Censorial System*, pp. 34–35.

81. See Altan's biography in *Dictionary*.

82. *Ta-Ming Hui-tien*, 129.23, 152.14.

83. Ibid., 28.26–28, 129.3–6.

84. Ch'i was feared on these grounds. See Chiao, *Kuo-ch'ao Hsien-cheng-lu*, 106.59.

85. This can be observed from his collection of correspondence, already summarized in my *Taxation and Governmental Finance*, pp. 297–98.

86. Hsü et al., *Huang-Ming Ching-shih Wen-pien*, 347.14; Hsieh and Ning, *Ch'i Chi-kuang*, 116.

87. Chiao, *Kuo-ch'ao Hsien-cheng-lu*, 106.60; Hsieh and Ning, *Ch'i Chi-kuang*, 124 n. Note that Chang Chü-cheng wrote: "We must let him [Ch'i] do the recruiting." See Chang Chü-cheng, *Shu-tu*, 1.4.

88. *Mu-tsung Shih-lu*, 0548, 0742; Chiao, *Kuo-ch'ao Hsien-cheng-lu*, 106.59; Chang, *Shu-tu*, 1.4, 5.

89. *Mu-tsung Shih-lu*, 0548, 0576, 0583.

90. *Ming-shih*, 212.2467.

91. *Mu-tsung Shih-lu*, 0581, 0609.

92. See Chang, *Shu-tu*, 1.9, 2.14, 4.16, 5.19.

93. Ibid., 1.19.

94. Ibid., 4.16, 20.

95. See Ch'i, *Lien-ping Shih-chi*, 258, 261; *Ta-Ming Hui-tien*, 193.13; Yü, *Cheng-ch'i-t'ang Chi*, 11. 9–14. Note that the same name did not always mean the same thing.

96. It is derived from "Farangi" or "Franks."

97. Ch'i, *Lien-ping Shih-chi*, 91, 230-33, and *Chi-hsiao Hsin-shu*, 15.24–25.

98. Ch'i, *Lien-ping Shih-chi*, 105–06, 260–61; Hsü et al., *Huang-Ming Ching-shih Wen-pien*, 349.4.

99. Ch'i, *Lien-ping Shih-chi*, 103, 221, 222, 223.

100. Hsü et al., *Huang-Ming Ching-shih Wen-pien*, 349.10. The same source, 349.4, indicates that the brigade held its fire until the enemy was within 250 feet. Ch'i, *Lien-ping Shih-chi*, 103, however, indicates that muskets could be fired when the enemy was twice that distance away.

101. Ch'i, *Lien-ping Shih-chi*, 226–28, 234–35, 244–45. Cf. Sung Ying-hsing, *T'ien-kung K'ai-wu*, chap. 15, and Ho Liang-ch'en, *Chen-chi*, 30.

102. Ch'i, *Lien-ping Shih-chi*, 103; Hsü et al., *Huang-Ming Ching-shih Wen-pien*, 349.4.

103. Ch'i, *Lien-ping Shih-chi*, 99–100.

104. For the minor engagements, see Hsieh and Ning, *Ch'i Chi-kuang*, 127–28; *Ming-shih*, 327.3767. Also see *Dictionary*, p. 335, for the split of the Mongols. But *Shen-tsung Shih-lu*, 10734, indicates that in 1599, 30,000 Chinese troops with battle wagons held back 100,000 enemy troops surrounding them. The details are unclear.

105. See Altan's biography in *Dictionary*, and that of Wang Ch'ung-ku.

106. Ou-yang, *Nien-p'u*, 128; Chang Chü-cheng, *Shu-tu*, 4.19–20.

107. Chang, *Shu-tu*, 5.9, 19.

108. *Ming-shih*, 212.2466; Hsü et al., *Huang-Ming Ching-shih Wen-pien*, 347.14–16. Cf. *Shen-tsung Shih-lu*, 0220.

109. Hsü et al., *Huang-Ming Ching-shih Wen-pien*, 349.12.

110. *Ming-shih*, 222.2560; Hsü et al., *Huang-Ming Ching-shih Wen-pien*, 349.17–18; Ou-yang, *Nien-p'u*, 113–14, 125; Hsieh and Ning, *Ch'i Chi-kuang*, 121–22. The last source indicates that 1,017 towers were constructed.

111. *Ming-shih*, 212.2466; *Shen-tsung Shih-lu*, 2113.

112. Hsü et al., *Huang-Ming Ching-shih Wen-pien*, 349.12; Ou-yang, *Nien-p'u*, 114–16, 125. The reference made in Chiao, *Kuo-ch'ao Hsien-cheng-lu*, 106.60, that "the construction was completed in a matter of tens of days and a month," is obviously untrue. The dimensions also differ from those described by Chang Chü-cheng (see *Shu-tu*, 1.4).

113. For instance, in 1587 it was still so. Regarding the deserters, see *Shen-tsung Shih-lu*, 3537.

114. Ch'i, *Lien-ping Shih-chi*, 251.

115. Hsü et al., *Huang-Ming Ching-shih Wen-pien*, 347.14, 350.13. See also such sentiments expressed in his poetry: Ch'i, *Chih-chih-t'ang Chi*, "heng-so-kao shang," 19, 26, 33.

116. *Ming-shih*, 212.2467.

117. Ch'i, *Lien-ping Shih-chi*, 210.

118. Ch'i, *Chih-chih-t'ang Chi*, "heng-so-kao shang," 18, 19.

119. Hsieh and Ning, *Ch'i Chi-kuang*, 129; *Dictionary*, p. 223.

120. Wang Shih-chen, *Yen-chou Shan-jen Ssu-pu-kao*, 62.18, 65.7; *Yen-chou Shan-jen Hsü-kao*, 38.20, 51.16. (These page numbers are based on *Ming-jen Chuan-chi Tzu-liao So-yin*, 504. They differ from those in some recent reprints.)

121. There was no more functional assignment to an army officer above this level. The holder of this position could, however, continue to advance in rank, as explained in my *Taxation and Governmental Finance*, p. 30. Also, Hucker has indicated that all tactical commanders were subordinate to civil officials (see his "Governmental Organization," p. 63).

122. *Shen-tsung Shih-lu*, 2474–75 (*chiao-k'an-chi*, 641), 2672, 2763, 2869; Hsieh and Ning, *Ch'i Chi-kuang*, 148. Cf. Ch'eng Ku'an-cheng, *Ch'i Chi-kuang*, 47–48; *Dictionary*, p. 223.

123. *Shen-tsung Shih-lu*, 2723, 3060, 3769.

124. Wang Shih-chen, *Yen-chou Shan-jen Hsü-kao*, 38.20.

125. Chiao, *Kuo-ch'ao Hsien-cheng-lu*, 17.60–108; it is reproduced from Wang Shih-chen, *Chia-ching I-lai Nei-ko Shou-fu-chuan*, chaps. 7 and 8. Their intriguing relationship may be seen from the fifteen letters that Chang wrote Wang, Chang, *Shu-tu*, 6.21–23.

126. Chiao, *Kuo-ch'ao Hsien-cheng-lu*, 17.74–75. Cf. Wang's biography in *Dictionary*, especially p. 1401.

127. Chiao, *Kuo-ch'ao Hsien-cheng-lu*, 106.62; Hsieh and Ning, *Ch'i Chi-kuang*, 149.

128. Chiao, *Kuo-ch'ao Hsien-cheng-lu*, 106.61–62; *Dictionary*, p. 223.

129. Ch'i, *Lien-ping Shih-chi*, 205, 210.

130. Sun, *Ch'un-ming Meng-yü-lu*, 6.65. The *Meng-yü-lu* does not identify Ch'i, but no one else fits the description.

131. Ch'i, *Chih-chih-t'ang Chi*, "heng-so-kao hsia," 20–22, 34, 38.

132. Chang Chü-cheng, *Shu-tu*, 4.20.

133. *Ming-shih*, 212.2465.

134. Chiao, *Kuo-ch'ao Hsien-cheng-lu*, 106.62.

135. Ch'i, *Lien-ping Shih-chi*, 185–94, and *Chi-hsiao Hsin-shu*, chap. 16.

136. The comment appears in *Ssu-k'u Ch'üan-shu Tsung-mu T'i-yao*, and is reproduced in Ch'i, *Chih-chih-t'ang Chi*, prelim. 1.

137. The doctrine usually led to elaborations on supernatural phenomena, which were quite common in Ming sixteenth-century publications, for instance, Chang Han, *Sung-ch'uang Meng-yü*, and Huang Wei, *P'eng-ch'uang Lei-chi*. On the other hand, Ch'i sometimes showed the ascendancy of his rationality over his superstition. On one occasion he said: "When we fulfill our human effort, there is no need to be inhibited by astrological considerations" (see *Lien-ping Shih-chi*, 191). On another occasion, he acknowledged that the intimidating effect of future punishment in hell had its utilitarian value (see *Lien-ping Shih-chi*, 212).

138. Hsü et al., *Huang-Ming Ching-shih Wen-pien*, 350.5. Note that some of Ch'i's publications are his lectures before those officers.

139. Ch'i, *Lien-ping Shih-chi*, 196.

140. See Chang Mou-hsiu's note to Chang Chü-cheng, in Chang, *Shu-tu*, 5.19. Hsieh and Ning, *Ch'i Chi-kuang*, 147.

141. Chiao, *Kuo-ch'ao Hsien-cheng-lu*, 106.62; Hsieh and Ning, *Ch'i Chi-kuang*, 149.

142. Wang was retired and therefore not involved in the controversy. See chap. 2, n. 45 above, and *Dictionary*, pp. 1427–30.

Chapter 7: Li Chih, A Divided Conscience

1. For instance, "in confrontations between peasants and large landholders, Li Chih supported the peasants." Chu Ch'ien-chih, *Li Chih*, 21.

2. Li Chih, *Hsü Fen-shu*, 11.

3. W. T. de Bary's essay is the first one to give consideration to cultural differences. See his *Self and Society in Ming Thought*, pp. 7, 220.

4. Yüan Chung-tao, "Li Wen-ling Chuan," appended to the present edition of Li Chih, *Fen-shu*, prelim. 4–5.

5. Ibid. prelim. 5.

6. Ibid., 3.130; for a similar statement, see 2.50.

7. "Li Chih ti Chia-shih, Ku-chü chi chi Ch'i Mu-pei," *Wen-wu* [Cultural Artifacts], no. 1 (1975), pp. 37–38; Needham, *Science and Civilisation in China*, vol. 4, pt. 3, p. 495 n.

8. Li, *Fen-shu*, 1.10, 37, 3.105, 6.232.

9. Ibid., 3.110. The context indicates that he was then hired as a teacher dependent on his employer for food. Even though the starvation was caused by severe winter weather, Li must have been destitute.

10. Jung Chao-tsu, *Li Cho-wu P'ing-chuan*, 2–10; and Li's biography in *Dictionary*.

11. See Li, *Fen-shu*, 2.52, 4.142. Cf. Chu Ch'ien-chih, *Li Chih*, 2.

12. See Li's comment in *Fen-shu*, 2.44.

13. For Li's dislike of hypocritical pretension, see ibid., 1.30, 36, 40, 2.46.

14. Ibid., 1.9, 2.57, 77–78; Jung, *Li Cho-wu P'ing-chuan*, 11–17.

15. See the translation of the poem. *Dictionary*, p. 809.

16. Li, *Fen-shu*, 2.45.

17. Ibid., 3.84.

18. See Ho Liang-Chün, *Ssu-yu-chai Ts'ung-shuo Tse-ch'ao*, 176.2; Kuei, *Kuei Yu-kuang Ch'üan-chi*, 96. Note that both men's biographies are included in *Dictionary*.

19. Cf. Ping-ti Ho, *The Ladder of Success in Imperial China*. But the family profession registered by a candidate at the Civil Service examination might differ from reality.

20. See *Ta-Ming Hui-tien*, 6.8–12.

21. Even though in practice it was not always so, a cultured gentleman was not supposed to shirk his obligation to his kindred. See Kuei, *Kuei Yu-kuang Ch'üan-chi*, 231.

22. Chu Ch'ien-chih, *Li Chih*, 29.

23. Li, *Fen-shu*, 2.52–53; Jung, *Li Cho-wu P'ing-chuan*, 25.

24. The extant copy has been worked on by many hands. Even though it extends to about 1800, the earliest handwriting on it is dated 1606. See "Li Chih ti Chia-shih," *Wen-wu*, no. 1 (1975), p. 34.

25. Ibid., p. 39; Li, *Fen-shu*, 4.181.

26. Based on Li's own assertion, in ibid., 1.25.

27. Ibid., 2.65, 4.150–53.

28. Ibid., 2.16, 82, 4.182, supplement 2.269; Li, *Hsü Fen-shu*, 1.8, 11, 19, 26.

29. He met Wang Chi, Lo Ju-fang, and Chiao Hung, as well as the Keng brothers. Li, *Fen-shu*, 3.123, 4.142.

30. Among them were Liu Tung-hsing, Chou Ssu-ching, Ku Yang-ch'ien, Mei Kuo-chen, and Li Shih-ta, who were canal commissioner, vice minister, governor, supreme commander, and censor-in-chief. See Li, *Fen-shu*, 2.57, 66, 69, 73, 77, 82. Also see Chang Chü-cheng, *Shu-tu*, 5.7.

31. Li, *Fen-shu*, 3.118, 123; Li, *Hsü Fen-shu*, 1.29–30, 2.55–56.

32. This has been pointed out by de Bary, *Self and Society*, pp. 5–8.

33. See Li's poem, *Fen-shu*, 6.243.

34. Ibid., 4.143.

35. See *Dictionary*, p. 718. For their relationship with Li Chih, see *Fen-shu*, 6.229; *Hsü Fen-shu*, 1.17, 22–23, 41, 45; Jung, *Li Cho-wu P'ing-chuan*, 11.

36. Huang Tsung-hsi, *Ming-ju Hsüeh-an*, 35.7–8. Cf. *Ming-shih*, 221.2553. The reference to Li Chih in the latter source is prejudiced and inaccurate.

37. Li, *Fen-shu*, 1.4.

38. Jung Chao-tsu, *Li Cho-wu P'ing-chuan*, p. 11. Note that Li Chih stated that Ting-li was missed. See Li, *Fen-shu*, 4.143.

39. Huang, *Ming-ju Hsüeh-an*, 35.1–7. Ming thinkers came close to what Joseph Needham calls the difference between the "law of nature" and "natural law" (*Science and Civilisation in China*, 2: 540–42). For instance, Ch'en Hsien-chang, as described by Jen Yu-wen seems to have had such a notion (see de Bary, *Self and Society*, p. 70). But the concept was never persistently pursued nor firmly established. See also my description of Ni Yüan-lu in de Bary, ibid., p. 442.

40. Li, *Fen-shu*, 1.27, 37, 4.150, 182–83; Li, *Hsü Fen-shu*, 1.19, 2.56–57; Jung, *Li Cho-wu P'ing-chuan*, 13.

41. Li, *Fen-shu*, 2.68, 3.130, 4.187.

42. Ibid., 4.185. This can also be seen from Ho Liang-chün, *Ssu-yu-chai Ts'ung-shuo Tse-ch'ao*, 176.8.

43. Li, *Fen-shu*, prelim. 3, 1.8, 4.192; Li, *Hsü Fen-shu*, 2.68; Jung, *Li Cho-wu P'ing-chuan*, 18.

44. *Hsü Fen-shu*, 1.11, 2.59. Jung Chao-tsu emphasizes that only after 1582 did Li seriously engage in writing for publication. See Jung, *Li Cho-wu P'ing-chuan*, 12.

45. Chu, *Yung-ch'uang Hsiao-p'in*, 16.365. Note that the author met Li.

46. Li, *Fen-shu*, 1.30.

47. Ibid., 2.50, 55, 3.130, 4.187, supplement 2.268.

48. Ibid., prelim. 7.

49. Arthur Waley, trans., *The Analects of Confucius*, p. 28.

50. James Legge, trans., *The Life and Works of Mencius*, p. 307, with slight modification.

51. See, for instance, Hu Shih's evaluation in H. F. MacNair, ed., *China*, p. 230. Cf. W. T. de Bary et al., *Sources of Chinese Tradition*, p. 480.

52. See Wing-tsit Chan, trans., *Reflections on Things at Hand*, and de Bary et al., *Sources*, pp. 479–502.

53. Chan, *Reflections*, pp. 12, 93.

54. This error was quite common even among thinkers of many centuries later (see, for example, my criticism of Ni Yüan-lu, in de Bary, *Self and Society*, p. 438).

55. Chu Hsi, *Chu-tzu Ch'üan-shu*, 43.2–3; de Bary et al., *Sources*, p. 495.

56. See Chu Hsi, *Chu-tzu Yü-lei*.

57. This has been emphasized by de Bary, *Self and Society*, p. 9.

58. De Bary et al., *Sources*, pp. 491–92, 496.

59. See Wing-tsit Chan's introduction to his translation, *Instructions for Practical Living and Other Neo-Confucian Writings*.

60. See Li, *Fen-shu*, prelim. 4–5.

61. His other name was Yen Chün. See Huang Tsung-hsi, *Ming-ju Hsüeh-an*, 32.1, 34.1–2, 18, 28; de Bary, *Self and Society*, pp. 178–79, 249–50. The quotation is found in Li, *Fen-shu*, supplement 1.260.

62. Li, *Fen-shu*, supplement 1. 260–64. Jung Chao-tsu wrote: "This is not absolutely without evidence" (*Li Cho-wu P'ing-chuan*, 25).

63. Huang, *Ming-ju Hsüeh-an*, 32.4.

64. De Bary et al., *Sources*, pp. 514–26. In *Dictionary*, Wang is entered under the name Wang Shou-jen. The story appears on p. 1409.

65. See Chan, *Instructions for Practical Living*, and Chun-i T'ang's analysis in de Bary, *Self and Society*, pp. 103–05.

66. Chan's introduction to *Instructions for Practical Living*.

67. This view was held by such late Ming scholars as Huang Tsung-hsi and Ku Yen-wu, and is also commented upon by the modern Western scholars Charles O. Hucker and Joseph R. Levenson.

68. I am afraid that some writers read their own sense of populism and even egalitarianism into Li's reference to livelihood. In reality, Li Chih was referring to "food and clothing" and "the people" no more than to material security and society in general. He discussed these matters entirely from the scholarly, bureaucratic point of view. Note that de Bary regards his so-called egalitarianism "confusing" and "doubtful." See *Self and Society*, pp. 195, 213. Cf. Chu Ch'ien-chih, *Li Chih*, 25; Jung Chao-tsu, *Ming-tai Ssu-hsiang-shih*, 250–55; Wu Tse, *Ju-chiao P'an-t'u Li Cho-wu*, 32.

69. Li, *Fen-shu*, 4.143–44. For more about the Chou family, see: *Fen-shu*, 1.31, 2.52, 69, 4.143–44; Li, *Hsü Fen-shu*, 1.23; *Ma-ch'eng Hsien-chih*, 8.17–19, 9.32.

70. Li, *Hsü Fen-shu*, 2.61.

71. Ibid., 1.42. Li declined the invitation.

72. Ibid., 4.96.

73. Ibid., 1.30.

74. Li Chih, *Ts'ang-shu*, 3.43, 57.953.

75. Li's admiration for Empress Wu is reflected in his comments on history. In the reproduced biography of Ti Jen-ch'ieh, when referring to the empress, Li repeatedly pays her the compliment of calling her a "saintly empress" (*Ts'ang-shu*, 9.158). In a biography on the empress herself, after quoting her self-glorifying statements, Li unreservedly agrees with her, writing, "This is true." Also, he calls her "ten times better than T'ang Kao-tsung, and myriad times than T'ang Chung-tsung" (*Ts'ang-shu*, 63.1049–50).

76. See ibid., 64.1063, 1066. On the other hand, he shows a certain disdain for Ts'ai Yen who, in the third century, because of circumstances married a Mongol and then a Chinese (*Hsü Fen-shu*, 4.95).

77. See Li's letter to Liu Tung-hsing, *Fen-shu*, 2.73.

78. Li, *Hsü Fen-shu*, 2.75, 4.94, 100; de Bary, *Self and Society*, pp. 210–11.

79. Li, *Hsü Fen-shu*, 76.

80. See Li, *Fen-shu*, 1.3, 3, 109, 4.162, supplement 2.272; Li, *Hsü Fen-shu*, 2.54.

81. Li, *Ts'ang-shu*, "Shih-chi Tsung-lun," 2.

82. Ibid., 9.146, 156–57, 162, 164. The theme is also mentioned in the preface by Keng Ting-li.

83. Li, *Fen-shu*, 5.217, and *Ts'ang-shu*, 9.146, 17.292–96.

84. Li, *Fen-shu*, 5.217.

85. Ibid., 4.162.

86. Li, *Hsü Fen-shu*, 4.99.

87. Li, *Fen-shu*, 1.15.

88. Ibid., 2.69. That both Keng Ting-hsiang and Chou Ssu-ching had been close to Chang Chü-cheng may be seen from their correspondence. In Chang Chü-cheng, *Shu-tu*, there are eight letters to Keng and five to Chou. The page numbers are, respectively: 1.1, 4.26, 5.1, 4, 8, 18, 6.5, 27, and 4.7, 18, 21, 5.3, 7.

89. *Shen-tsung Shih-lu*, 1651, 1732. For Chang Chü-cheng's national land survey, see my *Taxation and Governmental Finance*, pp. 299–301.

90. He was also known as Li Chung-hsi (Chiao, *Kuo-ch'ao Hsien-cheng-lu*, 89.39). Also mentioned in Robert Crawford's article on Chang Chü-cheng, in de Bary, *Self and Society*, p. 397. A brief reference appears in *Dictionary*, p. 721.

91. Li, *Fen-shu*, 3.119.

92. Huang Tsung-hsi, *Ming-ju Hsüeh-an*, 32.2, 11.

93. Li, *Fen-shu*, 1.15.

94. See Chang Chü-cheng, *Shu-tu*, 2.16; Crawford, in de Bary, *Self and Society*, p. 400; Chu Ch'ien-chih, *Li Chih*, p. 33.

95. Li, *Fen-shu*, 2.69.

96. Like "volitional ideas," the term has never been defined. Any attempt to elaborate on their good and evil aspects yields only poetic and disorganized attributes. The reader is never sure whether the philosopher is dealing with a concept or a substance. Cf. Chan, *Instructions for Practical Living*, prelim. 33.

97. See Huang, *Ming-ju Hsüeh-an*, 32.69–70; de Bary, *Self and Society*, pp. 162–170, especially 165.

98. Huang, *Ming-ju Hsüeh-an*, 12.2, 7. Chun-i T'ang's explanation, in de Bary, *Self and Society*, especially p. 114, is penetrating. However, from my particular view that late Ming philosophers were really searching for ideological tools as a substitute for statutory law, I am, aside from my inadequate philosophical training, naturally less inclined to make metaphysical speculations.

99. Li, *Fen-shu*, 3.117, 123.

100. Ibid., supplement 1.259.

101. Li Chih did use the term to describe himself (see Liu Tung-hsing's remarks in *Hsü Fen-shu*, 2.54). He also said this to Chu Kuo-chen (Chu, *Yung-ch'uang Hsiao-p'in*, 16.365).

102. See Li, *Hsü Fen-shu*, 1.45; also, Liu Tung-hsing's preface to Li's *Ts'ang-shu*.

103. Chu Ch'ien-chih, *Li Chih*, 9; *Dictionary*, pp. 813–14.

104. Li, *Fen-shu*, 4.167, 183, 184, 6.229, and *Hsü Fen-shu*, 1.5.

105. As pointed out by Yüan Chung-tao, "his misfortune followed his fame" (*Fen-shu*, prelim. 7).

106. Chu Ch'ien-chih, *Li Chih*, 8. Li himself mentioned the incident in several letters (see *Hsü Fen-shu*, 1.14, 17, 18, 25).

107. Jung Chao-tsu, *Ming-tai Ssu-hsiang-shih*, 232; Li, *Fen-shu*, 3.126, 6.228, and *Hsü Fen-shu*, 2.61, 4.98.

108. Li, *Fen-shu*, 2.79.

109. Li, *Hsü Fen-shu*, 2.68, 4.95, 5.118.

110. Li, *Fen-shu*, prelim. 4.

111. This is Li's thesis in *Ts'ang-shu*, 2.

112. *Shen-tsung Shih-lu*, 6917–19. Note that the records state that Li died from fasting. It is very likely that this was how his death was reported to the emperor.

113. Ibid., 3415, 3455–56, 3548.

114. Ibid., 6107–08. In a way, it was impossible to maintain the purity of Confucianism. Ricci wrote: "Because of the fact that they neither prohibit nor command anything relative to what should be believed regarding a future life, many who belong to this caste identify the other two cults with their own." This passage appears in Ricci, *China in the Sixteenth Century*, p. 97.

115. Li, *Fen-shu*, prelim. 4–5, based on Yüan Chung-tao, "Li Wen-ling Chuan," printed in ibid.

B IBLIOGRAPHY

This bibliography is neither a suggested reading list nor a complete listing of current literature on the subject. It is restricted to the titles cited in the Notes. For further study and for identification of the Chinese characters for the names and works cited, the reader is advised to consult Wolfgang Franke, *An Introduction to the Sources of Ming History* (Kuala Lumpur and Singapore, 1968) and L. Carrington Goodrich and Chaoying Fang, eds., *Dictionary of Ming Biography, 1368–1644* (New York, 1976; referred to in the Notes as *Dictionary*).

Bodde, Derk, and Morris, Clarence. *Law in Imperial China Exemplified by 190 Ch'ing Dynasty Cases.* Cambridge, Mass., 1967.

Chan Wing-tsit, trans. *Instructions for Practical Living and Other Neo-Confucian Writings* [by Wang Yang-Ming]. New York, 1963.

————, trans. *Reflections on Things at Hand: Chu Hsi and Lü Tsu-ch'ien.* New York, 1967.

Chang Chü-cheng. *Shu-tu.* Reprint. Shanghai: Ch'ün-hsüeh Shu-she, 1917.

Chang Han. *Sung-ch'uang Meng-yü (Wu-lin Wang-che I-chu* ed.).

Cheng Hsiao. *Chin yen (Chi-lu Hui-pien* ed.).

Cheng Mo. *Ching-hai Chi-lüeh* (bound under *Wo-pien Shih-lüeh*). Taipei, 1964.

Chiao Hung. *Kuo-ch'ao Hsien-cheng-lu.* Reprint. Taipei: Hsüeh-sheng Shu-chü, 1965.

————. *Tan-yüan-chi (Chin-ling Ts'ung-shu* ed.).

Chin-hua Fu-chih. Library of Congress microfilm, 1578 ed.

Chou Hsüan-wei. *Ching-lin Hsü-chi (Han-fen-lou Pi-chi* ed.).

Chou Wei. *Chung-kuo Ping-ch'i Shih-kao.* Peking, 1957.

Chu Ch'ien-chih. *Li Chih: Shih-liu Shih-chi Chung-kuo fan Feng-chien Ssu-hsiang ti Hsien-ch'ü-che.* Wuhan, 1956.

Chu Hsi. *Chu-tzu Ch'üan-shu (Ssu-pu Ts'ung-k'an* ed.).

————. *Chu-tzu Yü-lei.* (Changsha: Shang-wu Yin-shu-kuan ed.).

Chu Kuo-chen. *Yung-ch'uang Hsiao-p'in.* Reprint. Peking: Chung-hua Shu-chü, 1959.

Chu Tung-jün. *Chang Chu-cheng Ta-chuan.* Wuhan, 1957.

Chu Yüan-chang. *Huang-Ming Tsu-shün.* In *Ming-ch'ao K'ai-kuo Wen-hsien.* Reprint. Taipei: Hsüeh-sheng Shu-chü, 1966.

————. *Ta-kao.* In *Ming-ch'ao K'ai-kuo Wen-hsien.* Reprint. Taipei: Hsüeh-sheng Shu-chü, 1966.

Ch'eng K'uan-cheng. *Ch'i Chi-kuang.* Chungking, 1943.

Ch'en Hung-mo, *Chi-shih Chi-wen (Chi-lu Hui-pien* ed.).

————. *Chih-shih Yü-wen (Chi-lu Hui-pien* ed.).

Ch'en Wen-shih. *Ming Hung-wu Chia-ching Chien-ti Hai-ching Cheng-ts'e.* Taipei, 1966.

Ch'i Chi-kuang. *Chi-hsiao Hsin-shu* (1841 ed.).

_____. *Chih-chih-t'ang Chi.* Shantung: Shu-chü, 1888.

_____. *Lien-ping Shih-chi.* Reprint. Shanghai: Shang-wu Yin-shu-kuan, 1937.

Ch'ien Mu. *Kuo-shih Ta-kang.* 10th ed. Taipei, 1966.

Ch'ü, T'ung-tsu. *Local Government in China under the Ch'ing.* Cambridge, Mass., 1962.

de Bary, W. T., ed. *Self and Society in Ming Thought.* New York, 1970.

de Bary, W. T. et al., eds. *Sources of Chinese Tradition.* Text ed. New York, 1964.

D'Elia, Pasquale M., ed. *Fonti Ricciane.* Rome, 1942 and 1949. *See also* Ricci, Matteo.

de Gouveia. See Gouveia.

Fu I-ling. *Ming-Ch'ing Shih-tai Shang-jen chi Shang-yeh Tzu-pen.* Peking, 1956.

Goodrich, L. Carrington, and Fang, Chaoying, *Dictionary of Ming Biography: 1368–1644.* New York, 1976.

Gouveia, de Antonio. *Journal.* Unpublished partial translation by J. M. Braga. National Library of Australia. Supplied by L. Carrington Goodrich.

Hai Jui. *Hai Jui Chi.* Peking, 1962.

Ho Chung-shih. *Liang-kung Ting-chien-chi (Ts'ung-shu Chi-ch'eng ed.).*

Ho Liang-ch'en. *Chen-chi (Ts'ung-shu Chi-ch'eng ed.).*

Ho Liang-chün. *Ssu-yu-chai Ts'ung-shuo Tse-ch'ao (Chi-lu Hui-pien, ed.).*

Ho, Ping-ti. *The Ladder of Success in Imperial China: Aspects of Social Mobility, 1368-1911.* New York, 1962.

Hsiang Meng-yüan. *Tung-kuan Chi-shih (Ts'ung-shu Chi-ch'eng ed.).*

Hsiao, Kung-ch'üan. *Rural China: Imperial Control in the Nineteenth Century.* Seattle, Wash., 1960.

Hsiao-tsung Shih-lu. Reprint. Taipei: Chung-yang Yen-chiu-yüan, 1965.

Hsieh Ch'eng-jen, and Ning K'o. *Ch'i Chi-kuang.* Shanghai, 1961.

Hsieh Kuo-chen. *Ming-Ch'ing Chih-chi Tang-she Yün-tung-k'ao.* Shanghai, 1935.

Hsien-tsung Shih-lu. Reprint. Taipei: Chung-yang Yen-chiu-yüan, 1964.

Hsin Chung-kuo K'ao-ku ti Shou-huo. Peking: K'ao-ku Yen-chiu-so, 1962.

Hsi Shu, and Chu Chia-hsiang. *Ts'ao-ch'uan-chih (Hsüan-lan-t'ang Ts'ung-shu ed.).*

Hsi-tsung Shih-lu. Reprint. Taipei: Chung-yang Yen-chiu-yüan, 1967.

Hsüan-tsung Shih-lu. Reprint. Taipei: Chung-yang Yen-chiu-yüan, 1964.

Hsü Fu-yüan et al., eds. *Huang-Ming Ching-shih Wen-pien.* Reprint. Taipei: Kuo-feng Ch'u-pan-she, 1964.

Hsü Hsüeh-chü, ed. *Chia-ching Tung-nan P'ing-wo T'ung-lu* (author unknown; bound under *Wo-pien Shih-lüeh*). Taipei, 1964.

Huang, Ray. "Military Expenditures in Sixteenth-Century Ming China." *Oriens Extremus* 17 (1970): 1–2.

_____. *Taxation and Governmental Finance in Sixteenth-Century Ming China.* Cambridge, 1974.

Huang Shün, ed. *Huang-Ming Ming-ch'en Ching-chi-lu* (1551 ed.).

Huang Tsung-hsi. *Ming-ju Hsüeh-an (Ssu-pu Pei-yao ed.).*

Huang Wei. *P'eng-ch'uang Lei-chi (Han-feng-lou Pi-chi ed.).*

Hucker, Charles O. "Governmental Organization of the Ming Dynasty." *Harvard Journal of Asiatic Studies*, vol. 21 (1958).

————. *The Censorial System of Ming China*. Stanford, Calif., 1966.

————. *The Traditional Chinese State in Ming Times, 1368–1644*. Tucson, Ariz., 1961.

Hummel, A. W., ed. *Eminent Chinese of the Ch'ing Period*. Washington, D.C. 1943–1944.

Jen Ts'ang-ch'ang. *Ch'i Chi-kuang*. Shanghai, 1947.

Jung Chao-tsu. *Li Cho-wu P'ing-chuan* (*Jen-jen Wen-k'u* ed.). Taipei, 1962.

————. *Ming-tai Ssu-hsiang-shih*. Shanghai, 1941.

Kao Kung. *Ping-t'a I-yen* (*Chi-lu Hui-pien* ed.).

K'ao-ku, no. 7 (1959).

K'ao-ku T'ung-hsin, no. 7 (1958).

Kierman, Frank A., Jr., and Fairbank, John K., eds. *Chinese Ways in Warfare*. Cambridge, Mass., 1974.

Kuang-tsung Shih-lu. Reprint. Taipei: Chung-yang Yen-chiu-yüan, 1966.

Kuei Yu-kuang. *Kuei Yu-kuang Ch'üan-chi*. Reprint. Taipei: Tzu-li Ch'u-pan-she, 1959.

Kuno, Y. S. *Japanese Expansion on the Asiatic Continent*. Berkeley, Calif., 1937 and 1940.

Ku Yen-wu. *Jih-chih-lu Chi-shih* (*Wan-yu Wen-k'u* ed.).

————. *T'ien-hsia Chün-kuo Li-ping-shu* (*Ssu-pu Ts'ung-k'an* ed.).

Ku Ying-t'ai. *Ming-shih Chi-shih Pen-mo*. Reprint. Taipei: San-min Shu-chü, 1956.

Legge, James, trans. *The Life and Works of Mencius*. London, 1875.

Levenson, Joseph R. *Confucian China and its Modern Fate*. Berkeley, Calif., 1958.

Li Chih, *Fen-shu* and *Hsü Fen-shu*. Combined ed. Reprint. Peking: Chung-hua Shu-chü, 1975.

————. *Ts'ang-shu*. Reprint. Peking: Chuang-hua Shu-chü, 1974.

Li Kuang-ming. *Chia-ching Yü-wo Chiang-Che Chu-k'e-chün-k'ao*. Peking, 1933.

Li Tung-fang. *Hsi-shuo Ming-ch'ao* (*Wen-hsing Ts'ung-k'an* ed.). Taipei, 1964.

Liu Jo-yü. *Cho-chung-chih* (*Ts'ung-shu Chi-ch'eng* ed.).

Lu Jung. *Shu-yüan Tsa-chi* (*Chi-lu Hui-pien* ed.).

Lu Shien-chi. *Jen-jen-ts'ao* (*Ts'ung-shu Chi-ch'eng* ed.).

Ma-ch'eng Hsien-chih (1935 ed.).

MacNair, Harley F., ed. *China*. Berkeley, Calif., 1946.

Mao Yüan-I, *Wu-pei-chih* (K'ang-hsi era ed.).

Meng Shen. *Ming-tai-shih*. Taipei, 1957.

Ming-jen Chuan-chi Tzu-liao So-yin. Taipei: Chung-yang T'u-shu-kuan, 1966.

Ming-shih. Reprint. Taipei: Kuo-fang Yen-chiu-yüan, 1963.

Mu-tsung Shih-lu. Reprint. Taipei: Chung-yang Yen-chiu-yüan, 1966.

Needham, Joseph. *Science and Civilisation in China*. Cambridge, 1954 et seq.

Needham, Joseph, and Huang, Ray. "The Nature of Chinese Society: A Technical Interpretation." *Journal of Oriental Studies* (Hongkong) 12 (1974): 1–2; and *East and West* (Rome), n.s. 24 (1974): 3–4.

Ni Hui-ting. *Ni-wen-cheng-kung Nien-p'u* (*Yüeh-ya-t'ang Ts'ung-shu* ed.).

Ou-yang Tsu-ching. *T'an-hsiang-min-kung Nien-p'u.* Shanghai, 1936.

P'an Chi-hsün. *Ho-fang I-lan.* Reprint. Taipei, Hsüeh-sheng Shu-chü, 1965.

P'eng Hsin-wei. *Chung-kuo Huo-pi-shih.* Shanghai, 1954.

P'eng Shih, *P'eng-wen-hsien pi-chi (Chi-lu Hui-pien* ed.).

Reischauer, Edwin O., and Fairbank, John K. *East Asia: The Great Tradition.* Boston, 1958.

Ricci, Matteo. *China in the Sixteenth Century: The Journals of Matthew Ricci, 1583–1610,* translated by L. J. Gallagher. New York, 1953. *See also* D'Elia, Pasquale M.

Samedo, C. Alvarez. *The History of That Great and Renowned Monarchy of China,* anonymously translated. London, 1655.

Sansom, G. B. *A History of Japan.* Stanford, Calif., 1958 et seq.

Shen Pang. *Wan-shu Tsa-chi.* Reprint. Peking: Pei-ching Ch'u-pan-she, 1961.

Shen Shih-hsing. *Chao-tui-lu (Ts'ung-shu Chi-ch'eng* ed.).

————. *Tz'u-hsien-t'ang Chi.* Library of Congress microfilm.

Shen Te-fu. *Yeh-huo-pien.* Reprint. Fu-li Shan-fang, 1869.

Shen-tsung Shih-lu. Reprint. Taipei: Chung-yang Yen-chiu-yüan, 1966.

Shih-tsung Shih-lu. Reprint. Taipei: Chung-yang Yen-chiu-yüan, 1965.

Shun-te Hsien-chih. 1585 ed. Library of Congress microfilm.

Ssu-k'u Ch'üan-shu Tsung-mu T'i-yao (1930 ed.).

Sun Ch'eng-tse. *Ch'un-ming Meng-yü-lu.* Reprint. Hongkong: Lung-men Shu-chü, 1965.

Sung Ying-hsing. *T'ien-kung K'ai-wu.* Reprint. Taipei: Jen-jen Wen-k'u, 1966.

Su T'ung-ping, *Ming-tai I-ti Chih-tu.* Taipei, 1969.

Ta-Ming Hui-tien. Reprint. Taipei: Tung-nan Shu-pao-she, 1963.

T'ai-tsung Shih-lu. Reprint. Taipei: Chung-yang Yen-chiu-yüan, 1963.

T'ai tsu Shih-lu. Reprint. Taipei: Chung-yang Yen-chiu-yüan, 1962.

Teng Chih-ch'eng. *Chung-hua Erh-ch'ien-nien-shih.* Hongkong, 1964.

Ting I. *Ming-tai T'e-wu Cheng-chih.* Peking, 1950.

Ts'ai Chiu-te. *Wo-pien Shih-lüeh.* Reprint. Taipei: Kuang-wen Shu-chü, 1964.

Ts'en Chung-mien. *Huang-ho Pien-ch'ien-shih.* Peking, 1957.

Waley, Arthur, trans. *The Analects of Confucius.* 1938. Reprint. New York: Vintage Books, 1966.

Wan-li Ti-ch'ao. Reprint. Taipei: Hsüeh-sheng Shu-chü, 1968.

Wang Ao, *Chen-tse Ch'ang-yü (Chi-lu Hui-pien* ed.).

Wang Shih-chen. *Chia-ching I-lai Nei-ko Shou-fu-chuan.* Reprint. Taipei: Wen-hai Shu-chü, 1967.

————. *Yen-chou Shan-jen Ssu-pu-kao (Shih-ching-t'ang* ed.).

————. *Yen-chou Shan-jen Hsü-kao (Shih-ching-t'ang* ed.).

————. *Yen-chou Shih-liao Hou-chi.* Reprint. Taipei: Hsüeh-sheng Shu-chü, 1965.

Wei Ch'ing-yüan. *Ming-tai Huang-ts'e Chih-tu.* Peking, 1961.

Wei Huan, *Huang-Ming Chiu-pien-k'ao* (National Peking Library reprint, 1936).

Wen Ping. *Hsien-po Chih-shih (Ts'ung-shu Chi-ch'eng* ed.).

Wen-wu, no. 1 (1975).

Wu Han. *Chu Yüan-chang Chuan.* Reprint. Hongkong: Chuan-chi Wen-hsüeh-she, n.d.

————————. "Ming-tai ti Chün-ping." *Chung-kuo She-hui Ching-chi-shih Chi-k'an* 5 (1937): 2.

Wu Tse. *Ju-chiao P'an-t'u Li Cho-wu.* Shanghai, 1949.

Wu-tsung Shih-lu. Reprint. Taipei: Chung-yang Yen-chiu-yüan, 1965.

Ying-tsung Shih-lu. Reprint. Taipei: Chung-yang Yen-chiu-yüan, 1964.

Yü Ta-yu. *Cheng-ch'i-t'ang Chi* (Wei-ku-shih, 1884 ed.).

INDEX